FROMMER'S

COMPREHENSIVE TRAVEL GUIDE

NEW YORK '95

by Faye Hammel

MACMILLAN • USA

About the Author:
   Faye Hammel has been reporting on the New York scene for many years in books, magazines, and newspapers. In addition to Frommer's Travel Guides on New York and Hawaii, she is also the author of *The Dream Theater* and *The New York Lunch*.

The Greenwich Village Walking Tour in this book is adapted from *Frommer's New York State 4th Edition,* by John Foreman.

Macmillan Travel
A Prentice Hall Macmillan Company
15 Columbus Circle
New York, NY 10023

ISBN 0-671-88376-3
ISSN 0899-7675

Design by Robert Bull Design
Maps by Geografix Inc. and Ortelius Design

SPECIAL SALES
Bulk purchases (10+ copies) of Frommer's Travel Guides are available to corporations at special discounts. The Special Sales Department can produce custom editions to be used as premiums and/or for sales promotion to suit individual needs. Existing editions can be produced with custom cover imprints such as corporate logos. For more information write to Special Sales, Prentice Hall, 15 Columbus Circle, New York, NY 10023.

Manufactured in the United States of America

CONTENTS

LIST OF MAPS

WALKING TOURS

by Arthur Frommer

You will perhaps find it natural that I should myself read, use, and cherish all the Frommer's guides. But the one that most captivates me (apart from my "baby," *Europe On $50 a Day*) is the guidebook to New York City that is now in your hands. Like most New Yorkers, I carry on an intense and unwavering love affair with my city, and I plan to consult this book in the year ahead as often as any tourist would.

What I most admire is that the guide's author, Faye Hammel, doesn't confine her comments to the well-recognized sights of New York City, the places where the tours go (SoHo, Greenwich Village, Chinatown, the UN, Wall Street). She gives equal emphasis to another New York, the scores and scores of subtle, even secondary, attractions that often equal or even surpass the major locations in real interest and pleasure.

But may I add my own special recommendations, some of which overlap hers? To me, no visit to New York is complete unless it includes the areas frequented by residents of the city. Of the many such places, the following stand out.

- The shops and restaurants of the Upper West Side, along Broadway, from 72nd to 86th Street. See, in particular, the famous Zabar's, Citarella's, and Fairway.
- Nineteenth-century New York, in Brooklyn Heights. Take the 2 or 3 IRT subway train to Court Street–Borough Hall, then walk down Montague Street to the Promenade overlooking New York Harbor and Manhattan's financial district.
- The campuses of New York University (off Washington Square, at the southern tip of Fifth Avenue) and Columbia University (in Morningside Heights, just beyond the Upper West Side).
- The lobby of the Woolworth Building, my own favorite among the skyscrapers of New York, on Broadway near City Hall. Built in a Gothic style, the building has been called a "Cathedral of Commerce."
- The Winter Garden of the World Financial Center (not to be confused with the World *Trade* Center) in lower Manhattan. It's a glass-enclosed atrium with palm trees and seating. The promenade along the harbor just outside the Financial Center is another favorite spot.
- Brighton Beach, an area of recent Russian immigrants, just under the elevated subway tracks at the Brighton Beach station of the BMT. At night, you might visit a Russian nightclub nearby, such as Primorski or the National.

- The East Village (east of Greenwich Village), and especially the district of Indian restaurants on East 6th Street, between Second and First Avenues.
- Off-Off-Broadway theaters. They're listed in the weekly *Village Voice* and the Friday and Sunday editions of the *New York Times*. Attend an Off-Off performance—you haven't experienced the whole New York theater scene until you do.
- The dim sum restaurants of Chinatown, like the Silver Palace at 50 Bowery.
- Grand Army Plaza, near downtown Brooklyn, for a glimpse of the optimism that once characterized major U.S. cities. This great oval plaza was designed around 1870 by Frederick Law Olmsted and Calvert Vaux, who also planned Manhattan's Central Park.
- The ethnic Greek district of Astoria in Queens across the East River from midtown Manhattan.
- And if you have an extra day, take a trip to a summer haunt of New Yorkers in eastern Long Island. You can ride the Long Island Rail Road to Westhampton (an hour and a half from Manhattan) or Easthampton (two hours), and wander the sophisticated main streets of these warm-weather New York retreats.

As you'd expect, Faye has her own list of favorites. In preparing this 12th edition, she caps a 30-year career in New Yorkology. What has this supreme expert on New York come up with for the new edition? Well, in addition to scores of revisions and updated prices, she's included many new restaurants. In SoHo, she's discovered one of New York's best Japanese soba noodle houses, serene Honmura An, plus Kwanzaa, an exotic shrine to international soul food. She's found a great Cajun cook on the Lower East Side at the Ludlow Street Café; moving farther north, in the Flatiron District, Patria, the place for scintillating South American cuisine, and Bolo, with its flamboyant contemporary Spanish fare. Uptown, she marvels at the masterful European-Asian cuisine served at Lespinasse in the tony St. Regis Hotel. Near Lincoln Center, she raves about New York's most delightful natural gourmet restaurant, Josie's.

Regarding accommodations, she's given close attention to all listings. She recommends the newly renovated old-timer, the St. Moritz, with the best prices on Central Park South. And she advises parents with kids in tow to make tracks for Embassy Suites in the Times Square area; this all-suite hotel has dozens of amenities for traveling families, including kitchenettes, and a fully supervised daycare center.

I'm confident you'll enjoy reading this revised edition. Better yet, I know it will prove immensely helpful in the course of your New York stay.

Have a good trip!

WHAT THE SYMBOLS MEAN

 FROMMER'S FAVORITES—hotels, restaurants, attractions, and entertainments you should not miss

 SUPER-SPECIAL VALUES—really exceptional values

 FROMMER'S SMART TRAVELER TIPS—hints on how to secure the best value for your money.

IN HOTEL AND OTHER LISTINGS

The following symbols refer to the standard amenities available in all rooms:

A/C air conditioning   TEL telephone   TV television
MINIBAR refrigerator stocked with beverages and snacks

The following abbreviations are used for credit cards:

AE American Express   DISC Discover   JCB (Japan)
CB Carte Blanche   ER enRoute   MC MasterCard
DC Diners Club   EU Eurocard   V Visa

TRIP PLANNING WITH THIS GUIDE

Use the following features:

What Things Cost In . . . to help you plan your daily budget
Calendar of Events . . . to plan for or avoid
Suggested Itineraries . . . for seeing the city
What's Special About Checklist . . . a summary of the city's highlights—which lets you check off those that appeal most to you
Easy-to-Read Maps . . . walking tours, city sights, hotel and restaurant locations—all referring to or keyed to the text
Fast Facts . . . all the essentials at a glance: currency, embassies, emergencies, and more

OTHER SPECIAL FROMMER FEATURES

Cool for Kids—hotels, restaurants, and attractions
Did You Know . . . ?—offbeat, fun facts

INVITATION TO THE READERS

In researching this book, I have come across many fine establishments, the best of which I have included here. I am sure that many of you will also come across appealing hotels, restaurants, guesthouses, shops, and attractions. Please don't keep them to yourself. Share your experiences, especially if you want to comment on places that have been included in this edition that have changed for the worse. You can address your letters to:

Faye Hammel
Frommer's New York '95
c/o Macmillan Travel
15 Columbus Circle
New York, NY 10023

A DISCLAIMER

Readers are advised that prices fluctuate in the course of time and travel information changes under the impact of the varied and volatile factors that affect the travel industry. Neither the author nor the publisher can be held responsible for the experiences of the readers while traveling. Readers are invited to write to the publisher with ideas, comments, and suggestions for future editions.

SAFETY ADVISORY

Whenever you're traveling in an unfamiliar city or country, stay alert. Be aware of your immediate surroundings. Wear a moneybelt and keep a close eye on your possessions. Be particularly careful with cameras, purses, and wallets—all favorite targets of thieves and pickpockets.

INTRODUCING NEW YORK

New York—it's a great place to visit, as the saying goes, but it's not an easy city to know. Because there is so much happening here, such a wealth of things that bombard the visitor, it's easy to come to New York and leave it without having experienced the best of it. And when it comes to spending your dollar wisely in one of the world's most expensive cities, it takes some special knowhow. Here, then, is the inside information, the special tips that can make all the difference between feeling like a native or a newcomer. Read on to find which hotels offer the best values, from the Waldorf to the "Y"; which restaurants are worth declaring bankruptcy for and which will feed you well for a pittance; and how to obtain tickets for a top Broadway musical without paying scalper's rates or having an uncle who works for the producer. You'll discover how to enjoy the city's sights in the most efficient, relaxed manner possible; how to discover the shopping secrets of New York's out-of-the-way bargain meccas; and how to find the coziest pub, the latest disco, or the newest supper club. A series of walking tours will help you explore the city's rich architectural history. Hopefully, this catalog of the best New York has to offer will be useful to you, whether it's your first trip to the city or your 110th. First, though, a word of warning to newcomers.

There is one dangerous aspect of coming to New York for the first time—not of getting lost, mugged, or caught in a blackout, but of falling so in love with the city that you may not want to go home again. Or, if you do, it may be just to pack your bags. With most visitors to New York, it's love or hate at first sight. Either you are so enthralled by the dazzle, the tempo, the sense of adventure only a great city can give, that you immediately make it your own . . . or you may find the noise, the smog, the traffic, the poverty evidenced in the streets by the homeless, and the seeming callousness of the natives just too much. But New York is still the magic town, and the younger you are, the more potent is its spell. *Caveat emptor.*

WHAT MAKES NEW YORK TICK To describe New York City fully would take volumes—and besides, it's indescribable. New York simply must be experienced, in all its incredible variety, to be comprehended. It is unlike any other city in America—more like a country of its own. New York is a lot more like London than it is like Chicago or Los Angeles, but it is really an entity unto itself.

It is noted for its size (with a population of around 7.3 million, it is the nation's largest city); its diversity (more different kinds of people do their thing here than just about anywhere else); and perhaps most important of all, the magnetism that attracts the brightest, most

WHAT'S SPECIAL ABOUT NEW YORK

World-Class Attractions

- ☐ The Statue of Liberty, restored and shining brighter than ever.
- ☐ Ellis Island, the portal through which 12 million immigrants entered the United States from 1892 to 1954—now a restored shrine welcoming tourists.
- ☐ The United Nations, international enclave on the East River.

Architectural Highlights

- ☐ City Hall (1803–11), a formal Federal-style building.
- ☐ Federal Hall National Memorial (1842–62), a prime example of Greek Revival style.
- ☐ New York Public Library (1898–1911), a superb example of Beaux Arts design, with those famous lions.
- ☐ Flatiron Building (1902), shaped like a flatiron.
- ☐ Empire State Building (1931), at 102 stories high a symbol of the city.
- ☐ Seagram Building (1958), which heralded the arrival of the modern office tower in New York.

Museums

- ☐ Metropolitan Museum of Art, one of the major art palaces of the world.
- ☐ Museum of Modern Art, for the best of modern art.
- ☐ Whitney Museum of American Art, with an outstanding collection of 20th-century art.
- ☐ Guggenheim Museum, designed by Frank Lloyd Wright, an unconventional setting for modern art.

Jewish Museum

- ☐ Jewish Museum, with a great collection depicting 4,000 years of Jewish history and culture.

Shopping

- ☐ Macy's, the world's largest store, plus other major department and specialty stores.
- ☐ Madison Avenue and SoHo for elegant boutiques.
- ☐ Lower East Side for incredible bargains.

Zoos

- ☐ Bronx Zoo, one of the best in the world.
- ☐ Central Park Zoo, small and enchanting, a delight for kids.

Public Gardens

- ☐ Central Park, the city's great rural playground.
- ☐ New York Botanical Garden, in the Bronx, 250 splendid acres of natural and landscaped grounds.
- ☐ Brooklyn Botanic Garden, 52 glorious acres of flowers, trees, exotic plants, and Japanese cherry trees that blossom in spring.

After Dark

- ☐ Wonderful theater, music, dance, and films, plus an exciting club scene.

For the Kids

- ☐ *Intrepid* Sea-Air-Space Museum, a floating repository of naval history and technology.
- ☐ American Museum of Natural History, with exhibitions, giant-screen films, and the Discovery Center.
- ☐ The Children's Museum of Manhattan and the Brooklyn Children's Museum, for ages 3 to 15.

creative, most ambitious, most determined people from everywhere. For this is the central city, the megalopolis, the nerve center of the world's finance and trade; of advertising, publishing, and fashion; of theater, ballet, and music; and, with the United Nations here, of world diplomacy as well. It is the vortex that pulls into its center a lot of the best (and worst) people and projects and theories and schemes from everywhere. New York is the eye of the hurricane. This is what gives the city its special feeling of intensity, the high-powered vibration that is felt immediately by even the most casual visitor. It is what makes New York one of the most exciting places on the planet.

1. GEOGRAPHY, HISTORY & POLITICS

GEOGRAPHY New York City is the southernmost point in New York State, comprising more than 300 square miles just east of the state of New Jersey, on the northeast coast of the United States. Of the five boroughs that constitute the city, the Bronx is the only one that is solely on the mainland (the northern tip of Manhattan is on the mainland too). The island of Manhattan is bounded by the Hudson River to the west, the Harlem River to the north, the East River to the east, and Upper New York Bay to the south. Staten Island is surrounded by the Arthur Kill Channel and Upper and Lower New York Bays. Queens and Brooklyn are on westernmost Long Island.

Manhattan is primarily an island, and a rather small one at that (12 miles long, 2½ miles across at its widest point). You probably already know that New York City is divided into five boroughs: Manhattan, the most important; the Bronx, to the north; Brooklyn, to the south; Queens (where Kennedy and LaGuardia airports and Shea Stadium are), to the east; and Staten Island, southwest of New York harbor.

HISTORY & POLITICS New York is a city always in transition, the unofficial capital of the world. It is a leading world center for the arts; commerce; and, most of all, finance. It has always been a trading post, founded as such and named Nieuw Amsterdam in 1624 by the Dutch West India Company. Ever since Peter Minuit landed with his small group of Dutch settlers in 1626 and drove a shrewd bargain with the Native Americans for the purchase of Manhattan for $24 (60 guilders) worth of trinkets, trade has been the chief occupation. There had been earlier discoveries: In 1524, Italian explorer Giovanni da Verrazano had found New York harbor to be "an agreeable situation . . . in the midst of which flowed . . . a very great river." He sailed through the Narrows between Brooklyn and Staten Island, and the beautiful bridge that now spans the Narrows bears his name.

DATELINE

- **1524** Giovanni da Verrazano is first to explore the bay of New York.
- **1609** Henry Hudson sails as far as Albany in search of a route to the Orient.
- **1614** Adriaen Block charts the waters around Manhattan, naming the area "New Netherland."
- **1624** Nieuw Amsterdam becomes the first permanent white settlement in lower Manhattan.

(continues)

DATELINE

- **1626** Peter Minuit, governor of Nieuw Amsterdam, purchases Manhattan Island from Native Americans for about $24.
- **1644** Fences are built to keep cattle out of what is now Wall Street.
- **1647** Peter Stuyvesant becomes governor of the Nieuw Amsterdam colony.
- **1652** A fortified wall replaces the old fence on Wall Street to keep out the British.
- **1664** British invade Nieuw Amsterdam, renaming it New York after James, duke of York.
- **1667** British and Dutch sign the Treaty of Breda giving New York to England.
- **1709** The Wall Street Slave Market opens.
- **1710** Population nears 30,000.
- **1725** *The New York Gazette*, New York's first newspaper, makes its debut.
- **1732** The first theater is built.
- **1735** John Peter Zenger's acquittal on libel charges sets a precedent for freedom of the press.
- **1754** King's College—later Columbia University—is chartered.
- **1761** Oil lamps on posts are

(continues)

In 1609, Henry Hudson, an Englishman searching for a northwest passage to the Orient, sailed his *Half Moon* nearly to present-day Albany on the river later named for him.

From the beginning, Nieuw Amsterdam was run as a business. To attract new settlers, the Dutch offered land inducements to merchants willing to come and set up shop. As the population increased, new white settlements were established: Staten Island in 1630; Queens a year later; and, finally, in 1639, the Bronx. A fur trade flourished; in 1635 alone, $53,000 worth of pelts were exported. The town early earned a reputation for dissolution and lawlessness. Liquor stores lined the streets, drunkenness was rampant; there was blatant disregard for rules and ordinances, much to the chagrin of Gov. Peter Stuyvesant, who was constantly at odds with his unruly subjects.

Although rigidly autocratic, Stuyvesant was well regarded. Under his administration Nieuw Amsterdam acquired its first City Hall (a converted tavern) along with its first city government; its first building and fire codes; its first ferry service; the first ordinances against fast driving, excessive drinking, and fighting in the streets; and its first city police. A fortified wall was built along what is now Wall Street to keep out the Native Americans and the British; and a canal on Broad Street was designed to give the city more of a Dutch appeal.

When the British suddenly attacked in 1664, Stuyvesant was in no position to fight, since Fort Amsterdam was in a state of disrepair because the home government had not allocated funds for its defense. So Nieuw Amsterdam became New York, and though it was recaptured by the Dutch in 1673, it was returned to the British in 1674 in exchange for Java, considered a more valuable asset. In 1683, the city received its first British Charter and Official Seal. New York had its first pre-Revolutionary civil liberties battle in 1734–35, when John Peter Zenger, editor of the New York *Weekly Journal,* was prosecuted for libel for articles he had published criticizing British rule. Defended by Andrew Hamilton, Zenger was acquitted, and freedom of the press was born. For most of the American Revolution, the British were headquartered in New York, but when it was over, a victorious George Washington rode into town to cheering crowds and bade farewell to his troops at historic Fraunces Tavern "with a heart full of love and gratitude."

For a short time (1789–90) New York was the capital of the new United States, and George Washington was inaugurated as the country's first president at Federal Hall. New York's economic development continued with the beginning of the stock exchange and the founding of the Bank of New York by Alexander Hamilton. As a result of the population so rapidly expanding, the city water supply became a serious problem. Yellow fever and cholera killed thousands; survivors fled in droves to the "country" north of 14th Street. By 1799, when the city's population was about 60,000, the first public utility was established to supply the city with fresh water.

New York boomed after 1812, largely due to the 1825 opening of the Erie Canal, which gave the city a virtual monopoly on transportation to the American West. The City Planning Commission, organized in 1811, designed Manhattan's present-day grid system of streets. In 1858, Frederick Law Olmsted, a landscape architect, and Calvert Vaux, an architect, won the competition and $2,000 prize to design Central Park, a swampland then inhabited by squatters.

During the Civil War—although the well-to-do could buy their way out of the army by paying $300 for a substitute and the poor, resentful of this injustice, rioted in the streets—many of New York's 750,000 went to war. Afterward, economic recovery was rapid, and corruption commonplace; it existed in both the business and the public sectors. The money stolen from the city during William "Boss" Tweed's administration of Tammany Hall, the political organization that ran the city in the 1860s and '70s, has been estimated as high as $200 million.

From about 1880 to 1920, tremendous waves of immigration produced the manpower for building the elevated railway, the Brooklyn Bridge, and the first skyscrapers. The late 19th and 20th centuries brought stupendous expansion only temporarily interrupted by economic depressions and two world wars. In 1898, Brooklyn, Queens, and Staten Island were annexed to form Greater New York (the Bronx already had been annexed). Following the Tammany Hall regime, Mayor Fiorello LaGuardia, "The Lit-

DATELINE

Manhattan's first street lights.

- **1765** Stamp Act enforced; Congress convenes in New York to protest taxes.
- **1774** English ship loaded with tea turned back in New York's own "tea party."
- **1776** American Revolutionary War begins.
- **1783** British forces leave New York. George Washington delivers his farewell address at Fraunces Tavern.
- **1789** George Washington is sworn in as first president of the United States, at Federal Hall.
- **1790** The first census counts some 33,100 in Manhattan.
- **1791** Stock Exchange started.
- **1797** Capital of New York State moved from New York City to Albany.
- **1807** The *Clermont*, Robert Fulton's steamboat, voyages up the Hudson to Albany.
- **1817** New York State decrees that all slaves be freed by 1827.
- **1820** Population reaches 120,000.
- **1825** Erie Canal completed.
- **1831** New York University founded.
- **1840** Manhattan population reaches

(continues)

DATELINE

312,710; in 1850,
it's 515,550.

- **1848** Ireland's potato famine and Germany's political uprisings cause an influx of immigrants.
- **1851** *The New York Times* is founded.
- **1853** Crystal Palace houses the world's fair on the site of Bryant Park.
- **1858** Calvert Vaux and Frederick Law Olmsted win the competition to design Central Park.
- **1863** Less affluent New Yorkers stage Draft Riots when a law allows individuals to avoid conscription for the Civil War by paying $300.
- **1870** Manhattan population reaches 942,300.
- **1871** "Boss" Tweed and his political cronies are jailed for stealing millions from the city while in power.
- **1880** Metropolitan Museum of Art opens.
- **1882** Electric power plant built by Thomas Edison provides city with electricity.
- **1883** Brooklyn Bridge opens to traffic.
- **1885–86** United States receives and dedicates the Statue of Liberty, a gift from the French people.

(continues)

tle Flower," restored color, character, and optimism to an office lacking all three. Mayor during 1934–45, LaGuardia saw the city through the Depression years, creating jobs, improving buildings and parks, and securing federal aid for the poor.

In 1952, the United Nations moved to Manhattan, making it more than ever a political sounding board to the world. New York City was given a voice in the United States by well-known mayors like Robert F. Wagner, Jr., John V. Lindsay, and Edward I. Koch.

Today New York glitters as a bastion of capitalism, its mighty skyscrapers dominating the skyline with a zeal that out-of-towners find overwhelming, even terrifying. Yet New York is a beautiful city, beautiful of line, color, and dramatic impetus. There are incomparable museums, theaters, art galleries, and concert halls and every kind of antiques shop, bookseller, clock dealer, and jade carver. By common consent, New York restaurants are among the finest in the world. A seamless ritual of rejuvenation and hope still prevails, perhaps a carryover from the days of immigration, when America was the haven for all the world's oppressed. New York is America at its bold best, the noblest of symbols, the most exciting city on earth.

2. ARCHITECTURE & THE ARTS

ARCHITECTURE New York is a polyglot city, a rich warren of architectural styles that reflect the diversity of its culture and its historical heritage.

The Great Fires of 1776 and 1835 ravaged New York and destroyed many of the Georgian and early Federal buildings. Those that remain are scattered throughout the city. Some examples of buildings in these styles still to be found are St. Paul's Chapel (1764–66), the earliest surviving pre-Revolutionary nonresidential building in New York, and the Morris-Jumel Mansion (1765), an excellent example of Georgian Colonial, although it was remodeled in the Federal style in about 1810.

In the early 19th century, Greek and

Gothic Revival emerged. The Federal Hall National Memorial (1842–62) recalls an Athenian temple, and many attached town houses have facades decorated in the Greek style. Richard Upjohn's Trinity Church (1846) at the end of Wall Street is a classic example of Gothic Revivalism, while Stanford White's Washington Arch, along with the town houses along Washington Square North (1832–33), reflects a passion for Greek Revivalism.

After the Civil War, a resurgence of international travel and trade brought to New York a renewed interest in European architecture. Examples of Tudor, Romanesque, Italian Renaissance, and French Second Empire can be found—not infrequently in the same structure. The Villard Houses (1884; now part of a hotel), for example, were clearly inspired by the Palazzo della Cancelleria in Rome. Despite revolutionary technology, such as steel-pile foundations and steel frames, there was very little change in architectural styles at first, as well as a seeming unawareness of the possibilities this technology offered in terms of design. The invention of the hydraulic lift allowed for the erection of skyscrapers, but their steel frames were disguised with facades from other periods. The rusticated stone facade and the Florentine Renaissance cornices of the Flatiron Building (1902) are typical examples of the continued use of earlier architectural styles. Another building constructed in a similar vein is the Woolworth Building (1913), with its adaptation of a Gothic cathedral—complete with gargoyles—to skyscraper form.

In residential architecture, brownstone row houses reminiscent of those in Paris persisted, though available technology also produced such luxury high-rise residential buildings as the Chelsea and the Dakota (both 1884). The neoclassical decoration of the Metropolitan Museum of Art (1902) exhibited the strong interest in the Beaux Arts movement prevalent as the 20th century began.

Modernist architecture began to develop through the form-follows-function model of Louis Sullivan, who was the first to break from the idea that older architectural styles were necessary to the facades of skyscrapers. Art deco was the next major innovation. The 1930 Chrysler Building, the 1931 Empire State Building, and the 1932 RCA Build-

DATELINE

- **1887** Electric streetcars run on elevated railways.
- **1889** Wooden arch at Washington Square commemorates Centennial of George Washington's Inauguration. Permanent arch is erected in 1892.
- **1892** Immigration center established on Ellis Island.
- **1898** Greater New York City is formed by joining five boroughs. The population in 1900 is 3.4 million.
- **1899** Bronx Zoo opens.
- **1901** Macy's department store opens for business.
- **1904** First subway, the IRT line, runs from City Hall to 145th Street.
- **1911** New York Public Library at 42nd Street opens.
- **1917** United States enters WWI. New York City is chief port of embarkation for troops.
- **1920** Population is 5.6 million.
- **1923** Yankee Stadium—the House that Ruth Built—opens in the Bronx.
- **1929** Stock market crash precipitates Great Depression.
- **1930** Chrysler Building completed.
- **1931** George Washington Bridge

(continues)

ing (now the GE Building) are stunning examples of the heights to which skyscraper architecture rose.

Economic recovery after the Great Depression saw the development of glass-walled buildings, where the weight-bearing function rested on steel skeletons. Lever House (1952) and the Seagram Building (1958) are early examples of the glass-and-steel-curtain walls of the new International Style.

In recent times, sculptural planes and masses have become prevalent and are in evidence in such buildings as the Whitney Museum (1966) and the Waterside apartment complex (1974). An interest in decorative facades is currently being exhibited, such as the Chippendale cornice of the Sony (formerly AT&T) Building (1978–82). In the late 1980s and early 90s, the World Financial Center, designed by Cesar Pelli, and the Four Seasons Hotel New York, designed by I. M. Pei, won international acclaim.

THE ARTS No sooner was New York City settled than its artistic citizens found an avenue for expression. Theaters became increasingly popular from the time the first one opened on Maiden Lane in 1732. Few painters, however, saw New York as their venue until the 20th century. The city's lack of interest in art (commerce and trade were the chief foci) drove them to Europe, a pattern established by such artists as Benjamin West and John Singleton Copley.

However, with the growth of fascism in Europe in the 1930s, the trend reversed with the influx of a number of noted artists, including George Grosz and Hans Hoffman. After World War II, the New York School became prominent with artists like Jackson Pollock, Robert Motherwell, Mark Rothko, Willem de Kooning, Philip Guston, and Franz Kline.

As New York became an international center for the arts, artists gained almost unlimited support, and buildings were erected to showcase their talents. The Guggenheim Museum (1959) was constructed as a repository for modern painting and sculpture, while Lincoln Center (1966) was built to house the Metropolitan Opera; the New York Philharmonic; the city opera and ballet companies; a repertory theater; a concert hall for chamber music; and the Juilliard School for actors, musicians, and dancers.

The Metropolitan Museum and the Museum of Modern Art were expanded as well, and the Whitney Museum of American Art was built.

In an earlier time, the simultaneous progression of vaudeville and the legitimate theater started at Crystal Palace, then gradually moved uptown, finally reaching Times Square around the turn of the century. In music, Carnegie Hall (1891) established New York City as a major venue for performing artists.

In recent years, experimentation in the visual arts has been high, with a variety of new techniques and media strongly in evidence. This is an unrestrained and provocative scene that encourages much growth and innovation.

3. RECOMMENDED BOOKS & FILMS

BOOKS

GENERAL

Cudahy, Brian J. *Over and Back* (Fordham University Press, 1989).

Dolkart, Andrew S. *The Texture of TriBeCa* (TriBeCa Community Association, 1989).

Kinkead, Eugene. *Central Park: The Birth, Decline, and Renewal of a National Treasure* (Norton, 1990).

Kisseloff, Jeff. *You Must Remember This* (Schocken, 1989).

Miller, Terry. *Greenwich Village and How It Got That Way* (Crown, 1990).

Morris, Jan. *Manhattan '45* (Oxford University Press, 1987).

Schermerhorn, Gene. *Letters to Phil* (New York Bound, 1982).

Snyder, Robert. *The Voice of the City: Vaudeville and Popular Culture in New York* (Oxford University Press, 1989).

Trager, James. *West of Fifth: The Rise and Fall of Manhattan's West Side* (Atheneum, 1987).

ECONOMIC, POLITICAL & SOCIAL HISTORY

Allen, Oliver E. *New York, New York: A History of the World's Most Exhilarating & Challenging City* (Macmillan, 1990).

Asbury, Herbert. *The Gangs of New York* (Capricorn, 1989).

Baldwin, James. *Notes of a Native Son* (Beacon, 1990).

Blackmar, Elizabeth. *Manhattan for Rent, Seventeen Eighty-five to Eighteen Fifty* (Cornell University Press, 1988).

Brandt, Nat. *The Man Who Tried to Burn New York* (Syracuse University Press, 1986).

Cohen, B., S. Heller, and S. Chwast. *New York Observed* (Abrams, 1987).

DATELINE

Democratic and Republican mayoral endorsements, wins second term with 75% of vote.

● **1986** Refurbished Statue of Liberty celebrates its centennial.

● **1989** David Dinkins elected as New York's first black mayor.

● **1990** New York population is 7.3 million. Newly restored Immigration Museum opens to public on Ellis Island.

● **1992** Democratic National Convention held in New York.

● **1993** World Trade Center badly damaged in terrorist bombing but soon reopens. Rudolph Giuliani elected mayor.

Hood, Clifton. *722 Miles: The Building of the Subways & How They Transformed New York* (Simon & Schuster, 1993).

Jacobs, William Jay. *Ellis Island* (Macmillan, 1990).

Kazin, Alfred. *Our New York* (Harper & Row, 1989).

Kessner, Thomas. *Fiorello H. LaGuardia and the Making of Modern New York* (McGraw-Hill, 1989).

MacKay, Ernst A. *The Civil War & New York City* (Syracuse University Press, 1990).

Marshall, Richard. *Fifty New York Artists: A Critical Selection of Painters & Sculptors Working in New York* (Chronicle, 1986).

Patterson, Jerry E. *The Vanderbilts* (Abrams, 1989).

Rink, Oliver A. *Holland on the Hudson* (New York State Historical Association, 1986).

Whitman, Walt. *Walt Whitman's New York* (Macmillan, 1963).

ARCHITECTURE & THE ARTS

Bogart, Michele H. *Public Sculpture and the Civic Ideal in New York City, 1890–1989* (University of Chicago Press, 1989).

Boyer, M. Christine. *Manhattan Manners: Architecture & Style, 1850–1900* (Rizzoli International, 1985).

Goldberg, Paul. *Skyscraper* (Knopf, 1981).

Jacobs, Jane. *Death and Life of Great American Cities* (Random House, 1961).

Lieberman, Nathaniel. *Manhattan Lightscape* (Abbeville, 1990).

Mackay, Donald A. *The Building of Manhattan: How Manhattan Was Built Overground & Underground, from the Dutch Settlers to the Skyscrapers* (Harper & Row, 1987).

Orkin, Ruth. *More Pictures from My Window* (Rizzoli International, 1989).

Rosen, Laura. *Top of the City: New York's Hidden Rooftop World* (Thames & Hudson, 1990).

Silver, Nathan. *Lost New York* (American Legacy, 1982).

Valenzi, Kathleen D., ed. *Private Moments: Images of Manhattan* (Howell, 1989).

Watson, Edward B. *New York Then & Now: Eighty-three Manhattan Sites Photographed in the Past & Present* (Dover, 1976).

Willensky, Elliot, and Norval White. *AIA Guide to New York City, Third Edition* (Harcourt Brace, 1988).

FICTION
For Adults

Carr, Caleb. *The Alienist* (Random House, 1994).

Finney, Jack. *Time and Again* (Simon & Schuster, 1986).

James, Henry. *Washington Square* (G. K. Hall, 1980).

Liebling, A. J. *The Telephone Booth Indian* (North Point, 1990).

McInerny, Jay. *Brightness Falls* (McKay, 1992).

Powell, Dawn. *The Locusts Have No King* (Yarrow, 1989).

Wharton, Edith. *The Age of Innocence* (Macmillan, 1983).

Wolfe, Tom. *Bonfire of the Vanities* (Farrar, Straus & Giroux, 1987).

For Kids

Barracca, Sal. *The Adventures of Taxi Dog* (Halcyon, 1990).

Gangloff, Deborah. *Albert and Victoria* (Crown, 1989).

Jacobs, William Jay. *Ellis Island* (Macmillan, 1990).

Macaulay, David. *Underground* (Houghton Mifflin, 1976).
Selden, George. *The Cricket in Times Square* (Dell, 1970).
Swift, Hildegarde H. *The Little Red Lighthouse and The Great Gray Bridge* (Harcourt Brace Jovanovich, 1974).
Thomson, Kay. *Eloise* (Simon & Schuster, 1969).
Waber, Bernard. *Lyle, Lyle, Crocodile and The House on East 88th Street* (Houghton Mifflin, 1965).
White, E. B. *Stuart Little* (Harper & Row, 1973).

FILMS

Hundreds of movies have been made about New York and in New York—it's one of the most familiar movie sets in the world. Woody Allen's films, perhaps more than any others, catch the humor and angst of current-day New Yorkers, especially in *Annie Hall, Manhattan, Hannah and Her Sisters,* and *Manhattan Murder Mystery.* Nobody tells about growing up in the city better than Neil Simon in *Brighton Beach Memoirs.* Italian family life in New York is portrayed in *Moonstruck. Godfather III, Prizzi's Honor,* and *Goodfellas* deal with the world of organized crime in New York. Several scenes in *Ghostbusters* were shot at Columbia University; *Ghost* took place in SoHo, Brooklyn, and downtown Manhattan. *Tootsie* deals with the television world in New York. *Crossing Delancey* shuttles between the old-world Jewish culture of the Lower East Side and Manhattan's uptown literary set. Spike Lee portrays the seamy streets of Brooklyn in *Do the Right Thing* and, most recently, *Crooklyn.* Of course, there's the all-time New York classic— *Breakfast at Tiffany's.* And Martin Scorsese reaches even farther back in *The Age of Innocence,* which chronicles life in late 19th-century New York.

PLANNING A TRIP TO NEW YORK

Here's some basic information to work with as you start to plan your trip to New York. After deciding where to go, most people have two basic questions: What will it cost? and How do I get there? This chapter will answer both these questions, as well as provide information about when to go, what to pack, where to obtain special services, and where to get more information about New York.

1. INFORMATION & MONEY

As soon as you know you're going to New York, contact the **New York Convention and Visitors Bureau,** 2 Columbus Circle, New York, NY 10019 (tel. 212/397-8222), and ask for an information packet. The bureau will send you details on hotels, restaurants, shopping, tour packages, events, and lots more.

New York, in general, is an expensive city, among the most expensive in the United States. But don't let that deter you: You can choose where to save and where you really want to spend. Save money on hotels by staying at a B&B and splurge on the best French restaurants; go all out at luxury hotels and eat picnics in the park; enjoy free poetry readings and concerts and have a shopping spree; or get two in the orchestra for a Broadway musical and buy bargains on the Lower East Side. In short, what you'll spend in New York pretty much depends on your own tastes: The city can accommodate every reasonable budget.

2. WHEN TO GO

CLIMATE   New York winters tend to be unpredictable: most often they are relatively mild, but 1994 was severe and stormy. There are usually a few idyllic weeks in spring and fall when the temperature hovers around the 70° mark. Summer, hot and muggy, begins early and lasts late, often through September. But still, the city is great to visit at any time. Both central heating and air conditioning are practically universal, so the weather is never a problem indoors. The winter is the height of the theater and entertainment season, and if you come in summer you'll be ahead of the game, since many residents will be at the beach or in the mountains, and you have the city practically to yourself. It's much easier then to pick up tickets for Broadway plays at the last minute as well as to get into the charming little restaurants, and you have less trouble fighting off the mobs in the big stores.

WHAT THINGS COST IN NEW YORK	U.S. $
Taxi from Kennedy Airport to Manhattan (plus tip)	$30.00–$35.00
Carey bus from Kennedy Airport to Manhattan	$11.00
Local telephone call	25¢
Double at The Mark (very expensive)	$285.00–$340.00
Double at Mayflower Hotel (expensive)	$160.00–$180.00
Double at The Wyndham (moderate)	$130.00–$140.00
Double at Roger Williams Hotel (inexpensive)	$60.00–$75.00
Lunch for one at Contrapunto (moderate)	$22.00–$25.00
Lunch for one at Teachers Too (inexpensive)	$10.00–$12.00
Dinner for one, without wine, at Sign of the Dove (expensive)	$60.00–$70.00
Dinner for one, with wine, at American Festival Café (moderate)	$25.00
Dinner for one, without wine, at Dallas BBQ (inexpensive)	$10.00–$12.00
Bottle of beer (at a bar)	$3.00–$4.00
Coca-Cola	$1.50
Cup of coffee	$1.50
Roll of ASA 100 Kodacolor film, 36 exposures	$5.85
Admission to the Museum of Modern Art	$7.50
Movie ticket	$8.00
Theater ticket to *Sunset Boulevard*	$25.00–$65.00

Average Daily Temperature and Days of Rain

	Jan	Feb	Mar	Apr	May	June	July	Aug	Sept	Oct	Nov	Dec
Temp. (°F.)	38	40	48	61	71	80	85	84	77	67	54	42
Days of Rain	11	10	11	11	11	10	11	10	8	8	9	10

NEW YORK CALENDAR OF EVENTS

JANUARY

☐ **New York National Boat Show.** The 85th edition of the marine extravaganza, at the giant Jacob K. Javits Convention Center, will include hundreds of boats and marine products from the world's leading manufacturers. Jan 5–15.

☐ **New York Coliseum Antiques Show.** This new and exciting "collector's show" is the only ongoing event to take place in the well-loved Coliseum, at Columbus Circle. Dec 31 (94)–Jan 1 (also Oct 21–22 and Mar 25–26).

FEBRUARY

☐ **Chinese New Year** celebrations usher in the Year of the Pig 4693. Celebrations concentrated in Chinatown in Lower Manhattan the first two weeks of the month.

☐ **Manhattan Antiques and Collectibles Triple Pier Expo.** New York's largest and most comprehensive antiques event is held at three piers on the Hudson River: "The 20th-Century Pier" (Pier 88), "The Americana Pier" (Pier 90), and "The Classical Pier" (Pier 92). Feb 18–19 and 25–26 (also Nov 18–19 and 25–26).

MARCH

❂ *NEW YORK FLOWER SHOW   Annual harbinger of spring presented by the Horticultural Society of New York.* ***Where:*** *Piers 90 and 93, 51st Street and Twelfth Avenue.* ***When:*** *March 1–5.* ***How:*** *Buy tickets at the door—$10 adults, $4 children.*

☐ **St. Patrick's Day Parade.** More than 150,000 marchers join in the world's largest civilian parade, as Fifth Avenue from 44th to 86th streets rings with the sounds of bands and bagpipes. Mar 17.

APRIL

✪ **OPENING OF NEW YORK METS BASEBALL SEASON**
     Where: Shea Stadium, in Queens. **When:** April. **How:** For tickets and information, call 718/507-6387.

✪ **OPENING OF NEW YORK YANKEES BASEBALL SEASON**
     Where: Yankee Stadium, in the Bronx. **When:** April. **How:** For tickets, call Ticketmaster (tel. 212/307-1212) or Yankee Stadium (tel. 718/293-4300).

✪ **GREATER NEW YORK INTERNATIONAL AUTO SHOW**   The largest U.S. auto show spotlights the latest cars, trucks, and vans from all over the world.
     Where: Jacob K. Javits Convention Center. **When:** Apr 15–23. **How:** Buy tickets at the door—$8 adults, $2 children under 12.

MAY

☐ **Salute to Israel Parade,** beginning at Fifth Avenue and 57th Street. May 21.

JUNE

✪ **16TH ANNUAL MUSEUM MILE FESTIVAL**   Nine major cultural institutions including the Metropolitan Museum of Art, the Guggenheim Museum, the Jewish Museum, and the Museum of the City of New York, are open free to the public from 6:30 to 9pm. The streets become a pedestrian mall, with entertainment, musicians, and children's events on virtually every block.
     Where: Fifth Avenue, from 82nd to 102nd streets. **When:** June 13. **How:** All events and admissions free, so just come on over.

☐ **Shakespeare in the Park,** Delacorte Theater, in Central Park. Free. For information, call 212/598-7100. Through August.
☐ **Metropolitan Opera,** free concerts in parks in all boroughs. Through August.

JULY

✪ **SUMMERGARDEN CONCERTS OF CLASSICAL MUSIC**
     Where: Museum of Modern Art sculpture garden. **When:** Friday and Saturday evenings, from the first weekend in July through August. **How:** Free.

☐ **July 4th weekend.** Macy's great fireworks extravaganza near the tip of Manhattan is an annual cause for celebration. July 4.

AUGUST

✪ *25TH ANNUAL LINCOLN CENTER*
OUT-OF-DOORS FESTIVAL *A celebration of*
performing arts, held in the outdoor spaces of Lincoln
Center.
   Where: Lincoln Center. *When:* All of August. *How:*
Free. For information, phone 212/875-5400.

SEPTEMBER

☐ **Washington Square Outdoors Art Festival,** Greenwich
Village. A classic. Sept 2–4 and 9–10 (also May 27–29 and June
3–4).

OCTOBER

☐ **Columbus Day Parade** brings out the crowds from 44th to
86th streets. October 10.
☐ **Greenwich Village Halloween Parade.** It wouldn't be
Halloween without this flamboyant event. Sixth Avenue from
Spring to 23rd streets. October 31.

NOVEMBER

✪ *RADIO CITY MUSIC HALL CHRISTMAS*
SPECTACULAR *A fitting climax to Radio City's 63rd*
anniversary year.
   When: Mid-November to early January. *Where:* Radio
City Music Hall, Sixth Avenue at 50th Street. *How:* Buy
tickets at box office or via Ticketmaster's Radio City
Hotline: 212/307-1000.

☐ **New York City Marathon.** 25,000 hopefuls from around
the world will participate in the 25th running of the largest
U.S. marathon, and at least a million fans will cheer them on.
Nov 12.
☐ **Macy's Thanksgiving Day Parade.** A New York tradition.
Nov 23.

DECEMBER

☐ **Rockefeller Center Christmas Tree** is lit. Early December.
☐ **Giant Hanukkah Menorah** is lit at Manhattan's Grand
Army Plaza, Fifth Avenue, in front of the Plaza Hotel. Mid-December.
☐ **The Nutcracker.** Tchaikovsky's holiday favorite is performed
by the New York City Ballet, at Lincoln Center.
☐ **New Year's Eve.** Fireworks and midnight run in Central Park;
lighted ball drops from the top of One Times Square. Dancing
and performing-arts events throughout the city, part of the Fifth
Annual First Night. Dec 31.

3. WHAT TO PACK

Because New York weather is variable, you'll need to be flexible with your wardrobe. It's always best to dress in layers so you can quickly adjust to changing temperatures. In summer, try to wear very cool clothes—the city gets hot and muggy. New Yorkers wear everything from very sporty clothes to very dressy ones, so it all depends on your lifestyle. Jackets and ties are necessary for men in the fancier restaurants; denim is always out in these places. People tend to dress up for the theater and concerts. In some nightclubs, especially discos, the more outrageous the costume, the better. Basically, dress as you would in any American city: New Yorkers are amazingly tolerant when it comes to what other people wear. Bring an umbrella and raincoat—you never know.

4. TIPS FOR THE DISABLED, SENIORS, SINGLES, FAMILIES & STUDENTS

FOR THE DISABLED   New York has some of the most extensive services and programs for the disabled. For information about special events and programs, contact **The Lighthouse, Inc.,** 11 E. 59th St., New York, NY 10017 (tel. 800/334-5497), which serves people with impaired vision, or the **New York Society for the Deaf,** 817 Broadway, New York, NY 10003 (tel. 212/777-3900; for emergencies, 212/673-6500). *Access for All,* a guide to the city's cultural institutions, is available free from Hospital Audiences, Inc., 220 W. 42nd St., New York, NY 10036 (tel. 212/575-7676).

FOR SENIORS   Most hotels offer seniors a discount. Be sure to travel with your card issued by the AARP (1909 K Street NW, Washington, D.C. 20049; tel. 202/874-4700)—it opens the doors to many discounts. Few restaurants offer senior discounts, but they are available in many stores (look for signs) and at movie theaters during certain weekday hours. Most museums and attractions offer special prices. With your Social Security Health Insurance card (for those over 65), you need to pay only 65¢ on buses or subways.

FOR SINGLES   Unfortunately, the price of single and double hotel rooms are almost the same; singles save only a few dollars. Savings for singles are somewhat better in B&Bs, however. Traveling with a companion always saves money: To that end, **Travel Companion,** P.O. Box P-833, Amityville, NY 11701 (tel. 516/454-0880), tries to make you a match. For $36 to $66, you'll get a six-month listing of potential companions of either sex, as part of a most useful newsletter for solo travelers. A sample issue costs $4 postage paid.

FOR FAMILIES   In many of the hotels listed in this book, children (usually under 17) can stay free in their parents' room, when using existing bedding. Hilton Hotels have a unique deal: Children of *any* age can stay free with their parents in the same room. A few hotels offer a second room for children at a lower price.

FOR STUDENTS   High-school and college students with current I.D.s are often eligible for discounts at theaters, concert halls, museums, and other places. Look for signs.

5. GETTING THERE

BY PLANE   The major domestic carriers flying into the New York area are **American, America West, Continental, Delta, TWA, USAir,** and **United.** Most of the major international carriers also fly into New York.

The airports serving New York City are John F. Kennedy International Airport and LaGuardia Airport, both in Queens, and Newark International Airport in New Jersey. (See "Orientation" in Chapter 4 for details on arriving in the New York area.)

Obtaining the Best Prices   To get the best price on your airline ticket to New York, be prepared to do a little shopping around and always ask for the lowest fare. Fares are volatile; they vary from airline to airline and even for the same airline from day to day. Try to schedule your traveling for weekdays during the busy summer season and avoid major holiday periods, when fares go up. In general, the lowest fares are **Economy** or **APEX** fares—the former has no restrictions, while the latter (an advance-purchase excursion fare) requires you to reserve and pay for the ticket 7, 14, 21, or 30 days in advance and to stay for a minimum number of days; it also may have other restrictions, like flying before a specific date. APEX fares are usually nonrefundable, and there is a charge for changing dates; however, the savings are considerable. For example, on a day last summer, Continental's first-class Los Angeles–New York round-trip fully refundable fare was $1,320; its cheapest, nonrefundable APEX fare was $371 round trip. From Chicago to New York, the first-class fully refundable fare was $600 round trip; the cheapest, nonrefundable APEX fare was $290 round trip. There are a variety of prices in between these extremes, depending on how much of the payment is refundable, what days you travel, availability, and so on. Knowing all this, get on the phone, call your travel agent or a number of airlines, and work out a deal.

Another possibility is to call a discount travel agency like **Travel Avenue** in Chicago (tel. toll free 800/333-3335). Unlike most travel agencies, this one does not offer advice or itinerary planning; it does, however, offer cash rebates of 7% on fares from major airlines (over $300).

If you decide on a trip to New York at the last minute, give a call to 800/FLY-ASAP. This is a national reservation service that uses a new computer program to find the lowest fares available. You could realize substantial savings here.

A highly praised 5-year-old organization called **FreeFlier** may be

**FROMMER'S SMART TRAVELER:
AIRFARES**

1. Use a travel agent only if you know he or she will put in time and effort to get you the cheapest fare; otherwise, do your own homework or use a discount travel agency. It pays off!
2. Shop all the airlines that fly to New York.
3. Ask for the lowest fare, not just a discounted fare.
4. Keep calling: Airlines sometimes open up additional low-cost seats as a departure date nears.
5. Plan to travel during the week—avoid weekends and holiday periods as your travel dates.
6. Make sure to purchase your tickets at least 21 days in advance to take advantage of the cheapest APEX (advance purchase) fares; next cheapest are 14-day, then 7-day advance-purchase fares.

able to save you travel dollars—even if you're a relatively "infrequent flyer." For a small fee ($9.95 adults; $7.50 seniors, retirees, and students), it forwards the applications of travelers to more than two dozen frequent-flyer, car-rental, and hotel-stay programs. Owner Robert Reiner points out that many programs provide instant benefits and do not require long-term loyalty. Frequent-flyer programs often offer insider discounts or advance notice of lower fares that only members may obtain. Many car-rental programs offer free upgrades or an extra day's usage. Several hotel-stay programs reward members with a free weekend night when they stay on a weekday night. Reiner advises that they often receive extra coupons for frequent traveler bonuses that they will pass on to anyone sending a stamped, self-addressed #10 envelope. For more information, contact FreeFlier, P.O. Box 844, Bowling Green Station, New York, NY 10274-0844 (tel. 212/727-9675).

BY TRAIN **Amtrak** (tel. toll free 800/USA-RAIL) runs frequent service to New York City. Here are sample fares (subject to change) and travel times from four major cities. Boston: $52 unreserved, $57 reserved one way, $84 round trip; 4 hours, 30 minutes to 5 hours, 40 minutes. Chicago: $128 one way, $136–$224 round trip; 18 hours, 25 minutes to 26 hours, 49 minutes. Washington, D.C.: $68 one way, $92 round-trip excursion; 3 hours, 20 minutes. Philadelphia: $31 one way, $52 round trip; one hour, 20 minutes.

BY BUS Here are sample fares (subject to change) and travel times via **Greyhound Bus Lines** (tel. 800/231-2223, or check your local telephone book). Boston: $25.95 one way, $51.90 round trip; 4 to 5 hours. Chicago: $69 one way, $133 round trip; 16 to 24 hours. Philadelphia: $11.95 one way, $23.90 round trip; 2 to 3 hours. Washington, D.C.: one way $25.95, $51.90 round trip; 4 to 6 hours. *Note:* Ask about advance-purchase tickets to realize extra savings.

BY CAR From the south, the New Jersey Turnpike (I-95) leads to the Holland Tunnel, the Lincoln Tunnel, and the George Washington

Bridge. From the north, the New York Thruway (I-287 and I-87) leads to Manhattan's East and West Sides; the New England Thruway (I-95) leads via connecting roads to Manhattan and the other boroughs. From the west, the Bergen-Passaic Expressway (I-80) leads to Manhattan and the other boroughs. Driving times should be about the same as bus times (see above). *Note:* Having a car in Manhattan is not an asset. Hotels charge very high parking rates, usually with no in-and-out privileges; parking spaces on city streets are very difficult to come by; and garage rates in much of the borough are exorbitant. Drive only if you must.

CHAPTER 3

FOR FOREIGN VISITORS

Although American fads and fashions have spread across Europe and other parts of the world so that America may seem like familiar territory before your arrival, there are still many peculiarities and uniquely American situations that any foreign visitor will encounter.

1. PREPARING FOR YOUR TRIP

ENTRY REQUIREMENTS

DOCUMENT REGULATIONS   Canadian citizens may enter the United States without visas; they need only proof of residence.

Citizens of the United Kingdom, New Zealand, Japan, and most western European countries traveling on valid passports may not need a visa for fewer than 90 days of holiday or business travel to the United States, providing that they hold a round-trip or return ticket and enter the United States on an airline or a cruise line participating in the visa-waiver program.

(Note that citizens of these visa-exempt countries who first enter the United States may then visit Mexico, Canada, Bermuda, and/or the Caribbean islands and then re-enter the United States by any mode of transportation, without needing a visa. Further information is available from any United States embassy or consulate.)

Citizens of countries other than those stipulated above, including citizens of Australia, must have two documents: a valid passport, with an expiration date at least six months later than the scheduled end of the visit to the United States, and a tourist visa, available without charge from the nearest United States consulate.

To obtain a visa, the traveler must submit a completed application form (either in person or by mail) with a 1½-inch-square photo and demonstrate binding ties to a residence abroad. Usually you can obtain a visa at once or within 24 hours, but it may take longer during the summer rush from June to August. If you cannot go in person, contact the nearest U.S. embassy or consulate for directions on applying by mail. Your travel agent or airline travel agent or airline office may also be able to provide you with visa applications and instructions. The U.S. consulate or embassy that issues your visa will determine whether you will be issued a multiple- or single-entry visa and any restrictions regarding the length of your stay.

MEDICAL REQUIREMENTS No inoculations are needed to enter the United States unless you are coming from, or have stopped over in, areas known to be suffering from epidemics, particularly cholera or yellow fever.

If you have a disease requiring treatment with medications containing narcotics or drugs requiring a syringe, carry a valid signed prescription from your physician to allay any suspicions that you are smuggling drugs.

CUSTOMS REQUIREMENTS Every adult visitor may bring in free of duty: one liter of wine or hard liquor; 200 cigarettes or 100 cigars (but no cigars from Cuba) or three pounds of smoking tobacco; $100 worth of gifts. These exemptions are offered to travelers who spend at least 72 hours in the United States and who have not claimed them within the preceding six months. It is altogether forbidden to bring into the country foodstuffs (particularly cheese, fruit, cooked meats, and canned goods) and plants (vegetables, seeds, tropical plants, and so on). Foreign tourists may bring in or take out up to $10,000 in U.S. or foreign currency with no formalities; larger sums must be declared to Customs on entering or leaving.

INSURANCE

There is no national health system in the United States. Because the cost of medical care is extremely high, we strongly advise every traveler to secure health coverage before setting out.

You may want to take out a comprehensive travel policy that covers (for a relatively low premium) sickness or injury costs (medical, surgical, and hospital); loss or theft of your baggage; trip-cancellation costs; guarantee of bail in case you are arrested; costs of accident, repatriation, or death. Such packages (for example, "Europe Assistance" in Europe) are sold by automobile clubs at attractive rates, as well as by insurance companies and travel agencies.

MONEY

CURRENCY & EXCHANGE The U.S. monetary system has a decimal base: one American **dollar ($1)** = 100 **cents** (100¢)

Dollar bills commonly come in $1 ("a buck"), $5, $10, $20, $50, and $100 denominations (the last two are not welcome when paying for small purchases and are not accepted in taxis or at subway ticket booths). There are also $2 bills (seldom encountered).

There are six denominations of coins: 1¢ (one cent or "penny"), 5¢ (five cents or "a nickel"), 10¢ (ten cents or "a dime"), 25¢ (twenty-five cents or "a quarter"), 50¢ (fifty cents or "a half dollar"), and the rare $1 piece.

TRAVELER'S CHECKS Traveler's checks denominated in U.S. dollars are readily accepted at most hotels, motels, restaurants, and large stores. But the best place to change traveler's checks is at a bank. Do not bring traveler's checks denominated in other currencies.

CREDIT CARDS The method of payment most widely used is the credit card: VISA (BarclayCard in Britain), Mastercard (EuroCard in Europe, Access in Britain, Chargex in Canada), American Express, Diners Club, Discover, and Carte Blanche. You can save yourself trouble by using "plastic money" rather than cash or traveler's checks in most hotels, motels, restaurants, and retail stores (a growing number of food and liquor stores now accept credit cards). You must have a credit card to rent a car. It can also be used as proof of identity (often carrying more weight than a passport), or as a "cash card," enabling you to draw money from banks that accept them.

Note: The "foreign-exchange bureaus" so common in Europe are rare even at airports in the United States, and nonexistent outside major cities. Try to avoid having to change foreign money, or traveler's checks denominated other than in U.S. dollars, at a small-town bank, or even a branch in a big city; in fact, leave any currency other than U.S. dollars at home—it may prove more nuisance to you than it's worth.

SAFETY

GENERAL While tourist areas are generally safe, crime is on the increase everywhere, and U.S. urban areas tend to be less safe than those in Europe or Japan. Visitors should always stay alert. This is particularly true of large U.S. cities. It is wise to ask the city's or area's tourist office if you're in doubt about which neighborhoods are safe. Avoid deserted areas, especially at night. Don't go into any city park at night unless there is an event that attracts crowds—for example, New York City's concerts in the parks. Generally speaking, you can feel safe in areas where there are many people, and many open establishments.

Avoid carrying valuables with you on the street, and don't display expensive cameras or electronic equipment. Hold on to your pocketbook, and place your billfold in an inside pocket. In theaters, restaurants, and other public places, keep your possessions in sight.

Remember also that hotels are open to the public, and in a large hotel, security may not be able to screen everyone entering. Always lock your room door—don't assume that once inside your hotel you are automatically safe and no longer need to be aware of your surroundings.

DRIVING Safety while driving is particularly important. Question your rental agency about personal safety, or ask for a brochure of traveler safety tips when you pick up your car. Obtain written directions, or a map with the route marked in red, from the agency showing how to get to your destination. And, if possible, arrive and depart during daylight hours.

Recently more and more crime has involved cars and drivers. If you drive off a highway into a doubtful neighborhood, leave the area as quickly as possible. If you have an accident, even on the highway, stay in your car with the doors locked until you assess the situation or until the police arrive. If you are bumped from behind on the street or are involved in a minor accident with no injuries and the situation appears to be suspicious, motion to the other driver to follow you. *Never* get out of your car in such situations. You can also keep a pre-made sign in your car which reads: PLEASE FOLLOW THIS VEHICLE TO REPORT THE ACCIDENT. Show the sign to the other driver and go directly to the nearest police precinct, well-lighted service station, or all-night store.

If you see someone on the road who indicates a need for help, do *not* stop. Take note of the location, drive on to a well-lighted area, and telephone the police by dialing 911.

Park in well-lighted, well-traveled areas if possible. Always keep your car doors locked, whether attended or unattended. Look around you before you get out of your car, and never leave any packages or valuables in sight. If someone attempts to rob you or steal your car, do *not* try to resist the thief/carjacker—report the incident to the police department immediately.

You may wish to contact the local tourist information bureau in your destination before you arrive. They may be able to provide you with a safety brochure.

2. GETTING TO & AROUND THE U.S.

Travelers from overseas can take advantage of the **APEX (Advance Purchase Excursion)** fares offered by all the major U.S. and European carriers. Aside from these, attractive values are offered by **Icelandair** on flights from Luxembourg to New York and by **Virgin Atlantic Airways** from London to New York/Newark.

Some major American airlines (for example, TWA, American, Northwest, United, and Delta) offer travelers on their transatlantic or transpacific flights special discount tickets under the name **Visit USA,** allowing travel between any U.S. destinations at minimum rates. They are not on sale in the United States, and must, therefore, be purchased before you leave your foreign point of departure. This system is the best, easiest, and fastest way to see the United States at low cost. You should obtain information well in advance from your travel agent or the office of the airline concerned, since the conditions attached to these discount tickets can be changed without advance notice.

The visitor arriving by air, no matter what the port of entry, should cultivate patience and resignation before setting foot on U.S. soil. Getting through Immigration control may take as long as two hours on some days, especially summer weekends. Add the time it takes to clear Customs and you'll see that you should make very generous allowance for delay in planning connections between international and domestic flights—an average of two to three hours at least.

In contrast, travelers arriving by car or by rail from Canada will find border-crossing formalities streamlined to the vanishing point. And air travelers from Canada, Bermuda, and some places in the Caribbean can sometimes go through Customs and Immigration at the point of departure, which is much quicker and less painful.

For further information about travel to New York, see "Getting There" in Chapter 2.

International visitors can also buy a **USA Railpass,** good for 15 or 30 days of unlimited travel on Amtrak. The pass is available through many foreign travel agents. Prices in 1994 for a 15-day pass are $208 off-peak, $308 peak; a 30-day pass costs $309 off-peak,

$389 peak. (With a foreign passport, you can also buy passes at some Amtrak offices in the United States, including locations in San Francisco, Los Angeles, Chicago, New York, Miami, Boston, and Washington, D.C.) Reservations are generally required and should be made for each part of your trip as early as possible.

Visitors should also be aware of the limitations of long-distance rail travel in the United States With a few notable exceptions (for instance, the Northeast Corridor line between Boston and Washington, D.C.), service is rarely up to European standards: delays are common, routes are limited and often infrequently served, and fares are rarely significantly lower than discount airfares. Thus, cross-country train travel should be approached with caution.

The cheapest way to travel the United States is by **bus.** Greyhound, the nation's nationwide bus line, offers an **Ameripass** for unlimited travel for 7 days (for $250), 15 days (for $350), and 30 days (for $450). Bus travel in the United States can be both slow and uncomfortable, so this option is not for everyone.

FAST FACTS FOR THE FOREIGN TRAVELER

Automobile Organizations Auto clubs will supply maps, suggested routes, guidebooks, accident and bail-bond insurance, and emergency road service. The major auto club in the United States, with 955 offices nationwide, is the **American Automobile Association (AAA).** Members of some foreign auto clubs have reciprocal arrangements with the AAA and enjoy its services at no charge. If you belong to an auto club, inquire about AAA reciprocity before you leave. The AAA can provide you with an **International Driving Permit** validating your foreign license. You may be able to join the AAA even if you are not a member of a reciprocal club. To inquire, call toll free 800/336-4357. In addition, some automobile rental agencies now provide these services, so you should inquire about their availability when you rent your car.

Automobile Rentals To rent a car you need a major credit card, a valid driver's license, and you usually need to be at least 25. Some companies do rent to younger people but add a daily surcharge. Be sure to return your car with the same amount of gas you started out with; rental companies charge excessive prices for gasoline. All the major car rental companies are represented in New York (see "Getting Around" in Chapter 2).

Business Hours Banks are open weekdays from 9am to 3 or 4pm, although there's 24-hour access to the automatic tellers (ATMs) at most banks and other outlets. Generally, offices are open weekdays from 8am to 4 or 5pm. Stores are open six days a week with many open on Sunday, too; department stores usually stay open until 9pm at least one night a week.

Climate See "When to Go" in Chapter 2.

Currency See "Money" in "Preparing for Your Trip," above.

Currency Exchange You will find currency exchange services in all major airports with international service. Elsewhere, they may be quite difficult to come by. In New York, a very reliable choice is **Thomas Cook Currency Services, Inc.,** which has been in business since 1841 and offers a wide range of services. They also sell commission-free foreign and U.S. traveler's checks, drafts, and wire transfers, and they do check collections (including Eurochecks). Their rates are competitive and their service excellent. Cook maintains several offices in Manhattan (for the Fifth Avenue office, tel. 212/757-6915); at the JFK Airport International Arrivals Terminal (tel. 718/656-8444); and at LaGuardia Airport in the Delta Terminal (tel. 718/533-0784).

Drinking Laws   See "Liquor Laws" in "Fast Facts: New York," Chapter 4.

Electricity   The United States uses 110–120 volts, 60 cycles, compared to 220–240 volts, 50 cycles, in most of Europe. In addition to a 100-volt transformer, small appliances of non-American manufacture, such as hairdryers or shavers, will require a plug adapter, with two flat, parallel pins.

Embassies and Consulates   All embassies are located in the national capital, Washington, D.C.; some consulates are located in major cities, and most nations have a mission to the United Nations in New York City. Foreign visitors can obtain telephone numbers for their embassies and consulates by calling "Information" in Washington, D.C. (tel. 202/555-1212).

The Australian embassy is located at 1601 Massachusetts Ave. NW, Washington, DC 20036 (tel. 202/797-3000). The consulate-general is located in the International Building, 636 Fifth Ave., New York, NY 10111 (tel. 212/245-4000).

The Canadian embassy is located at 501 Pennsylvania Ave. NW, Washington, DC 20001 (tel. 202/682-1740). The consulate-general is located at 1251 Ave. of the Americas, New York, NY 10020-1175 (tel. 212/596-1600).

The Irish embassy is located at 2234 Massachusetts Ave. NW, Washington, DC 20008 (tel. 202/462-3939). The consulate-general is located at 345 Park Ave., New York, NY 10154-0037 (tel. 212/319-2555).

The New Zealand embassy is located at 37 Observatory Circle NW, Washington, DC 20008 (tel. 202/328-4000). There is no consulate in New York.

The British embassy is located at 3100 Massachusetts Ave. NW, Washington, DC 20008 (tel. 202/462-1340). The consulate-general is located at 845 Third Ave., New York, NY 10022 (tel. 212/745-0200).

Emergencies   Call 911 to report a fire, call the police, or get an ambulance.

If you encounter traveler's problems, check the local directory to find an office of the **Traveler's Aid Society,** a nationwide, nonprofit, social-service organization geared to helping travelers in difficult straits. Their services might include reuniting families separated while traveling, providing food and/or shelter to people stranded without cash, or even emotional counseling. If you're in trouble, seek them out.

Fax   See "Telephones," below.

Gasoline (Petrol)   One U.S. gallon equals 3.8 liters, while 1.2 U.S. gallons equals one Imperial gallon. You'll notice that there are several grades (and price levels) of gasoline available at most gas stations. And you'll also notice that their names change from company to company. The unleaded ones with the highest octane are the most expensive (most rental cars take the least-expensive "regular" unleaded), and leaded gas is the least expensive (if it is even available); but only older cars can take this, so ask if you're not sure.

Holidays On the following legal national holidays, banks, government offices, post offices, and many stores, restaurants, and museums are closed: January 1 (New Year's Day); third Monday in January (Martin Luther King, Jr. Day); third Monday in February (Presidents' Day); last Monday in May (Memorial Day); July 4 (Independence Day); first Monday in September (Labor Day); second Monday in October (Columbus Day); November 11 (Veterans' Day); last Thursday in November (Thanksgiving Day); December 25 (Christmas).

Finally, the Tuesday following the first Monday in November is Election Day and is a legal holiday in presidential-election years.

Languages Major hotels always have multilingual employees. Unless your language is very obscure, they can usually supply a translator on request.

Legal Aid The foreign tourist will probably never become involved with the American legal system. If you are pulled up for a minor infraction (for example, of the highway code, such as speeding), never attempt to pay the fine directly to a police officer; you may wind up arrested on the much more serious charge of attempted bribery. Pay fines by mail, or directly into the hands of the clerk of the court. If accused of a more serious offense, it's wise to say and do nothing before consulting a lawyer. Under U.S. law, an arrested person is allowed one telephone call to a party of his or her choice. Call your embassy or consulate.

Mail If you want your mail to follow you on your vacation and you aren't sure of your address, your mail can be sent to you, in your name, **c/o General Delivery** at the main post office of the city or region where you expect to be. The addressee must pick it up in person and produce proof of identity (driver's license, credit card, passport, etc.).

Generally to be found at intersections, mailboxes are blue with a red-and-white stripe and carry the inscription U.S. MAIL. If your mail is addressed to a U.S. destination, don't forget to add the five-figure postal code, or ZIP Code, after the two-letter abbreviation of the state to which the mail is addressed (NY for New York).

Newspapers/Magazines National newspapers include the *New York Times, USA Today,* and the *Wall Street Journal.* National news weeklies include *Newsweek, Time,* and *U.S. News & World Report.*

Radio and Television Audiovisual media, with four coast-to-coast networks—ABC, CBS, NBC, and Fox—joined in recent years by the Public Broadcasting System (PBS) and the Cable News Network (CNN), play a major part in American life. In big cities, televiewers have a choice of about a dozen channels (including the UHF channels), most of them transmitting 24 hours a day, without counting cable and pay-TV channels showing recent movies or sports events. All options are usually indicated on your hotel TV set. You'll also find a wide choice of local radio stations, each broadcasting particular kinds of talk shows and/or music—classical, country, jazz, pop, gospel—punctuated by news broadcasts and frequent commercials.

Safety See "Safety" in "Preparing for Your Trip," above.

Taxes In the United States there is no VAT (Value-Added Tax) or other indirect tax at a national level. Every state, and each city in it, has the right to levy its own local tax on all purchases, including hotel and restaurant checks, airline tickets, and so on. In New York City, sales tax is 8¼%.

Telephone, Fax, Telegraph, Telex The telephone system in the United States is run by private corporations; so rates, particularly for long-distance service and operator-assisted calls, can vary widely—especially on calls made from public telephones. Local calls in the United States usually cost 25¢.

Generally, hotel surcharges on long-distance and local calls are astronomical. You are usually better off using a **public pay telephone,** which you will find clearly marked in most hotels, public buildings, and private establishments as well as on the street. Outside metropolitan areas, public telephones are more difficult to find. Stores and gas stations are your best bet.

Most **long-distance and international calls** can be dialed directly from any phone. For calls to Canada and other parts of the United States, dial 1 followed by the area code and the seven-digit number. For international calls, dial 011 followed by the country code, city code, and the telephone number of the person you wish to call.

For **reversed-charge or collect calls,** and for **person-to-person calls,** dial 0 (zero, *not* the letter O) followed by the area code and number you want; an operator will then come on the line, and you should specify that you are calling collect, or person-to-person, or both. If your operator-assisted call is international, ask for the overseas operator.

Note that all phone numbers with the area code 800 are toll free.

For local **directory assistance** ("information"), dial 411; for **long-distance information,** dial 1, then the appropriate area code, and 555-1212.

Like the telephone system, **telegraph** and **telex** services are provided by private corporations like ITT, MCI, and above all, Western Union, the most important. You can bring your telegram in to the nearest Western Union office (there are hundreds across the country), or dictate it over the phone (a toll free call, 800/325-6000). You can also telegraph money, or have it telegraphed to you, very quickly over the Western Union system.

Telephone Directory There are two kinds of telephone directories available to you. The general directory is the so-called **White Pages,** in which private and business subscribers are listed in alphabetical order. The inside front cover lists the emergency number for police, fire, and ambulance, and other vital numbers (like the Coast Guard, poison-control center, crime-victims hotline, and so on). The first few pages are devoted to community-service numbers, including a guide to long-distance and international calling, complete with country codes and area codes.

The second directory, printed on yellow paper (hence its name, *Yellow Pages*), lists all local services, businesses, and industries by type of activity, with an index at the back. The listings cover not only such obvious items as automobile repairs by make of car, or drugstores (pharmacies), often by geographical location, but also restaurants by type of cuisine and geographical location, bookstores by special subject and/or language, places of worship by religious denomination, and other information that the tourist might otherwise not readily find. The *Yellow Pages* also include city plans or detailed area maps, often showing postal ZIP Codes and public transportation routes.

Time   The United States is divided into four **time zones** (six, if Alaska and Hawaii are included). From east to west, these are: eastern standard time (EST), central standard time (CST), mountain standard time (MST), Pacific standard time (PST), Alaska standard time (AST), and Hawaii standard time (HST). Always keep changing time zones in mind if you are traveling (or even telephoning) long distances in the United States. For example, noon in New York City (EST) is 11am in Chicago (CST), 10am in Denver (MST), 9am in Los Angeles (PST), 8am in Anchorage (AST), and 7am in Honolulu (HST).

New York observes eastern standard time. **Daylight saving time** is in effect from the last Sunday in April through the last Saturday in October (actually, the change is made at 2am on Sunday) except in Arizona, Hawaii, part of Indiana, and Puerto Rico. Daylight saving time moves the clock one hour ahead of standard time.

Tipping   This is part of the American way of life, on the principle that you must expect to pay for any service you get (many service personnel receive little direct salary and must depend on tips for their income). Here are some rules of thumb:

In **hotels,** tip bellhops at least $1 per piece ($2 to $3 if you have a lot of luggage) and tip the chamber staff $1 per day. Tip the doorman or concierge only if he or she has provided you with some specific service (for example, calling a cab for you or obtaining difficult-to-get theater tickets).

In **restaurants, bars, and nightclubs,** tip service staff 15% to 20% of the check, tip bartenders 10% to 15%, tip checkroom attendants $1 per garment, and tip valet-parking attendants $1 per vehicle. Tip the doorman only if he has provided you with some specific service (such as calling a cab for you). Tipping is not expected in cafeterias and fast-food restaurants.

Tip **cab drivers** 15% of the fare.

As for **other service personnel,** tip redcaps at airports or railroad stations at least 50¢ per piece ($2 to $3 if you have a lot of luggage) and tip hairdressers and barbers 15% to 20%.

Tipping ushers in cinemas and theaters or gas-station attendants is not expected.

THE AMERICAN SYSTEM OF MEASUREMENTS
LENGTH

1 inch (in.)	=	2.54cm				
1 foot (ft.)	=	12 in.	=	30.48cm	=	.305m
1 yard (yd.)	=	3 ft.	=	.915m		
1 mile (mi.)	=	5,280 ft.	=	1.609km		

To convert miles to kilometers, multiply the number of miles by 1.61 (for example, 50 mi. × 1.61 = 80.5km). Note that this conversion can be used to convert speeds from miles per hour (m.p.h.) to kilometers per hour (km/h).

To convert kilometers to miles, multiply the number of kilometers by .62 (for example, 25km × .62 = 15.5 mi.). Note that this same conversion can be used to convert speeds from kilometers per hour to miles per hour.

CAPACITY

1 fluid ounce (fl. oz.)	=	.03 liter		
1 pint	=	16 fl. oz.	=	.47 liter
1 quart	=	2 pints	=	.94 liter
1 gallon (gal.)	=	4 quarts	=	3.79 liter
	=	.83 Imperial gal.		

To convert U.S. gallons to liters, multiply the number of gallons by 3.79 (example, 12 gal. × 3.79 = 45.58 liters).

To convert U.S. gallons to Imperial gallons, multiply the number of U.S. gallons by .83 (example, 12 U.S. gal. × .83 = 9.95 Imperial gal.).

To convert liters to U.S. gallons, multiply the number of liters by .26 (example, 50 liters × .26 = 13 U.S. gal.).

To convert Imperial gallons to U.S. gallons, multiply the number of Imperial gallons by 1.2 (example, 8 Imperial gal. × 1.2 = 9.6 U.S. gal.).

WEIGHT

1 ounce (oz.) = 28.35 grams				
1 pound (lb.)	= 16 oz.	= 453.6 grams	= .45 kilograms
1 ton	= 2,000 lb.	= 907 kilograms	= .91 metric ton

To convert pounds to kilograms, multiply the number of pounds by .45 (example, 90 lb. × .45 = 40.5kg).

To convert kilograms to pounds, multiply the number of kilos by 2.2 (example, 75kg × 2.2 = 165 lb.).

AREA

1 acre	=	.41 hectare		
1 square mile (sq. mi.)	=	640 acres	=	259 hectares
	=	2.6km²		

To convert acres to hectares, multiply the number of acres by .41 (example, 40 acres × .41 = 16.4ha).

To convert square miles to square kilometers, multiply the number of square miles by 2.6 (example, 80 sq. mi. × 2.6 = 208km²).

To convert hectares to acres, multiply the number of hectares by 2.47 (example, 20ha × 2.47 = 49.4 acres).

To convert square kilometers to square miles, multiply the number of square kilometers by .39 (example, 150km² × .39 = 58.5 sq. mi.).

TEMPERATURE

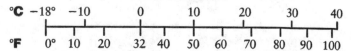

To convert degrees Fahrenheit to degrees Celsius, subtract 32 from °F, multiply by 5, then divide by 9 (example, 85°F − 32 × 5/9 = 29.4°C).

To convert degrees Celsius to degrees Fahrenheit, multiply °C by 9, divide by 5, and add 32 (example, 20°C × 9/5 + 32 = 68°F).

GETTING TO KNOW NEW YORK

This chapter will answer a number of questions you might have upon your arrival and during your stay in New York City—from how to find your way around to telephone numbers to call for information.

1. ORIENTATION

ARRIVING

BY PLANE   There are three major airports serving New York City: **John F. Kennedy International Airport (JFK),** which is in Queens, about 15 miles (or one hour's driving time) from midtown Manhattan; **LaGuardia Airport,** also in Queens, about 8 miles (or 30 minutes) from midtown; and **Newark International Airport,** in nearby New Jersey, about 16 miles (or 45 minutes) from New York.

For information on getting to and from the airports, call 800/AIR-RIDE.

Carey Transportation (tel. 718/632-0509) provides bus service between both JFK and LaGuardia airports and Manhattan. Buses leave from JFK every 30 minutes with midtown stops at 125 Park Avenue, near Grand Central Terminal between 41st and 42nd streets; or at the Airport Bus Center at the Port Authority Bus Terminal at 42nd Street between Eighth and Ninth avenues. The charge is $11 one way. Buses leave from LaGuardia every 20 to 30 minutes for the Park Avenue and Port Authority terminals. The charge is $8.50 one way.

New Jersey Transit (tel. 212/564-8484 or 201/762-5100) provides Airport Express service from Newark Airport to the Port Authority Bus Terminal's Airport Bus Center at 42nd Street and Eighth Avenue. **Olympia Trails** (tel. 212/964-6233) provides service to the Pennsylvania Station at Seventh Avenue and 33rd Street, to Grand Central Terminal at 41st Street and Park Avenue, and to One World Trade Center at the tip of Manhattan. Both bus services cost $7 one way from Newark to Manhattan. Buses leave every 20 minutes.

The **Gray Line Air Shuttle** operates daily from the three airports from 7am to 11pm and stops at all hotels between 23rd and 63rd streets. Going to the airports, it operates from 6am to 7pm from 51 midtown Manhattan hotels and two Gray Line terminals (526 W. 46th Street; Eighth Avenue and 49th Street). To take the shuttle, inquire at the Ground Transportation Desk at any airline terminal. For pickup from hotels, call toll free 800/451-0455 one day before departure. The buses leave approximately every half hour. The one-way fare is $18 to Newark Airport, $16 to JFK, and $13 to LaGuardia.

Taxis are available at designated taxi stands at the three New York airports. At JFK and LaGuardia, yellow taxis with the fare printed on the outside front doors are the only ones licensed by the New York Taxi and Limousine Commission. New Jersey cabs available from curbside dispatchers at Newark are various colors. Fares between JFK, LaGuardia, and Newark airports and New York City are metered, costing approximately $30 to $35, $20 to $25, and $30 plus tolls, respectively. (Going to Newark from New York, a trip that crosses state lines, the fare in a yellow cab is the amount on the meter plus $10.) There is a 50¢ surcharge between 8pm and 6am on all taxis. Metered fares include everyone in the taxi and are not per person.

Important advice: On the cab ride from the airports to the city, out-of-town and foreign visitors should be wary of cab drivers demanding huge sums; take only a metered cab and pay only *exactly* what the meter reads, plus a tip and toll charges. At the airports, take only the taxis at curbside or those available from official dispatchers, not from hustlers in the terminal halls themselves.

BY TRAIN   If you come to New York by train, you will arrive at either **Pennsylvania Station** (34th Street and Seventh Avenue) or **Grand Central Terminal** (42nd Street and Park Avenue). Both are located in mid-Manhattan, minutes from your hotel, and you'll be able to make subway connections or hail a cab easily.

BY BUS   If you come by bus, you will arrive at the **Port Authority of New York and New Jersey Bus Terminal** (41st Street and Eighth Avenue). It's in a seedy (though improving) neighborhood and not particularly safe at night, so try to schedule your arrival during daylight hours.

TOURIST INFORMATION

The **New York Convention and Visitors Bureau,** 2 Columbus Circle at 59th Street (212/397-8222), has a wealth of information about the city, including pamphlets and brochures on sightseeing, hotels, restaurants, shopping, and current activities, as well as city subway and bus maps and free tickets to TV shows and discount tickets to theaters. The office is open Monday to Friday from 9am to 6pm and Saturday and Sunday from 10am to 3pm.

The **Times Square Visitor and Transit Information Center,** at the corner of Seventh Avenue and 42nd Street, is a joint project of the Times Square Business Improvement District (BID) and the New York City Transit Authority. Its multilingual staff can offer a wide variety of information on the city, with special emphasis on the Times Square area. They can provide complete transit information for all five boroughs, with interactive computers to route you to a specific destination. Join them any Friday at noon, rain or shine, for an enjoyable behind-the-scenes walking tour exploring the history and architecture of the theater district, with stops at important landmark buildings. The center is open daily from 10am to 7pm; it cannot be reached by telephone.

The **Visitors Center** at A&S Plaza, 32nd Street and Herald Square, 7th floor (tel. 212/465-0600), also offers free information and services.

Traveler's Aid can provide many kinds of help for visitors and stranded travelers in New York City. Its offices are at 1481 Broadway, between 42nd and 43rd streets (tel. 212/944-0013), and in the lobby of the International Arrivals Building at JFK Airport (tel. 718/656-4870).

CITY LAYOUT
MAIN ARTERIES & STREETS

If you can count and you know your east from your west, you can find your way easily around most of Manhattan. All you have to remember is that streets run east and west and are numbered consecutively; avenues run north and south and most have numbers, although a few have names; and streets and avenues usually bisect one another at right angles. Unfortunately, this simplicity does not apply to Lower Manhattan—Wall Street, Chinatown, SoHo, TriBeCa, and Greenwich Village—since these neighborhoods developed before engineers came up with this brilliant grid scheme; take a map when you explore these areas.

As for the east and west street designations, the key to the mystery is **Fifth Avenue,** the big dividing line between the East and West Sides of town (below Washington Square, **Broadway** is the dividing line). So, for example, to get to 20 East 57th Street, you would walk about one block east of Fifth; to get to 20 West 57th Street, you'd walk about one block west. To get uptown of a certain point, simply walk north of, or to a higher-numbered street than, where you are; downtown is south of (or a lower-numbered street than) your current location. Got that? All that's left to learn are the names of the major avenues. Starting at Fifth Avenue and going east (toward the East River), they are **Madison; Park** (Park Avenue South below 34th Street); **Lexington; Third; Second; First; York** (from East 92nd to East 60th Street), which becomes **Sutton Place** (from East 59th to East 51st Street); and **East End** (from East 90th to East 79th Street). On the Lower East Side, First Avenue gives way to **avenues A, B, C,** and **D.** Starting again at Fifth Avenue and working west, we have **Avenue of the Americas** (widely known by its old name, **Sixth Avenue**); **Seventh Avenue; Broadway; Eighth Avenue** (called **Central Park West** above 59th Street); **Ninth Avenue** (called **Columbus Avenue** above 59th Street); **Tenth Avenue** (called **Amsterdam Avenue** above 59th Street); **Eleventh Avenue** (called **West End Avenue** from 59th to 107th streets); and **Riverside Drive,** beginning at 72nd Street. Note that Central Park intervenes between Fifth Avenue and the West Side from 59th to 110th streets.

FINDING AN ADDRESS
Avenue Addresses

New Yorkers have the following system for finding the cross street on an avenue address: Drop the last digit of the number of the address and divide the remaining number by two. Then add or subtract the following appropriate number:

Avenue A, B, C, or D	add 3
First Avenue	add 3
Second Avenue	add 3
Third Avenue	add 10
Park Avenue South (Fourth Avenue)	add 8
Fifth Avenue	
63 to 108	add 11
109 to 200	add 13
201 to 400	add 16
401 to 600	add 18
601 to 775	add 20
From 776 to 1286, cancel last figure and subtract 18; do *not* divide number by two.	
Avenue of the Americas (Sixth Avenue)	subtract 12
Seventh Avenue	
1 to 1800	add 12
above 1800	add 20
Eighth Avenue	add 9
Ninth Avenue	add 13
Tenth Avenue	add 14
Eleventh Avenue	add 15
Amsterdam Avenue	add 59
Broadway	
1 to 754	named street below 8th Street
755 to 846	subtract 29
847 to 953	subtract 25
Above 953	subtract 31
Columbus Avenue	add 59 or 60
Lexington Avenue	add 22
Madison Avenue	add 27
Park Avenue	add 34
Riverside Drive	divide number by 10 and add 72 (1 to 567) or 78 (above 567)
West End Avenue	add 59

For example, if you're trying to locate 645 Fifth Avenue, you'd drop the 5, leaving 64. Then you would divide 64 by 2, leaving 32. According to the chart, you would then add 20. Thus 645 Fifth Avenue is at about 52nd Street.

Street Addresses

BETWEEN 14TH & 59TH STREETS Here is a chart to help you locate street addresses between 14th and 59th streets:

East Side	**West Side**
1 at Fifth Avenue	1 at Fifth Avenue
100 at Park Avenue	100 at Sixth Avenue
200 at Third Avenue	200 at Seventh Avenue
300 at Second Avenue	300 at Eighth Avenue
400 at First Avenue	400 at Ninth Avenue
	500 at Tenth Avenue
	600 at Eleventh Avenue

59TH TO 110TH STREETS   Above 59th Street and all the way to 110th Street, things are different on the *Upper West Side only*. This is the region west of Central Park, where numbers on the streets start at Central Park West and continue upward all the way to West End Avenue or Riverside Drive (above 72nd Street), as outlined below:

> 1 at Central Park West (Eighth Avenue)
> 100 at Columbus Avenue (Ninth Avenue)
> 200 at Amsterdam Avenue (Tenth Avenue)
> 300 at West End Avenue (Eleventh Avenue).

MANHATTAN NEIGHBORHOODS IN BRIEF

Lower Manhattan/Financial District   This is the oldest part of New York, containing among other sights the Brooklyn Bridge, City Hall and courthouse area, South Street Seaport, Wall Street, New York Stock Exchange, World Trade Center, and World Financial Center in Battery Park City.

TriBeCa   Just south of SoHo is the *Tri*angle *Be*low *Ca*nal Street, west of Broadway. It's a newer artists' colony.

Chinatown   Located south of Canal Street, this Chinese community centers on Mott and Pell streets.

Little Italy   The heart of this once-ethnic enclave, just east of Broadway between Houston and Canal streets, is Mulberry Street.

SoHo   Centered around West Broadway and Spring and Greene streets between Houston (pronounced "house-ton") and Canal streets (just west of Little Italy), SoHo (*So*uth of *Ho*uston) is home to the world's largest collection of cast-iron commercial architecture and is a vital artists' colony.

Lower East Side   This area, also south of Houston Street but east of Little Italy, is where thousands of immigrants settled into the New World in the early 1900s—some to struggle and be engulfed, some to conquer. Most of the Jews, Irish, and Italians have moved uptown or to the suburbs, but little colonies still remain. Most of the population is now Hispanic. Around Grand and Orchard streets is still a Jewish neighborhood, known mostly for bargain shopping.

Greenwich Village   Centered between 14th Street and Houston, west of Broadway, this was the heart of old New York's Bohemia. Many noted writers and artists have lived here. In the evening the area can be noisy and crowded.

East Village   The one-time home of the hippies and flower children (now home to many young artists), this area extends from Broadway to First Avenue and beyond to avenues A, B, and C. The northern border is 14th Street and the southern is Houston.

Chelsea   In the West 20s, Chelsea contains the Flower Market, centered near 28th Street and a number of very popular weekend flea markets along Sixth Avenue, between 24th and 27th Streets.

Gramercy Park/Murray Hill   Flanked on the west by Fifth Avenue and on the east by First Avenue, on the south by 14th Street and on the north by 42nd Street, this is a mixed residential/commercial area containing some of Manhattan's finest old buildings.

Garment and Fur Districts   From the upper 20s to 40th Street along Seventh Avenue, the streets become crowded with trucks and throngs of people pushing minks and other garments on racks along the sidewalks. This is Manhattan's (and the nation's) vibrant, hectic, and legendary fashion capital.

Herald Square   The area around 34th Street and Broadway is home to Macy's, the world's largest department store. To the east are the shops of 34th Street and Fifth Avenue; to the west and south, A&S and A&S Plaza at 33rd Street and Sixth Avenue, and Madison Square Garden Center rising above Pennsylvania Station between Seventh and Eighth avenues and 31st and 33rd streets.

Midtown   The center of things and the heart of the city, this area runs, roughly, from the East River to the Hudson and from 33rd to 59th streets. In this neighborhood you'll find the Empire State Building, Rockefeller Center, Broadway theaters, major department stores, many business offices, and most large hotels.

Central Park   Starting north of 59th Street, this magnificent sweep of greensward, running between Fifth Avenue and Central Park West, is the great divide between the Upper East and Upper West Sides.

Lincoln Center   At 65th Street and Broadway, Lincoln Center for the Performing Arts is a great cultural center, containing the Metropolitan Opera House, Avery Fisher Hall, the New York State Theater, the Juilliard School of Music, the Vivian Beaumont Theater, and Alice Tully Hall.

Upper West Side   A mainly residential district, with the lovely buildings of Central Park West on one boundary and Riverside Drive on the other, it lies north of 59th Street. At about 116th Street and Broadway is the campus of Columbia University, and as you go up Riverside Drive, you will see the massive structure of Grant's Tomb and the great Gothic spires of Riverside Church.

Upper East Side   This neighborhood, also north of 59th Street, is the home of many well-to-do, fashionable schools and shops, and the prestigious Metropolitan Museum of Art. Included in this area is the once predominately German and Central European (notably Hungarian) section called Yorkville, centered around 86th Street between Park and First avenues.

Harlem   This area begins at 125th Street on the West Side and 96th Street on the East, and around East 110th Street is the center of sprawling **Spanish Harlem**, or **El Barrio**.

Washington Heights   This mixed residential neighborhood, near the northern tip of the island, embraces Fort Tryon Park and the beautiful Cloisters of the Metropolitan Museum of Art, a serene vantage point from which to contemplate the great diversity of New York.

STREET MAPS

The **New York Visitor's Guide and Map** is available (in six languages) at the New York Convention and Visitors Bureau, 2 Columbus Circle (tel. 212/397-8222). A map of the New York City subway system is also available at the visitors bureau, or you can pick one up at subway token booths. Excellent maps for sale are produced by H. M. Gousha, Hagstrom, and other publishers.

2. GETTING AROUND

New York is one of the few cities in the United States where walking is not only encouraged but also feasible, since most everything is so close together. Walking, in fact, is often the quickest way to get somewhere, especially during the midday lunch crush and the evening rush hour (5 to 6:30pm), when surface traffic seems to move at the rate of 2 miles per hour.

BY SUBWAY Everyone should ride the New York subway at least once—just for the experience. If you manage to survive a rush-hour crush (roughly 8 to 9:30 in the morning, 5 to 6:30 in the evening on weekdays), you'll have something to tell the folks back home. The rest of the time, the subway is relatively uncrowded and will take you where you want to go quickly (no traffic!), fairly efficiently, and at a cost of $1.25 per token. *Note:* Senior citizens (over 65) can show their Social Security Health Insurance Card and ride buses for 60¢ and subways for half-fare.

Use our map (see pages 42–43) or pick up a color map at a token booth. East Side trains (numbers 4, 5, and 6) run along Lexington Avenue; the line is known as the Lexington Avenue Subway. On the West Side, the trains (numbers 1, 2, 3, and 9) go along Broadway and Seventh Avenue. (The 1 and 9 go north to Columbia University and Washington Heights and wind up in the Bronx at Van Cortlandt Park; the 2 and 3 branch eastward north of 96th Street to Seventh Avenue and up Lenox Avenue through Harlem. Heading south, they reach Battery Park by way of Chelsea and Greenwich Village.) The east and west branches are connected by the Grand Central/Times Square Shuttle (the S train) and the 14th Street–Canarsie Line (the L). The Flushing line (number 7) runs beneath the shuttle from Times Square to Grand Central and then east into Queens. The Sixth and Eighth avenue lines (B, D, F, and Q, and A, C, and E trains, respectively) have major stops in Greenwich Village at West 4th Street, at the Port Authority Bus Terminal area at 42nd Street, and at Columbus Circle (59th Street).

For information on how to get from one place to another by subway, call 718/330-1234.

BY BUS Slower than subways but cheaper than taxis, the buses solve a lot of transportation problems. Almost every major avenue has its own bus. (They run either north or south: downtown on Fifth, uptown on Madison, downtown on Lexington, uptown on Third, and so on.) There are crosstown buses at strategic locations all around town: 8th Street (eastbound), 9th (westbound), 14th, 23rd, 34th, and 42nd (east- and westbound), 49th (eastbound), 50th (westbound), 57th (east- and westbound), 65th (eastbound across the West Side, through the park, then north on Madison, continuing east on 68th to York Avenue), 67th (eastbound on the East Side to Fifth Avenue, then south on Fifth, continuing west on 66th Street through the park and across the West Side to West End Avenue), 79th, 86th, 96th, 116th, and 125th (east- and westbound). Some of the buses, however, are erratic: The M104, for example, starts at the East River, then turns at Eighth Avenue and goes up Broadway. The buses of the Fifth Avenue line go up Madison or Sixth and follow various routes

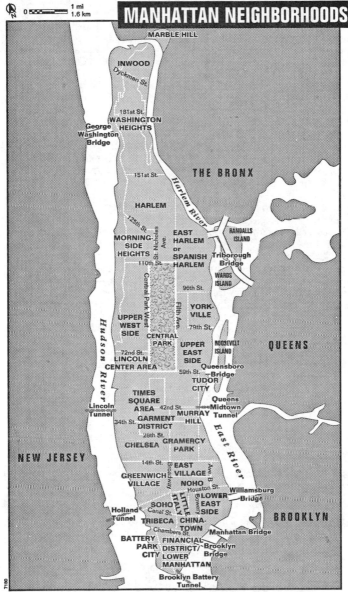

MANHATTAN NEIGHBORHOODS

around the city. Check the maps on the bus signs, or ask the driver, to be sure.

Note: Since bus drivers are no longer allowed to make change, you must have your exact fare ready: a subway token or $1.25 (in coins, not bills). Transfer tickets to intersecting bus lines are available; ask the driver for one when you board a bus. But there are no free transfers to the subway.

For information on how to get from one place to another by bus, call 718/330-1234.

BY TAXI The most convenient way to get around town is often by cab, which can be hailed on any street. Official New York taxis are yellow, have the rates on the outside front doors, and have a light on the roof. (When the light is on, the taxi is available.) Other cabs are best avoided.

Taxis are expensive. As soon as you step into the cab, the meter clicks to $1.50; the charge is then 25¢ for each one-fifth of a mile and 25¢ for each minute of waiting time in traffic. There is also a 50¢ surcharge between 8pm and 6am. You are expected to tip about 20% to 25%.

If you wish to have a cab come directly to your door (often helpful during rush hour), simply check the *Yellow Pages* under "Taxicab Service." If you wish to call a car service to take you to an airport, call, among others, **Carmel** (tel. 662-2222) or **Tel Aviv** (tel. 777-7777).

Note: It's often best to give a cab driver an intersection rather than a numbered address as your destination. You'll sound like a local, who can't be taken on a roundabout and expensive route.

BY CAR It is really not feasible to drive a car around Manhattan. Traffic is horrendous; parking in garages is exorbitant (between $18 and $25 per day), especially in the business and entertainment areas; and street parking is very difficult to find, except after 7pm, and then it usually involves moving the car in the morning when complicated alternate-side-of-the-street parking rules go into effect.

The main office of the **American Automobile Association** in Manhattan is at Broadway and 62nd Street (tel. 757-2000).

The major national **car-rental companies**—Alamo, Avis, Budget, Dollar, Hertz, and so on—have agencies in Manhattan. Consult the *Yellow Pages* of the phone book for offices close to your hotel. Rates are high. A one-day rate at Avis last summer for a compact with automatic shift was around $87. Prices are lower for longer rentals.

For discount rentals, try **A A M Car,** 303 W. 96th St. (tel. 222-5800), which provides a high level of personal service and will rent to customers without credit cards.

BY BICYCLE Many New Yorkers ride bikes through heavily trafficked areas, but, again, this is not recommended for visitors. Riding a bike in the parks, however, can be fun. The **Bicycle and Exercise Store,** 242 E. 79th St. (tel. 249-9218), charges $3 per hour, $10.50 per day, $50 per week. It also rents Rollerblades and exercise equipment. *New York* magazine recently called it New York's "Best Bike Store."

TRAINS TO THE SUBURBS The **PATH** (Port Authority TransHudson) rail transit system (tel. toll free 800/234-7284) is the primary mass-transit link between Manhattan and neighboring New Jersey urban communities, as well as with New Jersey's suburban commuter railroad (New Jersey Transit, with which it has connections at Newark and Hoboken). PATH operates four lines: Newark–World Trade Center; Journal Square–33rd Street; Hoboken–WTC, and Hoboken–33rd Street. PATH service, all air-conditioned, runs 24 hours a day, 7 days a week. The fare is $1.

Metro North (tel. 532-4900) provides train service from Grand Central Station at 42nd Street between Vanderbilt and Lexington avenues to Westchester County and other northern suburbs. The **Long Island Rail Road** (tel. 718/217-5477) serves Long Island from Pennsylvania Station on Seventh Avenue between 31st and 33rd streets. **Amtrak** (tel. toll free 800/USA-RAIL) links the New York City area with the rest of the United States.

FAST FACTS NEW YORK

Area Codes All telephone numbers in Manhattan have the **212** area code. In Brooklyn, Queens, the Bronx, and Staten Island, the area code is **718.** To dial outside the 212 area code, you must dial "1" before the area code. For instance, to call Information in Brooklyn, dial 1/718/555-1212.

Babysitters Most hotel concierges can recommend babysitters.

Business Hours Standard **office** hours are weekdays from 9am to 5pm. Most **stores** are in addition open late on some weekdays and are open on Saturday and often on Sunday.

Car Rentals See "Getting Around" in this chapter.

Climate See "When to Go" in Chapter 2.

Crime See "Safety," below.

Dentists Should you have a dental emergency, call **Preventive Dental Associates** at 683-2722; a dentist will return your call and give you professional advice. This service can also make same-day appointments at its office at 200 Madison Ave. (tel. 685-6628).

Doctors Should you need a physician when in New York, do not go to a hospital emergency room unless you are in a very serious or life-threatening situation. Waits in overcrowded, understaffed hospital emergency rooms can be agonizingly long. Nonemergency situations can be better handled at a place like **Manhattan Medical Care,** 152 W. 72nd St. (tel. 496-9620), where Dr. Richard Shepard and his staff provide expert care, without the necessity of an appointment. It is open weekdays from 8am to 8pm and Saturday from 9am to 5pm. A basic office visit is $85. If you are in doubt as to whether you should go to a hospital or can be taken care of here, phone and discuss your situation with the nurse.

In midtown, **Beth Israel Medical Center** runs Doctors Walk-In at 57 E. 34th St. (tel. 683-1000), which charges $65 for an office visit and is open weekdays from 8am to 6pm and Saturday from 10am to 2pm. No lab or X-ray work can be done after 4pm.

House calls are available from **Doctors on Call** (tel. 718/238-2100) 24 hours a day, 7 days a week, for a charge of between $80 and $95 a visit, depending on the time of day or night. Minimum waiting time is 1½ hours. If the situation appears serious, you will be advised to go to a hospital emergency room (see "Hospitals," below).

Drugstores Kaufman Pharmacy, Lexington Avenue at 50th Street (tel. 755-2266), is open 24 hours a day, 7 days a week, and will make emergency deliveries (you pay the cab fare).

Emergencies Dial **911** to reach the police or the fire department or to summon an ambulance. Call the **Poison Control Center** at 764-7667.

Eyeglasses LensCrafters with three stores in Manhattan, at 901 Sixth Ave. at 33rd Street, 425 Lexington Ave. at 44th Street, and

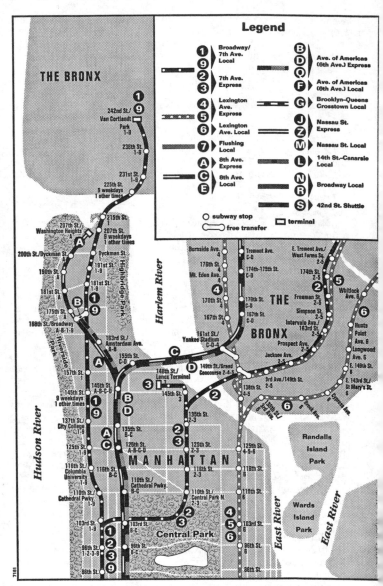

2040 Broadway at 70th Street, can replace a pair of glasses in about one hour.

Hospitals Excellent emergency care is provided at **St. Luke's–Roosevelt Hospital Center,** corner of 58th Street and Ninth Avenue (Roosevelt Hospital: tel. 523-4000) and 113th Street and Amsterdam Avenue (St. Luke's Hospital: tel. 523-4000); at **New York University Medical Center,** 550 First Avenue at 33rd Street (tel. 263-7300); and at **New York Hospital's** Emergency Pavilion at 510 E. 70th St. (tel. 746-5050). Prehospital emergency care and

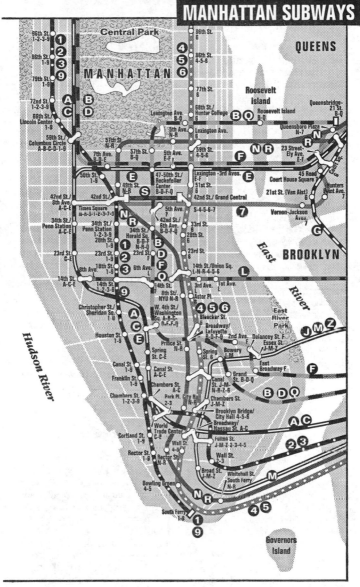

MANHATTAN SUBWAYS

transport to the hospital of your choice is obtained by calling the New York Hospital Paramedic Service at 472-2222.

Hotlines Crime Victims Hotline (tel. 577-7777); **Suicide Prevention Hotline** (tel. 718/389-9608); **Suicide Hotline Samaritans of New York** (tel. 673-3000); and **Youth Hotline** (tel. 683-4388).

Information See "Tourist Information" under "Orientation" in this chapter.

Laundry/Dry Cleaning Your hotel usually can take care

of this for you. Or try the closest cleaner at hand; there is at least one on most blocks.

Libraries   The main branch of the **New York Public Library** is at 42nd Street and Fifth Avenue.

Liquor Laws   Liquor and wines are sold only in licensed liquor stores. Neither can be sold to anyone under 21 in stores, bars, or restaurants. Liquor stores are closed on Sunday.

Newspapers/Magazines   New York has four daily papers: *The New York Times,* the *Daily News,* the *New York Post,* and *New York Newsday.* They all have information about what's going on about town. Several New York City–based weekly newspapers and magazines also provide comprehensive coverage: *The New Yorker, New York* magazine, the *Village Voice,* and *New York Observer.* These are all available at newsstands throughout the city.

Hotaling's, 142 W. 42nd St., between Sixth Avenue and Broadway (tel. 840-1868), carries hundreds of newspapers from out of town and around the world. Many international publications are available at **Gottfried's,** in Sony Plaza at 55th Street and Madison Avenue (tel. 755-0420).

Photographic Needs   Willoughby Peerless Camera Store, 110 W. 32nd St., near Herald Square (tel. 564-1600), can provide any kind of photographic service. Film can be purchased at any drugstore.

Police   Dial **911** for emergency calls to the police.

Post Office   The **General Post Office** is at Eighth Avenue and 33rd Street (tel. 967-8585); a convenient East Side station is the FDR, Third Avenue at 53rd Street (tel. 330-5665).

Religious Services   There are houses of worship of most faiths in Manhattan. Saturday's *New York Times* runs a limited listing of Sunday services. The Yellow Pages list houses of worship by denomination.

Restrooms   The best public restrooms are in hotels, department stores, and government buildings. Restaurants try to limit the use of their restrooms to customers, but if you are well dressed and ask nicely, they may allow you to use them. Never use the restrooms in subway stations.

Safety   Let's look at the facts. New York does have a high incidence of crime, but so does every other major U.S. city; crime in New York simply gets more publicity. Second, considering that more than 7.3 million people live in the city—and that all go about their business freely—the out-of-towner's frequent impression that New York is an extremely dangerous place just doesn't make sense. However, take precautions. Try not to look like a tourist, flashing a big camera and a big wallet. Keep your camera inconspicuous, put your money in traveler's checks, and leave your valuables in the hotel safe or at home. (Never leave your valuables in a hotel room unless there is an in-room safe.) Stay alert and be aware of your immediate surroundings. Wear a moneybelt and keep a close eye on your possessions. Watch your purse or wallet in crowded buses, subways, and hotel elevators.

There are certain areas to avoid late at night: One is the East Village, where there is drug traffic on the far eastern streets; the second is Amsterdam Avenue and its cross streets above about 120th Street on the West Side; and third is the area around Times Square, particularly between Seventh and Eighth avenues. The parks are taboo after sundown, unless you're going to a festival or theatrical performance in Central Park, in which case the access routes are well lighted. And it's safer to take a cab home late at night than a subway. You'll see beggars and homeless people on many streets, but they are generally not dangerous.

Taxes   New York City sales taxes are high—8¼% on many goods and services, including restaurant meals. Parking taxes are even higher. For hotel taxes, see Chapter 5.

Taxis   See "Getting Around" in this chapter.

Telegrams/Telex   For **Western Union,** dial toll free 800/325-6000.

Television   All national broadcast networks and most cable networks are available in New York. See local papers for listings.

Tipping   In restaurants, waiters are tipped about 15%, 20% in case of extraordinary service; taxi drivers are tipped 20% to 25%, never less than 25¢. Bellhops should be tipped $1 to carry a few bags to your room; airport porters should be tipped 50¢ for a small bag, $1 for a larger one.

Transit Information   Call the **MTA** at 718/330-1234 (24 hours a day, 7 days a week) for schedules and routes. (Phone 718/330-4847 to be connected to a foreign translator.) Bus and subway maps are available at Grand Central Terminal, Pennsylvania Station, and the Port Authority Bus Terminal. For information on getting to and from the area's three major airports, John F. Kennedy International, Newark International, and LaGuardia, see "Arriving" in Section 1 of this chapter or call toll free 800/AIR-RIDE.

Useful Telephone Numbers   For the correct **time,** dial 976-1616. For a **weather** report, dial 976-1212.

3. NETWORKS & RESOURCES

FOR STUDENTS   Visiting students might check the bulletin boards at Columbia University and New York University; many events will be open to them.

FOR GAY MEN & LESBIANS   Nearly 400 lesbian, gay, and bisexual organizations hold meetings at the **Lesbian and Gay Community Services Center,** 208 W. 13th St., in Greenwich Village (tel. 620-7310). The Center runs 25 programs of its own, including an orientation program for lesbians and gay men newly relocated to New York, as well as lectures, dances, readings, and films. Open daily from 9am to 11pm.

FOR WOMEN   A variety of information and help is available from the **Women's Psychotherapy Referral Service** (tel. 242-8597) and the **National Organization for Women** (tel. 807-0721).

FOR SENIORS   For information, call the **Gray Panthers** (tel. 799-7572).

NEW YORK ACCOMMODATIONS

New York City has more hotel rooms than some small countries have. In a city where at least a handful of establishments can each accommodate 2,000 guests, where a small hotel is one with fewer than 500 rooms, you needn't spend your nights sleeping in Central Park.

But—and it's a rather big but—getting exactly the kind of hotel room you want, in the location you want, at the price you want, is another cup of tea.

In general, the price picture breaks down like this. To stay in one of the top elegant hotels of the city, those geared to international business travelers and other members of the expense-account set, you can expect to pay $200 and up for a double room. To stay in one of the city's first-class, efficiently run, and comfortable hotels, expect to spend $150 and up for a double; to stay in a still comfortable but more modest establishment, prepare to part with around $125. You can also still find some pleasant and respectable establishments where you can reserve a double for $80 or less a night. Therefore, I have divided the hotels into four broad and somewhat overlapping categories: **very expensive,** $200 and up per night for a double room; **expensive,** $150 to $200; **moderate,** $80 to $150; and **inexpensive,** $80 and under.

I have described here some 60 hotels—which, in my opinion, offer excellent values in each price category and are representative of what you will find everywhere in New York.

I have made every effort to be accurate about prices, but the hotel business presents a highly competitive, changing situation, and prices may go up or down a bit, depending on the season and the demand for rooms. Since new labor contracts are usually settled around the middle of the year, some hotels may raise their prices in June.

All the rates listed, unless otherwise stated, are for European Plan only, which means that no food is included. The rates given are transient rates; for those who stay in some hotels on a weekly or monthly basis, lower rates are usually available. All rooms in the listings have **private baths** unless otherwise specified. Making **reservations** in advance is always a good idea, especially during the busy summer months. (From Easter to October is high season in New York.) If you haven't booked in advance, however, you will almost always be able to get some sort of room, but perhaps not just the one you would like. **Parking** rates are per night and usually refer to an enclosed garage.

Finally, I'm sorry to say that New York City's **hotel taxes** are among the highest in the country. Plan on paying an additional 13.25% plus $2 in taxes for your hotel room. Thus, if you're renting a room for $120 a night, your actual cost will be $137.90. High as these taxes are, they represent a significant decrease over last year.

WEEKEND PACKAGES   If you're coming to New York for just the weekend, you're in luck. That's when business travelers clear out and expensive hotel rooms go empty. Rather than let this happen, some of the loveliest hotels in town woo the vacationer with attractive weekend package rates, which often include some meals, sightseeing, theater tickets, and many extras. Because these packages vary greatly and change frequently, your best deal is to call the hotel you're interested in, and/or write the **New York Convention and Visitors Bureau,** 2 Columbus Circle, New York, NY 10019, requesting their brochure "New York City Tour Package Directory." Also note that many weekend packages are advertised in the travel section of the Sunday *New York Times,* available in most major cities.

RESERVATION SERVICES   Need to make a last-minute reservation? Need advice on what hotel best suits your particular needs? Hope to save a few dollars on your bill? A reservation service can help.

Accommodations Express works with 80% of all hotels in New York, in every price category from budget to luxury. Not only can they offer you immediate confirmation, but they can often help you realize a nice saving off rack (regular) rates—at least 10% and sometimes more. The service is free, and their toll-free 800 number is answered daily from 7am to 11pm. They can also help if you're continuing your travels farther south, to Atlantic City, Philadelphia, Washington, D.C.—or out west to Chicago or Las Vegas. For New York City reservations, call toll free 800/444-7666, ext. 114.

Large firms have always secured "corporate rates" for their employees. A Colorado-based firm, ✪ **Express Hotel Reservations,** does the same for individual travelers to New York and Los Angeles. They can save you from $29 to $80 per night at some 26 major New York establishments in every price category. On hotels whose rack rates are $99 to $290, they offer rates of $70 to $210. To contact the free service, call toll free 800/356-1123 Monday through Friday between 10am and 7pm Eastern Time.

BED & BREAKFASTS   If you'd like to get away from the glitzy atmosphere of New York hotels, you might want to consider using a bed-and-breakfast service. Staying in a B&B is a good way to get a firsthand sense of what it's like to actually live in New York City. Lodgings can be either hosted or unhosted. Hosts can range from struggling actors to doctors to New York yuppies. Who knows?— You might find yourself in a huge SoHo loft filled with Andy Warhol paintings or perhaps an Upper East Side pied-à-terre just off Central Park.

City Lights Bed & Breakfast, Ltd.,   P.O. Box 20355 Cherokee Station, New York, NY 10028 (tel. 212/737-7049 or 737-8251; fax 212/535-2755), is a well-established and highly praised service; they are moving into the moderate-to-luxurious price range as the city becomes more gentrified. In addition to accommodations, they also offer settings for small business meetings and conferences, a personalized shopping service for B&B clients, and individualized tours for art lovers and architecture buffs. Accommodations are available in Manhattan and parts of Brooklyn, on Long Island, and in Westchester. Rates for single occupancy range from $60 to $75, and doubles go for $70 to $90, depending on length of stay, location, and "opulence." They also rent unhosted apartments and book B&B accommodations in the major capitals of Europe.

City Lights' newest offering is a "Live Like a Millionaire" package in which guests can reside in a truly spectacular property, like a palatial apartment in a venerable Park Avenue building or a smart town house in the East 60s; some have working fireplaces and Jacuzzis. Priced from $160 to $225 per night, the package includes a bottle of champagne and gift basket upon arrival, a continental breakfast, and maid service. For an additional charge, they can arrange dinner reservations, theater tickets, limousine transportation, or the services of a private guide.

Another popular agency, **New World Bed & Breakfast,** 150 Fifth Ave., Suite 711, New York, NY 10011 (tel. 212/675-5600), has fewer listings, but an important difference: It is the only B&B agency in New York with a toll-free number (U.S. and Canada) for reservations and inquiries—800/443-3800. It also has toll-free numbers from Germany (01 30 811672), France (19 05 90 1148), and other countries. Their local number is 212/675-6000 (fax 212/675-6366). Rooms, in Manhattan only, go from $50 to $75 for a single and $60 to $90 for a double; unhosted apartments range from $70 to $117 per night single or double, plus $10 to $20 for each additional person. Owner Kathleen Kruger personally inspects each accommodation.

New York's oldest and largest B&B organization is **Urban Ventures,** P.O. Box 426, New York, NY 10024 (tel. 212/594-5650; fax 212/947-9320), which offers comfortable rooms in private apartments—mostly in Manhattan's Upper West Side, Upper East Side, and Greenwich Village and in close-to-Manhattan areas of Brooklyn—at rates that are often less than those at budget hotels. Singles cost from $50 to $70, doubles run from $65 to $90. A studio apartment costs from $70 to $90, and a one-bedroom apartment is $95 to $145. Mary McAulay is the helpful lady in charge.

1. LOWER MANHATTAN

In addition to the hotels listed below, note **The New York Vista,** 3 World Trade Center, New York, NY 10048 (tel. 212/938-9100, or toll free 800/258-2505), the flagship of Hilton International in the continental United States and a superb home base for business travelers during the week and a resort destination on weekends. Closed after sustaining damage in the early 1993 bombing of the World Trade Center, the hotel was scheduled for reopening sometime this year.

VERY EXPENSIVE

THE HOTEL MILLENIUM, 55 Church St., New York, NY 10017. Tel. 212/693-2001, or toll free 800/835-2220. Fax 212/571-2316. 561 rms and suites. A/C MINIBAR TV TEL

FROMMER'S SMART TRAVELER: HOTELS

1. Make a deal. It's almost never necessary to pay full "rack rates" that hotels quote. When you make reservations, always ask for any special discounts that might apply: corporate rates; family rates; package deals; senior-citizen rates (almost all hotels have these); or rates for students, military and government employees, clergy, airline employees, or whatever is appropriate.
2. When dealing with a national chain, if you call a hotel directly rather than phoning a toll-free 800 number, you have a better chance of negotiating a discount rate.
3. Remember that a hotel room is a perishable commodity. If it's not sold, the revenue is lost forever. Therefore, it is a fact that rates are linked to the hotel's occupancy level. If it's 90% occupied, the price goes up; if it's 50% occupied, the price goes down. So always try negotiating by stating your price.
4. Consider a bed-and-breakfast accommodation; their charges are usually much lower than hotel rates.
5. Try to schedule your trip for a weekend. Weekend package deals, even at some of New York's best hotels, are incredible bargains.
6. If you're staying for a week or longer, you can usually get a cheaper rate.
7. Book your room through a discount service: See information on Accommodations Express and Express Hotel Reservations, above.

SOME ADVICE ABOUT NEW YORK TELEPHONES

Long-distance calls from hotel rooms are no longer regulated by law. Even if you use lobby pay phones with your telephone cards you may be subject to unconscionably high fees, since the Operator Service Provider (OSP) chosen by the hotel can pretty much charge what it wishes. A possible alternative: investigate the ATN (American Travel Network) Discount Calling Card. There is no surcharge, as with other calling cards, and interstate rates are only 17.5¢ per minute, any time of day or night; the company states that card users can save as much as 67% over other major phone-card companies. There is no charge to obtain the card, which is already in wide use among airline pilots, flight attendants, and frequent business travelers. For more information, phone toll free 800/477-9692.

Note: If you are going to pay for a phone call from a public phone by a regular calling card, the New York State Public Service Commission advises that you pick up the receiver and look at the plastic card below the keypad for the toll-free number of the Operator Service Provider; first, call and ask what the call will cost. If you don't get an answer, dial "O" for the operator and ask to be connected to another carrier. Easiest of all: pay cash.

$ Rates: $225–$245 single; $245–$265 double; $305 Millenium room (junior suite); $295–$2,500 suites. Weekend: $149–$189 single or double, superior room/guaranteed high floor, free parking (no in/out); $189 single or double, Millenium Room (junior suite), complimentary continental breakfast, free parking (no in/out); $269 single or double, one-bedroom suite, complimentary continental breakfast, free parking (no in/out). Extra person $20. AE, CB, DC, DISC, JCB, MC, V. **Parking:** $24 weekdays.

There's no need to wait until the millennium—the good life is already here for travelers who pick this handsome hotel, the newest in the downtown area. Built at an estimated cost of $150 million, this sleek 58-story tower is directly across from the World Trade Center. It's within walking distance, and offers superb views, of downtown's major attractions, including the Statue of Liberty/Ellis Island ferries and South Street Seaport. An effort is made to provide the traveler with every amenity and service on an around-the-clock basis, in a setting of warmth, comfort, and charm.

From the gracefully understated lobby, done in rosewood and Minnesota granite, rosewood-lined elevators lead the way to the guest floors. The rooms, of generous size, are quiet and comfortably elegant, with excellent city views (rooms from the higher floors offer splendid views of the Brooklyn Bridge, the Statue of Liberty, and the entire Manhattan skyline to the north). Rooms are decorated in soft tones of taupe, peach, and platinum, with either teak or curly-maple furnishings. Each features ample workspace, with two-line phones in the bedroom and bath, plus dataports for fax and personal computers. The closets are stocked with bathrobes, a shopping bag (there's great shopping in the neighborhood!), and even an umbrella. The rooms also have safes and remote-control cable TVs.

Because the hotel welcomes many guests for "weekend escapes," there is a weekend planning service (tours, sightseeing, restaurant and shopping recommendations, and much more). Many themed weekends are also held throughout the year.

Dining/Entertainment: The premier dining room, Taliesin, offers American cuisine with Mediterranean and Asian accents in an American art deco setting. The Grille offers casual American food and ambience; the Connoisseur Bar, a popular downtown watering hole, serves light fare and snacks, as well as classic drinks and bottles from an impressive wine list.

Services: Multilingual staff, concierge, valet parking, 24-hour room service, free video checkout, valet parking, complimentary scheduled car service to midtown points.

Facilities: Fitness and business centers. The Personal Care Center offers a variety of services including facials and aromatherapy massage.

NEW YORK MARRIOTT FINANCIAL CENTER HOTEL, 85 West St., New York, NY, 10006. Tel. 212/385-4900, or toll free 800/242-8685. Fax 212/227-8136. 504 rms and suites. A/C MINIBAR TV TEL

$ Rates: $255 single; $275 double; $549 Executive Suite; $349 Hospitality Suite. Extra person free. Children 18 and under free in parents' room. Weekend packages available, including a "Two for Breakfast" deal at $139 per night, single or double, with free parking. AE, CB, DC, DISC, EU, JCB, MC, V. **Parking:** Free.

One of the newest of Marriott's megahotels, this 38-story property just two blocks south of the World Trade Center affords spectacular views. Besides being convenient to Wall Street, it's in a key location for the sightseeing attractions of Lower Manhattan, as well as the ferries to the Statue of Liberty and Ellis Island.

Beautifully decorated rooms and suites are large, comfortable, and nicely appointed in shades of peach and pearl gray, with the expected hotel furniture (polished walnut armoires substitute for closets) and writing desks. Standard amenities include clock radios, iron and ironing boards, and two phones with a dataport for computer and fax access. A Concierge Level has its own lounge and business center.

Dining/Entertainment: JW's at the Financial Center is a good option for informal meals, served all day and evening. An all-you-can-eat lunch buffet runs about $13. Also on the premises is the Liberty Lounge for a light lunch, cocktails, and evening snacks, and Pugley's Pub.

Services: Room service, concierge, laundry/valet, express video checkout, babysitting referral, AT&T Language Line, guest relations desk.

Facilities: Indoor lap pool, business center, health club, gift shop.

EXPENSIVE

BEST WESTERN SEAPORT INN, 33 Peck Slip, New York, NY 10038. Tel. 212/766-6600, or toll free 800/HOTEL NY. Fax 212/766-6616. 65 rms. A/C TV TEL
$ Rates (including continental breakfast): $140–$225 single, $160–$245 double. Special weekend packages, government and military rates available. Children under 18 stay free in parents' room using existing beds; cribs $8. Rollaways, $10. AE, CB, DC, DISC, MC, V. **Parking:** $25 nearby.

You won't have to walk very far to the South Street Seaport from this hotel; it's right in the heart of one of New York's most popular visitor attractions. In keeping with the Early New York ambience of the Seaport, this landmark 1843 building has been meticulously restored. Indoors, there's the feeling of a quaint country inn, with a (laser-disc) fireplace "blazing" in the lobby and lovely Federal-style furnishings throughout. Because it's a landmark building, each room is unique in size and shape and larger than those in the usual New York hotel. Almost all have views—of the East River, Brooklyn Bridge, New York skyline, and Seaport. The nicest rooms, on the sixth floor, have Jacuzzis; some have terraces. Each nicely decorated guest room boasts a safe; a phone with dataports; and a tasteful armoire concealing the remote-control TV, VCR, and small refrigerator. Beds are either king or queen or two queens; some rooms have sofabeds, making them good choices for families. Bathrooms are knockouts, with heat lamps, hairdryers, retractable clothes lines, and other amenities. This small hotel specializes in personalized attention. Business services are available at the desk, there's a video-rental library, and guests have privileges at a nearby health club. Handicapped-accessible and no-smoking rooms are available.

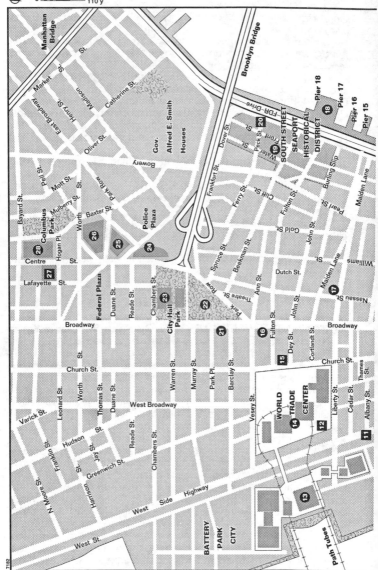

S The best prices downtown are found in a sparkling hotel that sits on the border of Chinatown and SoHo, blending Eastern and Western influences in a tasteful setting: a marble lobby, rosewood furnishings, paneled elevators, oversized arched windows, and a classic exterior. The high-ceilinged guest rooms are of different sizes and shapes, nicely appointed, and each offers computer fax dataports, two phones, a safe, and a personal voice mail system. Baths contain the traditional Holiday Inn amenities plus their Hospitality

LOWER MANHATTAN ACCOMMODATIONS & ATTRACTIONS

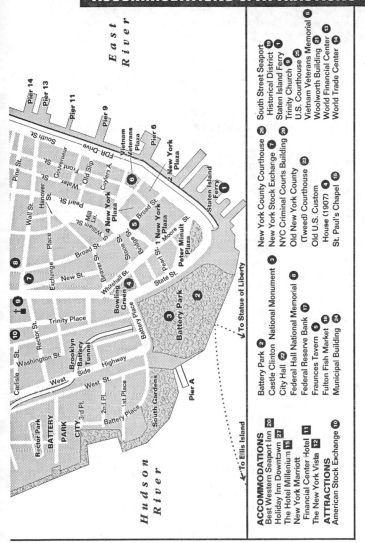

South Street Seaport Historical District ⓳
Staten Island Ferry ❶
Trinity Church ㉘
U.S. Courthouse ㉕
Vietnam Veterans Memorial ❻
Woolworth Building ㉑
World Financial Center ⓭
World Trade Center ⓮

New York County Courthouse ㉖
New York Stock Exchange ❼
NYC Criminal Courts Building ㉘
Old New York County (Tweed) Courthouse ㉓
Old U.S. Custom House (1907) ❹
St. Paul's Chapel ⓰

Battery Park ❷
Castle Clinton National Monument ❸
City Hall ㉒
Federal Hall National Memorial ❽
Federal Reserve Bank ⓱
Fraunces Tavern ❺
Fulton Fish Market ⓲
Municipal Building ㉔

ACCOMMODATIONS
Best Western Seaport Inn ⓴
Holiday Inn Downtown ㉗
The Hotel Millenium ⓯
New York Marriott Financial Center Hotel ⓫
The New York Vista ⓬

ATTRACTIONS
American Stock Exchange ⓾

MODERATE

HOLIDAY INN DOWNTOWN, 138 Lafayette St., New York, NY 10013. Tel. 212/966-8898. Fax 212/966-3933. 223 rms. A/C TV TEL
$ Rates: $88–$160 single; $99–$175 double. Bed & Breakfast Special: $99 for any room except those with king or queen size beds. AE, DC, DISC, JCB, MC, V. **Parking:** Valet, $20.

Promise: If you've forgotten any standard toiletry item (razor, comb, toothbrush), they'll give you one free. There's a high level of personal service here. The Pacifica Lounge just off the handsome lobby presents a menu of both Eastern and Western cuisine, with a popular Sunday brunch at $19.95.

2. GREENWICH VILLAGE

MODERATE

WASHINGTON SQUARE HOTEL, 103 Waverly Place, New York, NY 10011. Tel. 212/777-9515, or toll free 800/222-0418. Fax 212/979-8373. 180 rms. A/C TV TEL

$ Rates (including continental breakfast): Standard: $58 single; $85 double; $105 twin; $112 quad. Deluxe: $67 single; $95 double; $103 twin; $123 quad. AE, MC, JCB, V.

Just a few steps away from famed Washington Square, the Village's only hotel boasts a perfect location on a quiet street, yet a short stroll from the Off-Broadway theaters, clubs, and restaurants that have made the area famous. The hotel was built in 1902, but it has been thoroughly renovated, and work on the rooms steadily continues. Each room has cable color TV, individually controlled air conditioning, and a bath with shower or tub. Even though all are compact and pretty, the renovated "deluxe" rooms are much nicer and cost a bit more.

The hotel's exterior is plain, but a brass and wrought-iron gate leads to a small lobby with a marble floor and a winding staircase, in the style of turn-of-the-century hotels. The canopy at the entrance was painstakingly carved to revive the 1902 features. CIII, an affordable contemporary American restaurant, serves all three meals, at which hotel guests receive a 10% discount. Practical details include in-room safes, a room with storage lockers, an ice and vending machine, and public phones. Guests may use the copy and fax machines in the office. There's a new fitness center. And manager Sonny Christopher takes delight in briefing guests on where to go in the Village and even helping them secure tickets to special attractions and clubs.

3. PENN STATION/ HERALD SQUARE

MODERATE

HOTEL STANFORD, 43 W. 32nd St., New York, NY 10001. Tel. 212/563-1500. Fax 212/629-0043. Telex 24283. 135 rms. A/C TV TEL

$ Rates: $80 single; $90 double; $100 twin; $120 larger double with extra bed; $130 larger twin; $180 and up suite for four to six persons. Children under 12 stay free in parents' room; extra person $15. AE, DC, JCB, MC, V. **Parking:** $15 nearby.

The somewhat Asian Hotel Stanford is a tasteful and inexpensive place to stay, especially for families. Korean-owned, the hotel caters to an international trade and maintains high standards. The rooms were completely renovated a few years back, and now the Stanford offers many of the amenities of a large hotel while maintaining the friendliness and security of a small one. The lobby is bright and compact, featuring a small Japanese garden. Also available are a travel agency that sells local sightseeing tours; a limo and shopping haulage service to the airport; and the Garden coffee shop, which offers three meals a day. Sorabol, a Korean restaurant, offers authentic specialties for under $10. On the second floor is Maxim's, a very cozy piano bar with quite low prices.

The tastefully decorated rooms have cable color TVs, individually controlled air conditioning, and small refrigerators. All the baths are new. Suites, some with lovely Asian-style partitions dividing the space, are available. The Stanford is practically next door to Macy's and A&S.

NEW YORK'S HOTEL PENNSYLVANIA, a Best Western Hotel, 401 Seventh Ave., at 33rd Street (across from Madison Square Garden), New York, NY 10001. Tel. 212/736-5000, or toll free 800/223-8585. Fax 212/502-8798. 1,705 rms and suites. A/C TV TEL

$ Rates: $99–$115 single; $109–$135 double; $200–$1,000 suite. Children 18 and under stay free in parents' room. Weekend and other special packages available. AE, DC, DISC, ER, JCB, MC, V. **Parking:** $26.

This 21-story hotel is one of the largest in the city as well as one of its prime convention and exhibit hotels. Designed by McKim, Mead, and White, it began life as the Hotel Pennsylvania in 1919 and became famous as the setting for lavish parties during the "Roaring" 1920s and for Big Band concerts during the 1930s and '40s. After several changes in ownership, it's now a Best Western Hotel; a major renovation was completed last year.

The guest rooms are done in soft colors with custom-designed traditional and contemporary furnishings. Most of the rooms are not large, but they are designed to give a feeling of comfort. Larger suites are accented with special features, including bars, living and dining areas, and kitchenettes. Conveniences include color TVs with in-room movies and individually controlled air conditioning.

Dining/Entertainment: Eamon Doran's is an Irish/American pub-restaurant; the Moghul Room offers Indian cuisine; the Penn Bar, with a sports theme, features nightly karaoke sing-along; and the Globetrotter serves a buffet breakfast daily from 6:30am.

Services: Electronic security system, multilingual staff.

Facilities: Sixth-floor center and meeting rooms; use of nearby Vertical Club, a health club with an Olympic-size heated pool.

SOUTHGATE TOWER SUITE HOTEL, 371 Seventh Ave., at 31st Street, New York, NY 10001. Tel. 212/563-1800, or toll free 800/637-8483. Fax 212/643-8028. Telex 220939. 522 apts. A/C TV TEL

$ Rates: $99–$119 guest room single; $146–$180 studio suite single; $179–$220 one-bedroom suite single; $166–$200 studio suite double; $199–$240 one-bedroom double; $395–$495 two-bedroom double. Each extra person $20; up to four for one-bedroom suite. AE, DC, DISC, MC, V. **Parking:** $19.

Just across the street from all the excitement at Madison Square Garden and the Paramount Theater is a hotel with the ambience of a quiet, gracious home. The spacious suites, some with terraces, are beautifully furnished, all containing color cable TVs with in-room movies and kitchens with coffeemakers (VCRs and microwave ovens are available). The housekeeping is tops. Southgate Mall, the main lobby, is like a European street with fountains, plants, shops, and services lining each side of the plaza. It's so comfortable that many relocating executives stay here for extended periods. Considering all you get here, and the savings of eating in, this has to be among the better values in town. Southgate Tower is part of Manhattan East Suite Hotels, which means that you can often realize substantial savings (as much as 50% on weekends); summer and holiday rates are also often significantly lower. Contact the hotel for information.

Dining/Entertainment: Niles serves continental cuisine; the Penn Garden Coffee Shop provides all three meals; and Goldberg's Famous Delicatessen provides deli favorites.

Services: Room service, concierge, business services.

Facilities: Fitness center.

INEXPENSIVE

HERALD SQUARE HOTEL, 19 W. 31st St., New York, NY 10001. Tel. 212/279-4017, or toll free 800/727-1888. 112 rms (most with bath). A/C TV TEL

$ Rates: $40 single with shared bath; $50–$55 small single or double with private bath with shower; $70 standard single with bath with shower and tub; $75–$80 standard double with bath with shower and tub; $90 large double; $95 large double with three beds; $99 large double for four with one double bed and two singles or two double beds (all large doubles have private bath). AE, DISC, JCB, MC, V.

Ⓢ Located near the Empire State Building and a block from Macy's and A&S, this beautifully renovated hotel is a real find for the budget-minded. The once-rundown hotel has been lovingly transformed by the Puchall family, also in charge at the Portland Square Hotel in the Times Square area (see below). Back in 1937, the building housed the offices of *Life* magazine. Focusing on this theme, the hotel now has a restored statue of *Winged Life* over the entrance, and tasteful reproductions of old *Life* covers adorn the small lobby, halls, and rooms. Rose gardens bloom in front of the building. The environmentally conscious management made it the first hotel in New York to install a filtration system so that all drinking and bathing water is chlorine-free. The rooms are small but comfortable and well decorated in pastels and wainscoting. Each has a cable color TV and an AM/FM radio.

The hotel is small enough so guests can get plenty of attention from the multilingual staff. Manager Abraham Puchall can often be found in the lobby advising guests on where to sightsee and shop.

4. GRAMERCY PARK/ MURRAY HILL

MODERATE

GRAMERCY PARK HOTEL, 2 Lexington Ave., at 21st Street, New York, NY 10010. Tel. 212/475-4320, or toll

+ Thrift.

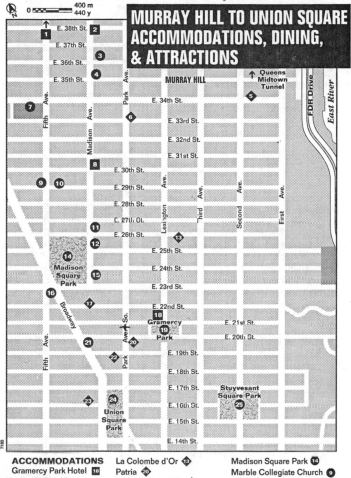

0 |___| 400 m / 440 y

MURRAY HILL

Queens Midtown Tunnel

FDR Drive

East River

E. 38th St.
E. 37th St.
E. 36th St.
E. 35th St.
E. 34th St.
E. 33rd St.
E. 32nd St.
E. 31st St.
E. 30th St.
E. 29th St.
E. 28th St.
E. 27th St.
E. 26th St.
E. 25th St.
E. 24th St.
E. 23rd St.
E. 22nd St.
E. 21st St.
E. 20th St.
E. 19th St.
E. 18th St.
E. 17th St.
E. 16th St.
E. 15th St.
E. 14th St.

Fifth Ave.
Madison Ave.
Park Ave.
Lexington Ave.
Third Ave.
Second Ave.
First Ave.
Broadway

Madison Square Park
Gramercy Park
Stuyvesant Square Park
Union Square Park

7183

ACCOMMODATIONS
Gramercy Park Hotel 18
Jolly Madison Towers Hotel 2
Quality Hotel by Journey's End 1
Roger Williams Hotel 8

DINING
Bolo 17
Café Beulah 22
El Parador 5
Fiore 6
La Colombe d'Or 13
Patria 20
Union Square Cafe 23

ATTRACTIONS
Appellate Division of the State Supreme Court 12
Church of the Incarnation 4
Church of the Transfiguration 10
Empire State Building 7
Flatiron Building 16
Gramercy Park 19
Madison Square Park 14
Marble Collegiate Church 9
Metropolitan Life Insurance Tower 15
New York Life Insurance Building 11
Pierpont Morgan Library 3
Stuyvesant Square Park 25
Theodore Roosevelt Birthplace 21
Union Square Park 24

free 800/221-4083. Fax 212/505-0535. 509 rms and suites. A/C TV TEL

$ Rates: $125–$135 single; $130–$140 double; from $160 one-bedroom family suite. Extra person $10. Children 12 and under stay free in parents' room. Weekend packages available. AE, CB, DC, DISC, EU, JCB, MC, V.

⭐ This charming European-style hotel overlooks New York's only private residential park (guests have access), so you can request a room with a view. The Gramercy Park has both character and history: It opened in 1924 and retains some of the marble fireplaces from the Stanford White brownstones it replaced. It has since hosted celebrities like Humphrey Bogart; James Cagney; Irish actor Siobhan McKenna, remembered by a plaque in the lobby; and, more recently, actor Matt Dillon. The wraparound lobby has been restored to its original look, with burnished pine-paneled walls, crystal chandeliers, and dramatic potted plants. The guest rooms, although undistinguished, are spacious enough, their typical vintage hotel furniture brightened by pastel-printed bedspreads and matching drapes.

Accommodations vary in size from a standard double-bedded room to a family suite, consisting of two double beds and a queen-size sofabed. Suites are equipped with mini-refrigerators. The Gramercy Park is also one of only a few New York hotels that offer monthly rates for long-term residential guests, either in studio apartments or in suites, both of which come with small kitchens.

Dining/Entertainment: Le Parc, the hotel's elegant restaurant, is popular with the neighborhood cognoscenti, who are attracted by the combination of gorgeous ambience—grape-velvet furniture, deep-green carpet, stunning flower arrangements, exquisite service—and better-than-average food at moderate prices. Hours are continuous daily from 7:30am to 10:30pm. Definitely worthwhile.

Services: Room service, laundry/valet.

Facilities: Newsstand, sundry shop, beauty salon.

JOLLY MADISON TOWERS HOTEL, 22 E. 38th St., at Madison Avenue, New York, NY 10016. Tel. 212/685-3700, or toll free 800/225-4340 outside New York State. Fax 212/447-0747. 225 rms, 10 suites. A/C TV TEL

$ Rates: $130–$150 single; $150–$170 double; $275 suite. Lower rates sometimes available; inquire when you make reservations. Extra person $20. Weekend packages available. AE, DC, EU, MC, V. **Parking:** $19 nearby.

Clean, cheerful, well priced, and located in a charming, safe, and convenient neighborhood—what more could the price-conscious traveler ask for in a hotel? That's what you'll find at the Jolly Madison Towers, the happy result of a $5-million renovation of a hotel that's now more than 60 years old. It sparkles from its small, pretty lobby with marble floors and mirrored ceilings, to the 18 stories of guest rooms above. The rooms are irregularly shaped, which makes them interesting; they are decorated with European-style fabrics and tones that blend effectively with the warmth of traditional rosewood furniture. Most of the beds are queens, although twins, double-doubles, and kings are also available. Each bath has a marblelike sink, a full tub and shower, and an extra phone.

Many guests are involved in the fashion industry (the Garment District is just across town), and you can often find them having a drink or entertaining clients in front of the baronial wood-burning fireplace at the Whaler Bar, a stunning re-creation of a popular New York cocktail lounge of the 1940s and '50s. The Tower Restaurant serves dinner nightly.

Facilities: Asian-style health spa offering Shiatsu massage.

Ⓕ FROMMER'S COOL FOR KIDS: HOTELS

Embassy Suites (see p. 67). The Cool Cats Kids Club is a one-of-a-kind place, a fully supervised daycare center for kids 3 to 13, with a playroom, arts and crafts room, "bubble room" for little kids, computer games for older ones. Family Friendly suites are childproof; free use of cribs and strollers, free diapers, formula, bibs, and other kid necessities.

Paramount (see p. 71). Here kids have a wonderful play room filled with plush stuffed animals (parental supervision necessary).

Travel Inn Hotel (see p. 75). An Olympic size pool, a large recreation area, and plenty of space in which the kids can let off a little steam make this a family favorite.

The Park Inn International (see p. 74). Kids adore the open-to-the-sky rooftop pool at this hotel. They may not want to go anywhere else!

Days Hotel Midtown (see p. 74). This place also has an open-air rooftop pool. There are indoor pools the kids will like at **Holiday Inn–Crowne Plaza** (see p. 69), **Parker Meridien** (see p. 64), and **Sheraton Manhattan Hotel** (see p. 71).

QUALITY HOTEL BY JOURNEY'S END, 3 E. 40th St., New York, NY 10016. Tel. 212/447-1500, or toll free 800/668-4200. Fax 212/213-0972. A/C TV TEL

$ Rates: $143.99 single, $153.99 double. $99 weekend rate, Fri, Sat, Sun. Extra person $10. Children under 18 stay free in parents' room. AE, DC, MC, V. **Parking:** $18 nearby.

Ⓢ Journey's End opened its first location in New York four years ago, and although the name has changed slightly, this hotel has all the qualities that have made the 15-year-old Canadian company so successful. Their concept of "limited service lodging" means they do not have meeting rooms, pools, or fancy amenities; what they do have are handsome new buildings; clean, comfortable rooms; and plenty of friendly, personal service. Considering its moderate rates and superb location—just off Fifth Avenue across the street from the New York Public Library, around the corner from Grand Central Terminal, and within walking distance of Broadway theaters—this hotel is a very good deal indeed.

Perfect for both families and business travelers, this 29-story high-rise has a small, attractive lobby and a mezzanine where guests can have complimentary coffee and read the local newspapers in the morning. On the weekends, they get complimentary coffee and muffins. The average-size rooms are attractively furnished, most with queen-size beds and a sofa that can convert into a small bed; some have two double beds. A nice touch is that each room has a large worktable where a businessperson can spread out. Rooms are wheelchair accessible and 10 rooms are fitted out for the handicapped. Room service is available from 7am to 10pm.

INEXPENSIVE

ROGER WILLIAMS HOTEL, 28 E. 31st St., New York, NY 10016. Tel. 212/684-7500, or toll free 800/637-9773. Fax 212/576-4343. 211 rms. A/C TV TEL

$ Rates: $55–$65 single; $60–$70 double; $65–$75 twin; $75–$80 triple; $80–$90 quad. Children under 12 stay free in parents' room. Weekly rates sometimes available. AE, MC, V. **Parking:** $17.70 nearby.

There's a one-of-a-kind find in this neighborhood: The Roger Williams is an old building in a quiet, safe, and central location, and each of its rooms has a kitchenette (two-burner gas stove, sink, refrigerator, cabinet space). Each also has a large bath with tub and shower, simple but new furnishings, a color cable TV, individually controlled air conditioning, and a direct-dial phone. Staying here is like having your own studio apartment in this pleasant Murray Hill area. Across the street is the American Academy of Dramatic Arts, as well as a 24-hour deli salad bar, which solves the problem of what to eat in that kitchenette.

Why is this place so inexpensive? Mainly because for years the hotel housed mostly long-term residents, some from the United Nations and some temporary American Red Cross disaster victims. With the resurgence of Murray Hill, the Roger Williams renovated its interior and upgraded its service, as have many of the older hotels in the area. The lobby was redone in art deco style, all the rooms were redone, and they began accepting many more transient guests.

The rooms vary in size, but most are large and all are comfortable. Some have terraces. As for the kitchenettes, a "Kitchen Kit" sets you up with a kettle; paper plates; cups; plastic cutlery; and tea, coffee, sugar, and salt. (You're on your own for pots and pans, if you need them.)

Genial manager Peter Arest and his staff, mainly old-timers, are very friendly and like to help guests. If possible, they will give you a room with a terrace, advise you where to shop, or suggest what to eat in the Chinese restaurant in the lobby. Flanked by churches, this is exactly the kind of hotel that budget tourists pray for.

5. MIDTOWN WEST

If you've come to New York to go to the theater, to see the sights, to conduct business, or just to be in the heart of everything, you can't pick a more convenient location than Midtown West. Since it's bounded on the north by the West 50s, passing through the Broadway theater district in the 40s, and bordered on the south by Madison Square Garden Center, you'll be within walking distance of just about everything, including Rockefeller Center, Carnegie Hall, and Lincoln Center, not far north; as well as the art galleries and elegant shops of 57th Street and Fifth Avenue.

Several national chain hotels are represented in this area, including the popular **Howard Johnson Plaza-Hotel,** 851 Eighth Ave. at 50th Street (tel. 212/581-4100 or toll free 800/426-HOJO), well located, within walking distance of Broadway theaters, with rates from $106–$142 single, $118–$154 double or twin, $195 and up suite.

VERY EXPENSIVE

THE NEW YORK HILTON AND TOWERS AT ROCKEFELLER CENTER, 1335 Avenue of the Americas, between 53rd and 54th streets, New York, NY 10019. Tel. 212/586-7000, or toll free 800/HILTONS. Fax 212/315-1374. Telex NYHUR 238492. 2,041 rms and suites. A/C MINIBAR TV TEL

$ Rates: $176–$235 single; $201–$260 double or twin. Extra person $30. No charge for children occupying same room as parent. Tower: $201–$260 single; $226–$285 double; $400–$2,500 suite. Weekend packages available. AE, CB, DC, DISC, ER, JCB, MC, V. **Parking:** $30.

This is one of New York's major hotels, an international center with a huge array of services and facilities for both business and pleasure travelers within its soaring glass-sided column. Its Grand Ballroom is big enough for small armies to parade in (up to 3,300 people). A $120-million renovation, completed in 1993, has made the hotel, with its extensive art collection in public areas and guest accommodations, more handsome than ever.

The wall-to-wall blue-tinted windows in the guest rooms provide dramatic vistas of New York's skyline. The rooms, nicely decorated with a modern touch, have color cable TVs with in-house movies at a nominal charge, refreshment centers, voice mail, and computer dataports. Special rooms are available for the disabled, and 1,000 rooms on 18 floors are reserved for nonsmokers. The Tower, a hotel within a hotel on the 39th through 44th floors, features its own registration desk, a private lounge and boardroom, concierge service, and many special amenities. Continental breakfast, afternoon tea, and hors d'oeuvres are served here.

Dining/Entertainment: Grill 53 offers prime beef, fresh seafood, and pasta at lunch and dinner, and a Sunday "Bruncheon" buffet with entertainment; Café New York, a reasonably priced restaurant, has both Japanese and American menus, including buffet breakfasts every morning; Mirage is a lobby cocktail lounge; and the International Promenade is great fun for cocktails, express breakfast, and people-watching through floor-to-ceiling windows.

Services: Multilingual staff (some 25 languages are spoken); International Visitors Information Service; foreign-currency exchange 24 hours a day; room service.

Facilities: Fitness center, business center, sightseeing and theater ticket desks, beauty salon, barbershop, boutiques, American Express desk.

NEW YORK MARRIOTT MARQUIS, 1535 Broadway, between 45th and 46th streets, New York, NY 10036.

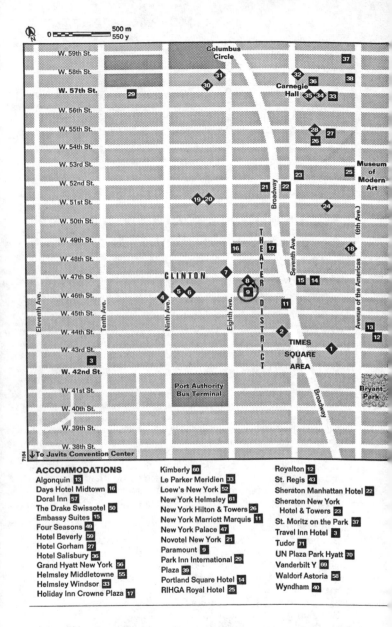

Tel. 212/398-1900, 212/704-8700 (reservations), or toll free 800/228-9290. Fax 212/704-8930. 1,874 rms, 147 suites. A/C MINIBAR TV TEL

$ Rates: Sun–Thurs: $300 single; $315 double. Fri–Sat: usually $159–$199 single or double. Concierge Room: $275 single; $295 double; $425–$3,500 suite. Other special packages and rates sometimes available. AE, CB, DISC, JCB, MC, V. **Parking:** $30.
The opening of the Marriott Marquis 10 years ago signaled the

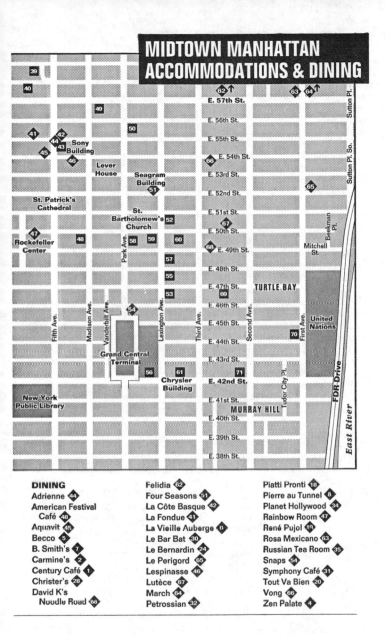

MIDTOWN MANHATTAN ACCOMMODATIONS & DINING

DINING

Adrienne 44
American Festival
  Café 48
Aquavit 45
Becco 5
B. Smith's 7
Carmine's 2
Century Café 1
Christer's 28
David K's
  Noodle Road 68

Felidia 62
Four Seasons 51
La Côte Basque 42
La Fondue 41
La Vieille Auberge 6
Le Bar Bat 30
Le Bernardin 24
Le Perigord 65
Lespinasse 46
Lutèce 67
March 64
Petrossian 32

Piatti Pronti 18
Pierre au Tunnel 8
Planet Hollywood 34
Rainbow Room 47
René Pujol 19
Rosa Mexicano 63
Russian Tea Room 35
Snaps 54
Symphony Café 31
Tout Va Bien 20
Vong 66
Zen Palate 4

glamorous rebirth of Times Square. Located in the heart of the theater district, this is Marriott's flagship and one of New York's largest hotels, with the world's tallest atrium (half the height of the Empire State Building). Architect/developer John Portman's $450-million 50-story colossus is a dazzling city-within-a-city where one could sleep in comfort, dine in style, attend a business convention, take in a Broadway show, work out in the fitness center, and shop in a wealth of specialty stores, with no need ever to venture outdoors.

Although the hotel does cater to many business and convention travelers with its state-of-the-art facilities, it also provides a world of excitement and glamour for the vacationer. Glass-enclosed elevators rise eight stories to the spectacular atrium lobby, which suggests a wondrous indoor park with giant trees, abundant plantings, and fountains—all creating a feeling of tropical, rather than urban, splendor. The guest rooms are oversize by New York standards, each with two views (an exterior one overlooking the city, an interior one overlooking the atrium lobby). All with two telephones, love seats, armchairs, and desks, they are done in traditional walnut woods and deep-purple and green color schemes. The baths have many luxurious amenities. Rooms for the disabled are available. If you need to conduct a small business meeting in your room, get one of the 24 parlors that feature Murphy-type sleeping units and double as small meeting rooms. Concierge Rooms offer even more amenities and services.

Dining/Entertainment: Lining the atrium are a variety of restaurants, lounges, and people-watching spots: the revolving Broadway Lounge; the Encore sidewalk-like cafe for casual dining (and New York's largest lunchtime salad buffet); the sunken Atrium Café with built-in deli; and the elegantly understated JW's Steakhouse. It's become a New York tradition to meet friends "under the clock"—the 3½-story centerpiece of the dramatic Clock Lounge, an intimate seating area amid the trees. On the top of the hotel is The View, a three-story rooftop revolving restaurant and lounge, offering excellent food and some of the grandest views in New York (see the review under "Specialty Dining" in Chapter 6).

Services: Video express checkout, 24-hour room service, newspaper delivered every morning.

Facilities: Full-service business center; health club with Universal equipment, whirlpool, and sauna.

LE PARKER MERIDIEN, 118 W. 57th St., New York, NY 10019. Tel. 212/245-5000, or toll free 800/543-4300. Fax 212/708-7477. Telex 680-1134. 700 rms, 200 suites. A/C MINIBAR TV TEL

$ Rates: $225–$240 single; $255–$275 double; $325–$425 Tower Suite; $350 Corner Suite; $700 2-bedroom suite: Weekend packages available. AE, DC, EU, JCB, MC, V. **Valet parking:** $28 (at a nearby garage).

If you love Paris in the springtime, then you're surely going to love Le Parker Meridien, for that's the feeling one gets anytime of the year at New York's first French hotel. This $75-million 41-story beauty is the North American flagship of Meridien Hotels, a division of Air France. From its splendid entrance promenade with 65-foot-high gold-leaf ceiling and marble arch, to the lobby and balconied atrium alive with trees and plantings, to the elegant restaurants, guest rooms, and rooftop pool, there's a special ambience here: the good life, *à la française.*

The newly renovated rooms and suites are decorated in a contemporary, sophisticated style, with black accents on an oatmeal background, furniture in deep-wood shades, and Greco-Roman borders and artwork.

Dining/Entertainment: Shin's, a handsome restaurant with an open kitchen on the lobby floor, introduces Japanese fusion cuisine to New York, an exquisite blending of tastes from Asia and the West, with an emphasis on sushi. Bar Montparnasse, with its magnificent oak bar, subtle furnishings, and whimsical canvas murals, is open from 10am to midnight for light fare, specialty coffees, and champagne by the glass. Every night there's live music and a tapas menu.

Services: Multilingual staff, Japanese Assistance Network, business services, concierge service, laundry and dry cleaning, 24-hour room service, in-room massage available from health club staff.

Facilities: Club La Racquette, with regulation racquetball, squash, and handball courts, aerobics classes, and fitness equipment; splendid glass-enclosed swimming pool; indoor and outdoor sun decks; jogging path.

RIHGA ROYAL HOTEL, 151 W. 54th St., New York, NY 10019. Tel. 212/307-5000, or toll free 800/937-5454. Fax 212/765-6530. 500 suites. A/C MINIBAR TV TEL

$ **Rates:** $290–$390 standard one-bedroom suite; $420 Pinnacle Suite; $900 Crown Royal Suite; $1700 Grand Royal Suite. Weekend rates from $205, including parking. AE, DC, DISC, JCB, MC, V. **Parking:** $28 nearby.

One of New York's tallest hotels, the 54-story RIHGA Royal opened in 1990 and was immediately hailed as one of the most architecturally splendid of the city's newer hotels. With its facade of rose-beige brick and granite and a horizontal array of bay windows creating a set-back effect and offering panoramic views of the Manhattan skyline and the rivers, the hotel is a classic form reminiscent of the skyscrapers of the 1920s and '30s. The small, exquisite lobby is in the style of Park Avenue apartment house lobbies built in that period. This hotel contains only deluxe suites with full service. Security is excellent throughout—a computer-controlled, timed key system is used.

The suites themselves are custom-designed, done in peach or teal, the latter with an especially cool, restful effect. They are very quiet, since six inches of wall space between the units blocks out the noise from one's neighbors and double-pane windows eliminate street noise. Each suite has an octagonal-shaped living room, good for a small gathering, and one or two luxurious bedrooms. They all contain VCRs, under-the-counter refrigerators and icemakers with soft drinks and snacks, three telephones with two separate lines, computer and fax lines, and electronic safes. The rose-beige–marble baths, with separate tubs, shower stalls, and dressing areas with vanity, are surely among the most luxurious in New York. Guests in the Pinnacle Suites (50 suites on the top floors) have their own complimentary cellular phone and fax machine with private numbers; they are given personalized business cards listing these numbers as well as their private room phone number. They also receive private town-car service to and from the airport. The six Grand Royal Suites are uniquely designed and furnished as if they were exquisite private apartments.

Opulence and elegance extend to every area of the RIHGA Royal, with marble, mahogany, and brass touches and glorious flowers everywhere. The hotel represents the entry into the United States of a Japan-based luxury hotel chain, the Royal Hotel, Ltd.

Dining/Entertainment: The award-winning Halcyon Restaurant serves contemporary American cuisine, with pre- and post-theater menus and a spectacular Sunday brunch on the 54th floor; the Halcyon Lounge offers music, cocktails, and light meals.

Services: 24-hour in-suite dining service, served butler style on the finest china and crystal; multinational staff; free shoeshine; valet and laundry service; free morning paper and shuttle to Wall Street.

Facilities: Banquet and meeting rooms on the top floors; business center, fitness center with sauna, exercise machines, and massage service.

THE ROYALTON, 44 W. 44th St., between Fifth and Sixth avenues, New York, NY 10036. Tel. 212/869-4400, or toll free 800/635-9013. Fax 212/869-8965. Telex 213875. 167 rms, 24 suites. A/C MINIBAR TV TEL

$ Rates: $210–$335 single; $235–$360 double; $380 alcove suite. Penthouse and weekend rates available on request. AE, DC, ER, MC, V. **Parking:** $25.

A small hotel that makes a large design statement, the Royalton is one of the most talked about of the newer hotels in New York City. The $40-million makeover of the cozy old theatrical residential hotel has made the Royalton like something out of a futuristic stage set, with an almost surreal, dreamlike quality; it could be of the next century or something out of antiquity, a hotel in which the cutting edge meets the classic.

Architect Philippe Starck's concept of "hotel as theater" has created some extraordinary results: a long, low lobby with a wall of seemingly endless mahogany doors, a cobalt-blue carpet forming a runway-style path, club chairs covered with white slipcovers as in a deserted house, light fixtures that look like projecting rhino horns, and a sunken library table; and with all the standard hotel fixtures—guest registration, porters, elevators—tactfully concealed. There is no name on the door outside, and "doormen" are black-clad youths who dare not smile.

Upstairs, dark, mysterious hallways with deep-blue walls and carpeting lead to the guest rooms, which also make a design statement: Huge, luxurious beds are surrounded by wraparound mahogany headboards and nightstands shaped like portholes. There are velvet banquettes; working fireplaces in many rooms, with wood supplied by room service; arched mantelpieces with a single candleholder and lighted taper set atop a strange wall sculpture. Above it, just one small frame holds an art postcard that is changed daily—the only picture in the room. Among the most spacious in New York (they average 400 square feet), all rooms and suites have separate areas for entertaining and working, as well as sleeping. Each room has a writing desk; a dining table; a queen- or king-size bed; VCR; a cassette deck player; and two-line telephones. And each bathroom is a pièce de résistance; many have five-foot custom bathtubs, usually circular, built in a concave slate wall. There are mirrored dressing rooms, Italian cut-glass vanities, and luxurious amenities.

Dining/Entertainment: At the end of the fantastical lobby is "44," a critically acclaimed restaurant serving New American cuisine, a haven for smart celebrities, magazine editors, and theater folk, the 1990s answer to the Round Table of the Algonquin Hotel across the street. The Round Bar in the lobby, inspired by Ernest Hemingway's favorite bar at the Ritz in Paris, is the setting for "lobby socializing." Food and beverage service is available throughout the lobby all day.

Services: Impeccable service includes 24-hour room service, valet parking, nightly turndown, valet/laundry service, in-room delivery of the *New York Times*.

Facilities: Fitness Room open 24 hours a day, with state-of-the-art equipment; personal trainers and massage therapists available. LifeCycle equipment is in some of the rooms.

EXPENSIVE

ALGONQUIN HOTEL, 59 W. 44th St., between Fifth and Sixth avenues, New York, NY 10036. Tel. 212/840-6800, or toll free 800/548-0345. Fax 212/944-1419. 142 rms, 23 suites. A/C TV TEL

$ Rates: $195 single; $215 double; from $165 weekend; $300 suite. Extra person $25. Children 12 and under stay free in parents' room. AE, CB, DC, DISC, EURO, ER, JCB, MC, V. **Parking:** $25.

I know of no other hotel lobby in New York that is so full of fascinating ghosts as the Algonquin's. Every time I sit down at one of the plush little sofas in the oak-paneled lobby-lounge and ring the bell for a drink—or a spot of tea—I am reminded of the generations of actors and writers and celebrated wits who have held forth here since 1902. Although Robert Benchley, James Thurber, H. L. Mencken, and Dorothy Parker are part of the Algonquin's storied past, this place is still as much a literary and artistic club as it is a hotel. But it is a hotel, very much in the manner of an inn, where you needn't be a celebrity to feel at home.

The recently updated guest rooms—the entire hotel has undergone a $20-million complete renovation—welcome with Chippendale-style mahogany antique and reproduction furniture; Chinese porcelain lamps; and, in many rooms, upholstered window seats with colorful throw pillows. The effect is homey and cozy, a refreshing change from the modern megahotel chains. Theatrical drawings and caricatures by Algonquin habitués James Thurber and Al Hirschfeld decorate rooms and halls. Guests are pampered with free in-room movies through remote-control TVs, electronic key cards, personal safes, and complimentary copies of the *New York Times,* the *Wall Street Journal,* and *The New Yorker*.

Dining/Entertainment: The Rose Room serves breakfast, lunch, dinner, pre- and post-theater supper, and Saturday and Sunday brunch in posh Louis XVI surroundings. At night the Oak Room turns into a cabaret showcasing some of the best talent in the country. Drinks and light meals and snacks are available at the Blue Bar from noon to midnight. But the Algonquin's highlight remains the lobby, alive all day and evening, for drinks, conversation, and even afternoon tea.

Services: Room service, concierge, theater tickets, laundry/valet, babysitting, multilingual staff, business services.

Facilities: Newsstand; use of nearby health club for a fee.

EMBASSY SUITES, 1568 Broadway, at 47th Street and 7th Avenue, New York, NY 10036. Tel. 212/719-1600 or toll free 800-EMBASSY. Fax 212/921-5110. 460 two-room suites. A/C MINIBAR TV TEL

$ Rates (including complete American breakfast): $159–$225 single, $179–$245 double. $350–$450 Corporate Class and Conference Suites. Packages available. Extra person $20. Children under 12 free with parents. Cribs free. Special suites for the disabled available. AE, DISC, DC, JCB, MC, V. **Parking:** $28.

If somebody told you that for the price of a regular hotel room you could stay in a handsome suite, enjoy a lavish buffet breakfast and a daily cocktail party free, and have access to all kinds of amenities for your kids, including a supervised daycare center—all in the heart of the Broadway theater district—you might think you were dreaming. But wake up and smell the coffee (that's free, too). Embassy Suites offers one of the best hotel deals in New York. The four-year-old, 43-story hotel, built around a handsome indoor atrium, offers all these features, and more.

Embassy Suites has no rooms—just two-room suites; and each consists of a nicely decorated private bedroom with either a king- or queen-size bed or two doubles, a separate living room with a queen-size sofa, a dining worktable area, a wet bar, microwave oven, small refrigerator, coffeemaker with free coffee, decaf, and tea. (Plates, cups, and saucers, and cutlery available on request.) There are two remote-control televisions with cable and in-room movies, and three telephones with call waiting and voice mail. Conference and Corporate Class suites are larger, spacious enough to host a small business meeting, and feature a workstation with multiple two-line phones with fax and modem hookups.

For families traveling with kids, the hotel is the next best thing to a visit from a fairy godmother. An entire floor consists of childproof suites; there's a special kid's room service menu; and if you need a stroller or a crib, or run out of formula or diapers or bibs or whatever, they're all available, and all free. Best of all is the Cool Cats Kids Club, a supervised daycare center for ages 3 to 13, with a playroom, an arts and crafts room, a "bubble room" for little kids and computer and video games for the older ones. Kids adore it. It's available by appointment and costs are $5 per hour or $20 per day. Kids can take their favorite toys back to their suite, too.

Dining/Entertainment: The Broadway Museum Café serves Continental and American food in a handsome setting decorated with theatrical murals. A $9.95 pasta lunch is a bargain. A piano bar provides entertainment, evenings, at the Broadway Museum Cabaret. A lavish breakfast buffet, featuring many hot and cold dishes and made-to-order omelets, is served exclusively to guests. Drinks are unlimited at the nightly Manager's Reception.

Services: Room service, concierge, free morning newspaper, Cool Cats Kids Club (see above).

Facilities: State-of-the-art fitness center: $15-a-day access to nearby Vertical Club, with Olympic-size swimming pool.

HELMSLEY WINDSOR, 100 W. 58th St., New York, NY 10019. Tel. 212/265-2100, or toll free 800/221-4982. Fax 212/315-0371. 208 rms, 36 suites. A/C TV TEL

$ Rates: Sun–Thurs, $135–$145 single; $145–$155 double or twin; $215–$225 one-bedroom suite; from $325 two-bedroom suite. AE, CB, DC, MC, V. **Parking:** $21.

This is the kind of gracious small hotel that people tell their friends about. A favorite for almost half a century, the Windsor is close to Central Park and has a beautiful old-world lobby with a mirrored ceiling, a fireplace, and chandeliers. The old-world theme is carried out in the generously sized rooms (even the singles have king-size beds!) with traditional furniture, wall-to-wall carpeting, and good closets (most rooms have two). Computerized no-key locks assure absolute protection. You'll find performing artists (the hotel is near the major music and theater centers), corporate types, and international visitors enjoying the peacefulness of a stay here.

HOLIDAY INN CROWNE PLAZA, 1605 Broadway, at 49th Street, New York, NY 10019. Tel. 212/977-4000, or toll free 800/243-NYNY. Fax 212/333-7393. 746 rms, 24 suites. A/C MINIBAR TV TEL

$ Rates: $149–$199 single or double; $199–$219 Crowne Plaza Club single or double; $350–$1,100 suite; $149–$189 per night Stress Reduction Weekend, including continental breakfast, use of health club, parking. AE, DC, MC, V. **Parking:** Valet, $29.

With a 100-foot granite archway that recalls the proscenium arch of Broadway theaters and 12 stories of dazzling lights and signage, this $300-million hotel is perhaps the most architecturally lavish new building in New York. Whether one thinks it's gorgeous or garish or would fit in better in Las Vegas is a matter of opinion, but everyone does agree that it's a major boost to the revitalization of the Times Square area. They also agree that this flagship hotel of Holiday Inn Crowne Plaza's worldwide system is a splendid full-service environment for tourists and business travelers alike.

All the good-size guest rooms are tastefully decorated, with marble baths, remote-control color cable TVs, in-room safe, direct-dial two-line phones with voice mail, and many nice touches. Families will like the convenience of two double beds. Four floors are devoted to Concierge Rooms, where guests receive complimentary continental breakfast, evening hors d'oeuvres, and many other amenities. No-smoking rooms and rooms for the disabled are available.

Dining/Entertainment: The Balcony Café offers breakfast and lunch daily in a greenhouse setting. The opulent Broadway Grill, created by David Liederman (of David's Cookies fame), offers fresh grilled meats, seafood, thin-crust pizzas, and a premier wine selection. Samplings Bar, a multitiered room with a splendid panorama of Broadway, offers entertaining light fare and a lavish Sunday brunch buffet. The Lobby Bar is an intimate lounge.

Services: Same-day cleaning, 24-hour room service, concierge, babysitting.

Facilities: A spectacular 50-foot glass-domed pool is centerpiece of the New York Sports Club, a large state-of-the-art fitness center, complete with exercise physiologists; comprehensive business center.

HOTEL GORHAM, 136 W. 55th St., New York, NY 10019. Tel. 212/245-1800. Fax 212/582-8332. 70 rms, 50 suites. A/C MINIBAR TV TEL

$ Rates: $150–$240 single; $160–$260 double; $188–$300 suite. Extra person $20; children under 16 stay free with parents. Weekend packages available. AE, CB, DC, JCB, MC, V. **Parking:** $25.

The Gorham has recently completed a multimillion-dollar overhaul that includes everything from new windows to custom-designed furniture. Its rooms and suites (this is a small property styled for easy living) are freshly painted and decorated in either pale gray and white or lavender and white. Custom-built armoires in burgundy lacquer conceal the TVs and provide extra drawers to supplement the already ample closets. Other built-ins include desks and luggage storage units. The rooms are spacious, large enough for either one king or two queen-size beds; suites have separate living areas with pullout couches accommodating as many as five.

Besides the expected features, the Gorham offers two-line phones (three per room) with call waiting and computer/fax access, custom-designed wet bars with refrigerators and microwaves, and in-room safes (security is tight here). Brand-new, sleek beige-marble-and-glass baths provide such luxuries as deep oval tubs (with whirlpools in many rooms and all suites), hairdryers, digital water-temperature control valves, and telephone extensions.

Dining/Entertainment: The on-premises Castellano's is an attractive upscale restaurant that serves lunch and dinner. The charming Breakfast Room offers a buffet breakfast for $10.50.

Services: Nightly turndown, concierge, laundry/valet, business services.

Facilities: Health club.

NOVOTEL NEW YORK, 226 W. 52nd St., at Broadway, New York, NY 10019. Tel. 212/315-0100, or toll free 800/NOVOTEL. Fax 212/765-5369. 474 rms. A/C MINIBAR TV TEL

$ Rates: Sun–Thurs, $159–$199 single or double. Fri–Sat, $129–$159 single or double. AE, CB, DC, EN, JCB, MC, V. **Parking:** $10.50 nearby.

Novotel New York caters to a sophisticated traveler who appreciates comfort, security, a Gallic flair, and a realistic tariff. The tiny street-level entrance hardly suggests what awaits above (the Novotel was built over an already existing four-story building), but in the seventh-floor Sky Lobby, a whole new world opens up—soaring glass windows, 10-foot-high dramatic French impressionist-style murals, rose-colored sofas, beautiful plantings, and chic style.

The newly renovated guest rooms, many with views of the Hudson, feature contemporary furnishings and accessories in rich hues of moss, Wedgwood blue, violet, taupe, and rose, with black accents. Bedding is either a king-size bed and a pullout sofa or two double beds. First-class touches include large worktable desks, new baths with environmentally friendly European Yves Rocher amenities and hairdryers; 100 movies to choose from on Cablevision and Spectravision; video account review and checkout; in-room safe; two telephones; a dataport for personal computers; and more. Security is excellent, with two levels of checkpoints. The efficiency and courtesy of the multilingual staff (who are given European training and rotate their assignments) have been given high marks by many repeat visitors.

Dining/Entertainment: You can visit the handsome glass-sided, two-tiered Café Nicole during the day or before and after the theater to see the lights and stars (celestial and celebrity—Jerry Ohrbach or Christopher Reeves might also be dining here). An extensive outdoor terrace affords a spectacular view of Times Square. The piano bar features live entertainment Monday to Saturday: Jazz artist Sarah McLawler performs every Thursday to Saturday.

Services: Guest Service assists with theater and airline tickets, transportation, and more; comprehensive Business Corner; room service.

Facilities: Fitness center.

PARAMOUNT, 235 W. 46th St., between Broadway and Eighth Avenue, New York, NY 10036. Tel. 212/764-5500, or toll free 800/225-7474. Fax 212/354-5237. 610 rms, 12 suites. A/C TV TEL

$ Rates: $185 single; $155–$205 double; $330–$440 suite. Children 12 and under stay free in parents' room. Weekend packages, some including parking, available. AE, DC, MC, V. **Parking:** $16 nearby.

In the heart of the heart of the Theater District, here's a hotel-as-theater: French interior-designer Philippe Starck has turned an older hotel into a striking, high-style ocean liner in the middle of Manhattan. There's no sign outside, so look for the fresh-faced young doormen in white T-shirts and black jackets. The lobby is not so much a lobby as an environment, with a dark palette and a "floating" marble staircase right out of 1930s Hollywood. The guest rooms, like ships' staterooms, are small but compact, done in white, gray and black, with curvy green chairs adding to the witty, slightly zany decor. The swivel cyclops-eye armoire is a showstopper. So are the headboards in the single rooms: oversize silkscreen reproduction of a famous Vermeer painting framed in gilt and glowing above the pristine white bed. Fresh flowers grace every room, and even the smallest accommodations have color cable TVs, two-line phones with computer capability, and VCRs (tapes can be rented from the desk).

Dining/Entertainment: The Paramount's "very in" dining spots include the stylish Mezzanine; the Dean & Deluca Café; and the Whiskey Bar. All are great for before- or after-theater dining and mingling.

Services: Room service, concierge, laundry/valet; babysitting; limo service.

Facilities: Children's playroom, business center, fully equipped sports room, meeting room, newsstand.

SHERATON MANHATTAN HOTEL, Seventh Avenue at 52nd Street, New York, NY 10019. Tel. 212/581-3300, or toll free 800/325-3535. Fax 212/541-9219. Telex 640-458. 650 rms, 7 suites. A/C TV TEL

$ Rates: $155–$240 single; $155–$285 double; with 14-day advance $149 weekdays, $145 weekend, single or double. $350–$430 one–bedroom suite; $525–$645 two-bedroom suite. AE, CB, DC, ER, JCB, MC, V. **Parking:** $18.75.

A $50-million renovation has turned an older establishment into a stunning boutique hotel, tailored for the needs of business travelers, with well-thought-out business amenities in each room—everything from a generous desk with phone to a dataport hookup for portable PCs and fax machines. Each handsome new room features an oversize bed, a brightly lit bath, a sofa or lounge chairs, a coffeemaker with free coffee and a TV that can be viewed from both bed and sitting areas; some have pullout sofas in the sitting areas, handy for business travelers accompanied by their families. All have an iron and ironing board, hairdryer, refreshment center, phones with voice mail, and video checkout. Solicitous attention is paid to each guest, with the aim of providing the facilities of a large hotel and the personal touch of a small one. No-smoking rooms and handicapped facilities are available.

Dining/Entertainment: Adjoining the lobby is Bistro 790, a popular American/Mediterranean restaurant with a lively bar and a show kitchen, serving all three meals, as well as pre- and post-theater dining.

Services: In-room video account review and checkout; voicemail; concierge service—including in-depth itinerary and activity planning; morning newspaper.

Facilities: Glass-enclosed pool, Fitness Center with state-of-the-art exercise equipment, sauna, and locker rooms with facilities for the handicapped; fax machines and PCs available for in-room rental.

SHERATON NEW YORK HOTEL & TOWERS, Seventh Avenue at 53rd Street, New York, NY 10019. Tel. 212/581-1000, or toll free 800/325-3535. Fax 212/262-4410. Telex 421130. 1,750 rooms, 51 suites. A/C MINIBAR TV TEL

$ **Rates:** $150–$240 single, $155–$225 double; with 14-day advance notice, $149 weekdays, $145 weekends, single or double. $350–$430 one-bedroom suite. AE, CB, DC, MC, V. **Parking:** $24.

This 50-story hostelry has recently completed a $150-million construction and renovation program that assures its stature as one of New York's premier convention and business travelers' hotels, with state-of-the-art facilities and superior service. The guest rooms and suites, all completely renovated and re-outfitted, are each handsomely furnished and boast king- and/or queen-size beds, well-defined work and relaxation areas with a full-size writing desk, comfortable sofas or lounge chairs, a safe, and individually controlled heating and cooling units. They all have a hairdryer, iron and ironing board, refreshment center, coffeemaker with free coffee, phones with voice mail, and video checkout. Wheelchair-accessible and no-smoking rooms are available. Rooms in the Sheraton Towers, a luxury hotel within the main hotel, boast English Regency–style furnishings and such touches as fresh flowers and plush bed and bath linens. Sheraton Towers has its own express elevators and a grand expanded lounge where complimentary breakfast and hors d'oeuvres are served.

Dining/Entertainment: The large glass-enclosed Streeter's New York Café on the lobby level offers three American-style meals a day. Hudson's Sports Bar and Grill features intimate booths and 30 TV screens, autographed sports memorabilia and interactive sports trivia games. The Lobby Court is the place for evening cocktails and nightly entertainment, with Irving Fields at the piano Tuesday through Saturday evenings. The "Broadway Hour" radio show originates here every Thursday at 5pm.

Services: Multilingual staff, room service, concierge. For Sheraton Towers guests: bar and breakfast buffet, pantry, butler service, cocktail hour.

Facilities: 3,500-square-foot health club with locker rooms, sauna, and steam; free use of swimming pool at the Sheraton Manhattan Hotel, across the street.

ST. MORITZ ON THE PARK, 50 Central Park South, New York, NY 10019. Tel. 212/755-5800 or toll free 800/221-4774. Fax 212/371-5838. 589 rooms, 125 suites. A/C TV TEL

$ **Rates:** $135 single, $150 double, courtyard; $165 single, $180 double, avenue; $195 single, $205 double, park; $275–$450 one-bedroom suite; $595 two-bedroom suite. AARP discount 20%. Inquire about special promotional rates. Weekend packages:

$205 per person double occupancy for a three-day two-night Central Park Dream Package that includes a horse-driven carriage ride through Central Park, daily continental breakfast and dinner for two, nightly dessert at Rumpelmayer's, champagne upon arrival. Children under 12 stay free with their parents. AE, CB, DC, DISC, JCB, MC, V. **Parking:** $23.

Central Park South, that posh avenue facing the greensward of Central Park, has long been known for its luxury hotels; happily, one of these is still surprisingly affordable—and it has more parkview rooms than any of the others. The St. Moritz on the Park, a venerable hotel dating back to 1930, has recently undergone a major renovation and emerged as what *Entrepreneur* called the "Best Individual Hotel Value" in town for its combination of price, service, and location. The historic building (once home to columnist Walter Winchell and many other celebrities) has refurbished all of its guest rooms while still maintaining the feeling of an older New York. Attractive rooms have either a desk or table, voice mail, video checkout and message service, Spectrodyne movies available via the color cable TV, and even Japanese TV channels. The suites, particularly those facing Central Park South, are particularly attractive.

Dining/Entertainment: Beloved of generations of New York children, Rumpelmayer's still serves up the best chicken potpie and the best hot chocolate and hot fudge sundaes in town, along with a sophisticated menu at all three meals. Café de la Paix is famous for its Around the World cocktail lounge and its charming sidewalk cafe, open from spring through early fall, and one of New York's best venues for people-watching.

Services: Multilingual staff, valet parking, gift shop.

Facilities: Business Center, health club privileges at nearby New York Health and Racquet Club.

MODERATE

COMFORT INN MURRAY HILL, 42 W. 35th St., New York, NY 10001. Tel. 212/947-0200, or toll free 800/228-5150. Fax 212/594-3047. 120 rms. A/C TV TEL
$ Rates: $85–$94 single; $89–$129 double; $99–$129 room with double bed and pullout sofa; $99–$129 room with queen-size bed; $129 room with king-size bed (all for one or two people). Extra person $12. Weekend packages available. AE, CB, DC, DISC, ER, JCB, MC, V. **Parking:** $20 nearby.

Small luxury hotels abound in New York—at rates of $200 per night and over! What a treat, then, to find an "affordable luxury hotel" like the Comfort Inn, which boasts European charm, personal service, and moderate rates. Located just around the corner from Fifth Avenue department stores, near Seventh Avenue's Garment District and the Jacob Javits Convention Center, it's considered an "in" find among fashion buyers and other smart business and vacation travelers. Most of its rooms are sold out every night, and over 60% of its guests are repeat customers.

Built more than 70 years ago (meaning thick walls and relative quiet), the building was treated to a $4.5-million renovation and opened as a hotel some 10 years ago. A deluxe complimentary continental breakfast is served every morning in the charming small lobby with its winding marble staircase, Greek columns, and plush furnishings. Manager Anthony Longano can often be found there; he likes to get to know his guests, and he and his front-desk staff are concerned that guests have a good time during their stay. (He prefers individual travelers and will not take large groups.) The 12-story hotel has no more than 12 rooms per floor, which makes for a cozy feeling (women traveling alone seem to feel especially safe), and these rooms are very pleasantly decorated in soothing pastels; all have individually controlled air conditioning and newly tiled baths. A floor for nonsmokers is available. *Note:* The manager advises that you call the hotel directly (rather than the 800 number); you may qualify for AARP, AAA, senior-citizen, corporate, fashion industry, or other discount.

DAYS HOTEL MIDTOWN, 790 Eighth Ave., between 48th and 49th streets, New York, NY 10019. Tel. 212/581-7000, or toll free 800/572-6232. Fax 212/974-0291. Telex 147182. 366 rms. A/C TV TEL

$ Rates: $99–$130 single; $115–$142 double; $170–$205 one-bedroom suite; $235–$255 two-bedroom suite. Extra person $20. Children under 18 stay free in parents' room. AE, DC, DISC, MC, V. **Parking:** $7.75.

Here's a good place to stay with the kids. There's no fancy formality here, and kids will love the open-air pool up on the roof with its cozy cabana deck and snack bar for poolside lounging. The rooms are nicely furnished, with picture windows, color TVs featuring in-room first-run movies, oversize beds, and good-size closets. Metro Restaurant and Bar, an informal American deli, provides three meals a day.

THE PARK INN INTERNATIONAL, 440 W. 57th St., between Ninth and Tenth avenues, New York, NY 10019. Tel. 212/581-8100. Fax 212/581-8719. 590 rms and suites. A/C TV TEL

$ Rates: $79–$139 single; $99–$154 double; $225–$275 suite. Discounts of 20% for senior citizens. AE, CB, DC, DISC, ER, MC, V. **Parking:** $7.

Ⓢ One of New York's best hotel pools opens to the sun on the roof of the Park Inn International, and that's just one plus for this pleasant hotel. Well located within minutes of Carnegie Hall, Lincoln Center, the Jacob Javits Convention Center, Fifth Avenue shops, and Rockefeller Center, the hotel is on a lively residential street, so guests can feel safe about going out at night—perhaps to the Hard Rock Café, just a few blocks away. Security is excellent; the card locks are changed every time a guest leaves. There's a multilingual staff at the front desk. The rooms and suites, quite large by New York standards, are done in soft pastel and earth tones, and each has a desk. Most rooms have two double beds, a few have kings; King Leisure or Deluxe rooms all have sofas, and a few of these even have balconies. Facilities are available for the disabled. The hotel is currently undergoing an extensive renovation.

The Greenery Restaurant offers reasonably priced dinner specials; the rooftop cafe, opposite the pool, also offers moderately priced specials daily (summer only). The Apples Lounge has daily drink specials and a large-screen TV.

HOTEL SALISBURY, 123 W. 57th St., New York, NY 10010. Tel. 212/246-1300, or toll free 800/223-0680 in the U.S., 800/228-0822 in Canada. Fax 212/977-7752. 320 rms, 86 suites. A/C TV TEL

$ Rates (including continental breakfast): $134–$144 single; $144–$154 double; $154–$174 one-bedroom suite single; $164–$184 one-bedroom suite double; $225 two-bedroom suite. Extra person $15. AE, CB, DC, JCB, MC, V. **Parking:** $15 nearby.

Just about the closest hotel to Carnegie Hall is the Salisbury, across the street from the venerable concert hall; since 1931, it's been attracting not only musicians but businesspeople, politicians, internationals, and sophisticated travelers who appreciate its old-fashioned courtesy and competitive rates (a one-bedroom suite here compares to the cost of a bedroom in other midtown hotels).

Because it was once essentially a residential hotel, its rooms are quite large, with generous closet space, traditional American furnishings, and personal safes. Almost all rooms have serving pantries with sink and small refrigerator; those on the top four floors also have coffeemakers and microwave ovens; these cost $5 more per day. The newly remodeled Executive Floor features attractive rooms with in-room fax machines, desk speaker phones, and dataport connections for computers; these cost $15 more per day. The one-bedroom suite—a living room with queen-size sofabed and a bedroom with two double beds—is an excellent choice for a family. Two-bedroom suites, with living and dining rooms, are spacious enough to sleep six and hold a small business meeting. A free newspaper is delivered each day, and guests have access to the hotel's fax services. For a small fee, they also have privileges at La Racquette, a handsome health club with swimming pool at the Parker Meridien Hotel. The newly remodeled lobby and the Breakfast Room on the third floor are both attractive; room service is available via the nearby New York Deli.

TRAVEL INN HOTEL, 515 W. 42nd St., New York, NY 10036. Tel. 212/695-7171, or toll free 800/869-4630. Fax 212/967-5025. 160 rms. A/C TV TEL

$ Rates: From $80 single; $90 double; each additional person $10. Children 16 and under sleep free. AE, DC, MC, V. **Parking:** Free.

You'd hardly know you were in the heart of New York once you step inside the Travel Inn—it's very much the typical American motor hotel, with an Olympic-size outdoor pool and recreation areas, lots of family groups, and free self-parking that allows you to use your car as often as you like with no extra charge. (At most New York hotels there are in-and-out charges.) Just 3½ short blocks from the Jacob Javits Convention Center, Travel Inn is situated in the Off-Off-Broadway theater area of New York, several blocks (or a short bus ride) west of Times Square. All the rooms have been done in first-class fashion, with custom draperies, imported furnishings, and new baths. Many face a courtyard overlooking the pool and sunning area, which are surrounded by a lovely garden and outdoor furniture. The River West Café/Deli is on the premises. The hotel will assist with any sightseeing or ticket requests.

THE WYNDHAM, 42 W. 58th St., between Fifth and Sixth avenues, New York, NY 10019. Tel. 212/753-3500 or toll free 800/257-1111. Fax 212/754-5638. 144 rms, 70 suites. A/C TV TEL

$ Rates: $115–$125 single; $130–$140 double; $175–$205 one-bedroom suite; $290–$340 two-bedroom suite. Inquire about summer rates of $110 double, $150 suites, which are sometimes available. Monthly rentals available. AE, DC, MC, V. **Parking:** $28 nearby.

⭐ The rooms are usually booked far in advance at the Wyndham, because word-of-mouth and an appreciative press have made this homey hotel into a favorite address for visiting film, theater, and literary people. Sir Laurence Olivier used to stay here when he was appearing on Broadway. Eva Marie Saint, Sir Alec Guinness, Peter O'Toole, Philip Roth, Eva Gabor, and Peter Ustinov are among the celebrated names on the guest list. Famous people flock here, despite its relatively low prices and limited services, because of resident owners John and Suzanne Mados and their staff, who provide guests with old-fashioned hospitality, warmth, and friendship; staying here is akin to being a guest in a private club where everybody knows your name. And the Madoses have created a world of charm, from the plush lobby that looks like the living room of a European country inn, to the rooms and suites, each with a distinctive personality. All rooms are European in feeling, with a tasteful mixture of antiques and one-of-a-kind pieces, good paintings, good-size baths, and graceful touches throughout. But the suites are the real glory of this hotel, and it's well worth a splurge for these graceful dwellings, each with a pantry (refrigerator, sink, and cabinet). Sir Laurence's favorite was Suite 1401, handsome with its chandeliers, huge bed, gilt-edged mirrors, and Persian carpets.

The Wyndham has its own restaurant, Jonathan's, which serves three reasonably priced meals a day. The Plaza Hotel is just across the street. Security is excellent: The front door is always locked, and guests are buzzed in. The two elevators are manned. With Mr. and Mrs. Mados usually on duty, this tasteful "Mom-and-Pop" hotel offers one of the best values in New York in its price range.

INEXPENSIVE

PORTLAND SQUARE HOTEL, 132 W. 47th St., New York, NY 10036. Tel. 212/382-0600, or toll free 800/388-8988. Fax 212/382-0684. 104 rms (most with bath). A/C TV TEL

$ **Rates:** $40 single with shared bath; $60 single with private bath; $75 double with one bed and private bath, $85 double with two beds and private bath; $90 double for three persons with private bath; $95 double for four persons with private bath. AE, MC, V. **Parking:** $20 nearby.

$ The Portland Square was formerly called the Rio. Both the hotel, built in 1904, and the block had declined from the early 1900s, when the area attracted famous theatrical names. But the block and the hotel are a Cinderella story, for they are both now highly desirable. The area, well-lit and with new buildings, is a short stroll from the Broadway theaters, the Diamond District, and Radio City. The hotel has been completely renovated, and its rooms, although tiny, are tidy and among the best budget buys in New York. The lobby is simple, the photos adorning the walls showing how New York looked earlier in this century. This motif is carried into the halls, which pictorially re-create old New York. Certainly the prices re-create it, especially the four small single rooms with sink (bathroom down the hall) on each floor for an incredible rate of $40. The rooms are tastefully furnished and spanking clean; all have color remote-control cable TVs, direct-dial phones, individually controlled air conditioning, and comforters on the beds. Thanks to a new filtration system, all drinking and bathing water is chlorine-free.

The building is owned by the Puchall family, who operate a similar "Cinderella" hotel, the Herald Square Hotel on West 31st Street (see above). They make every effort to service their guests in the old-fashioned way. They provide lockers where guests may store luggage after they've checked out, and a comfortable sitting area, a rarity in budget hotels. The Portland Square describes itself as a "classic limited-service budget hotel." There's no room service.

6. MIDTOWN EAST/ UPPER EAST SIDE

New York's East Side is traditionally known for being a bit more peaceful, a bit less frenzied than the West Side. Some—especially women—feel it's safer at night. The location couldn't be better. You're near Grand Central Terminal, the United Nations, and the Fifth Avenue department stores. Plus, the posh specialty shops of Madison Avenue and trendy boutiques of Lexington and Third avenues are nearby.

VERY EXPENSIVE

THE DRAKE SWISSOTEL, 440 Park Ave., at 56th Street, New York, NY 10022. Tel. 212/421-0900, or toll free 800/DRAKE-NY. Fax 212/688-8053. Telex 14178. 487 rms, 65 suites. A/C TV TEL

$ Rates: $215–$265 single; $240–$290 double; $375–$1200 one- and two-bedroom suites. Extra person $20. Children under 14 stay free in their parents' room. Inquire about entertaining and innovative weekend packages, like "Dining Out With The Drake" and "Shopping With The Drake." AE, CB, DC, DISC, ER, JCB, MC, V. **Valet parking:** $24.

This premier North American unit of Swissotel, the prestigious Swiss chain, is the result of a $52-million 1981 renovation of one of New York's landmark hotels. Currently, it is undergoing a $35-million capital-improvement program, adding "high technology to high touch" and making it more than ever a magnet for the international business traveler as well as the vacationer.

Because the Drake was once a residential hotel, its rooms are bigger—and nicer—than many elsewhere. Subtle ivory-toned rooms boasting soft coral, celadon green, and ivory prints; fruitwood furniture, desks, full-length mirrors, and plants all give the feeling of guest bedrooms in a country home. Special extras include foolproof locks, peepholes, individual safes, three telephones with call waiting, jacks for computers and fax machines in some rooms (eventually all phones will have two-way facsimile modem capability units), options for video check-in and checkout, ice buckets, and digital AM/FM clock radios in addition to color TV (complimentary HBO plus pay movies) concealed in the cabinetry. Each room also has small refrigerators, irons and ironing boards, coffeemakers, and beautiful marble baths with hairdryers and scales. No-smoking and wheelchair-accessible rooms are available. Several Park Avenue suites feature spacious terraces overlooking Manhattan (one even has a wood-burning fireplace). Rooms with Murphy beds are available.

Dining/Entertainment: The Drake Bar and Lounge, which overlooks Park Avenue like a sidewalk cafe, serves all three meals, featuring Swiss, European, and American specialties.

Services: Complimentary limousine service to Wall Street weekday mornings, multilingual concierge staff, 24-hour room service.

Facilities: Business Center. Guests may use (for $21 per day) the nearby Atrium Club, with its swimming pool. At the hotel is a state-of-the-art fitness center.

FOUR SEASONS HOTEL NEW YORK, 57 E. 57th St., New York, NY 10022. Tel. 212/758-5700, or toll free 800/332-3442 in the U.S., 800/268-6282 in Canada. Fax 212/758-5711. 309 rms, 58 suites. A/C MINIBAR TV TEL

$ Rates: $390–$490 single; $430–$530 double; $695–$4,000 suite; $50 extra room with terrace. AE, CB, DC, ER, JCB, MC, V.
Parking: Valet, $30.

Hailed as an architectural masterpiece of the late 20th century, the Four Seasons is the tallest hotel in New York, rising 52 stories and 682 feet into the sky. The I. M. Pei–designed skyscraper, whose walls are clad in Magny limestone from France (the same used in Pei's expansion of the Louvre), boasts an indoor Lobby Court with marble floors and a 33-foot-high backlit onyx ceiling; it is one of New York's grandest indoor spaces. All this, coupled with some of the largest guest rooms in New York and the top-notch hospitality skills of the international Four Seasons chain, made it an instant success when it opened in June 1993.

Guest rooms are spacious (averaging 600 square feet) and handsome, done in an understated contemporary decor of warm colors and custom-designed furniture and English-sycamore cabinetry. Each features an entrance foyer; a dressing room; and a wall-to-wall marble bath with color TV, glass-enclosed shower, and oversize steeping tub that fills in 45 seconds! Each room has a large partners-style desk; some have splendid terraces; all have windows that open, fully stocked refrigerators, fresh flowers, personal safes, terry robes, bathroom scales, umbrellas, two dual-line telephones with speaker capability and modem, and a complete color-cable TV system with movie and closed-circuit channels. Wheelchair-accessible rooms are available.

Dining/Entertainment: The extraordinary talents of chef Harry Gabel, formerly of The Four Seasons Maui, are evident at Fifty Seven Fifty Seven, a contemporary American grill that serves all three meals. Adjacent to it is The Bar, a popular spot for lunch, cocktails, and evening snacks. The graceful Lobby Lounge is the setting for breakfast, light lunch, and a lovely tea from 3 to 5pm daily.

Services: 24-hour concierge and room service, nightly turndown, complimentary shoeshine, one-hour pressing, use of VCRs and videos; fax machines in all suites and in rooms on request.

Facilities: Spa and Fitness Center offers exercise and cardiovascular equipment, saunas, whirlpools, steam rooms, and services like facials and massages. Business Center is fully equipped.

+ Thrift Shops.

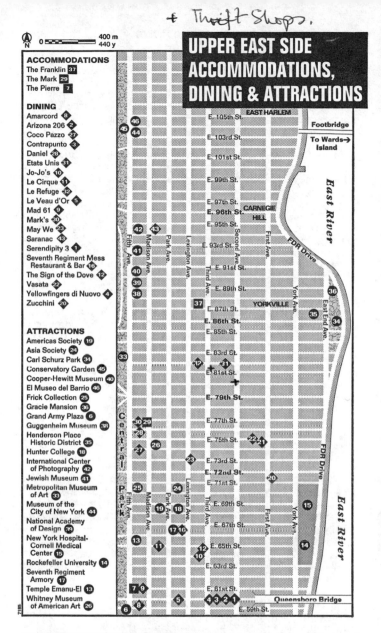

UPPER EAST SIDE ACCOMMODATIONS, DINING & ATTRACTIONS

0 — 400 m / 440 y

ACCOMMODATIONS
The Franklin **37**
The Mark **29**
The Pierre **7**

DINING
Amarcord **8**
Arizona 206 **2**
Coco Pazzo **27**
Contrapunto **3**
Daniel **28**
Etats Unis **31**
Jo-Jo's **10**
Le Cirque **11**
Le Refuge **32**
Le Veau d'Or **5**
Mad 61 **9**
Mark's **30**
May We **23**
Saranac **43**
Serendipity 3 **1**
Seventh Regiment Mess Restaurant & Bar **16**
The Sign of the Dove **12**
Vasata **22**
Yellowfingers di Nuovo **4**
Zucchini **20**

ATTRACTIONS
Americas Society **19**
Asia Society **24**
Carl Schurz Park **34**
Conservatory Garden **45**
Cooper-Hewitt Museum **40**
El Museo del Barrio **46**
Frick Collection **25**
Gracie Mansion **36**
Grand Army Plaza **6**
Guggenheim Museum **38**
Henderson Place Historic District **35**
Hunter College **18**
International Center of Photography **42**
Jewish Museum **41**
Metropolitan Museum of Art **33**
Museum of the City of New York **44**
National Academy of Design **39**
New York Hospital-Cornell Medical Center **15**
Rockefeller University **14**
Seventh Regiment Armory **17**
Temple Emanu-El **13**
Whitney Museum of American Art **26**

EAST HARLEM
Footbridge
To Wards→ Island
East River
CARNEGIE HILL
FDR DRIVE
YORKVILLE
Central Park
East River
Queensboro Bridge

E. 105th St.
E. 103rd St.
E. 101st St.
E. 99th St.
E. 97th St.
E. 96th St.
E. 95th St.
E. 93rd St.
E. 91st St.
E. 89th St.
E. 87th St.
E. 86th St.
E. 85th St.
E. 83rd St.
E. 81st St.
E. 79th St.
E. 77th St.
E. 75th St.
E. 73rd St.
E. 72nd St.
E. 71st St.
E. 69th St.
E. 67th St.
E. 65th St.
E. 63rd St.
E. 61st St.
E. 59th St.

Fifth Ave.
Madison Ave.
Park Ave.
Lexington Ave.
Third Ave.
Second Ave.
First Ave.
York Ave.
East End Ave.

GRAND HYATT NEW YORK, Park Avenue at Grand Central Terminal, New York, NY 10017. Tel. 212/883-1234, or toll free 800/233-1234. Fax 212/692-3772. Telex 645601. 1,407 rms, 42 suites. A/C TV TEL

$ Rates: $205–$235 single; $235–$265 double. Weekend package (including parking) $145–$179 single or double. Hyatt Business Plan $15 surcharge. Regency Club $25 surcharge. AE, CB, DC, DISC, JCB, MC, V. **Parking:** $34.

⭐ The striking hotel that heralded the renaissance of East 42nd Street, Grand Hyatt is perhaps the most dramatically modern of New York hotels, a 34-story building that has been hailed as a triumph of modern architectural design. From the silver-mirrored facade that reflects such neighborhood landmarks as the Chrysler Building and Grand Central Terminal to the four-story plant-filled atrium with its cascading waterfall and 100-foot bronze abstract sculpture, the effect is one of dazzle and glitter.

In contrast, the guest rooms are quiet and subdued, done in soft pastels and decorated with handsome prints. All have color TVs with in-room movies, clock radios, plush carpeting, skirt hangers in the closets, and luxurious baths with amenity baskets of toiletries. Deluxe king rooms have separate seating areas, desks, and chairs. Even more luxurious are the 110 rooms in the Hyatt Regency Club, which occupies the entire 31st and 32nd floors and offers a special concierge and a hospitality lounge. Hyatt Business Plan rooms include fax machines, hairdryers, and irons with ironing boards. Guests on the Business Plan also enjoy free access to local and 800 telephone calls, morning coffee, newspaper delivery, complimentary continental breakfast in the Crystal Fountain, and 24-hour access to a photocopier and laser printer.

Dining/Entertainment: Dining rooms and lounges continue the glamour theme of the lobby, especially the Sun Garden Lounge, a sidewalk cafe and cocktail spot cantilevered spectacularly right over busy 42nd Street. The Crystal Fountain, the hotel's full-service restaurant, is handsome, with a reflecting pool and a mirrored ceiling that reflects the busy goings-on of the street. Sunday brunch is a lavish treat here. The decor at Trumpets, an elegant haven of regional American cuisine, is more traditional and subdued.

Services: Concierge, Hyatt Passport Service for preregistration and express checkout, 24-hour room service, complimentary week-day morning paper, same-day valet/laundry, Japanese welcome service, multilingual staff.

Facilities: Business Center; guest privileges at nearby health clubs.

THE MARK, 25 E. 77th St., between Fifth and Madison avenues, New York, NY 10021. Tel. 212/744-4300, or toll free 800/THE MARK; in Canada, 800/223-1588. Fax 212/744-2749. 120 rms, 60 suites. A/C TV TEL

$ **Rates:** $285–$340 single or double; $610–$2,400 suite. Extra person $20. Children 15 and under stay free in parents' room. Special summer rates available. AE, DC, JCB, MC, V. **Parking:** $30 nearby.

⭐ One of the prettiest and most deliciously elegant of the city's circle of small luxury hotels, The Mark is a worthy rival of that grande dame of the genre just across the street, the Carlyle. Elegant maybe, but it's definitely not stuffy. (Madonna stayed here.) Art and antiques dealers favor it, as do museum buffs (the Metropolitan, Whitney, and Frick are within a few blocks) and serious Madison Avenue shoppers. The original hotel was built in 1929 (the copper tower and black-vitro-glass marquee, spectacularly floodlit at night, are very art deco), later became the Madison Avenue Hotel, and in 1989 it was acquired by the Rafael Group, which spent $35 million transforming the property down to the most minute detail. Now its rooms and suites pamper with king-size beds and custom-designed Queen Anne furniture, with museum-quality Piranesi architectural drawings decorating the walls. Rooms also feature remote-control Sony Trinitron TVs (with in-room movies) in custom-designed cabinets, clock radios, and two or four double-line direct-dial phones with fax capability. There's even an umbrella in every room, compliments of the management. Most guest rooms come with pantries, stoves, and small refrigerators. The large and luxurious baths have telephones, deep-soak tubs, separate stall showers, heating lamps, hairdryers, scales, and crystal boxes that contain the finest toiletries.

Dining/Entertainment: Mark's restaurant serves French/American cuisine in an exquisite setting for breakfast, lunch, afternoon tea, and dinner. Mark's Bar, with a separate entrance on 77th Street, offers pre- and post-theater hors d'oeuvres and cocktails from 5pm to midnight.

Services: 24-hour room service, concierge, laundry/valet, limousine, business services.

Facilities: Meeting and banquet rooms.

THE NEW YORK HELMSLEY, 212 E. 42nd St., New York, NY 10017. Tel. 212/490-8900, or toll free 800/221-4982. Fax 212/986-4792. 800 rms, 10 suites. A/C TV TEL

$ Rates: Sun–Thurs, $190 single; $215 double; $400 suite. Fri–Sat, $144 single or double. AE, DC, MC, V. **Parking:** $33.

This 41-story brick-and-bronzed–glass tower is a model of grace in both its luxurious appointments and its efficiency, the kind that top-level business executives demand. Each beautifully appointed guest room has a 25-inch color TV with cable and remote control, a digital clock radio with an alarm, and such amenities as oversize down pillows and skirt hangers in the closet. The baths are luxurious, with both phones and scales, full-length mirrors, bath sheets, and the usual package of toiletries found in luxury hotels. All the suites are situated on corners on the top five floors.

Dining/Entertainment: Breakfast, lunch, and dinner are served at Mindy's, the hotel's full-service restaurant, which offers fine French cuisine in a glorious multilevel setting with many trees and plantings and an entire glass wall overlooking an open-air landscaped plaza. Harry's New York Bar is a popular gathering spot for lunch and cocktails—plus free hors d'oeuvres.

Services: Concierge, fast check-in and checkout service, currency exchange, multilingual business services.

Facilities: Nearby health club.

NEW YORK PALACE, 455 Madison Ave., at 50th Street, New York, NY 10022. Tel. 212/888-7000, or toll free 800/NY-PALACE. Fax 212/644-5750. 863 rms, 100 suites. A/C MINIBAR TV TEL

$ Rates: $195–$320 single; $220–$320 double; $400–$3,000 Tower suite. Weekend packages from $195 per night available. AE, CB, DC, JCB, MC, V. **Parking:** $46.

Perhaps the grandest of the city's newer hotels is the New York Palace. Above the landmark 1884 Villard Houses, Neo-Renaissance Italian palazzi built in American brownstone for railroad tycoon and journalist Henry Villard, rises a 51-story bronzed-glass tower. While the painstakingly and magnificently restored public rooms have won nothing but praise from critics, the new tower has been dubbed, in contrast, a "mediocrity." But no matter. The rooms inside are lovely, and the public rooms are perhaps the finest in New York. Guests enter through the Villard cobblestone courtyard and proceed up the grand marble staircase to view the red Verona marble fireplace of Augustus Saint-Gaudens. And they are surrounded by the works of such noted artists as Louis Comfort Tiffany, John La Farge, and George Breck. A renovation is now under way by the new owners, the Business Advisory Group of Singapore.

Amid all this splendor are all the conveniences of modern hotel living. Some of the oversize guest rooms have king-size beds with gilded headboards, and others have two doubles. Interior colors are soft pastels, with velvet chairs and carpeting. Rooms have remote-control color TVs and in-house movies, digital clock radios, dual telephone lines with fax and PC hookups, VCRs on request, and minirefrigerators, a welcome extra. Electric blankets are available, and the baths are sumptuous. The suites include one-bedroom apartments and fairy-tale triplexes with roof gardens and solariums.

Dining/Entertainment: Le Trianon is the elegant fine dining room; Harry's New York Bar and the Hunt Bar are popular watering holes; the lovely Gold Room is the setting for high tea in the afternoon.

Services: Multilingual staff, 24-hour concierge and room service.

Facilities: Business Center and conference facilities; guest passes to New York Health & Racquet Club, portable telephones and fax machines.

THE PIERRE, Fifth Avenue at 61st Street, New York, NY 10021-8402. Tel. 212/838-8000, or toll free 800/332-3442. Fax 212/940-8109. 146 rms, 57 suites. A/C TV TEL
$ Rates: $280–$460 single; $310–$490 double; from $630 suite. Extra person $25. Children 18 and under stay free in parents' room. Holiday, summer, and weekend packages available. AE, CB, DC, ER, EU, JCB, MC, V. **Parking:** $30.

A reminder of the city's more gracious and dignified past, The Pierre dates from 1930. Since 1981, it has been managed by Four Seasons Hotels and Resorts, which has recently completed a spectacular $30-million renovation, restoring the hotel to its famous European grandeur. You can still rub elbows with the haut monde and occasional member of royalty (after all, the Pierre *is* a world-class hotel). For all its elegance and grandeur, its lovely European lobby and Italianate rotunda, the Pierre is warm and hospitable.

There are 28 types of accommodations interspersed with privately owned apartments on 42 floors. Rooms and suites vary in size, configuration, and views, and decor runs the gamut from English country cottage to splendid baronial mansion. A typical single room, very charming, might have walls papered in palest blue and trimmed in white, blue-gray carpet, and a romantic floral-chintz bedskirt (with drapes to match) under a white heirloom coverlet. Suites have fully furnished living rooms (many with fireplaces) boasting lovely mahogany antique furniture and reproductions, mirrors, and paintings. In-room amenities include digital clock radios, direct-dial two-line phones, remote-control color cable TVs with in-room movies, and individual safes. Baths, while not lavish (they retain the streamlined simplicity of their art deco origins) provide many nice touches.

Dining/Entertainment: Like a room in a French château, with its ceiling and wall murals, ornate mirrors, and gray-and-gold color scheme, the intimate (and very swanky) 54-seat Café Pierre is open for breakfast, lunch, dinner, pre-theater dinner (prix-fixe $34) and after-theater supper, and Sunday brunch. The Café Lounge offers nightly piano music to sip champagne by, and the Rotunda is a stunner for afternoon tea ($19.50), light meals, and snacks.

Services: 24-hour room service, twice-daily cleaning service, multilingual concierge, laundry/valet service, one-hour pressing, theater desk, complimentary shoeshine, unpacking service (on request), currency exchange, notary public, secretarial services.

Facilities: Sundries shop, barber, hair salon.

THE PLAZA, 768 Fifth Ave., between 58th and 59th streets, New York, NY 10019. Tel. 212/759-3000, or toll free 800/759-3000. Fax 212/759-3167. Telex 236938. 805 rms, 96 suites. A/C MINIBAR TV TEL

$ Rates: $235–$475 single or double; $500–$15,000 suite. Weekend packages sometimes available. AE, DC, DISC, JCB, MC, V. **Valet parking:** $35.

Synonymous with New York elegance, the Plaza has been attracting the cognoscenti since early in the century. Built in 1907, it has officially been designated as a "landmark of New York." Frank Lloyd Wright called it his home-away-from-home; Eloise grew up there; Donald Trump took it over; Ivana Trump supervised its redecoration (pre–Marla Maples); and it is a favorite choice of visiting royalty. Looking incongruously like a European château on the New York skyline, the French Renaissance structure is full of splendid touches, inside and out. All rooms have been totally restored to their original luxurious ambience. Some have 14-foot ceilings, crystal chandeliers, ornamental plaster moldings, and thick mahogany doors, while some parlors also have carved marble fireplaces. Modern conveniences include in-room safes, electronic keys, two telephones—each with two-line service and data jack, remote control TV with complimentary HBO and pay-per-view movies; custom Frette bed and bath linens. Many of the rooms afford spectacular views of Central Park and Fifth Avenue.

Dining/Entertainment: The Plaza's dining rooms include the romantic, gardenlike Palm Court, especially popular for Sunday brunch and afternoon tea; the classic Edwardian and Oak Rooms (the Oak Bar is the place to celebrity-watch and be seen); and the casual Oyster Bar, a cross between an English pub and a fish house.

Services: Concierge services (concierges are members of the prestigious Les Clefs d'Or), business services including secretarial services, morning delivery of the *New York Times,* laundry/valet, 24-hour room service, shoeshine, money exchange, theater ticket booth.

Facilities: State-of-the-art exercise room, plus use of Atrium Health Club (with pool) and Cardio-Fitness Center, both nearby.

THE ST. REGIS, 2 East 55th St., at Fifth Avenue, New York, NY 10022. Tel. 212/753-4500, or toll free 800/759-7550. Fax 212/787-3447. 227 rms, 90 suites. A/C MINIBAR TV TEL

$ Rates: $350 superior; $395 deluxe; $450 grande luxe; from $550–$3,500 suite. Weekend rates available. Children 17 and under free in parents' room. AE, CB, DC, ER, EU, JCB, MC, V, and more. **Parking:** $30.

⭐ The doyen of New York hotels has reopened after a three-year $100-million restoration that has returned it to the opulence of its original and glorious past, its decor scrupulously restored down to the last detail. In 1904, when John Jacob Astor opened the St. Regis, it was the city's tallest hotel building—18 stories. The hotel was finished in marble (even in the walls of the boiler room) and furnished with Louis XV antiques, rare Flemish tapestries, crystal chandeliers, Oriental rugs, and a library fully stocked with gold-tooled books bound in leather. Such architectural details as the Astor Court with its vaulted ceiling, trompe-l'oeil cloud murals, and faux marble, ornate brass cashier's windows, and yard upon exquisite yard of real 22-karat gold leafing have been either preserved or restored.

The St. Regis is probably New York's most expensive hotel, the rationale being that stand-out luxuries usually costing extra are included in the tariff here, like tea brought to your room on arrival, maître d'étage (butler) service (each floor has its own pantry and butler), fresh flowers daily, complimentary local phone calls, and a different-each-day amenity in your room. All rooms also offer international direct-dial phones that can be programmed in six languages. Suites come with fax machines. The guest rooms and suites (60 sizes) wear an elegant, essentially Louis XV decor, with crystal chandeliers, silk wall-coverings with matching draperies, contrasting printed bedspreads and upholstery, and accents of gleaming gilt. Colors are muted greens or blues with eggshell (suites are done in silver-blue and ruby). European deep soaking tubs, two sinks, and separate shower areas distinguish the all-marble baths.

Dining/Entertainment: Afternoon tea is an art at the splendid Astor Court. The old King Cole mural has been restored and returned to the King Cole Bar and Lounge, where Fernand Petit invented the Bloody Mary some 60 years ago. At Lespinasse, the hotel's highly praised formal restaurant, Swiss chef Gray Kunz adapts classical cuisine with flavors and textures from the Far East. The St. Regis Roof is New York's only rooftop ballroom.

Services: 24-hour room service, laundry/valet, nightly turn-down, butler, concierge, secretarial and confidential office service, multilingual staff.

Facilities: Business center; barber shop; health club; florist; information library on local commerce; Bijan, Christian Dior, La Boutique, and Godiva boutiques.

UN PLAZA PARK HYATT HOTEL, One United Nations Plaza, on East 44th Street just west of First Avenue, New York, NY 10017-3575. Tel. 212/758-1234, or toll free 800/233-1234. Fax 212/702-5051. 428 rms, 45 suites. A/C TV TEL

$ Rates: $240–$260 single; $260–$280 double; $175 weekend (including American breakfast and parking); $350–$660 suite; $200–$450 weekend suite. AE, CB, MC, JCB, V. **Parking:** $24.

⭐ This masterpiece of understated elegance perfectly befits the ambassadors, diplomats, and heads of state who choose it for the kind of serenity and security that few other New York hotels possess. Just across the street from the United Nations (although its rates are too steep for most U.N. personnel), the hotel was designed by Kevin Roche of Kevin Roche–John Dinkeloo and Associates, and his fine hand is seen everywhere. The guest rooms begin on the 28th floor (offices occupy the first 27 floors), so there's scarcely a whisper of traffic noise, and all have beautiful views, subtly modern decor, radios, and every amenity. Many have kitchens. Rooms and halls are decorated with tapestries and textiles from around the world.

Dining/Entertainment: The stunning Ambassador Grill and Lounge has a ceiling of mirrored glass that refracts light in a series of prisms within prisms, making the 14-foot ceiling seem cathedral-high. Breakfast, lunch, and dinner are served, as well as an immensely popular Sunday Champagne Brunch, featuring lobster, smoked salmon, and omelets made to order ($38 for adults and $19 for children under 12; reservations are necessary). The Ambassador Lounge serves a weekday sandwich buffet and offers piano entertainment nightly.

Services: Multilingual staff, business services, shoes polished overnight, 24-hour room service, complimentary weekday limousine service to Wall Street and the Garment District, complimentary transportation to theater district, the *New York Times* delivered to your door every day.

Facilities: Glorious glass-enclosed pool in the sky, health club, tennis for a fee at 39th-floor regulation-size indoor court.

THE WALDORF-ASTORIA, 301 Park Ave., at 50th Street, New York, NY 10022. Tel. 212/355-3000, or toll free 800/HILTONS. Fax 212/421-8103. Telex WUI 666747-RCA275797. 1,140 rms, 200 suites. A/C MINIBAR TV TEL

$ Rates: $245–$305 single; $270–$330 double or twin; $350 minisuite; $400–$850 suite. Waldorf Towers: $350–$375 single; $375–$400 double; $500–$4,000 suite. (Rates subject to change without notice.) AE, CB, DC, DISC, MC, V. **Parking:** $34.

Could there be anyone who has not heard of the Waldorf-Astoria? As much a part of the New York scene as the Empire State Building (the site of the original Waldorf-Astoria), it's legendary among New York's luxury hotels. Its lushly carpeted and beautifully furnished lobby, with meandering arcades and quiet little corners, is one of the few classic hotel lobbies left in the city. Waldorf guests have always included the world famous: You might run into Frank Sinatra or any head of state.

Not content to rest on its laurels, however, the Waldorf, under the Hilton banner, has refurnished and redecorated all of its rooms and equipped them, of course, with the necessities: color TVs (with first-run cinema service), direct-dial telephones, and old-world amenities. A bottle of champagne and an American breakfast in bed are offered at no extra charge with the "Romance Package."

Dining/Entertainment: Oscar's, the famous coffee shop at the Waldorf, is decorated as an indoor garden. The Bull & Bear has a giant Maltese-cross bar of African mahogany with a footrail and serves both British and American food. Sir Harry's Bar has an African safari setting; Inagiku serves Japan's finest food. And, of course, there's still Peacock Alley, which has always been one of the nicest *intime* spots in town for elegant dining. Featuring Cole Porter's own piano, it is the scene, every Sunday, of mind-boggling brunches that are among the most lavish in town ($38.50 for adults, $19.25 for children under 12).

Services: International concierge service, 24-hour room service, theater desk, tour desk, beauty salon, barber shop, nightly turndown.

Facilities: Plus One Fitness Center, with state-of-the-art equipment, six personal trainers, and two massage therapists; comprehensive business center.

EXPENSIVE

HOTEL BEVERLY, 125 E. 50th St., at Lexington Avenue, New York, NY 10022. Tel. 212/753-2700, or toll free 800/223-0945 outside New York State, including Canada. Fax 212/753-2700, ext. 48. Telex 66579. 175 suites, 25 rms. A/C TV TEL

$ Rates: $129–$149 single; $149–$159 double. Junior suite; $139–$159 single; $149–$169 double. One-bedroom suite; $170–$190 single; $180–$200 double. Weekend packages available. AE, CB, DC, JCB, MC, V. **Parking:** $25 nearby.

The European-style Beverly is a longtime favorite on the East Side. There's a quiet, calm feeling about this family-owned hotel, refreshingly unusual in the hubbub of the city. Also unusual is the fact that this is largely a suite hotel. For the cost of a bedroom in other hotels, you can have all the comforts of a private apartment—living room; bedroom; bath; and full kitchenette, complete with refrigerator, cooking unit, dinnerware, and utensils, as well as coffeemakers with complimentary tea and coffee. And even the regular rooms, without kitchenettes, all have refrigerators. The rooms are individually decorated in fine taste, and although the decor varies from traditional to contemporary, all are spacious and lovely. Some of the junior suites have sofas and desk areas. The hotel is especially proud of its security walk-in closets (you have the only key). Many corporations keep permanent rooms here for their executives; it seems they find the location and ambience congenial. So, too, do international tourists, U.N. people, and visiting families (all groups of three or more must take suites).

The Beverly's lobby has warm fruitwood-paneled walls, an Oriental-pattern carpet, and traditional furnishings that create the feeling of an 18th-century English living room. A concierge is at the ready; there is room service; and Kenny's Steak & Seafood and a 24-hour pharmacy are off the lobby.

DORAL COURT, 130 E. 39th St., New York, NY 10016. Tel. 212/685-1100, or toll free 800/22-DORAL. Fax 212/889-0287. Telex 679-9532. 189 rms, 50 suites. A/C TV TEL

$ Rates: $179–$199 single; $199–$219 double; $255 suite single/double. Weekends: $115–$135 single/double. AE, DC, MC, V. **Parking:** $34.50 nearby.

The Doral Court is a quiet, personal hotel featuring attentive service. The rooms are spacious and sunny, with walk-in closets, king-size beds, writing desks, comfortable chairs, foyers, and separate dressing alcoves that also house refrigerators. Kitchenettes are available upon request, as is an exercise bicycle. For more serious fitness buffs, use of the exemplary Doral Fitness Center, a block away, is complimentary. The suites are cozy enough to settle down in for a good stay; all have walk-in kitchens, and some have balconies. The Courtyard Café serves breakfast, lunch, dinner, and Sunday brunch; there's an intimate bar area and delightful indoor-outdoor seating.

DORAL INN, 541 Lexington Ave., at 49th Street, New York, NY 10022. Tel. 212/755-1200, or toll free 800/22-

DORAL. Fax 212/319-8344. Telex 236641. 652 rms, 55 suites. A/C
TV TEL

$ Rates: $135 single; $145 double; $170–$450 suite. Executive
Club Level: $150 single; $160 double. Weekends: $115 single/
double. AE, DC, ER, JCB, MC. **Parking:** $23.

The location for this East Side favorite couldn't be more convenient,
since it's smack in the midtown shopping area, across the street, in
fact, from the Waldorf-Astoria. It's a busy, with-it hotel, the first in
New York to have indoor squash courts available at a nominal fee.
When you're not chasing the ball around the court, you can enjoy the
feeling of quiet comfort in the well-appointed rooms, decorated in
smart beige motifs. Small refrigerators are available on request. Two-
and three-room suites are perfect for family living; some of the newer
suites contain their own saunas, and the penthouse floor has
executive rooms and suites, subdivided by terraces. The new Executive Club Level on the 6th and 8th floors provides many special
amenities, including express check-in and checkout, complimentary
continental breakfast, complimentary personal computers, fax machines, newspapers, and more. A laundry room and ice machines are
available. Downstairs, the Equinox Café, serving American cuisine, is
open 24 hours; and the lovely Mormandos Restaurant offers Italian
cuisine until 1am. Christos Steak House is for hearty eaters.

The same Doral management is also in charge at two other
gracious small hotels in the Murray Hill area: **Doral Park Avenue
Hotel,** 70 Park Ave., at 38th Street, New York, NY 10016 (tel.
212/949-5924, or toll free 800/22-DORAL), and **Doral Tuscany
Hotel,** 120 E. 39th St., New York, NY 10016 (tel. 212/686-1600, or
toll free 800/22-DORAL). All three are comparable in charm and
comfort and charge similar tariffs.

**THE KIMBERLY, a Suite Hotel, 145 East 50th St., be-
tween Lexington and Third avenues, New York, NY
10022. Tel. 212/755-0400,** or toll free 800/683-0400. Fax
212/486-6915. 34 rms. 158 suites. A/C TV TEL

$ Rates: $170 single or double; $205 studio suite; $265 one-
bedroom suite; $370 two-bedroom suite. Extra person $20.
Children under 12 stay free in parents' room. Weekend rates:
$135 single or double; $159 one-bedroom suite; $295 two-
bedroom suite. Weekly and monthly rates available. Summer
Specials, $100 less on all suites. AE, DC, MC, V. **Parking:** $25
nearby.

Here's a charming way to have a pied-à-terre in New York:
Stay at the Kimberly. Although this is mostly a suite hotel, even
the regular guest rooms give you that feeling of being able to
settle in for a long, comfortable stay. All accommodations are
handsomely decorated in rich classical furnishings of brocade, velvet,
and warm woods. The beds are mostly double/doubles, with some
kings; the stunning baths are done in marble and have deep soaking
tubs. The regular guest rooms have minirefrigerators; the suites have
fully equipped kitchens, complete with utensils, silverware, and
china. Each suite also has two televisions and a rare luxury for New
York—a private balcony affording stunning views. The Spectrodyne
movie system is available in all rooms. Everything about the hotel,
beginning with its small lobby, done in rich Italian marble with fine
Oriental carpetings, is calm, quiet, and elegant. No wonder it's a big
hit with people from the United Nations and with visiting Europeans

and South Americans. When the special summer rates are in force (see above), a suite here is often less than a bedroom alone in many other New York hotels.

Dining/Entertainment: Adjoining the hotel is the exquisite Paradis Barcelona, a restaurant in the classical Spanish tradition, which provides extraordinary room service. At night, it features a popular tapas bar. Tatou is a fabulous supper-club restaurant with cabaret, blues music, and nightclub dancing, as well as astonishingly good contemporary American cuisine at both lunch and dinner.

Services: Concierge, free newspapers, 24-hour room service, same-day valet, secretarial and business services on request.

Facilities: Complimentary privileges at nearby New York Health & Racquet Club (excellent swimming pool) and five other NYHRCs; from May through October, free 2½-hour cruise aboard the HRC Yacht (docked at Pier 13, near South Street Seaport).

LOEW'S NEW YORK, 569 Lexington Ave., at 51st Street, New York, NY 10022. Tel. 212/752-7000, or toll free 800/23-LOEWS. Fax 212/758-6311. 688 rms, 38 suites. A/C TV TEL

$ Rates: $185 single, $205 double. Concierge Floor: $205 single; $225 double. $225–$245 junior suite; $250 one-bedroom suite; $350 two-bedroom suite. Extra person $20. Children under 16 stay free in parents' room. AE, CB, DC, DISC, JCB, MC, V. **Parking:** $28.

Casual, comfortable, and exciting—these describe this three-star hotel, a popular gathering place for sports teams and sports fans alike. The Denver Broncos, the Washington Capitals, the Harlem Globetrotters, and many other teams stay here. The nine big-screen TVs in the handsome circular bar are often tuned in to a game. A $26-million renovation has transformed the hotel, giving it a new art deco lobby and beautifully equipped rooms of good size. Each room has its own refrigerator, desk area, personal safe, custom furnishings, remote-control TV with in-house movies, and two phones in every room (three in the handsome suites).

Dining/Entertainment: The Lexington Avenue Grill has become one of the city's "hot" new restaurants for breakfast, lunch, and dinner. Adjoining it is the lively Lexington Avenue Lounge.

Services: Concierge Floor for Extra Special Patrons has its own lounge serving continental breakfast, hors d'oeuvres and wine in the evening. Children can get games from the concierge and special menus and games in the restaurant. Room service is from 6:30am to midnight.

Facilities: Fitness center with personal trainers, sauna, Jacuzzi; full-service business center; theater/transportation desk.

ROGER SMITH, 501 Lexington Ave., at 47th Street, New York, NY 10017. Tel. 212/755-1400, or toll free 800/445-0277. Fax 212/319-9130. 110 rms, 26 suites. A/C TV TEL

$ Rates (including continental breakfast): $160–$190 single; $180–$210 double; $225–$300 one-bedroom suite; $130 single or double, weekend and holidays. Extra person $20. AE, CB, DC, MC, V. **Valet Parking:** $23 nearby.

Art is in the air at the Roger Smith—abstract bronze panels, life-size busts and bronze sculptures greet you in the lobby; vibrant murals adorn the hotel's restaurant, Lily's; there's an art gallery in the corner of the lobby, and oil paintings decorate the public rooms and corridors. James Knowles, the proprietor and sculptor, sees his hotel as a "work-in-progress," a place of warmth and wit, where creators of art and lovers of art can come together. A multimillion-dollar top-to-bottom renovation has made this comfortable, 17-story old-timer snuggled amid the skyscrapers better than ever; values here are among the best on the East Side. If what you cherish in a hotel is a feeling of space, comfort, and quiet relaxation, you're going to love this hotel with an "art bias."

Guest rooms are very large by New York standards (this was once a residential hotel) and are elegantly designed in a classic continental style. Design schemes make use of deep-fruitwood furniture; dusty rose chairs and sofas; thick carpeting; and, in many rooms, two-poster or four-poster (sometimes canopied) queen-size, king-size, twin, or double/double beds. Many rooms have large walk-in closets. The spacious rooms are furnished with desks, original artworks, antiques, and quality 18th-century reproductions. All have automatic coffeemakers, mini-refrigerators, renovated baths, and color TVs with radio, cable, and VCR; there's a library of 2,000 videos. On request, an exercise bike or rowing machine will be brought to the room. The two- and three-room suites, some boasting fireplaces and terraces, all have a butler's pantry. Many guests from Europe and Asia, as well as diplomats and U.N. personnel, frequent the Roger Smith.

Dining/Entertainment: Lily's, the hotel's attractive restaurant, is the scene of generous continental breakfast buffets (free to guests) every day. During the week, Chef Dietmar Schluter serves up Swiss-German lunches. Chef Bob Giordano creates New American Art Cuisine dinners, noted for a $39 tasting menu with wine.

Services: Weekday-morning newspapers, concierge, business services, passes to nearby Excelsior Health Club with swimming pool.

THE TUDOR, 304 E. 42nd St., New York, NY 10017. Tel. 212/986-8800, or toll free 800/TRY-TUDOR. Fax 212/986-1758. 300 rms, 14 suites. A/C MINIBAR TV TEL

$ Rates: $195–$245 single; $215–$265 double; $295–$595 suite. Weekend packages: $125 room for two; $139 with buffet or full American breakfast; $159 with Sunday Jazz Brunch. AE, CB, DC, DISC, JCB, MC, V. **Parking:** $15 weekends, $18 weekdays; valet parking available.

Choicely located amid the private residences and park of the Tudor City historic district and overlooking the United Nations and the East River (near Grand Central Terminal, Fifth Avenue shopping, and the theater district), the once-dowdy Tudor has undergone a multimillion-dollar renovation and emerged as one of the most charming small hotels in New York. The Sarova Hotel Group of London and Kenya has spared no expense in creating an enclave where quiet luxury, highly personalized service, meticulous attention to detail, and state-of-the-art conveniences hold forth. Guest rooms are furnished classically, each with individual climate control, cable and in-room movies, a high-tech lighting system, a personal safe, a trouser press, and a hairdryer in the opulent marble bath. Many executive rooms and suites have Jacuzzi tubs and private terraces. Business travelers have the convenience of dual-speaker telephones with voice mail and outlets for personal computers and fax machines. Some rooms have their own fax machines. Wheelchair-accessible and no-smoking rooms are available.

Dining/Entertainment: Cecil's Restaurant, an English-style carvery, offers imaginative cuisine for lunch and dinner, monthly wine-tasting dinners, as well as a very popular Sunday Jazz Brunch. High tea and cocktails are served in the Regency Lounge.

Services: Concierge, multilingual staff, 24-hour room service.

Facilities: Business Center, including professional secretarial service; Fitness Center, with exercise equipment, saunas, private massage rooms.

MODERATE

THE FRANKLIN, 164 E. 87th St., between Lexington and Third avenues, New York, NY 10128. Tel. 212/369-1000. Fax 212/369-8000. 46 rms. A/C TV TEL

$ Rates (including continental breakfast): $85–$95 single or double. AE, MC, V. **Parking:** Free nearby.

The Franklin is a small hotel that makes a large design statement. A complete renovation of an older hotel has turned this into a little charmer, from the pots of geraniums outside and the bouquet of fresh tearoses that sits at the front desk, to the breakfast room (where tea and coffee are hot all day), to the cozy library where daily newspapers are available, to the petite but ingeniously designed guest rooms. Each has a striking illuminated canopy bed; custom-designed cherrywood furnishings; a cedar closet; and a luxurious bath with a stainless-steel sink, deep reglazed cast-iron tub, hand-held European shower fixtures, hairdryer, and Neutrogena bath amenities. There's always a fresh rose on the desk. A call to the front desk brings American and foreign tapes to be played on the VCR. There is a high level of personal service.

The Franklin is well located, within walking distance of the Metropolitan, Jewish, Frick, Whitney, and other museums (museum associates often stay here) as well as Sotheby's, Christie's, and Doyle's auction galleries. Restaurants abound throughout the neighborhood. A few blocks west is Central Park; a few blocks east are Carl Schurz riverside park and Gracie Mansion, the residence of New York's mayor.

HELMSLEY MIDDLETOWNE HOTEL, 148 E. 48th St., New York, NY 10017. Tel. 212/755-3000, or toll free 800/843-2157. Fax 212/832-0261. 147 rms, 47 suites. A/C TV TEL

$ Rates: $135–$145 single; $145–$155 double; $175 executive; $195 junior suite; $225–$380 larger suite. AE, CB, DC, JCB, MC, V. **Parking:** $23.

The Helmsley Middletowne is one of the real finds in the New York hotel scene. Since it was converted from an apartment building, its rooms still have apartment amenities; they're spacious, each with two large closets and minirefrigerators; best of all, the larger suites boast fully equipped walk-in kitchens, wonderfully handy for those who must entertain as well as for visitors who wish to save on the high cost of always eating out. The rooms are prettily furnished with bright colors and have two-line direct-dial phones with fax and computer hookups, TVs with in-room movies, as well as bathroom phones. Twelfth-floor rooms have tiny terraces. The services include a multilingual staff, fax service at the front desk, and laundry and valet service.

THE DE HIRSCH RESIDENCE AT THE 92ND STREET YM-YWHA, 1395 Lexington Ave., at 92nd St., New York, NY 10128. Tel. 212/415-5650, or toll free 800/858-4692 in the U.S. and Canada. Fax 212/415-5578. 295 rms (with shared bath).

$ Rates: With a minimum stay of three nights, $40 per night, $280 per week single room; $30 per person per night in a shared room, $210 per person per week in a shared room. $3-a-day surcharge for air conditioning. For stays of two months or longer: $595 single room, $420–$500 per month per person in a shared room. Group rates available for stays of at least three days. AE, MC, V. **Parking:** Nearby garages, around $20.

Here's one of New York's best-kept secrets for the budget traveler. Although most of the guests at the prestigious De Hirsch Residence are long-term residents (students or young working adults), there are always openings, year-round, for short-term visitors, with no age restrictions. Rooms are clean and comfortable, attractively furnished with a single bed or beds, dressers, bookshelves, and lamps. Baths are communal; public phones are in the hall. Each floor has its own large self-service kitchen and a laundry room; bed linens are provided, and there is weekly cleaning service. But that's just for starters. Guests often get discount or even free tickets to the Y's outstanding cultural events— classical music concerts, lectures, readings by noted authors and poets—and can partake of special resident activities, such as weekly coffee houses, video nights, and more, which take place in the Residents' Lounge, with large-screen TV. They also have use of a splendid health-club facility with aerobic classes, Nautilus and free weights, racquetball courts, steamroom and sauna, and a 75-foot swimming pool.

The Y is located in one of New York's finest residential neighborhoods—the Upper East Side—and is convenient to public transportation. Prospective guests must phone or write for an application in advance.

VANDERBILT YMCA, 224 E. 47th St., New York, NY 10017. Tel. 212/756-9600. Fax 212/755-7579. 415 rms (none with bath). A/C TV

$ Rates: $42–$55 single; $52–$65 double; $62–$72 triple; $82–$92 quad. MC, V. **Parking:** Around $20 nearby.

The fully coed Vanderbilt Y boasts an excellent East Side location not far from the United Nations and a popular health club free to guests: You might find yourself sharing the two pools, sauna, and gym with U.N. personnel and business people who work in the area. The atmosphere is like that of a streamlined European youth hostel—relaxed, young, and friendly—but visitors of any age can stay. The newly renovated guest rooms, small but very clean, are located off attractive carpeted hallways. All accommodations have single or bunk beds, dressers, and desks. Some have sinks in the room, but shared bath accommodations are down the hall, as are phones. The desk staff will take messages.

The new International Café offers reasonably priced, generous, tasty meals and freshly baked goodies. Guests are given automatic Y membership for the length of their stay and can use all facilities free of charge. Reservations can be made here for YMCAs in major cities around the world through the "Y's Way" International.

7. LINCOLN CENTER/ UPPER WEST SIDE

EXPENSIVE

THE MAYFLOWER HOTEL ON THE PARK, 15 Central Park West, New York, NY 10023. Tel. 212/265-0060, or toll free 800/223-4164 (U.S. & Canada), 0-800-891-256 (U.K.). Fax 212/265-5098. Telex 4972657 MAYFLOW. 177 rms, 200 suites. A/C TV TEL

$ Rates: $145 single; $160 double; $195 suite. Parkview: $165 single; $180 double; $250 suite; $300–$500 penthouse terrace suite. "Weekend at the Park" (including continental breakfast and valet parking): $135–$145 single, $145–$155 double, $165–$175 triple, $155–$165 single in suite, $165–$175 double in suite, $175–$185 triple in suite; "No Frills Weekend": $98 single/double, $140 single/double in suite. Weekend rates are per night—Friday, Saturday, or Sunday. AE, DC, DISC, JCB, MC, V. **Parking:** $15 nearby, $18 valet parking.

⭐ Music makers and music lovers alike sing the praises of this venerable hotel, the only one on Central Park West, about a five-minute walk from Lincoln Center and Carnegie Hall. Built in 1925 as a residential hotel, it has spacious rooms, thick walls, a sense of peace and quiet, and the kind of dedicated service that can come only from a loyal staff who have been here for many years and know the large number of returning guests by name. Celebrity guests abound: At a recent visit, the Bolshoi Opera Company had just left and the Royal Ballet had just arrived. Liza Minnelli and Cher have been guests, and so has Robert De Niro, who lived at the hotel for a year and a half.

Since the Mayflower has so many suites, it's quite possible that your room may be upgraded. All of the rooms are nicely decorated—large enough for king-size, queen-size, or two double beds—and have individually controlled air conditioning, radio alarms, and voice-mail messaging. There are two to three enormous walk-in closets in many rooms, plus a refrigerator (with coffeemakers on request). Suites are gracious, some have terraces overlooking the city skyline. If you're planning a small wedding reception or other function, request one of the 17th-floor suites, where you have a choice of terraces overlooking Central Park or the Hudson River.

Dining/Entertainment: The Conservatory Café, facing Central Park, is a sunny spot for breakfast, lunch, and dinner, with excellent food. It's a favorite after–Lincoln Center gathering place.

Services: Room service, business services, valet service, voice mail.

Facilities: Fitness center.

RADISSON EMPIRE HOTEL, 44 W. 63rd St., New York, NY 10023. Tel. 212/265-7400, or toll free 800/333-3333. Fax 212/315-0349. 375 rms, 25 suites. A/C MINIBAR TV TEL

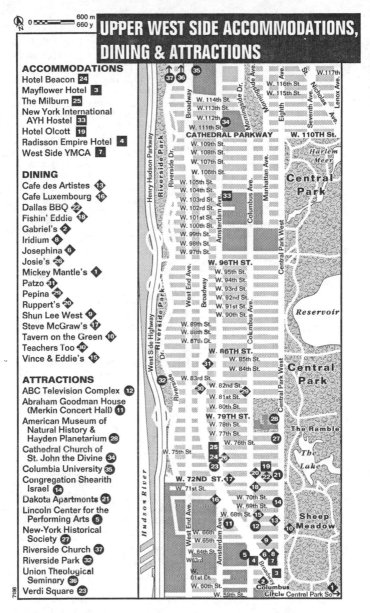

UPPER WEST SIDE ACCOMMODATIONS, DINING & ATTRACTIONS

0 — 600 m / 660 y

ACCOMMODATIONS
Hotel Beacon **24**
Mayflower Hotel **3**
The Milburn **25**
New York International AYH Hostel **33**
Hotel Olcott **19**
Radisson Empire Hotel **4**
West Side YMCA **7**

DINING
Cafe des Artistes **13**
Cafe Luxembourg **16**
Dallas BBQ **22**
Fishin' Eddie **18**
Gabriel's **2**
Iridium **8**
Josephina **6**
Josie's **26**
Mickey Mantle's **1**
Patzo **31**
Pepina **29**
Ruppert's **20**
Shun Lee West **9**
Steve McGraw's **17**
Tavern on the Green **10**
Teachers Too **30**
Vince & Eddie's **15**

ATTRACTIONS
ABC Television Complex **12**
Abraham Goodman House (Merkin Concert Hall) **11**
American Museum of Natural History & Hayden Planetarium **28**
Cathedral Church of St. John the Divine **34**
Columbia University **35**
Congregation Shearith Israel
Dakota Apartments **21**
Lincoln Center for the Performing Arts **5**
New-York Historical Society **27**
Riverside Church **37**
Riverside Park **32**
Union Theological Seminary **36**
Verdi Square **23**

$ Rates: $135–$200 single or double; from $250 suite. Extra person $20. Children 13 and under stay free in parents' room. Weekend packages available. AE, CB, DC, DISC, JCB, MC, V. **Parking:** $20.50.

You can't get much closer to all the excitement of Lincoln Center than the Radisson Empire Hotel. The Empire is, in fact, the "official" Lincoln Center hotel, and it has emerged after a $35-million renovation as one of the better hotel values in the city for comfort, service, quality, and rates. Music and dance groups (the Bolshoi Ballet has stayed here), international types, and visitors who enjoy being away from the midtown madness all favor this place.

The small lobby, with its dioramas in the hallway and magnificent fresh flowers, has a gracious quality about it; so, too, do the guest rooms, which look as though they belong in a lovely country home. Traditional furnishings, two-poster beds, floral-chintz bedspreads and drapes, and down comforters set a homey scene, yet every high-tech convenience is at hand, including Nakamini CD and cassette stereo systems, NEC VCRs and color TVs (you can rent your favorite CDs and videos from the front desk), two-line telephones with dataports for computer link-up, voice-mail messaging, and bathroom phones. The baths are especially lovely, with deep soaking tubs. The rooms, although not large, are adequate in size; most have queen-size beds, and some of the smaller rooms have twins or a double bed.

Dining/Entertainment: The Empire Lounge is the place for evening cocktails, billiards, and entertainment. There is a restaurant on the premises.

Services: 24-hour room service, laundry/valet, concierge.

Facilities: Adjacent health club, complimentary for hotel guests.

MODERATE

HOTEL BEACON, 2130 Broadway at 75th Street, New York, NY 10023. Tel. 212/787-1100, or toll free 800/572-4969. 80 rms, 40 suites. A/C TV TEL

$ Rates: From $89 single, $99 double; $120 suite for up to four. $15 each additional person. Inquire about specials on weekdays and for longer stays. AE, MC, DISC, V. **Parking:** $15 nearby.

One of the best choices on the Upper West Side (just one subway stop from Times Square and the heart of the Theater District on the 2 or 3 train), this gracious residential hotel offers excellent value for the visitor. It's easy to cook in or take out food from nearby gourmet emporiums like Zabar's, since each of the large, comfortably appointed rooms and one-bedroom suites (with separate living room) contains kitchen facilities and a dining area. Kitchenettes and bathrooms have been completely renovated; the bathrooms now boast hairdryers. Dishes and cutlery are provided on request. Rooms are attractive and have individual climate control. Families can spread out here—and the hotel is near the American Museum of Natural History. The attractive neighborhood, home to many artists and performers, is alive 24 hours a day.

ESPLANADE HOTEL AND SUITES, 305 West End Ave., at 74th Street, New York, NY 10023. Tel. 212/874-5000. Fax 212/496-0367. 20 studios, 100 suites. A/C TV TEL

$ Rates: $85–$99 single or double; $120–$140 one-bedroom suite, $200–$220 two-bedroom suite. Additional person $10 (up to four in one-bedroom, up to six in two-bedrooms). Children under 12 free with parents. **Parking:** At nearby garage, $10.

An excellent value in this Lincoln Center/Upper West Side area, the Esplanade is known for an especially helpful and friendly staff and for the size and comfort of its rooms. Artists performing at nearby Lincoln Center, students at the nearby dance companies, people who are having their apartments redone, as well as many guests from Europe enjoy staying at this spacious hotel on a lovely, tree-lined residential street, just a block from Broadway and major bus and subway lines.

Last year saw a complete renovation of the lobby and all the guest accommodations. Suites and rooms are all nicely furnished in traditional motifs, and many have walk-in closets. All feature refrigerators, burners, and microwave ovens, which make fixing light meals with food from the nearby gourmet emporiums easy. Best deals here are the suites: Each has a large living room with queen-size sofa bed, one or two bedrooms with double beds, and kitchenettes. There's a restaurant on the premises.

HOTEL OLCOTT, 27 W. 72nd St., New York, NY 10023. **Tel. 212/877-4200.** Fax 212/580-0511. 45 studios, 55 suites. A/C TV TEL

$ Rates: $85 daily, $500 weekly studio for one person; $95 daily, $535 weekly studio for two persons; $115 daily, $680 weekly one-bedroom suite for one or two persons. Extra person $15 daily, $70 weekly. No credit cards. **Parking:** $15 nearby.

This undiscovered hotel right off Central Park West is a true find. Most out-of-towners don't know about this place because it's largely a residential hotel—most guests are longtime residents or entertainers, diplomats, U.N. people, and the like in New York for a few months. But there are studios and suites available to transients, and as anyone who's discovered the Olcott will tell you, they are among the top buys in the city for the money. These are full one-bedroom apartments, comfortable enough to live in for a long time, and their size ranges from large to enormous. Each has a living room; a twin-bedded bedroom; a private tile bath and shower; and that great money-saver, a kitchenette, complete with dishes and cooking utensils. Additional rollaway beds can be added, for a small charge, to comfortably accommodate up to four. Single and double bedrooms are also available. All rooms have pantries, cable color TVs, and direct-dial phones. Furnishings are attractive and comfortable, and service is excellent. There's a fantastic budget restaurant off the lobby, Dallas BBQ (see Chapter Six for a review). In addition to all this, 72nd Street abounds with coffee shops, restaurants, and gift boutiques, and it's in the very heart of the bustling Columbus Avenue scene. A short bus or subway ride will take you to midtown and the theater district; a short walk, to Lincoln Center.

The management states that weekly rentals, reserved in advance, are given preference; however, with luck, you may get a room or suite for a night or two on short notice.

THE MILBURN, 242 W. 76th St., New York, NY 10023. **Tel. 212/362-1006,** or toll free 800/833-9622. Fax 212/721-5476. 52 studios, 38 suites. A/C TV

$ Rates: $85–$100 studios single or double; $112–$160 suite. Children under 12 stay free in parents' room. Extra person $10. AE, CB, DC, MC, V. **Parking:** $14 nearby.

While midtown hotel prices soar out of sight, rates at Upper West Side hotels stay realistic. More and more visitors are thrilled to discover places like the Milburn, actually a fine West Side apartment building that recently spent about $4 million converting some 90 of its 120 apartments into attractive hotel accommodations. Both studios and suites are available, and all of them have fully equipped kitchenettes with microwave ovens and in-room coffee service. The rooms are large, fully carpeted, and cheerfully decorated with modern furniture and attractive posters. There's a choice of twin-, queen-, and king-size beds; and all units sport new baths with hairdryers. Each suite consists of a living room (the sofa opens up into a queen-size bed) plus a bedroom.

Many extras make a stay at the Milburn especially pleasant. Room phones have speed-dialing to nearby takeout/delivery restaurants; press a button and you can order Chinese food, pizza, or meals around the clock from a nearby deli. Milburn Dining offers discounts at many neighborhood restaurants. For $10 per day, guests have privileges at the nearby Equinox Club. VCRs are available, and tapes can be rented nearby.

INEXPENSIVE

HOSTELLING INTERNATIONAL NEW YORK, 891 Amsterdam Ave., at 103rd Street, New York, NY 10025. Tel. 212/932-2300. Fax 212/932-2574. 480 beds. A/C

$ Rates: $20 ($22 June 1–Sept 30) AYH members, $3 additional non-members. Non-members may purchase a welcome stamp for $3 a night, which can be applied to the purchase of an AYH membership (around $25). Stays usually limited to seven days. JCB, MC, V. **Parking:** Free on street; commercial parking nearby.

Surely, the best news for budget travelers in many a New York moon was the 1990 opening of this youth hostel. In a city where one is lucky to find a room for $100 a night, its rates do not top $25. This facility is the first American Youth Hostel in New York, the largest in the nation, and the most ambitious hostel project in the world. It is housed in a century-old neoclassical landmark structure, transformed with a $15-million renovation from a sad state of disrepair into a gracious building with almost an acre of gardens in back for sunning and sitting. The building is just a block from a subway station, in a multiethnic neighborhood that will most certainly improve as a result of the presence of the hostel.

As in all AYH hostels, there are common rooms, self-service kitchens, a cafeteria, and a friendly atmosphere designed to foster cross-cultural exchange between visiting foreigners and Americans. HI–NY is different from most other hostels in several ways: It has no curfew and no closing time and operates on a full 24-hour schedule.

INTERNATIONAL HOUSE OF NEW YORK, 500 Riverside Drive, at 122nd Street, New York, NY 10027. Tel. 212/316-8436. Fax 212/316-1827. 700 rms (shared baths). TEL

$ Rates: $25–$35 per night for stays of 1–14 days; $18 per night for stays of 15–30 days (academic, trainee, or intern affiliation required for stays of over 30 days). MC, V. **Parking:** Free on street.

During the academic year, International House is home to graduate students and interns from over 80 countries. When they go home for the summer, from mid-May through August, however, rooms become available for the budget traveler. Here's a chance to enjoy a stimulating cultural, social, and recreational atmosphere, as guests are welcome to take part in trips around the city, films, ballroom dancing, aerobic classes, team sports, and more—at no extra charge; they have use of the gym, cafeteria, pub with dancing, and TV lounges. It's a great place to meet other travelers. The single rooms are simple but neat and clean; most have sinks; bath and shower facilities are shared; linens are provided. There is cross-ventilation but no air conditioning or fans.

Note: Among the best deals are a small number of guest rooms ($58 single, $68 double) and guest suites ($75 single, $84 to $105 double), each with a private bath, air conditioning, a color TV, maid service.

International House is located on Riverside Park near Columbia University, Teachers College, and the Jewish and Union Theological Seminaries. It's about a 20-minute subway ride from midtown Manhattan.

No chores are required. And although most of the sleeping rooms, with bunk beds, will be for four, six, and eight people, there are some rooms for couples, even a few with queen-size beds. Family rooms are sometimes available at around $60. Hostelers should bring a sheet sleeping sack with them, or they can rent bedsheets for $3 and towels for $2. There are no private bathrooms, but there is a laundry room, long-term storage space, bicycle storage rooms, and telephones on each floor. The hostel is fully accessible to the disabled. And, of course, it is open to people of all ages and nationalities.

The hostel operates a number of daily programs, including walking tours, bike rides, video nights, pub crawls, and other social events. The building also contains conference rooms for nonprofit groups, a full-service travel agency, a travel shop, and an Information Desk run by local volunteers. The hostel is also the home of the New York Student Center, operated by CIEE (Council on International Educational Exchange).

WEST SIDE YMCA, 5 W. 63rd St., New York, NY 10023. Tel. 212/787-4400, or toll free 800/348-YMCA. Fax 212/580-0441. 500 rms (shared baths), 50 rms (private baths). A/C TV.

$ Rates: $42 single without bath, $65 single with bath; $55 double without bath, $75 double with bath. MC, V. **Parking:** $10–$20 at garage next door; street parking free.

Close to Lincoln Center, this attractive building (a National Historic Landmark) right off Central Park West is steps away from the trendy restaurants and shops of the Upper West Side and close to major bus and subway lines. A multimillion-dollar renovation has modernized and upgraded all the public areas and guest rooms, which are now bright and attractive, with new furniture, lighting, air conditioners, and TVs. Students and tourists can feel comfortable in this congenial environment. Guest rooms are offered to men and women 18 years or older, with special rates for group bookings of ten or more rooms. Maid service and 24-hour uniformed security are pluses. So is an attractive cafeteria/dining room with fireplace, which serves all three meals. There's even room service at this upscale Y and an off-Broadway theater right on the premises.

All overnight guests of the West Side YMCA are entitled to complimentary use of fitness centers, gyms, two heated pools, cushioned indoor running track, Cybex and Eagle weight systems, plus handball, racquetball, squash courts, a steamroom, a sauna, and much more. A good inexpensive choice if you want to get in shape while visiting New York!

NEW YORK DINING

New York City is the restaurant capital of the country, but unless you have time on your hands and money to burn, you will have to be very selective. To help you make your way through the perplexing maze of the New York restaurant world, I have followed some very simple guidelines. I have chosen those restaurants that, in my opinion, offer the best buys in dining in New York, regardless of how much you spend. (Some other New Yorker might come up with a very different selection; but no matter—getting two New Yorkers to agree on their favorite restaurants is like getting Yankees fans and Mets fans to agree on their favorite players. That's part of the fun.) And because the price range in New York restaurants is enormous, I have grouped these selections first by neighborhood and then by price category. Dining in New York City can be expensive. New Yorkers expect to pay at least $25 to $30 for a good dinner, and that's before cocktails, wine, tax, and tip; if they get by with less, they consider themselves lucky. Thankfully, restaurants have recently lowered prices a bit. Still, there seems to be no limit to how much restaurants will charge or people will spend; at a very posh restaurant a $125 meal is not uncommon, especially with a good bottle of wine. My price categories for dinner, then, allowing for inevitable overlapping, since prices for à la carte items vary considerably within the same establishment, are **expensive,** $50 and up for one, without wine; **moderate,** $25 to $50; **inexpensive,** less than $25.

LUNCH A good way to stretch your food budget is to eat your main meal at lunch, when the values are always best—usually 15% to 20% less costly than dinner. Even some of the most expensive restaurants offer reasonable prix-fixe lunches.

BEVERAGES Cocktails cost about $6 or more per drink. Be careful when you order wine: A prize vintage in a luxury restaurant could skyrocket your bill by $50 to $100 or more. If you are not familiar with the subtleties of wine, put yourself in the hands of the waiter or wine steward and ask him or her to suggest the proper wine in your price range to accompany dinner. For four people, order a full bottle; for two or three, a half bottle will do nicely. To save on the tab, order the "vin de maison," or house wine, which is good and less expensive than bottled wines; it can be bought by the glass or in a carafe.

TIPPING Leave your slide rule at home and relax. At most places, the rule is to give the waiter about 15% of your check (just double New York's 8¼% tax added to all meal tabs). At a very posh establishment, consider 18% to 20%. If a captain is involved, he should receive 5% more.

HOURS The dinner hour stretches rather late in New York, and many restaurants also serve after-theater suppers. Many are closed on Sunday, and, during summer, some take rather long vacations. So it's always best to check before you go.

CALL AHEAD New York restaurants have a very high rate of mortality, all due to the craziness that makes one place "hot" and "trendy" for a few months, then causes it to fall out of favor while the restless crowds move on to another venue. As a result, closings are not infrequent. Always call in advance.

1. FINANCIAL DISTRICT/ TRIBECA

FINANCIAL DISTRICT

Windows on the World (on the 107th floor of One World Trade Center), once the crowning glory of the New York restaurant scene, was forced to close as a result of the early 1993 terrorist bombing of the World Trade Center. At press time, plans were not definite for the shape of the dining complex when it reopens, hopefully this year. Most likely it will include a large international restaurant, a cocktail lounge and light-food area, a private luncheon club, and perhaps a boutique Japanese restaurant. For the latest information, telephone 938-1111.

EXPENSIVE

HUDSON RIVER CLUB, 4 World Financial Center, 250 Vesey St., at the West Side Highway. Tel. 786-1500.
   Cuisine: HUDSON VALLEY REGIONAL. **Reservations:** Recommended, especially for lunch.
$ Prices: Appetizers $9–$16; main courses $22–$34. Hudson Valley Dinner $60; Sun brunch $23. AE, CB, DC, MC, V.
   Open: Lunch Mon–Fri 11:30am–2:30pm; dinner Mon–Sat 5–9:30pm; brunch Sun 11:30am–3pm. **Subway:** E to World Trade Center. Follow signs to World Financial Center.
The premier dining room of the World Financial Center (just southwest of the World Trade Center) is a very clubby place, an "in" spot for the Wall Street crowd. Weekdays at lunchtime, the bankers, brokers, and assorted CEOs from capitalism-central pack the long, sleek dining room. It's a handsome setting, with light-oak paneling, brass accents, and glass-walled wine caves; and it's triple-tiered so that all 40 tables face south and every diner has a waterfront view. At dinnertime the place is much quieter, so that's a good time to come and gaze at the Statue of Liberty and the excellent menu, which focuses on the food and wine of the Hudson River Valley. (Appropri-

ately, art from the Hudson River School lines the walls.) Chef Waldy Malouf buys from boutique farms and vineyards whose standards are the highest, and he varies his menus to reflect the finest available produce.

You might begin with sautéed Hudson Valley foie gras, salad of seared tuna and crisp squid, or heady pumpkin-apple soup with spiced croutons. Follow this with a main course of salmon in woven potatoes or venison-and-apple "chili" or grilled paillards of sword-fish, chicken, venison, or veal. Desserts are wonderful, especially the "tear of the clouds" (a poached pear with apricot sorbet and sabayon). The wine list focuses on American vintages at fair prices. At lunch, you can dine a bit more lightly, with perhaps a lobster, potato, and onion omelet or a salad of grilled quail and warm goat cheese.

MODERATE

BRIDGE CAFE, 279 Water St., at the corner of Dover Street. Tel. 227-3344.
Cuisine: CONTEMPORARY AMERICAN. **Reservations:** Recommended, especially for lunch.
$ Prices: Appetizers $4.95–$7.95; main courses $11.95–$18.50; Sun brunch $12.95; Sun prix-fixe dinner $19.95. AE, DC, MC, V.
Open: Lunch Mon–Fri 11:45am–5pm; dinner Tues–Sat 5pm–midnight; Sun–Mon 5–10pm; brunch Sun 11:45am–5pm. **Subway:** 2 or 3 to Fulton St., 4 or 5 to Fulton St. or Brooklyn Bridge.

Perfect for a meal after you've toured the South Street Seaport or other downtown attractions is Bridge Café, under the Brooklyn Bridge and just north of the Seaport. It's on the first floor of an old clapboard house, now painted a deep red, but a coat of paint is about the only visible sign of remodeling that's been done in many a year, and this is all part of the charm. A long, dark bar; red-checkered tablecloths; clay pots filled with flowering plants sitting in the windows; and wainscoting on the walls—all add to the decor of this waterfront bistro/restaurant.

The congenial group that works here makes you feel at home, and the prices make you relax. The menu changes every two weeks. Typical appetizers include chilled fennel-and-cucumber soup and herb-breaded calamari with spicy tomato mayonnaise. Popular main dishes include grilled marinated chicken with Riesling and roasted garlic; spinach linguine putanesca; and pan-seared mahimahi and citrus-marinated sliced beef with endive and watercress. Brunch features imaginative dishes and desserts, such as blueberry cobbler and fresh fruit cheesecake. The Bar Menu, served after 2pm, features half a chilled lobster for $3.25. Come on a Tuesday night for "Wine Discovery Tuesdays" and receive 30% off any bottle of wine from a selection of 65 American wines.

SLOPPY LOUIE'S, 92 South St., in the Fulton Fish Market, Tel. 509-9694.
Cuisine: SEAFOOD. **Reservations:** Recommended for groups of 10 or more.
$ Prices: Appetizers $2.15–$6.25; main courses $11.95–$22.95. AE, DC, MC, V.
Open: Mon–Sat 11am–9pm, Sun noon–7pm. **Subway:** 2, 3, 4, or 5 to Fulton St. Walk east toward the river.

Another good choice if you're touring the financial district or visiting the South Street Seaport, Sloppy Louie's is practically a New York institution, like the Brooklyn Bridge or Staten Island Ferry. Its prices are cheap and its seafood is wonderful, but perhaps best of all, it is still as unadorned and unpretentious as it was more than 60 years ago when Louie took over (there has been a restaurant in this building since 1811). The restoration done in this block by the South Street Seaport has made Louie's a little more comfortable but hasn't changed the style very much: Everyone still has a grand time, sitting at long wooden tables, feasting on succulent plates of hot fish, and brushing shoulders with the Wall Street executives, fish market truck drivers, and others who throng the place. The main attraction is, of course, the fish. Everything is à la carte, but the main courses come with potatoes and vegetables, so they are almost a meal in themselves. Ask the waiter what's in season before you order. The shad roe, when they have it, is delicate and lovely, and also good are the Florida red snapper and the shrimp Creole. I'm especially partial to Louie's famous bouillabaisse, a huge, steaming concoction ($18.45). The big, hearty bowls of fish soup, like Maine lobster soup and Long Island clam chowder, are also a treat. The freshest of lobsters are served at very fair prices. Liquor is available, along with beer and wine.

TRIBECA

MODERATE

BOULEY, 165 Duane St., between Hudson and Greenwich streets. Tel. 608-3852.
Cuisine: FRENCH/AMERICAN. **Reservations:** Required, well in advance.
$ **Prices:** Appetizers $7–$22; main courses $23–$27; prix-fixe tasting menu $75 and up.
Open: Lunch Mon–Fri noon–3pm; dinner Mon–Sat 5:30–11:30pm. **Subway:** 1, 2, or 9 to Chambers St. Walk two blocks north to Hudson St.

Some fans and food critics call Bouley the best restaurant in America; I certainly rank it one of New York City's finest. Chef/owner David Bouley trained with such superstars as Paul Bocuse and Roger Vergé before opening the chic Montrachet (see below) in 1985, and he struck out on his own again two years later. He redefines French cooking here, harmonizing organically grown ingredients from hand-picked produce into exquisite combinations that are virtually free of cream or butter. Although the menu changes constantly, recent offerings included such appetizers as Alaskan spot prawn ravioli with fresh Florida shrimp, steamed mussels in an ocean herbal broth, and roasted Maine Pemaquid oysters with crunchy vegetable chips. Among the main courses were Maine black bass with wild mushrooms in papillottes, ratte potatoes with lemon thyme juice, and organic baby lamb with a fricassée of root vegetables and a purée of fingerling potato. The desserts—creations like hot raspberry soufflé and tart of glazed shredded apples—are quite marvelous. You'll enjoy it all on Limoges china in a flower-filled room that transports you to a gentler, more romantic place and time. To savor the full spectrum of Bouley's wizardry, we recommend the dinner tasting menu at $75 and up, or the five-course prix-fixe lunch at $32 (appetizers and main courses are slightly lower at lunch than at dinner).

MONTRACHET, 239 W. Broadway. Tel. 219-2777.
Cuisine: FRENCH. **Reservations:** Recommended.

FROMMER'S SMART TRAVELER: RESTAURANTS

1. Eat your main meal at lunch when prices are as much as 15% to 20% lower. At some of the most fancy restaurants, prix-fixe lunches are quite affordable.
2. Look for "pre-theater" menus. Comparable to "early bird" specials in other cities, they offer considerable savings.
3. Eat ethnic: Chinese, Indian, and Thai restaurants abound. Look for Japanese noodle shops as opposed to fancier Japanese places.
4. Eat where the students do, near the campuses of New York University or Columbia University.
5. Get picnic fare at numerous take-out places or at the salad bars found in almost every grocery shop—then head for the parks.
6. Make reservations. At any of the better restaurants (and this includes even moderately priced ones that have heavy neighborhood trade or have caught on with the cognoscenti), reservations are a must. For the hotter ones, even calling a week in advance will not be enough. New Yorkers consider 7:30 to 9:30pm prime dining hours, so last-minute reservations at those times can be hard to come by. But you may be in luck if you want to dine earlier or later (in fact, you may find a "hot" restaurant totally empty at 6pm), or if you're here in August when New Yorkers flee the city.

$ Prices: Appetizers $9–$22; main courses $20–$29; prix-fixe dinners at $28, $36, $60 (tasting menu).
Open: Lunch Fri noon–2:30pm; dinner Mon–Thurs 6–10:30pm, Fri–Sat 6–11pm. **Subway:** 1 or 9 to Franklin St. Walk one block to W. Broadway.

In April 1985, Montrachet opened in TriBeCa to well-deserved raves, including a three-star rating from the *New York Times*. Since then, they've managed to keep that rating and add more stars from *Forbes* magazine, as well as an award of excellence from the *Wine Spectator* for an outstanding (but not outrageously priced) list of fine French and California vintages. Stressing simplicity in decor and elegant modern French cuisine, they offer three prix-fixe dinners, as well as à la carte main courses. The $28 meal typically includes an arugula salad as appetizer; a main course of pasta with wild mushrooms; and chocolate-and-banana gratin for dessert. For $36, the appetizer will probably be seared tuna with tomato fondue and a vegetable terrine with a hot tomato butter; the main course may be roast duck with ginger sauce, and the dessert, crème brûlée. For $60, the appetizer might be a choice of black sea bass with roasted peppers and lemon butter or grilled quail salad, and the main course perhaps venison in peppercorn sauce (game is often served in season), roast lobster, or rack of lamb. Dessert might be blood-orange cheesecake with a dried cherry sauce. Lunch is served only on Friday and features salads, lighter foods, and fresh fish dishes like Norwegian salmon.

TRIBECA GRILL, 375 Greenwich St., at the corner of Franklin Street. Tel. 941-3900.
Cuisine: CONTEMPORARY AMERICAN. **Reservations:** Required several days in advance for dinner; recommended for lunch.
$ Prices: Appetizers $7–$12; main courses $16–$26. AE, MC, V.
Open: Lunch Mon–Fri noon–2:30pm; dinner Mon–Thurs 5:30–11pm, Fri–Sat to 11:30pm, Sun to 10pm; brunch Sun 11:30am–3pm. **Subway:** 1 or 9 to Franklin St.

⭐ For several years, this has been one of the hottest restaurant scenes in New York. With owners like Robert De Niro, Sean Penn, Bill Murray, Christopher Walken, and Mikhail Baryshnikov in the picture, it was inevitable that the place would become a celebrity hangout. Dustin Hoffman is a regular, so are Stephen Spielberg, Martin Scorsese, and Tom Selleck. But star-gazing is not the only reason people flock to TriBeCa Grill: The atmosphere is warm and inviting, and the food just happens to be terrific.

TriBeCa Grill is the brainchild of Drew Nieporent, the managing partner, who is also responsible for the wonderful French restaurant Montrachet (see above). Although the food is simple, focusing mostly on grills, whatever chef Don Pintabona does is quite special. The heart of the dinner menu is very fresh fish—salmon, mahimahi, snapper, or whatever is best in the market. Then there's a roasted chicken, veal with real old-fashioned whipped potatoes, breast of duck with wild-mushroom canneloni, and a nightly lobster special. Appetizers are also memorable, like the warm goat cheese salad, gazpacho, or arugula salad with bocconcini and basil oil. Desserts are ethereal, especially the warm mascarpone blintz with fresh fruit and the chocolate torte. Lunch starts off with similar salads ($7 to $8), features a fish special and a grilled chicken special and grilled focaccia salads ($10–$18). Desserts are the same as at dinner.

TWO ELEVEN, 211 W. Broadway. Tel. 925-7202.
Cuisine: CONTEMPORARY AMERICAN. **Reservations:** Recommended.
$ Prices: Appetizers $5.50–$8.50; main courses $8.50–$22. Lunch prix fixe $19.95. Bar Menu $6–$7.50.
Open: Lunch Mon–Fri 11:30am–6pm; dinner Sun–Thurs 6pm–midnight. Fri–Sat 6pm–1am; brunch Sat–Sun 11:30am–4pm. **Subway:** 1 or 9 to Franklin St.; A, C, or E to Canal St.

⭐ It takes art to turn a cavernous, columned room into a cozy and intimate restaurant, and art is in abundance at Two Eleven, both in the decor (handsome modern paintings, whitewashed walls, a long, curved panel following the lines of the long, curved bar), and in the wonderful food dreamed up by Chef Guy Cerina, one of New York's most intriguing young chefs. Drawing on his experience at Café des Artistes, Le Cygne, Maxims, and The Sign of the Dove, Cerina utilizes contemporary cooking methods to create a menu that is wholesome and exciting. Vegetable juices, purées, and herb-infused oils are used throughout the menu. He insists that the natural flavors of meat, fish, and poultry stand out in dishes that are simply and beautifully presented—almost too pretty to eat. Among the entrées, pan-seared swordfish with red lentil salad, sautéed Swiss chard, and curry oil is a winner; so, too, is the smoked muscovy duck breast with horseradish mashed potatoes, broccoli rabe, and grilled apples. Tuna carpaccio with fried rice noodles, lime-and-coriander-cured salmon with a tingling jalapeño oil, and a mixed green salad,

with the lightest of raspberry vinaigrettes and chives, are good starters. To end the meal, there are sinful desserts like chocolate hazelnut cake with fudge sauce and ice cream, or a warm almond pound cake with poached pear and caramel sauce. Lunch offers similar dishes at lower prices and a three-course prix-fixe menu. The bar menu is one of the best deals in town for those who might be dining alone: grilled sausage with potato salad, chicken tostada, penne with spicy vodka tomato sauce are some of the choices under $10. Around 6:30pm, when "Happy Hour" is in full swing, the

SOHO, TRIBECA, LITTLE ITALY & CHINATOWN DINING & ATTRACTIONS

bartender often brings out gourmet appetizers—free! Brunch, featuring such dishes as cold smoked chicken salad, crabcakes or fried oysters and eggs, is another treat.

INEXPENSIVE

NOSMO KING, 54 Varick St. Tel. 966-1239.
  Cuisine: AMERICAN. **Reservations:** Recommended.
$ Prices: Appetizers $4–$8; main courses $11–$17. AE, MC, V.

Open: Lunch daily noon–3pm; dinner Mon–Fri 6–11pm, Sat–Sun 5:30–11pm. **Subway:** 1 or 9 to Canal St. Walk south across intersection of Varick and Canal Sts.

At Nosmo King (*No smoking*—get it?), your preconceptions of "health food" will melt away like so many inches off your waistline; dining here promises decadence with none of the morning-after regrets. Using local, free range, and organic ingredients, chef Alan Harding composes dazzling dishes that taste as wonderful as they look. Most of the items are gourmet vegetarian, but there are also a few fish and fowl choices. Splendid samplings from a recent seasonal menu include a chili and goat cheese burrito; cannelloni of chanterelles with pumpkin and truffle oil; pan-roasted duck with chickpea pancakes and chicory lentil salad; seared tuna with spinach, white beans, and lime marjoram vinaigrette. Don't miss the desserts here, especially the warm chocolate tart with hazelnut ice cream or the basmati rice pudding with orange rum sauce. Inquire about various tasting menus. A thoughtfully selected wine list boasts an international array.

RIVERRUN, 176 Franklin St. Tel. 966-3894.
   Cuisine: AMERICAN. **Reservations:** Recommended.
 $ **Prices:** Appetizers $5–$7.50; main courses $8.25–$15.90. AE, CB, DC, MC, V.
   Open: Lunch daily 11:30am–5pm; dinner Sun–Thurs 5pm–midnight, Fri–Sat 5pm–1am. **Closed:** Thanksgiving and Christmas. **Subway:** 1 or 9 to Franklin St.

★ Riverrun caters to a neighborhood crowd—but when that neighborhood is TriBeCa, near City Hall and home to lots of celebrities, that means you may find former mayor Ed Koch or actor Robert De Niro dining there. Riverrun was one of TriBeCa's first restaurants, and now the area and the restaurant are both "hot." It's no wonder—the food is delicious and thankfully non-nouvelle, the service is friendly and attentive, and, wonder of wonders, the prices are modest. There's a very popular bar up front (it keeps winning all sorts of awards) and simple, semienclosed tables in the rear. Hanging on the walls are paintings and photographs of high quality (some for sale) by local artists.

The dinner menu provides everything from sandwiches (like blackened chicken on rye, with roasted red pepper and fries) and burgers to grilled prawn and caesar salad, and on to such main dishes as roast chicken tarragon with homemade mashed potatoes, fresh Washington State oysters, and steamed mussels Chardonnay with garlic and tomato. You might start with fried calamari, end with the house's wickedly fattening chocolate mud cake for dessert. There's a full lunch menu at slightly lower prices, and Saturday and Sunday brunch specials run $6.25 to $9.95. The service is friendly yet professional, and there's an overall good feeling about this one. There's plenty of street parking.

2. CHINATOWN

Manhattan is dotted with Chinese restaurants, and you can have an adequate Chinese meal almost anywhere in the city. But make the trek down to Chinatown, not only to combine a little sightseeing with your meal (see details in Chapter 7) but also because the city's best, most authentic Chinese kitchens are here.

For a real experience in Chinese eating, choose a dim sum lunch at **Silver Palace,** 50 Bowery (tel. 964-1204); **Golden Unicorn,** 18 E. Broadway (tel. 941-0911; see more details below); or **Mandarin Court,** 61 Mott St. (tel. 608-3838)—the most "in" establishments at this moment. All are jammed on weekends, so come as early as you can for the best selections. Dim sum, in case you haven't heard, is the umbrella term for dumplings and other exotic morsels that are served early in the day, always accompanied by pots and pots of tea. The correct procedure for a tea lunch is to choose whatever appeals to you from the carts and trays that are constantly whisked by your table (dim sum never offers a menu). Your bill is tallied by counting the number of empty plates you've amassed. It's perfectly proper to linger over tea lunch and continue eating until you're thoroughly sated. You'll be seated communal style with lots of other diners, all happily eating away. Individual selections average about $1.80 to $5.95. At the Silver Palace, dumpling hours are 9am to 4pm; at Golden Unicorn, 8am to 3:30pm; at Mandarin Court, 7:30am to 3:30pm. To reach Chinatown, take the 6 to Canal Street.

MODERATE

GOLDEN UNICORN, 18 E. Broadway. Tel. 941-0911.
Cuisine: CHINESE. **Reservations:** Recommended.
$ Prices: Appetizers $5.95–$9.95; main courses $9–$30. AE, V.
Open: Daily 8am–midnight; dim sum served 8am–3:30pm.
Subway: F to E. Broadway.

When you enter the spotless marble lobby of 18 E. Broadway, a security guard with a walkie-talkie will direct you to the proper floor. The elevator doors will open on a beehive of activity at Golden Unicorn, one of the busiest dining spots in Chinatown.

Skip the usual soups and start with an intriguing dish like subgum winter-melon soup and braised shark's fin soup with shredded chicken or crabmeat. Then move on to an appetizer like fried stuffed bacon rolls or sliced coldmeat with jellyfish. Main courses like steamed chicken with ham and vegetable or beef with black mushrooms and bamboo shoots are fabulous. More esoteric tastes can pick from sautéed fresh conch and sliced fresh abalone with black mushrooms.

Golden Unicorn also features an extensive lunch menu with an amazing assortment of familiar and not-so-familiar dishes including pan-fried noodles, rice noodles, and mai fun dishes. For more than a few patrons, the dim sum is the best reason to come here: It's fresh, it's prepared to order (fairly unusual in Chinatown), and it ranges from bacon roll stuffed with shrimp paste to fried crisp egg-cream bun.

ORIENTAL PEARL, 103 Mott St. Tel. 219-8388.
Cuisine: CHINESE. **Reservations:** Recommended.
$ Prices: Appetizers $1.75–$8.95; main courses $6.50–$30. Buffet dinner $18.95. MC, V.
Open: Daily 8am–11pm. **Subway:** N or R to Canal St.; B, D, or Q to Grand St.

Chinatown's outdoor markets brim and bustle with all kinds of edible creatures and exotic produce, much of it unrecognizable to the outsider. If you'd like to sample as many of these as possible, and at a reasonable price, then head for Oriental Pearl, which features a $17.95 buffet dinner with an incredible array of choices. You select from a veritable groaning board of over 100 items, including vegetables, chicken, seafood, beef, soup, sushi, and dim sum. Many of these you cook yourself at the table in a communal hot pot. The restaurant itself gives the impression of utter chaos, and service is perfunctory at best; but never mind, this is a dining experience you cannot find anywhere else. If you want to stick to the regular menu, start with the triple seafood cocktail or the special Chinese-style corned beef. Savory main courses might include assorted seafood in a bird's nest or braised squab with mushrooms and bamboo shoots. Desserts are unusual, perhaps sweet black-sesame soup, waterchestnut cake, or sesame ball with lotus cream.

INEXPENSIVE

GREAT SHANGHAI, 27 Division St. Tel. 966-7663.

Cuisine: CHINESE. **Reservations:** Required for groups of 10 or more.

$ Prices: Appetizers $2.60–$8.95; main courses $7.95–$14.45; weekday lunch special $4.95–$8.50. AE.

Open: Sun–Thurs 11:30am–10pm, Fri–Sat 11:30am–11pm. Dim sum lunch, daily 11:30am–3pm. **Subway:** 6 to Canal St. Walk several blocks to Bowery; turn right on Bowery. Cross Bowery east of Division St.

Great Shanghai is a large, crowded, modern restaurant specializing in Soo-hang food, one of the most delicate of the Chinese cuisines, which originated in the southern part of China along the Yangtze River. The innovation here, available only in winter, is the Chinese fondue, a cook-it-yourself affair. A simmering broth in a large pot is brought to your table and placed on a gas burner. You order a variety of small meat, fish, and vegetable dishes—the ones we like best are the fish balls, squid, and paper-thin chicken—which you cook yourself in the broth, dipping them into the steaming brew with a wire-mesh basket. The waitress brings a tray of condiments and mixes you a sauce—hot or mildly spicy, as you designate. We thought it was wonderful. (Depending on how many ingredients you choose, the price should be about $12 to $14 per person.)

Any time of the year, enjoy such dishes as sautéed prawns, sea bass, and classic Peking duck (a $29 duck should feed two to four hungry people). You'll want to order steamed dumplings and spring rolls as appetizers and maybe fried bananas for dessert. For dim sum, come at lunchtime.

You can also have the same Peking duck at another restaurant under the same management called **Peking Duck House Restaurant,** 22 Mott St. (tel. 227-1810).

NHA TRANG VIETNAMESE RESTAURANT, 87 Baxter St. Tel. 233-5948.

Cuisine: VIETNAMESE. **Reservations:** Recommended on weekends.

Ⓕ FROMMER'S COOL FOR KIDS: RESTAURANTS

Mickey Mantle's (see p. 160) The legendary New York Yankees slugger often drops by to soak up the atmosphere and autograph baseballs and the like for young fans.

Two Boots (see p. 121) Even the staff has fun at this playful East Village Cajun/Italian emporium, whose tasty offerings include dinner and brunch specials—and coloring books—for the little ones.

Dallas BBQ (see p. 162) Parents will enjoy the stylish setting, and kids will love the barbecued chicken and ribs and the wonderful onion rings.

Saranac (see p. 175) It looks like summer camp in the Adirondacks and welcomes the stroller set, and those older, with a special children's menu.

Serendipity 3 (see p. 176) Little girls tend to favor the whimsical food here—Ftatateeta's toast, a foot-long chili hot dog, lemon ice-box pie, and unforgettable frozen hot chocolate.

Tavern on the Green (see p. 161) Like a trip to fairyland, all silver and glass and glitter, this is the kind of place of which childhood memories are made. Kids are given balloons to take home. Every spring, giant topiaries of fanciful animals dominate the garden—children love playing with them.

Chinatown After marveling at the pagoda-style phone booths and the exotic shops, kids will find the restaurants here a treat.

McDonalds [160 Broadway, near the World Trade Center, tel. 385-2063.] Kids will be in awe as moon-headed MacTonight dances on weekends, and they'll love the gift boutique with T-shirts, french-fry radios, and Ronald McDonald dolls. Adults will like it, too; there's a doorman, piano player, and fresh flowers on all the tables. Adults can enjoy cappuccino and espresso, and everyone will be pleased with the great dessert menu.

$ Prices: Appetizers and main courses $2.75–$12.50.
Open: Daily 10am–10pm. **Subway:** 6 to Canal St.

Nha Trang has to be one of the best bargains in Chinatown, maybe in the whole city. It's hopping with tourists and locals alike who are drawn by delicious Vietnamese food so inexpensive it's hard to make dinner for two exceed $20. Dip the cool, light spring rolls with rice vermicelli in sweet peanut sauce to start; follow them with flavorful barbecued shrimp on real sugar cane, frog legs in chile-and-lemongrass sauce with rice, or—an incredible bargain—a big plate of seafood with vegetables and white rice for all of $3.75! Try some of the unusual beverages, like the green bean with coconut milk, sweet enough to be a dessert; and the French black coffee, good and strong. There's nothing fancy about this place—glass covers over white tablecloths, paper napkins, and plastic flowers—but the service is fast and friendly (often a rarity in Chinatown), and the value is just wonderful.

Right next door, **Pho Pasteur,** 85 Baxter St. (tel. 608-3656), also serves delicious Vietnamese food at low prices, but in a simpler setting. You can't go wrong at either place.

SAY ENG LOOK, 5 East Broadway, off Chatham Square. Tel. 732-0796.

Cuisine: CHINESE. **Reservations:** Required for large groups.
$ Prices: Appetizers $1.25–$4; main courses $9–$24.50. AE, DC, MC, V.
Open: Sun–Thurs 11:30am–10:30pm, Fri–Sat 11:30am–11pm.
Subway: 6 to Canal St.

This restaurant is one of the best places in Chinatown to sample Shanghai delicacies. *Say eng look* means "four, five, six" in Shanghai dialect—an unbeatable combination in Chinese games of chance. Indeed, owner/chef A. K. Chang leaves nothing to fate as he fixes such surefire winners as finely sliced deep-fried pork cutlets, special mixed vegetables, shrimp with sizzling rice, sweet-and-sour sliced fish, and shrimp with kidney. You might also try the casseroles—another Shanghai specialty—particularly the fishhead casserole or the chicken with cashew nuts.

Say Eng Look's interior is spotless and attractive. Subdued lighting tones down the flamboyant red walls, and the beamed ceiling gives the restaurant a homey charm.

3. LITTLE ITALY

For those who love lusty, truly ethnic Italian food, the greatest neighborhood in Manhattan has to be Little Italy, a subway stop or two below Greenwich Village. The streets are lined with homey, family-style restaurants where they make the fried mozzarella, lobster Fra Diablo, clams in garlic sauce, steak in hot peppers, and fried zucchini the way they did back in Naples or Sicily. Come for lunch after you've been touring downtown Manhattan and join the local politicians and legal eagles (City Hall and the courts are just a few blocks away) wheeling and dealing over the steaming pastas. If you come for dinner on a weekend, be prepared to join the hungry throngs standing in long lines, since most of these restaurants do not accept reservations. Prices here are slightly lower than those uptown, and you can probably get a good meal for $15 to $20. In addition to **Grotta Azzurra** (detailed below), consider also **Paolucci's,** 149 Mulberry St., long a personal favorite. Other delicious choices are **Forlini's,** 93 Baxter St.; **Puglia,** 189 Hester St., which boasts live entertainment nightly; and **Vincent's Clam Bar,** 119 Mott St., for the best Italian fish dishes anywhere. It's nice to walk around the streets a little bit beforehand, poke your head into the grocery stores, and smell the marvelous cheese and sausages, perhaps listen to a strain of a Caruso recording. Finish your evening with a heavenly pastry and espresso at any of the wonderful Italian coffeehouses that line the streets: Two of our favorites are **Café Roma,** 385 Broome St., and the oldest "pasticceria" (pastry shop) in the country, **Ferrara's,** 195 Grand St., where, in summer, you can sit at the sidewalk cafe and pretend that you're on the Via Veneto.

MODERATE

GROTTA AZZURRA, 387 Broome St. Tel. 226-9283 or 925-8775.

> **Cuisine:** ITALIAN. **Reservations:** Not accepted.

$ **Prices:** Appetizers $8–$11; main courses $11–$18.

> **Open:** Tues–Thurs noon–11pm, Friday noon–midnight, Sat noon–12:30pm, Sun noon–11pm. **Subway:** 6 to Canal St.; walk east several blocks, then turn left on Mulberry St.

This is the most popular restaurant in Little Italy, and the one where the lines are the longest. But you won't be disappointed: The place is attractive, the service professional, and the crowd lively. The food is excellent, especially such standbys as steamed mussels or clams and stuffed artichokes among the appetizers, veal scaloppine with mushrooms, chicken rollatini, and saltimbocca à la Fiorentina among the main courses. For dessert, the cold zabaglione with strawberries is a must.

4. SOHO

In this eclectic, electric neighborhood, it pays to choose carefully, so here are some of my favorites in addition to those below. For clever, clean American fare, gallery gawkers flock to **Jerry's,** 101 Prince St. (tel. 966-9464), where people-watching qualifies as an Olympic sport. A few doors east, **Fanelli,** 94 Prince St. (tel. 226-9412), in continuous business at this location since the mid-1870s, serves homey, hearty pub fare in a memorabilia-packed saloon atmosphere. The interior is original, and prices are on the low side. Lines form early at the bright, cheery **Elephant & Castle,** 183 Prince St. (tel. 260-3600), for Saturday and Sunday brunch; mammoth omelets make the wait worthwhile. For European ambience (and attitude), light a Gauloise and head to **Lucky Strike,** 59 Grand St. (tel. 941-0479), or to its next-door rival, **La Jumelle,** 55 Grand St. (tel. 941-9651). Both turn out surprisingly serious French fare for the young, rich, and thin set through the wee hours. In an Italian mood? Within a three-block stretch, you'll find the warm **Amici Miei,** 475 W. Broadway (tel. 533-1933); hip **I Tre Merli,** 463 W. Broadway (tel. 254-8699); and convivial **Vucciria,** 422 W. Broadway (tel. 941-5811)—all of which have earned the loyalty of locals, no mean feat down here. Subway: Take the 6 to Spring Street or R to Prince Street.

MODERATE

ALISON ON DOMINICK STREET, 38 Dominick St., one block south of Spring Street, between Varick and Hudson streets. **Tel. 727-1188.**

> **Cuisine:** FRENCH. **Reservations:** Required well in advance.

$ **Prices:** Appetizers $8–$17; main courses $23–$28. Sun prix-

fixe dinner for two $49; pretheater dinner Mon–Sat, $29. AE, DC, MC, V.
Open: Dinner only, Mon–Thurs 5:30–10:30pm, Fri–Sat 5:30–11pm, Sun 5:30–9:30pm. **Subway:** 1 or 9 to Canal St.; E or C to Spring St.

Why are all those limos double-parked on a nondescript street that nobody has ever heard of just north of the Holland Tunnel? Dominick Street is the home of a stylish bistro so good that people go out of their way to enjoy the soul-satisfying food of southwestern France that chef Scott Bryan creates here. Proprietor Alison Price Becker, an actor turned restaurateur, has created an old-fashioned restaurant—a cozy, candlelit spot with creamy white walls, midnight-blue banquettes, silvery black-and-white photos of France on the walls, and a long white taper on each table. Soft, unobtrusive jazz plays in the background.

Against such a harmonious background, the food can really shine—and it does! Chef Bryan prefers to go light on the butter, heavy cream, and cheese sauces but still turns out wonderful dishes from Gascogne, Languedoc, and the Basque country. Braised lamb shank with white beans, aromatic vegetables, and sautéed spinach, and roast squab with green lentils and garlic confit are widely praised; also quite fine is the crisp skate with roasted eggplant purée in a bouillabaisse vinaigrette. Appetizers are satisfying, too, especially the almond-and-currant couscous. The menu changes with the seasons; game in season is featured. Be prepared to linger and enjoy. Artists and theatrical folk come here at night, so you may spy a celebrity or two.

L'ECOLE, 462 Broadway, at Grand Street. Tel. 219-8890.
Cuisine: FRENCH. **Reservations:** Recommended.
$ Prices: Prix-fixe lunch Mon–Fri, three courses $17; five courses $21; prix-fixe dinner Mon–Sat, three courses $27, five courses $33. Also à la carte: appetizers $4.50–$9; main courses $10–$20.50. AE, DC, MC, V.
Open: Lunch Mon–Fri noon–1:45pm; dinner Mon–Sat 6–9:30pm. Closed major hols. **Subway:** 6 to Spring St. walk one block.

To enjoy the best in classic French cuisine, it pays to go to school. And the school we're talking about is L'Ecole, the student-operated restaurant of the French Culinary Institute of New York, in SoHo. Here, in a light and airy two-tiered dining room, with white-napped tables well-spaced for conversation and colorful artwork on the walls, you can enjoy the classic cuisine of France at a fraction of the price you would pay at one of the great restaurants of New York or Paris. Students get to hone their skills, and patrons get to enjoy sumptuous food and save money: Everybody benefits.

The French Culinary Institute of New York was founded in conjunction with prestigious Ferrandi in Paris. Students undergo a rigorous 600-hour curriculum and are so well trained, in fact, that, upon graduation, many land jobs in some of New York's most prestigious kitchens—Lutèce, Le Bernardin, Le Cirque, and Montrachet among them. Some, like Bobby Flay of Mesa Grill, own their own establishments. Here's a chance to catch them at the beginning of their careers.

The five-course lunch or dinner always includes an appetizer or a soup, a fish course, a meat course, a green salad, and a dessert. The menu changes daily. You might start with Alsatian potato salad with garlic sausage, puréed fresh vegetable soup, or Maryland crab cakes. Fish and meat courses include pan-seared salmon on braised endive, country lamb shank with cassoulet beans, or Mediterranean fish stew with garlic mayonaisse. The desserts are wonderful, too. They could be chocolate sponge cake filled with chocolate mousse, poached pears with ice cream, crème brûlée, or perfect fresh fruit tarts. L'Ecole's wine list has won the *Wine Spectator's* Award of Excellence; each week, four bottled wines are offered by the glass at wine-shop prices.

INEXPENSIVE

HONMURA AN, 170 Mercer St., near Houston. Tel. 334-5243.

Cuisine: JAPANESE. **Reservations:** Recommended.

$ Prices: Appetizers $4.75–$19.75; main courses $8.75–$21.75. MC, V.

Open: Lunch Wed–Sat noon–2:30pm; dinner Tues–Sat 6–10pm; Fri–Sat 6–10:30pm; Sun 6–9:30pm. **Subway:** 6 to Bleecker St.

Although it's only on the second floor, Honmura An has a unique Japanese penthouse feel, with high ceilings, brick walls, simple decor, and a great view of New York University. At the top of the wooden steps leading to the dining area is a simple stone sculpture that holds a stream of water and a flower. The dining room is warmly, yet simply, decorated with a few arrangements of tulips. Numerous Japanese families and couples will be in evidence.

Honmura An specializes in authentic soba noodles, all handmade on the premises; from your table you can watch these nutritious buckwheat noodles being made in a special glass-walled room in the corner.

Start with finger food like *edamame,* Japanese summer green soybeans that you snap open to push the beans out; or *itry so age,* small prawns rolled with soba, shiso leaf, and nori, deep fried—and utterly delicious. Main courses include hot soba dishes topped with sliced duck and scallions in a duck-based soup, cold soba topped with button mushrooms, and several rice dishes. Some soba dishes come with a steaming kettle of liquid rich in vitamins and minerals; after you finish your noodles, you're instructed to pour the liquid into the soup bowl and drink it. Desserts show an exquisite appreciation for moderation and include small soba dumplings in a sweet red bean sauce and homemade ice creams and sorbets.

KWANZAA, 19 Cleveland Place, at Lafayette St. Tel. 941-6095.

Cuisine: INTERNATIONAL SOUL FOOD. **Reservations:** Recommended for parties of 5 or more.

$ Prices: Appetizers $3.75–$8; main courses $8–$15. AE, MC, V.

Open: Lunch Mon–Thurs noon–4pm; dinner Mon–Thurs 5pm–midnight; Sat–Sun 5pm–3am; brunch Sat–Sun 11am–5pm. **Subway:** 6 to Spring St.

All the gorgeous art you'll see at this exotic place is for sale: Kwanzaa doubles as an art gallery/shop, so you can replicate the African motif in your own home. Bold strips of kente cloth hang from the ceilings, and tables are handmade with cut marble; the beautiful lamp in the alcove is Moroccan, and the back dining room is a replica of an adobe hut of the Fanti tribe in Africa. Incense and jazz fill the air; downstairs you can enjoy cabaret, poetry, and performance art.

Kwanzaa serves up Caribbean and American Southern fare with a touch of African and New Orleans inspiration. Appetizers in great demand are the incredible jerk chicken wings and out-of-this-world Maryland crabcakes; or sample the Caribbean shrimp tossed with codfish and served on a bed of radicchio, endive, and arugula. Of the entrées, the braised oxtails are highly recommended; a prime cut is stewed with fresh vegetables and served with coconut rice and gonga peas, sweeter than black-eyed peas. The old-fashioned lentil loaf is perfect for vegetarians who want to try something different. For dessert, folks rave about the sweet-potato cheesecake and the German chocolate cake, but the hands-down favorite is the Guinness Stout ice cream. Kwanzaa gets very busy on weekends and draws many celebrities—you might spot Spike Lee, Christy Turlington, or Wesley Snipes.

SOHO KITCHEN AND BAR, 103 Greene St. Tel. 925-1866.

Cuisine: INTERNATIONAL. **Reservations:** Required for large groups.

$ Prices: Appetizers $2.75–$7.25; main courses $6.75–$15.75. AE, DC, MC, V.

Open: Mon–Thurs 11:30am–2am (kitchen serves until midnight), Fri–Sat 11:30am–3am (kitchen serves until 1:45am), Sun noon–11pm (kitchen serves until 10pm). **Subway:** 6 or E to Spring St.; N or R to Prince St. Walk west to Greene St.

Next door to Greene Street and under the same management, SoHo Kitchen and Bar offers one of the finest and most extensive selections of wines by the glass anywhere in the world—a total of 110. Along with tasting the wines, dedicated oenophiles can munch on salads, omelets, pizzas, burgers, pastas, and sandwiches, plus weekend brunch specials and a few dinner grill items, all at low prices.

SPRING STREET NATURAL RESTAURANT, 62 Spring St., at the corner of Lafayette. Tel. 966-0290.

Cuisine: NATURAL FOODS. **Reservations:** Not accepted.

$ Prices: Appetizers $5.25–$8; main courses $6.75–$16. AE, CB, DC, MC, V.

Open: Sun–Thurs 11:30am–midnight, Fri–Sat 11:30am–1am; brunch Sat–Sun 11:30am–4pm. **Subway:** 6 to Spring St.

It would be difficult to improve on this SoHo favorite; it just keeps getting better. Spring Street Natural is a great big, airy place, with windows overlooking both sides of the two-level cafe; wooden tables, exposed-brick walls with paintings by local artists, tall plants, and overhanging fans set the mood for dining on wonderful food that is wholesome, unprocessed, beautifully prepared, and reasonably priced. Everything is homemade, superfresh, and prepared from all-natural ingredients. And the service is friendly and efficient. An excellent regular menu plus a long printed sheet of daily specials make it difficult to choose among the wide array of fish and seafood, pasta, and vegetarian and natural gourmet specials. At a recent meal, our party started with thick, chunky Tahitian chicken soup with fresh basil; sampled yummy appetizers like yucca fritters with a roasted jalapeño tomato relish; then moved on to a flavorful Caesar salad and pesto ravioli with green onions and shiitake mushrooms and garlic-cured sundried tomatoes.

Our main courses were a wonderful sautéed shrimp with tomato-cream sauce, sautéed breast of chicken with miso-jalapeño sauce, and roasted acorn squash stuffed with scallions, apples, tofu, wild rice, and curried yogurt. The desserts ($4–$4.50) were wondrous: sweet-potato Grand Marnier pie, chocolate soufflé torte, and warm walnut-bourbon tart. Saturday or Sunday brunch is a special treat, with a large menu of soups, salads, appetizers, egg dishes, and great desserts, in addition to the regular menu. You can have drinks at the big, friendly bar up front, crowded with locals.

5. GREENWICH VILLAGE

The Village has, in addition to those highlighted below, a vast variety of places to eat or people-watch. In a vein similar to The Grand Ticino (see below), you might want to try **Rocco's,** 181 Thompson St. (tel. 677-0590); **Villa Mosconi,** 69 MacDougal St. (tel. 673-0390); and **Cucina Stagionale,** 275 Bleecker St., off Seventh Avenue (tel. 924-2707), where there's always an eager line waiting to get in (no bar, so BYOB). Inexpensive and very tasty Spanish fare can be found at **Rio Mar,** 7 Ninth Ave., at Little West 12th Street (tel. 246-9105), where there's live entertainment on Saturday nights. The famous Italian caffès of the Village are ideal for a cappuccino on ice or a piping-hot espresso; they are great places to sit, talk, play a game of chess, read the papers—or just watch the world whirl by. Our favorite caffès on MacDougal Street are **Caffè Dante** at no. 79 and **Caffè Reggio** at no. 119. Another pleasant place to linger is **The Peacock,** 24 Greenwich Ave. Subway: A, B, C, D, E, F, or Q to West 4th Street, where all are a short walk away.

EXPENSIVE

GOTHAM BAR AND GRILL, 12 E. 12th St. Tel. 620-4020.
   Cuisine: AMERICAN. **Reservations:** Strongly recommended.
$ **Prices:** Appetizers $9.25–$18; main courses $26.50–$31. AE, CB, DC, MC, V.
   Open: Lunch Mon–Fri noon–2pm; dinner Mon–Thurs 5:30–10pm, Fri–Sat 5:30–11pm, Sun 5:30–9:45pm. **Bus:** Fifth Ave. No. 5. **Subway:** 4, 5, 6, N, or R to 14th St./Union Square.

The beautiful, chic Gotham Bar and Grill celebrated its eleventh anniversary recently, and the crowds, limos, and celebrities are still there. The hurrahs are for one of New York's best restaurants and the exquisite presentations of its young chef de cuisine, Alfred Portale, a veteran of Troisgros and other stellar restaurants in France. Diners are seated at small tables placed among huge, soaring columns, in an art deco postmodern atmosphere that is at once soothing and exciting. As a first course, the seafood salad comes highly recommended, as does the morrel ravioli and the smoked duck breast. Among the main courses, Atlantic salmon with grilled fava beans, charred hedgehog mushrooms, and roasted corn custard, and the Muscovy duck breast are given top billing, along with the grilled swordfish with puréed potatoes. For dessert, the profiterole with vanilla, banana, and peanut-butter ice cream is quite lovely—as is the warm plum tart with vanilla ice cream and brown-sugar streusel.

MODERATE

NEW DEAL RESTAURANT AND GARDEN, 133 W. 13th St., between Sixth and Seventh avenues. Tel. 741-3663.
    Cuisine: CONTEMPORARY AMERICAN. **Reservations:** Recommended.
$ **Prices:** Appetizers $4.50–$8.50; main courses $13.50–$22.50; Prix-fixe dinner $16.75. AE, DC, DISC, MC, V.
    Open: Brunch Sun 11:30am–3pm; dinner Sun 5–9pm, Mon–Thurs 5–10pm, Fri–Sat 5–11pm. **Subway:** 1, 2, 3, or 9 to 14th St.

    In its previous incarnation in SoHo, WPA murals of the 1930s dominated the decor at the New Deal. There's no room for them in this new space in a Greenwich Village town house, but no matter: The narrow brick-walled room with its fireplace and grand piano (there's music to dine by Thursday, Friday, and Saturday night) is invitingly cozy, and the outdoor garden with its umbrellaed tables is one of the most relaxing al fresco dining spots around. Chef Jeffrey Nathan's seasonal menus, using fresh herbs from the garden, turn up some invigorating surprises. Among the appetizers are wild mushrooms under glass and a very popular sizzling duck-and-sausage salad. Among the main courses are lobster steak with stir-fried vegetables in a Thai yellow curry sauce and parmesan-crushed lamb chops. The prix-fixe menu, which includes an appetizer, a main course from a varied list, coffee, and dessert, is a great buy. Fall brings their annual game festival. The desserts are special: homemade ice creams with fresh fruits and berries, sinfully rich chocolate decadence cake, and mud pie. Nothing beats an outdoor weekend brunch, especially if you can have zucchini-and-parmesan frittata or eggs Callet (Virginia ham, chiffonade of spinach, and scrambled eggs atop a warm croissant). There's a full bar and a sensibly priced wine list.

ONE IF BY LAND, 17 Barrow St., between Seventh Avenue and West 4th Street. Tel. 228-0822.
    Cuisine: CONTINENTAL. **Reservations:** Recommended.
$ **Prices:** Appetizers $6–$14; main courses $26–$34. AE, MC, V.
    Open: Dinner only, 7 days, 5:30pm–midnight. **Subway:** 1 or 9 to Christopher St. or A, B, D, E, F to West 4th.

Stepping into One If By Land, you'll feel as though you've entered the dining room of someone's plush mansion, with a roaring fireplace to your immediate right and a pianist playing grandly to your left. This 250-year-old colonial town house was once the carriage house of Aaron Burr. During the American Revolution (hence the name of the restaurant), the tunnel in the wine cellar ran out to the Hudson River; revolutionaries used it to escape from the British to a boat they kept at the ready.

    With four working fireplaces, a bounty of fresh flowers and candlelight, One If By Land is surely one of the most romantic restaurants in New York. Women shouldn't be surprised if the incredibly gracious and charming maitre d', Richard, kisses their hand. He and the waiters sport tuxedos, and the service is impeccable.

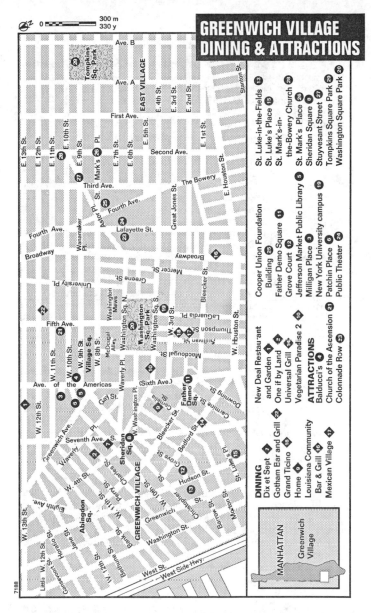

GREENWICH VILLAGE DINING & ATTRACTIONS

0 | 300 m
0 | 330 y

MANHATTAN
Greenwich Village

DINING
Dix et Sept ⟨7⟩
Gotham Bar and Grill ⟨22⟩
Grand Ticino ⟨9⟩
Home ⟨8⟩
Louisiana Community Bar & Grill ⟨16⟩
Mexican Village ⟨17⟩
New Deal Restaurant and Garden ⟨1⟩
One if by Land ⟨4⟩
Universal Grill ⟨3⟩
Vegetarian Paradise 2 ⟨10⟩

ATTRACTIONS
Balducci's ⟨21⟩
Church of the Ascension ⟨23⟩
Colonnade Row ⟨25⟩
Cooper Union Foundation Building ⟨26⟩
Father Demo Square ⟨11⟩
Grove Court ⟨12⟩
Jefferson Market Public Library ⟨5⟩
Milligan Place ⟨19⟩
New York University campus ⟨6⟩
Patchin Place ⟨24⟩
Public Theater ⟨27⟩
St. Luke-in-the-Fields ⟨13⟩
St. Luke's Place ⟨15⟩
St. Mark's-in-the-Bowery Church ⟨28⟩
St. Mark's Place ⟨26⟩
Sheridan Square ⟨27⟩
Stuyvesant Street ⟨29⟩
Tompkins Square Park ⟨20⟩
Washington Square Park ⟨20⟩

For starters, rock shrimp ravioli with spring greens and basil in a clear tomato broth is unbeatable. Herbivores can opt for grilled vegetables and goat cheese gratin with warm lentil salad and smoked tomato vinaigrette. Entrées are classics, splendidly turned out, and include a superb beef Wellington in Bordelaise sauce. Fresh seafood is flown in daily from Maine. Desserts include a blissful traditional chocolate ganache with a light vanilla sauce and classic New York–style cheesecake, on the menu for 25 years.

INEXPENSIVE

DIX ET SEPT, 181 W. 10th St., corner of Seventh Avenue. Tel. 645-8023.

Cuisine: FRENCH. **Reservations:** Accepted.

$ **Prices:** Appetizers $5–$7.50; main courses $10–$18.50. AE, CB, DC, MC, V.

Open: Dinner only, Sun–Thurs 6pm–midnight, Sat–Sun 6pm–2am; bar menu always available. **Subway:** 1 or 9 to Christopher St.

★ This could be your typical little Parisian "corner restaurant," except that here the corner is at 10th Street and Seventh Avenue (Dix et Sept). Maître d' François Feynerol and chef de cuisine Michael Brown are veterans of some of the city's finest restaurants; their own place is cozy and inviting, with white-brick walls, soft wall sconces, and photos by Brassaï on the walls. It's just like Paris, but "without the attitude"—and at very affordable prices. Menus vary with the season: In winter you might dine on cassoulet or venison, pheasant or *boeuf bourguignon;* in summer it could be *salade niçoise* or poached salmon, maybe roast monkfish with a saffron-fish broth. The plat du jour is always special—if you come on Saturday, you'll feast on couscous; on Friday, it's bouillabaisse. You can start with a wonderfully hearty onion soup. For dessert, try the chocolate-and-raspberry charlotte if they have it that day or the classic *poire Belle Hélène* or *Paris-Brest,* a praline-cream–filled pastry. A bottle of wine is agreeably priced, and of course there's a full list of French apéritifs and digestifs.

GRAND TICINO, 228 Thompson St. between West 3rd and Bleecker streets. Tel. 777-5922.

Cuisine: ITALIAN. **Reservations:** Recommended.

$ **Prices:** Appetizers $4–$8; main courses $11–$19. AE, CB, DC, MC, V.

Open: Lunch Mon–Fri noon–5pm; dinner Mon–Fri 5–11pm, Sat–Sun 3–11pm; brunch Sat–Sun noon–3pm. **Subway:** A, B, C, D, E, F, or Q to W. 4th St.; walk south two blocks, east one block.

This is your classic Greenwich Village Italian restaurant, typical of many where the prices are moderate and the food is rich and hearty in the grand old southern Italian tradition. This restaurant may look familiar if you've seen the movie *Moonstruck.* Try the assorted hot antipasto to begin, then follow with a bowl of their famous minestrone or tortellini in brodo. Main courses include sweetbreads with capers, breast of chicken with prosciutto and fontina cheese, and an excellent veal chop. Saturday and Sunday brunch is festive, with pastas, soups, main courses, and hearty *frittata del giorno* (omelet of the day).

HOME, 20 Cornelia St., near Sixth Avenue at West 4th Street. Tel. 243-9579.

Cuisine: AMERICAN REGIONAL. **Reservations:** Recommended.

$ **Prices:** Appetizers $5–$8; main courses $13–$16. No credit cards.

Open: Breakfast 9–11am, Mon–Fri; lunch 11:30am–3pm Mon–Fri; dinner Mon–Sat 6–11pm, Sun 5:30–10pm; brunch Sat–Sun 11am–4pm. AE. **Subway:** A, B, C, D, E, F, or Q to West 4th St.

★ It's a pretty incredible restaurant that can continually play the blues and still provide one of the more positive dining experiences in New York. With its vintage 1930s glass wall sconces and tiny dining area, Home also proves that good things can come in small, hotly lit packages. Owner David Page delivers a primarily free-range and organic menu as well as "the best onion rings on Cornelia Street" in keeping with Home's philosophy of having a few things on the menu that people really crave.

For appetizers, the wildly popular onion rings are lighter than air and more crisp and delicious than imaginable. Natural flavors emerge wonderfully with the sparingly seasoned main courses. The grilled New York State trout with a wild mushroom and sweet potato hash and peppered steak in natural juice with garlic-potato cake and escarole are beyond compare. You have only to glance up to watch the chefs at work in the open kitchen; they'll even prepare special vegetarian plates on request.

For dessert, prepare to regress to childhood by sampling the most incredible chocolate pudding in the universe. The strawberry short-cake and ginger cake are equally fantastic. Brunch is scrumptious: You can choose from main courses like potato and sardine cake, poached egg and a smoky red pepper sauce, or scrambled eggs with leeks and spinach, and pan-fried oysters on the side.

LOUISIANA COMMUNITY BAR & GRILL, 622 Broadway, between Bleecker and Houston streets. Tel. 460-9633.

Cuisine: CAJUN. **Reservations:** Recommended for Fri–Sat.

$ **Prices:** Appetizers $4.95–$6.95; main courses $8.95–$19.95. AE, DC, MC, V.

Open: Dinner only, Mon–Thurs 6–11pm, Fri–Sat 6pm–midnight, Sun 5–10pm. Bar opens at 5pm. Happy Hour specials until 7pm. **Subway:** 6 to Bleecker St.; N or R to Prince St.

If you can imagine a place that looks like a Louisiana roadhouse bar, offers live musical groups and big bands that play jazz and blues and zydeco, and serves up four-star Cajun cuisine at refreshingly moderate prices, you'll get some idea of the spirit of Louisiana Community. It's a cavernous place, with a 35-foot bar, red-and-white-checkered tablecloths, outlandish papier-mâché sculptures on the walls, and a nonstop fun and funky mood. The kitchen here was set up, and the staff trained, by Paul Prudhomme of K-Paul's New Orleans—so you know the food is authentic, and delicious.

The menu changes daily, so you might start with one of the great soups, like classic gumbo or "totally hot" Cajun jambalaya with sauce piquant. Don't miss Cajun popcorn—fried puffs of battered crayfish with sherry sauce. Or begin with warm spinach salad, beautifully seasoned with mushrooms and andouille dressing. Then proceed to such main courses as roasted chicken roulade with cornbread stuffing, blackened yellowfin tuna with mashed potatoes, or classic crayfish étouffée with rice. Desserts are sweet and lovely, especially the warm bread pudding topped with whipped cream. There's always live music from about 9:30pm on; late Friday night it's the Loup Garou Zydeco band, and late Saturday night it's the Harlem All Stars.

MEXICAN VILLAGE, 224 Thompson St. Tel. 475-9805.

Cuisine: MEXICAN. **Reservations:** Not necessary.

$ **Prices:** Appetizers $4.95–$8.95; main courses $8.25–$13. AE, CB, DC, MC, V.

Open: Daily noon–midnight. **Subway:** A, B, C, D, E, F, or Q to West 4th St. Walk south two blocks, east one block.

S Mexican Village is always busy, even on a cold winter weeknight when everyplace else is practically empty. Its popularity has continued for over 32 years, and with good reason. Not only is the atmosphere *muy simpático,* with lots of wood and brick and Mexican glass lanterns, but also the food is authentic and reasonably priced. To the traditional Mexican favorites, they often add new dishes not done in New York before, like *enchiladas Oaxaca;* shredded beef chimichangas; *chiles rellenos poblanos* (stuffed with cheese and sweet pork); and *enchiladas de mer* (flour tortillas stuffed with seafood). Be sure to ask about the daily specials. Vegetarians can enjoy meatless *enchiladas supremas,* as well as vegetarian tacos, enchiladas, and burritos. The chile sauces on the table are hot, so use them sparingly; to cool off, you can always order some iced mint tea or a bottle of Carta Blanca—the ideal accompaniment. It's pleasant to linger over your tequila while you're waiting for the delicacies to emerge from the hole-in-the-wall kitchen.

UNIVERSAL GRILL, 44 Bedford St. Tel. 989-5621.
  Cuisine: AMERICAN. **Reservations:** Limited.
$ Prices: Appetizers $3.75–$6.95; main courses $9.95–$16.95. AE.
  Open: Lunch Mon–Fri 11am–3:30pm; dinner daily 6pm–midnight; brunch Sat–Sun 11am–3:30pm. **Subway:** 1 or 9 to Christopher St.; walk two blocks south.

As the sound system blares Abba's "Dancing Queen," tambourine-toting waiters serenade a shocked diner and gingerly deliver a birthday dessert. That's just another night at Universal Grill, a West Village newcomer so hot the waiting crowds could fill a subway station. For a "scene" restaurant, Universal delivers surprisingly solid comfort food: curried shrimp, pan-roasted half chicken with gravy, and the Universal Club sandwich rank among the tastiest anywhere. Downtown hipsters have already made brunch a neighborhood institution; reasonably priced, massive platters of French toast, pancakes, omelets, and heavenly biscuits keep them coming. The room isn't decorated as much as accumulated, with knick-knacks that could have come from a maiden aunt's attic; take it all in as you pass the inevitable moments in line.

VEGETARIAN PARADISE 2 [V P 2], 144 W. 4th St., between Fifth and Sixth avenues. Tel. 260-7130.
  Cuisine: CHINESE/VEGETARIAN. **Reservations:** Not necessary.
$ Prices: Appetizers $3–$4.95; main courses $6.95–$12.95. AE, CB, DC, MC, V.
  Open: Sun–Thurs noon–11pm, Fri–Sat noon–midnight. **Subway:** 1 or 9 to Christopher St.; A, B, C, D, E, F, or Q to West 4th St.

S ✪ They began with a vegetarian restaurant in their native Hong Kong, moved on to Chinatown, and now they have a restaurant here in Greenwich Village. The Tang family, the people in charge at V P 2, are creative cooks whose vegetarian cuisine stems from both their Buddhist beliefs in nonviolence and their commitment to a healthful low-cholesterol cuisine that uses no fish, animal, or dairy products; no white sugar; and no preservatives. Besides the usual Chinese vegetarian dishes, they also create mock "meat" main courses—lemon chicken (made with Chinese yams), deep-fried oysters (based on eggplant), and prawns in black-bean sauce (really baby corn). And the food is delicious. Their Paradise Hot Clay Pots are a special treat. The desserts are surprisingly good, especially the lemon tofu and banana-date puddings. The place is plain and narrow, with a minimum of decor, but pleasant enough. Two doors away, at **VP-2-GO** (tel. 260-7049), 140 W. 4th St., they make authentic vegetarian dim sum take-out—a special treat if you're planning a picnic.

6. EAST VILLAGE/ LOWER EAST SIDE

EAST VILLAGE

It's not just a meal, it's an adventure. Dining in the East Village can take you from India to Poland to Jamaica—in one block. Since locals are mostly working-class folk, artists, and students, the restaurants down here offer wonderful fare that's cheaper than in almost any other neighborhood. In addition to those below, I suggest the following for a quick culinary trip around the world. In what feels like a loony Swiss cottage, **Roettele AG,** 126 E. 7th St. (tel. 674-4140), surrounds you with cuckoo clocks and kitsch and pampers you with Alpine soul food like goulash and Wienerschnitzel. For fine Indian fare, skip the all-Indian strip on East 6th Street and head for **Haveli,** 100 Second Ave. (tel. 982-0533), a standout for its snazzy decor and equally appealing food. With a Mexican accent, **Maryann's Distrito Federal,** 300 E. 5th St. (tel. 475-5939), dishes out delicious, inexpensive fare and terrific drinks to a youngish crowd. For authentic Polish and Ukrainian favorites like pierogi and kielbasa—and an even more authentic staff—check out **Kiev,** 117 Second Ave. (tel. 674-4040), or **Veselka** (tel. 228-9682), 144 Second Ave., both open 24 hours and such bargains you'll think you're still in the old country. And at **Two Boots,** 37 Ave. A (between Second and Third streets, tel. 505-2276), exciting Cajun-Italian cuisine is offered at affordable prices. They serve outrageous Cajun pizza, seafood jambalaya, vegetarian entrées, and a full children's menu. **Cucina di Pesce,** 87 E. 4th St. (tel. 260-6800), and **Frutti di Mare,** 84 E. 4th St. (tel. 979-2034), both under the same management, offer fresh pasta and seafood dishes that may be among the best bargains in New York; both have some sidewalk seating, friendly crowds, and sometimes free hors d'oeuvres at the bar to tide you over while waiting.

INEXPENSIVE

LA SPAGHETTERIA, 178 Second Ave., between 11th and 12th streets. Tel. 995-0900.
   Cuisine: ITALIAN REGIONAL. **Reservations:** Recommended, especially on weekends.

$ Prices: Appetizers $3.50–$6.95; main courses $8.95–$13.95; pretheater special $13.95.
Open: Lunch Mon–Fri noon–3:30pm, Sat–Sun noon–4pm; dinner daily 5pm–midnight. **Bus:** Any Second Ave. bus. **Subway:** 4, 5, 6, N, or R to 14th St./Union Square then walk east and south.

⭐ Casually elegant, La Spaghetteria is a second home to neighborhood artists, writers, and actors playing at the Public and other local theaters. A beautiful flower arrangement, with desserts—including a big basket of fruit—temptingly displayed on a white-linened table commands the center of the room; candlelight sets the mood, and in summer, although there's no al fresco dining area, windows overlook a lovely garden.

The menu—supplemented by daily specials—changes seasonally. You might begin with a scrumptious antipasto misto; be sure to ask for oil and vinegar and soak it all up with chunks of Spaghetteria's terrific Tuscan breads. Pasta courses include penne tossed with grilled fresh tuna, coarsely chopped tomatoes, and black olives in a light tomato sauce. At dinner there's always a gnocchi special—for example, pesto dumplings in fresh tomato purée garnished with thin strips of roasted red and yellow peppers. Secondi piatti (main courses) include *pollo arrosto*—roasted half chicken marinated in garlic and rosemary-scented olive oil, then served with oven-roasted potatoes and the vegetable du jour (perhaps grilled broccoli fleurets). At lunch there are also frittatas and sandwiches. The Italian/Californian wine list highlights eight premium wines by the glass. And the dessert list usually offers a heavenly tiramisù and an assortment of delicious tortas, such as an orange tart with thick chocolate crust.

THE MIRACLE GRILL, 112 First Ave., near 7th Street. Tel. 254-2353.
Cuisine: SOUTHWESTERN. **Reservations:** Accepted only for parties of six or more.
$ Prices: Appetizers $5.25–$8.50; main courses $9.95–$17.95. Brunch main courses $5.95–$8.95. AE, MC, V.
Open: Dinner Mon–Thurs 5:30–11:30pm, Fri–Sat 5:30pm–midnight, Sun 5:30–11pm; brunch Sat–Sun 11:30am–3pm. **Subway:** 6 to Astor Place. Walk three blocks east, one block south.

💲⭐ It is indeed a miracle that the small kitchen at this East Village restaurant turns out such terrific food. The Miracle Grill is a great find for devotees of the chile pepper who like their food hot, their prices moderate, and their atmosphere cool and casual. It's great fun, especially in warm weather, when you can sit in the rambling garden out back. The place is decorated in southwestern minimal, and the kitchen is kept open, so that patrons can watch the chef work his magic. Miracle Grill presents the hearty foods of the Southwest in a style better suited to health-conscious New Yorkers: They go easy on the butter, cheese, and salt, giving the food a clean, sharp, lighter taste. The menu is changed every six months, but the basic dishes remain similar.

To begin, dig right in and try the spicy black-bean soup with roasted garlic; go for the equally delicious quesadilla with chiles, corn, zucchini, two cheeses, and smoked tomato salsa; or try the chile-rubbed chicken skewers with grilled pineapple and tomatillo salsa. While you're sipping a Mexican beer to go along with this, consider such main courses as grilled chicken breast in soy-and-ginger marinade, served with crispy southwestern fries; grilled vegetable salad with herbed goat cheese and balsamic vinaigrette, a top choice for vegetarians; or a burrito with shrimp and black beans, served with salsa verde. Dessert might be a chocolate *buñuelos*—deep-fried cinnamon-and-sugar tortillas served with two scoops of vanilla ice cream and topped with chocolate sauce. Saturday and Sunday brunch feature a wonderfully varied and exotic menu.

103 NYC, 103 Second Ave., near 6th Street. Tel. 777-4120.
Cuisine: CONTEMPORARY AMERICAN. **Reservations:** Recommended for dinner.
$ Prices: Appetizers $4–$8; main courses $13.50–$16. Three-course pretheater dinner $21.
Open: Lunch Mon–Sat 11:30am–3:30pm; dinner daily 6pm–midnight; late supper Fri–Sat midnight–2am; brunch Sun 11am–3:30pm. **Subway:** 6 to Astor Place. Walk three blocks east, two blocks south.

If you didn't know better, you might mistake 103 NYC for your ordinary East Village restaurant—a big softly lit space with black booths and tables and a hip young crowd at the bar—but make no mistake: Once the food starts coming out of the kitchen, cheerfully delivered by a great-looking wait staff, you know you're in for something out of the ordinary. This is an extraordinary dining experience at a very affordable price. Chef Lincoln Engstrom turns out sophisticated American regional cuisine with international accents. The burrito with grilled shrimp, black beans, and sweet potato with spicy avocado vinaigrette is outstanding among the appetizers. Several pizzas and pastas are available every day. Old-fashioned grilled chicken with mashed potatoes and winter vegetables is a soul-satisfying main course; grilled salmon with new potatoes and tomato-fennel coulis is light and sophisticated. For dessert, go for the pumpkin cheesecake with warm caramel sauce or the warm chocolate cake with vanilla ice cream, toasted coconut, and macadamia nuts. The three-course pre-theater dinner, served from 6 to 7:15pm, is a great idea if you're catching an Off-Broadway show.

Lunch offers sophisticated sandwiches ($5 to $7.50), pizzas, omelets, several main courses, and those luscious desserts. The wine list offers a good selection of American, Italian, and French wines at reasonable prices.

PISCES, 95 Avenue A, at the corner of 6th Street Tel. 260-6660.
Cuisine: SEAFOOD. **Reservations:** Recommended.
$ Prices: Appetizers $4.25–$6.50; main courses $6.95–$14.95. AE, MC, V.
Open: Lunch daily 11:30am–4:30pm; dinner daily 5:30–11:30pm. **Subway:** 4, 5, 6 to Astor Place. Walk east.

Pisces resembles a ship that has been deposited onto Avenue A by a great flood. With its blue awning, low wooden ceilings, a few lantern-like lamps, and colorful primitive mural of the sun and sea life, it feels separate from, yet integrated with, the East Village. It's a fantastic spot from which to watch the parade of hair colors and tattoos down Avenue A. You could hear anything from flamenco to classical music as you eat among the bohemian types who bring their visiting parents here for a square meal.

All Pisces' seafood is purchased fresh daily at market and includes such appetizers as barbecued octopus salad with squash and paprika, and tuna sliced very thin and seasoned with cumin, with a baby artichoke and mashed potatoes—a surprisingly good combination seldom encountered. Entrées such as cod with corn, smoked garlic, and red bliss potatoes or spaghetti with fresh tomato and smoked onion are solid, yet inventive, and even more incredible at these low prices. All smoked items are prepared on the premises.

Of the desserts, don't miss the flourless chocolate cake; it's addictive enough to be declared illegal. All desserts are beautifully presented, with fresh fruit and colorful sauces. The "cannoli," made from a nest of phyllo dough, are divine; they're filled with a rich crème brûlée, topped with a bold splash of strawberry sauce, and big enough for two. The relaxed, adept wait staff are so attuned to diners' needs that they seem to be almost psychic. Pisces offers a predominantly American wine list.

SUGAR REEF, 93 Second Ave., between 5th and 6th streets. Tel. 47-SUGAR (477-8427), or 477-8754 for reservations.
  Cuisine: CARIBBEAN. **Reservations:** Recommended.
$ **Prices:** Appetizers $3–$6.50; main courses $9.25–$14.50. AE.
  Open: Dinner only, Mon–Thurs 5–11:45pm, Fri 5pm–1am, Sat 3pm–1am, Sun 3–11:45pm. **Subway:** 6 to Astor Place. Walk three blocks east, two blocks south.

The food and the mood both sizzle at Sugar Reef, which is as invigorating as a quick trip to the islands. Loud, lively, crowded, Sugar Reef sports a bar whose base is made of multicolored steel drums and lots of fake bananas and birds to accompany the vibrant island music. The food is wonderful for those who like it hot. Vegetable fritters, coconut shrimp, and mango pepperpot are among the tasty appetizers. Favorite main dishes include curried chicken and coconut with pumpkin rice and smothered cabbage; shrimp-and-vegetable brochette; and jerk pork or steak with hot and spicy Jamaican flavors. Vegetarians might have the vegetable roti (curried vegetables wrapped in roti bread, with peas, rice, and cucumber salad). For an unusual side dish, try island yams, mashed with rum, butter, and coconut milk; for dessert, have the sweet plantain tart served warm with coconut ice cream. Jamaican ginger beer goes well with a meal like this, and café con leche would be a good finale. Come before 8pm on Monday to Thursday and get a complete meal for $15.95 or under.

TELEPHONE BAR & GRILL, 149 Second Ave., between 9th and 10th streets. Tel. 529-5000.
  Cuisine: ENGLISH. **Reservations:** Recommended for parties of six or more.
$ **Prices:** Appetizers $2.75–$6.25; main courses $7–$15; Sun brunch $6–$12. AE, MC, V.
  Open: Sun–Thurs 11:30am–2am, Fri–Sat 11:30am–4am; Brunch Sun 10:30am–4pm. **Bus:** Any Second Ave. bus. **Subway:** 6 to Astor Place. Walk three blocks east, 2 blocks north.

You'll recognize Telephone by the row of authentic shiny red British phone booths imported from Plymouth, England, out front. Within, there's an atmosphere of cozy elegance; exposed-brick walls adorned with whimsical murals, fleur-de-lis–

topped columns, stained-glass windows, and a handsome marble-and-cherrywood bar. The back room features a bibliothèque decor, complete with fireplace. And in good weather you can also dine at cafe tables out front on Second Avenue.

Telephone is often the scene of publishing and celebrity parties, but it's more than just another chic party venue. The food is great, portions are enormous, and prices are moderate—most items are under $10. In line with the English theme, items like shepherd's pie and fish and chips are featured—along with appetizers such as Scotch eggs and Stilton cheese fritters. However, there are also scrumptious salads (try the Waldorf goat-cheese salad with green-apple slices and walnuts), and hearty fare such as half a roast chicken with challah-apple stuffing. You can get great soups and burgers here, too. Salads, sandwiches, and under-$6 main courses are featured at lunch. The desserts range from ultrarich chocolate cake topped with raspberry sauce to English trifle. And, on Sunday, a brunch menu proffers everything from a bagel/salmon/cream cheese platter to scrambled eggs with kippers, bacon, or bangers (sausages).

LOWER EAST SIDE

MODERATE

SAMMY'S FAMOUS ROUMANIAN STEAK HOUSE, 157 Chrystie St., north of Delancey. Tel. 673-0330.

Cuisine: JEWISH/ROUMANIAN. **Reservations:** Recommended.

$ Prices: Appetizers $4.95–$6.95; main courses $10.95–$28.95. AE, MC, V.

Open: Daily 4pm–midnight ("Jewish time"—maybe a little earlier, maybe a little later). **Closed:** Yom Kippur. **Subway:** B, D, or Q to Grand St. Walk two blocks north.

You don't have to be Jewish to love Sammy's, but it sure helps. Who else could understand the zany humor of the emcee or appreciate the food fragrant with garlic and chicken fat or the *freiliche* atmosphere that reminds you of your cousin Irving's noisy, long-forgotten Bar Mitzvah? Surprisingly, however, many of Sammy's most devoted patrons are not Jewish. "Do you have to be Japanese to like Japanese food?" asks owner Stanley (there is no Sammy) Zimmerman. "People come because they love the food and the friendliness, and they know they can relax here."

Sammy's is a one-of-a-kind restaurant, a happening, a seven-nights-a-week show for which no tickets are required, as heartwarming as it is sometimes heartburning. Stanley knows everybody; many of New York's top politicians dine here regularly. The decor is wall-to-wall people, especially on weekends. Don't come to Sammy's for a quiet, sedate evening. Come for a party and bring all your relatives.

Oh, yes, the food. It's Jewish style without being kosher, and Roumanian—this refers mostly to such dishes as a very flavorful Roumanian tenderloin, mush steak (the eye of the rib), and a sausage called karnatzlack—for garlic eaters only. Sammy's eggplant salad with fresh green peppers is authentic and delicious. As soon as you sit down, a bottle of seltzer and huge bowls of sour pickles, sour tomatoes, and roasted peppers are brought to your table along with assorted breads, including challah. You could happily make a meal on the appetizers alone—chopped liver, grated radish and chopped onions with chicken fat, broiled chicken livers, and unborn eggs—all rich, greasy, and unforgettable. A bottle of chicken fat is put on the table, just in case you like it greasier.

Main dishes might include flanken with mushroom-barley gravy, stuffed cabbage, broiled veal chops (excellent!), or Roumanian tenderloins. Side dishes are memorable: mashed potatoes with grieven and schmalz, potato latkes with applesauce, and kasha varnishkes. What's for dessert? You really don't need it after all this. They'll replace your bottle of seltzer and bring out a bottle of Fox's U-Bet Chocolate Syrup, plus a container of milk; you mix your own egg creams at the table.

Now you can sit back and enjoy the entertainment. On Friday, Saturday, and Sunday, a soprano and tenor from the New York City Opera perform. And on Monday and Tuesday, when the mood is much quieter, Reuben Levine plays the violin.

INEXPENSIVE

LUDLOW STREET CAFE, 165 Ludlow St., between East Houston and Stanton streets. Tel. 353-0536.
   Cuisine: CAJUN. **Reservations:** Not necessary.
$ **Prices:** Appetizers $2–$5.95; main courses $6.50–$15.
   Open: Dinner Tues–Thurs 6pm–midnight: Fri–Sat 6pm–1am; limited lunch menu noon–5pm; limited bar menu midnight to closing; brunch Sat–Sun 11am–4pm. **Subway:** F to Second Ave. Exit right, walk two blocks east and ½ block south.

The big news here is that the wonderful cuisine of the late, lamented Texarkana restaurant is alive and well and available downtown at about one-third of what it used to cost before. Master Cajun chef Abe de La Housaye has brought his skillets and his following to this quintessential downtown fixture, so now the crowd is an uptown-downtown mix, pin stripes and black-on-black clad types mingling in the warm wood-paneled dining room/bar. The menu has all the great Cajun dishes—hearty gumbos, fried or blackened chicken and catfish, crawfish étouffée and the like, as well as salads, pastas, and steaks. Add live music daily from around 10pm (regularly featuring local favorites, The Niagaras), and you've got a very New York night on the town. Lunch and the late-night bar menu offer sandwiches, burgers, and the like—not the Cajun menu. One of the pioneers behind the recent Lower East Side revival, Ludlow Street Café also offers a $7.95 brunch that merits a special trip to this slightly outré block—choices include huevos rancheros, yapingachos (a traditional Ecuadoran breakfast of fried eggs, potatoes, and spicy peanut sauce), and frittatas (the best in town, says the *New York Times*). A mimosa or champagne costs an extra dollar.

RATNER'S, 138 Delancey St., between Norfolk and Suf-folk streets. Tel. 677-5588.
   Cuisine: JEWISH DAIRY. **Reservations:** Not necessary.
$ **Prices:** Appetizers $5–$7; main courses $8–$16. AE, MC, V.
   Open: Sun–Thurs 6am–midnight, Friday 6am–3pm, Sat after sundown. **Subway:** F to Delancey St.

Should you find yourself downtown, bargain hunting on the Lower East Side (an activity we heartily recommend), you can have a great dairy-vegetarian-fish meal at Ratner's. The prices are moderate—

most items are $7 to $12—and the food is fresh and delicious. Don't miss the pastries!

7. CHELSEA

Once a staid industrial/commercial neighborhood, east Chelsea, also known as the Flatiron District (14th through 28th streets from Fifth to Seventh avenues), has evolved into a 1990s Restaurant Row, with some of the loveliest, loveliest spots in town. Many buildings used to house warehouses (some still do), so restaurants have taken advantage of loftlike, airy spaces to create one-of-a-kind dining rooms. In addition to those below, I recommend the bright, busy **Cal's,** 55 W. 21st St., (tel. 929-0740), perpetually packed with publishing, modeling, and ad folk; unlike most New York restaurants, there's actually breathing room between tables. From a late-1980s scene, **Le Madri,** 168 W. 18th St. (tel. 727-8022), has evolved into a full-fledged institution where the thin and rich crowd roosts for earthy Northern Italian cuisine. Tables here are a rare commodity, so reservations are recommended. The same is true at **Mesa Grill,** 102 Fifth Ave. (tel. 807-7400), which is still hot as a jalapeño for chef Bobby Flay's nouvelle creations and a whimsical southwest/surrealist decor. A New York restaurant address since 1899, the wonderful old building at 108 W. 18th St. is now **Nite Café** (tel. 924-4222), three floors full of action; dine on contemporary American cuisine downstairs, dance to a live band or play pool upstairs.

Farther west, Seventh, Eighth, and Ninth avenues boast a dazzling range of cuisines for a gamut of budgets. **Kaffeehaus,** 131 Eighth Ave. (tel. 229-9702), is pure Vienna, from old-world decor to classical Viennese cuisine, including fantastic coffees and authentic desserts: while enjoying your Café Schokolade and Dobosch Tort, watch the people go by through the window-doors. Others among my favorites include **Cola's,** 148 Eighth Ave. (tel. 633-8020), a smart little trattoria beloved by locals for creative, inexpensive pasta dishes; **Eighteenth & Eighth,** 159 Eighth Ave. (tel. 242-5000), a sort of upscale coffee shop whose young regulars don't seem to mind waiting in line for fresh, inexpensive American food; **Meriken,** 189 Seventh Ave. (tel. 620-9684), arguably New York's hippest sushi joint, whose front door boasts a strobe-lit Statue of Liberty crown; **Bright Food Shop,** 216 Eighth Ave. (tel. 243-4433), a kitschy converted diner that cross-breeds Chinese and Mexican cuisines on an imaginative, well-priced menu; and the stalwart **Man Ray,** 169 Eighth Ave. (tel. 627-4220), still trendy after all these years, whose deco-from-another-planet decor and French-accented food draw hipsters from all over the city.

MODERATE

FLOWERS, 21 W. 17th St., just west of Fifth Avenue. Tel. 691-8888.
   Cuisine: CLASSIC AMERICAN. **Reservations:** Recommended.
$ **Prices:** Appetizers $7–$10; main courses $15–$25. AE, MC, V.
   Open: Lunch Mon–Fri 11:30am–3pm; dinner Mon–Wed 6pm–

midnight, Thurs–Sat 6pm–1am. **Subway:** 1 to 18th St or F to 14th St.

⭐ What do Al Pacino, Oliver Stone, Robert De Niro, Ed Koch, the most gorgeous long-legged fashion models in town, and the stars of the New York Knicks and the Chicago Bulls have in common? Besides all being celebrities, they all like to hang out at one of the trendiest "scene" restaurants in town: Flowers. Come late for dinner—around 9 or 10—and you're apt to see some famous faces (Was that really Jack Nicholson at the bar?). But whether or not the "scene" continues at Flowers, this place will always be a good bet.

The front room is simple but charming with French windows opening out onto the street, and a semicircular bar at the rear; the back room has the feeling of a country restaurant, with its splashy bouquets of dried and fresh flowers, its rustic wood siding and rafters from an old barn in Pennsylvania.

But the food is the real scene-stealer here. Twenty-six-year-old Chef Jimmy Bradley, who learned to cook from his Italian grandmother and then apprenticed at restaurants in Chicago and Cape Cod, believes in "the beauty of simplicity"; his creations, which change just about every other week, are often inspired. Crisp matchsticks of zucchini lightly sautéed with toasted almonds and pecorino, and a salad of bitter greens with slices of pear, Gorgonzola, and spiced walnuts in a light sherry-vinaigrette dressing are among his signature appetizers. Pastas are lovely, especially the cellophane noodles with chili spiced prawns and red onion in a rice wine broth, and can be ordered in half portions. Among the entrées, pan-crisped salmon with a cucumber, tomato, and green salad in a light sauce is a delight. Vegetarians are welcomed with dishes like a warm chickpea cake with ratatouille, braised onion, baby greens, and goat cheese. Lunch offers similar dishes, plus several sandwiches under $10. Bradley is his own pastry chef, too, and promises always to keep the elegant cold lemon soufflé with fresh berries and whipped cream on the menu; you might also be treated to the richest rum-soaked tiramisù in town, or a simple, homey dessert like a warm apple wrapped in phyllo dough, drizzled with caramel sauce and served with vanilla ice cream.

Upstairs is a bar/lounge and above that a rooftop cafe where, in warm weather, guests can choose from the raw bar, the juice bar, and a menu of salads and light natural foods.

LUMA, 200 Ninth Ave., between 22nd and 23rd streets. Tel. 633-8033.
  Cuisine: SEASONAL/ORGANIC. **Reservations:** Recommended.
$ **Prices:** Appetizers $8–$11; main courses $13–$21. AE, CB, DC, MC, V.
  Open: Lunch Tues–Sat noon–2:30pm; dinner Mon–Sat 5:30–10pm, Sun 5–10pm. **Subway:** A, C, or E to 23rd St.

People come from all over to sample the "healthful elegant dining" here, including many celebrities. Luma uses organic ingredients whenever possible; avoids dairy, sugar, and eggs; and maintains a strict no-smoking policy. There is no bar, but wine and beer are served. Start with soup of the day or any one of their unusual salads, like *Luma Verde*, 16 varieties of wild and cultivated baby greens, for a first course. Grilled portobello mushrooms with charred endive and radicchio is a popular appetizer, and smoked-duck cavatelli with caramelized onion and roasted garlic is a favorite among the pastas. For a main course you might try the roasted salmon with horseradish mashed potatoes and watercress-parsley sauce or, for vegetarian tastes, the tempeh scallopine with wild mushrooms, white wine, and lemon. Desserts substitute organic maple syrup and rice syrup for sugar, and the improvement in taste is notable. At lunch, main courses and sandwiches are offered in a range of $6.50–$8.

PERIYALI, 35 W. 20th St., between Fifth and Sixth avenues. Tel. 463-7890.

Cuisine: GREEK. **Reservations:** Recommended.

$ **Prices:** Appetizers $7–$10; main courses $17–$25. AE, DC, MC, V.

Open: Lunch Mon–Fri noon–3pm; dinner Mon–Sat 5:30–11pm.

Subway: B or F to 23rd St., 1 to 18th St.

Here you can enjoy Greek "home-cooking" in a charming Mediterranean setting, with burnished red-oak floors, a billowed fabric ceiling (to help minimize noise), banquettes, and whitewashed walls hung with antique wooden cooking utensils. Exotic plants and cut flowers complete the soothing interior, and an outdoor garden is available in summer. Chef Charles Bowman, a graduate of the Culinary Institute of America, worked at La Côte Basque and the River Café before taking command of Periyali's kitchen in 1987.

For starters, try *pikantikes salates,* a tangy vegetable assortment, or the giant white beans with garlic sauce. The filet of salmon baked in phyllo with spinach and feta cheese is a delicious main course, as is an exceptionally light moussaka. Daily specials always include one or two seafood choices not on the menu, so be sure to ask your waiter. (Service at Periyali is always cheerful and efficient.) The wine list, reasonably priced, features a full page of regional Greek wines as well as the usual international selections. The extraordinary desserts are baked on the premises: Classic baklava, here made with toasted almonds rather than walnuts, is a delight, as is an uncommonly moist lemon cake.

INEXPENSIVE

EMPIRE DINER, 210 Tenth Ave., at 22nd Street. Tel. 243-2736.

Cuisine: AMERICAN. **Reservations:** Not accepted.

$ **Prices:** Appetizers $2.95–$5.95; main courses $8.50–$14.95. Weekend brunch $9.95. AE, DC, DISC, MC, V.

Open: 24 hrs. **Subway:** A, C, or E to 23rd St.; walk two blocks west, one block south.

This gleaming art deco diner is one of New York's liveliest after-hours scenes. From nearby nightclubs and bars, patrons stroll in wearing anything from black tie to black leather. In warm-weather months, the spectacle spills onto the sidewalk as well. If the crowd seems trendy, the food isn't, relying on basics like a generous home-roasted turkey platter, stir-fried vegetables, a vegetarian lentil burger, and overstuffed sandwiches. Brunch here includes fresh juice, one drink, and coffee, plus wonderful omelets, or bagels and lox, or French toast dipped in egg and vanilla ice cream. There's live piano every day, though it's sometimes inaudible over the din; when he first came to New York, a very young Harry Connick, Jr., found work as their piano player.

T-REX, 358 W. 23rd St. Tel. 620-4620.
  Cuisine: AMERICAN REGIONAL. **Reservations:** Recommended.
$ **Prices:** Appetizers $4.95–$7.50; main courses $13.95–$18.95. AE, DC, DISC, JCB, MC, V.
  Open: Lunch Mon–Sat 11:30am–3pm; dinner Sun–Mon 5–11pm; Tues–Sat 5pm–midnight; brunch Sun 11:30am–3:30pm.
  Subway: A, C, or E to 23rd St.

Although its interior does resemble a prehistoric cave—curved low ceilings, dim lights, petroglyphs resembling those at the Lascaux Caves on the walls, and a head of *Tyrannosaurus rex,* eyes flashing and teeth bared, jutting right into the room—don't be fooled: Neanderthal man never ate food this good. This is first-rate cooking whose quality belies the modesty of the tariff. No wonder the place is so popular, not only with people from nearby recording and photography studios, but with a before and after off-Broadway, Broadway, and Madison Square Garden crowd.

Late nights are especially festive. Chef William Silsdorf reinterprets regional American dishes in a unique and wonderfully appealing style—and these dishes look as good as they taste. His menu changes seasonally, but you can usually count on, among the appetizers, the jumbo ravioli of sun-dried tomatoes, goat cheese, and arugula in a heavenly toasted hazelnut butter; the four-cheese quesadilla with a tomato-onion confit is also a treat. You could almost make a meal of the huge salad of pear, crumbled blue cheese, and toasted walnuts, over arugula, frisée, and radicchio; it's best when two share.

As for the main courses, the chef does a delicious tri-colored fusili with smoked chicken, a tangy chicken satay salad with Thai peanut sauce, and a fine grilled Atlantic salmon, served over steamed brown rice and a three-sprout stir-fry. Desserts are not to be missed: pastry chef Joan Winters is known in gourmet circles for her legendary warm chocolate bread pudding. The wine list is well priced, with bottles beginning at just $14; and at both lunch and dinner, an $11 tasting of four different wines is available.

Lunch features some imaginative sandwiches, a terrific 10-oz. sirloin burger on a homemade focaccia roll with "elephant" fries and grilled onion rings (also available at dinner), salads, and a handful of T-Rex "daggers"—skewered chicken, scallops, turkey, veggies, even fruit; most items are $8.95 to $10.95. The Sunday Chelsea Homestyle Brunch features outsized portions of just about everything, including a giant "Bloody Rex."

T-Rex serves festival meals at all holidays, from Passover to Mother's Day to Thanksgiving, Christmas, and New Year's Eve; return visitors are plentiful. A gardenlike room in back is available for regular diners as well as private parties.

8. GRAMERCY PARK/ MURRAY HILL

MODERATE

BOLO, 23 E. 22nd St. Tel. 228-2200.

Cuisine: CONTEMPORARY SPANISH. **Reservations:** Recommended.

$ Prices: Appetizers $6–$9.50; main courses $13.50–$16.50. AE, MC, V.

Open: Lunch Mon–Fri noon–2pm; dinner Mon–Sat 5:30pm–midnight; brunch Sun 11:30am–2:45pm. **Subway:** N, R, or 6 to 23rd St.

Like a flamenco dancer clicking through Gramercy Park, Bolo brightens East 22nd Street with Iberian pizzazz. Columns are covered with oversized sections of Spanish newspapers and the walls with a bold yellow, cobalt, and red Matisse-like collage. A list of appetizers is painted on the mirror above the lively bar and a deck oven dominates the center of the restaurant, so dishes sizzle before you, whisked straight from oven to table.

The striking, earnest wait staff is keen to the after-work crowd's every culinary whim. Although Bolo is definitely "hot," you'll find no nose rings here. The clientele tends to be more buttoned down, but the mahogany bar does pick up around 9pm, when a slightly more casual set invades. The menu is more Spanish-inspired than authentic, although any Spaniards you might see dining here are certain to look quite content. Chef Bobby Flay of Mesa Grill fame uses the lightest of American ingredients to render Spanish food more health-conscious in some incredibly inventive ways.

Of the appetizers, the warm octopus salad (although reminiscent of the movie *Alien*) is delicious; and the Bolo salad with chorizo, Cabrales blue cheese, tomatoes, and 25-year-old sherry vinaigrette, is a true crowd pleaser. First courses and entrées are splashily presented on big orange plates, and portions are just right. Paella is jazzed up with lobster; beautifully grilled scallops with angel hair pasta in squid ink are made more flamboyant with yellow pepper–saffron sauce. The tapenade-crusted salmon in a saffron-tomato broth is succulent—perfect. Red or white homemade sangrias are available, along with a fine selection of Spanish and American wines.

For dessert, don't expect standard issue flan at this Iberian food fantasyland; here it's chocolate, with burnt orange and cinnamon syrup. The pistachio ice cream sandwich, with chunks of chocolate in pistachio ice cream, is light and sublime; the Catalan custard is served with toasted almonds and dried fruits.

LA COLOMBE D'OR, 134 E. 26th St. Tel. 689-0666.

Cuisine: FRENCH/PROVENÇAL. **Reservations:** Recommended.

$ Prices: Appetizers $5.75–$11.50; main courses $15–$24.50. AE, DC, MC, V.

Open: Lunch Mon–Fri noon–2:30pm; dinner Mon–Sat 6–11pm, Sun 5:30–9:30pm. **Subway:** 6 to 28th St.

Even a brief visit to Provence does wonders for the palate and spirit, and a trip to La Colombe d'Or is the next best thing. The handsome restaurant (rated two stars by the *New York Times*) has been called "the most romantic restaurant in New York," and it is Provençal all the way—from the traditional print fabric used for chairs, banquettes, and waitresses' aprons to the ratatouille and *soupe de poisson* on the menu. The foods of southern France are marked by an imaginative use of garlic and tomatoes, and, of course, seafood is a highlight. Provence is the home of bouillabaisse, and La Colombe d'Or's version, available at both lunch and dinner, does not disappoint. You might start here with ratatouille or green salad with roasted peppers and goat cheese. Soups are so filling that only the biggest eaters should start with one. Main courses include hearty winter cassoulet, grilled breast of duck, monkfish sautéed with tomatoes and fresh herbs, and grilled spring lamb chops with rosemary potatoes. A tempting dessert cart offers a luscious array of homemade pastries. Lunch offers similar dishes in a slightly lower price range.

PATRIA, 250 Park Avenue South, at 20th St. Tel. 777-6211.
  Cuisine: SOUTH AMERICAN/CUBAN. **Reservations:** Required.
$ Prices: Appetizers $6–$12; main courses $17–$25. AE, MC, V.
  Open: Lunch Mon–Sat 12 noon–2:30pm; dinner Mon–Sat 6–11pm. **Subway:** N, R, or 6 to 23rd St.

This glamorous corner restaurant with enormous windows draws a stylish and dramatic crowd; it has created an uninterrupted demand for reservations since it opened last year. The largely South American wait staff moves nimbly through tight quarters and packed tables of ebullient diners. Chef Douglas Rodriguez, fresh from conquering Miami with his "New Latin" cuisine, reigns over the kitchen. At Patria, you're likely to encounter tastes and textures you've never experienced before.

The appetizers have south-of-the-border zing and sass, from Ecuadorian ceviche with shrimp, tomato, avocado, and crunchy corn nuts (yes, popcorn) to the Colombian empañada, filled with snails, on a fennel orange salad with aguardiente sauce. Portions are quite large, so some prefer to order side dishes like a banana lentil salad instead. Main courses are served on big, bright plates, and could be chicken escabeche—grilled breast with black bean muñeta, green bean salad and patacones, or sugar cane tuna, coconut-glazed with malanga purée, chayote and dried shrimp salsa. There's also a vegetarian tasting menu with appetizer selections like mushroom picadillo empañada with sweet corn sauce, and entrées including quinoa-stuffed cabbage.

End your meal with a bit of whimsy and try the chocolate-cigar dessert truffle: it comes with a matchbook made of sugar and cookie dough, plus matches that some say can actually be lit. Or sate your sweet tooth with the marvelous piña colada pudding or any number of exotic sorbets.

UNION SQUARE CAFE, 21 E. 16th St. Tel. 243-4020.
  Cuisine: AMERICAN. **Reservations:** Required at dinner; accepted up to six weeks in advance. Parties of eight are the maximum.
$ Prices: Appetizers $5.95–$9.50; main courses $16.50–$24.
  Open: Lunch Mon–Sat noon–2:30pm; dinner Mon–Thurs 6–10:30pm, Fri–Sat 6–11:30pm, Sun 6–10:30pm. **Subway:** 4, 5, 6, N, or R to 14th St./Union Square.

Union Square Café is hot!—so much so that the house will accept your reservations up to six weeks in advance, and they keep a waiting list. For lunch, several days in advance is usually enough, so maybe that's when you'll come down to sample the exuberant American with overtones of Italian fare that has won this place three coveted stars from the *New York Times*. In the seven years since genial owner Danny Meyer opened his doors, nearby publishing and ad people, Village painters and writers, and a chic crowd have become regulars. Everyone gets a warm welcome, and the food just keeps getting better all the time.

The decor is warm, country-style, and not at all fancy. The attractive young staff in their button-down shirts and aprons have been thoroughly trained, so they can really be of assistance—and they move fast. Appetizers are the same at lunch and dinner: Try the fried calamari to dip in anchovy mayonnaise or the penne with roast eggplant. For a main dish at lunch, how about a yellowfin tuna burger with ginger-mustard glaze? Or herb-roasted chicken with tomato-laced mashed potatoes? You could happily make lunch just on some of the side dishes ($4.50 to $4.95), like the irresistible hot garlic potato chips, mashed turnips with crispy shallots, or bruschetta. Dinner presents such main courses as crisp-roasted lemon-pepper duck with pecan rice, pears poached in Port, and peppery greens, as well as roast salmon fillet with citrus-balsamic vinaigrette and three-grain almond-mushroom pilaf. The menu changes with the seasons. Desserts are stellar, especially the homemade mocha-caramel tartufo. The wine list is one of the best in town.

INEXPENSIVE

CAFE BEULAH, 39 E. 19th St. Tel. 777-9700.
Cuisine: AMERICAN SOUTHERN. **Reservations:** Recommended.
$ Prices: Appetizers $4–$10; main courses $10–$23. AE, MC, V.
Open: Lunch Mon–Fri 11am–3pm; dinner Mon–Thurs 6–11pm, Fri–Sat 6–midnight; brunch Sat–Sun 11am–3:30pm. **Subway:** N or R to 23rd St.

You can take a trip 70 years backward in time at Cafe Beulah, among the old black-and-white photographs of the smartly attired Small family and the gleaming mirrors that deck the soft yellow walls, as old blues and jazz tunes play in the background. Former opera singer Alexander Small is now a restaurateur and executive chef, luckily for Cafe Beulah's fiercely devoted following. This is one place with a distinctively Southern lilt and the feel of an instant classic.

Cafe Beulah combines North Carolina cooking with European technique for some amazing results. Of the appetizers, the highly praised she-crab soup is creamy and delicious. Fried chicken wings and sautéed chicken livers with peppered turnip greens and barbecue mustard sauce are also big favorites with the regulars. For an entrée, the smothered shrimp is delectable and deeply satisfying in a down-home way; and Alexander's Gumbo Plate is a Southern masterpiece: A deep dish plate of spicy duck, jumbo shrimp, and fresh lump crabmeat simmered with vegetables in a well-seasoned Creole sauce. Desserts are smooth and heaven-sent: you won't find a more glorious sweet-potato custard pie anywhere, and the chocolate pecan cake and pecan pie will have pecan lovers clamoring for more. The sweet-potato buttermilk pancakes are but one of the big draws on the brunch menu.

EL PARADOR, 325 E. 34th St., between First and Second avenues. Tel. 679-6812.
Cuisine: MEXICAN. **Reservations:** Not accepted.
$ Prices: Appetizers $5.95–$9; main courses $13.50–$16.95. AE, CB, DC, MC, V.

Open: Mon–Sat noon–11pm; Sun 1–10pm. **Subway:** 6 to 33rd St.

There's no need to fly to Mexico City for a great meal—the aficionados consider El Parador on a level with the best anywhere. It's done in a Mexican colonial motif, but it's so jammed with people that you probably won't notice the decor; be prepared to wait in line on weekends unless you arrive early—between 5 and 7pm. But you *will* notice the food: It's excellent. You'll find the old Mexican standbys, as well as fancier dishes, like the superb *pollo Parador* (one of the three Spanish dishes on the menu, steamed with onions and heady with garlic), *pollo mole poblano* (chicken in a spicy chocolate sauce), chicken fajitas (marinated, charcoal-broiled strips), and *camarones en salsa verde* (shrimp in a green parsley-and-wine sauce). The appetizers are almost as good as the main dishes: You'll find it hard to choose between the guacamole, the ceviche (whitefish marinated in lime juice), and the nachos. The classic Mexican and Spanish desserts, flan and natilla, are here, as well as mango and guava shell preserves. And, of course, you'll want a cooling pitcher of sangría or some Carta Blanca, Negra Modelo, or Dos Equis, imported Mexican cervezas, to go with the hot and spicy delicacies.

FIORE, 4 Park Ave., at 33rd Street. Tel. 686-0226.
   Cuisine: ITALIAN. **Reservations:** Not accepted.
$ **Prices:** Appetizers $3.50–$6.50; main courses $8.50–$12.95. AE, MC, V.
   Open: Mon–Fri 11:30am–11pm. **Subway:** 6 to 33rd St.

What a find Fiore is! The smart, stylish midtown watering hole is perfect when you're out shopping or sightseeing (it's two blocks from the Empire State Building), and it's near many midtown hotels. The large room, with its vaulted ceilings and wide columns, was once the rathskeller of the old Hotel Vanderbilt. It has a subterranean feeling—in fact, in an earlier incarnation, it was actually a subway station! Now it's an attractive restaurant with a large bar and tables nicely spaced for conversation and comfort. The modestly priced menu is the same at lunch and dinner.

Among the appetizers, popcorn shrimp and grilled sausage with roasted peppers are both very good. The delicious pizza with sun-dried tomatoes, smoked mozzarella, and fresh basil is easily a complete meal. Of the pastas, the most popular is the angel hair with shrimp in pesto-cream sauce; another excellent one is penne with broccoli, sun-dried tomatoes, and pignoli nuts. Recommended main courses include the fish of the day (I've had the succulent grilled salmon) and the grilled boneless breast of chicken. The desserts are marvelous—especially the Mississippi mud pie (triple-dense chocolate).

---

9. MIDTOWN WEST

The heart of New York's busy tourist scene, the midtown area offers hundreds of restaurant choices. In addition to those described below, some of my favorites include: **Ollie's Noodle Shop & Grill,** 200 W. 44th St. (tel. 921-5988), for primo Cantonese and Szechuan cuisine at modest prices in Times Square; and **Trattoria Dellarte,**

900 Seventh Ave. (tel. 245-9800), a moderately priced high-energy eatery serving a mixed Italian fare, with over 20 seafood and vegetable antipasto selections. For Nouvelle Chinese cuisine within walking distance of the Museum of Modern Art, there's **China Grill,** 52 W. 53rd St. (tel. 333-7788). If you're craving an old-fashioned burger, **Stardust Diner,** 1377 Sixth Avenue, at 56th Street (tel. 307-7575), with its sprightly 1950s decor and music provides the setting for the quintessential American diner experience; five video screens ensure that teenagers won't get bored. Stardust Diner has blue-plate specials and real, fluffy omelets. For a taste of Italy, **Palio,** 151 W. 51st St. (tel. 245-4850), is home to an expensive but remarkable Italian contemporary-style menu, and **Remi,** 145 W. 53rd St. (tel. 581-4212), lives up to its reputation for fabulous Northern Italian cuisine.

EXPENSIVE

AQUAVIT, 13 W. 54th St., just off Fifth Avenue. Tel. 307-7311.
Cuisine: SCANDINAVIAN. **Reservations:** Recommended.
$ **Prices:** Café: Appetizers $5–$14.50; main courses $13.50–$17.50; two-course pre-theater dinner $19. Dining room: lunch à la carte; prix-fixe dinner $62; three-course pre-theater dinner $39. AE, DC, MC, V.
Open: Dining room: Lunch Mon–Fri noon–2:30pm; dinner Mon–Sat 5:30–10:30pm. Café: Lunch Mon–Fri noon–3pm; dinner Mon–Sat 5:30–10:30pm. **Subway:** E or F to Fifth Avenue.

★ Scandinavian restaurants are a rare commodity in New York, so a hardy *Skal!* or two is definitely in order for Aquavit, handsomely ensconced in the former town house of John D. Rockefeller. The ground floor houses a long, sleek bar and cafe where a huge cooler dispenses some 14 flavors of aquavit, that potent vodkalike distillate flavored with fruit or spices and served ice cold. The luxurious downstairs dining room is a marvel of contemporary Scandinavian decor—cool and serene, with a glassed-in atrium, birch trees, and a real waterfall.

In the upstairs Café, my favorite, a homecooked meal might include open-faced Danish sandwiches or peel-and-eat Scandinavian shrimp with lemon mayonnaise and caviar sauce. The sensational smorgasbord plate includes several herrings treated to sauces of caviar, cream, or wine vinegar; home-cured gravlax; and liver pâté.

In the downstairs atrium dining room, menus are prix fixe, and a few dishes carry supplements. To start, consider the traditional gravlax in mustard sauce and dill and wash it down with a shot of mixed-berry aquavit (essential!). Try the blini: Swedish buckwheat pancakes garnished with trout roe, crème fraîche, and onions. Also sample the superb thinly sliced loin of Arctic venison with diced apples, mushrooms, Swedish lingonberries, and carrot purée. At least three different salmon dishes are available each day, all imaginatively prepared and beautifully presented.

Leave room for dessert—creamy chocolate cake with burnt-almond crust and raspberry sauce or homemade brambleberry sorbet in a baked almond shell shaped like a crown and dripping with fresh vanilla sauce. Wines cover a broad price range.

Aquavit's take-out counter sells the restaurant's own seafood, caviar, salads, and sandwiches.

LE BERNARDIN, 155 W. 51st St., between Sixth and Seventh avenues. Tel. 489-1515.
Cuisine: FRENCH/SEAFOOD. **Reservations:** Required far in advance.
$ Prices: Prix-fixe lunch $42; prix-fixe dinner $68. AE, DC, JCB, MC, V.
Open: Lunch Mon–Fri noon–2:30pm; dinner Mon–Thurs 6–10:30pm; Fri–Sat 5:30–11pm. **Subway:** 1 or 9 to 50th St; N or R to 49th St.

Since its opening 8 years back, Le Bernardin has won rhapsodic praise from critics and the sophisticated international set alike; many consider it the best seafood restaurant in New York. This four-star brainchild of Maguy Le Coze and her late brother Gilbert, descended from a long line of Breton restaurateurs, serves fish and seafood exclusively, all prepared with dazzling flair and presented with low-keyed but impeccable style. Posh, expensive, and very French but distinctly New York (waiters are bilingual, menus are in English), Le Bernardin is so popular that tables are booked months in advance—be forewarned.

Don't be fooled by the sterile facade of the Equitable Assurance Tower that houses the restaurant. Enter through the cozy cocktail lounge to the spacious dining room, where the decor is elegant but decidedly "clubby." Your prix-fixe meal automatically begins with a heavenly sampling of seafood canapés, accompanied by the crustiest French rolls this side of the Atlantic. Next, order an appetizer of sparkling carpaccio of tuna: thin, flat slices of the raw fish served in gingered mayonnaise. The chef has a mania for freshness, scavenging the markets at 3am to select the catch, so menu items vary slightly from day to day. By all means, try the famous fricassée of shellfish, lightly done in cream, white wine, and shallots, or the seared tuna with truffled herb salad. Chinese spiced red snapper is delicious in a Port sauce and crèpes, and roasted monkfish arrives layered on a bed of leeks. Among the desserts, the Caramel Variation, which includes a floating island, caramel ice cream in a pastry shell, caramel mousse, and crème caramel, is pure inspiration. A tall stand of petits fours is offered to crown a truly royal meal.

PETROSSIAN, 182 West 58th St., at Seventh Avenue Tel. 245-2214.
Cuisine: RUSSIAN/CONTINENTAL. **Reservations:** Required.
$ Prices: Caviar $18–$58; appetizers $7.50–$18; main courses $24–$34; prix-fixe lunch $29; prix-fixe dinner $35; "Les Années Folles" dinner $135. AE, DC, MC, V.
Open: Lunch Mon–Fri 11:30am–3pm; dinner Mon–Sat 5:30pm–midnight, Sun 5:30–11pm. Sat–Sun brunch 11:30am–3pm. **Subway:** N or R to 57th St.

In a gleaming art deco setting worthy of royalty, Petrossian serves up the royalty of foods—their own world-renowned brands of caviar, smoked salmon, and foie gras—to an appreciative audience that includes everyone from music and theater celebrities (Carnegie Hall is just a block away) to foreign potentates and businessmen, to New Yorkers and visitors hungry for a reminder of the days of Imperial Russia and the roaring '20s. Those were the years when the Petrossian brothers arrived in Paris from Moscow and introduced a new taste sensation from the waters of the Caspian Sea: caviar.

The setting—all Erté bronze sculptures from the '30s, Erté-inspired mirror etchings over the black granite caviar bar, Lalique crystal wall sconces, Limoges china, massive floral arrangements—does not disappoint. Courtly waiters anticipate your every need.

Clearly, this is a place where, by concentrating on the caviar and champagne and vodka, you could easily spend several hundred dollars for a meal. But it is also a place where you can have a quite respectable $29 lunch or $35 dinner and still sample exquisite delicacies. One might start dinner with 30g of Seruga caviar (supplement charge of $8), served on warm toast points; or a lovely borscht with crème fraîche and pirojkis, or smoked river trout salad with a sprightly horseradish dressing. For main courses, it's hard to choose between the Large Petrossian Teaser, an array of caviars and salmon roe with blini and crème fraîche; or the small salmon sampling; or the *zakouski*, a choice of roast salmon and sturgeon delicacies; or New York State organic chicken with potato purée and fricassée of summer vegetables; or roasted East Coast salmon with artichokes and French green beans in a basil broth. It's fun to come with several people and sample all. Desserts like the lemon tart with lemon custard and caramel and the New England cranberry spice cake with cinnamon ice cream are all but irresistible. Right on the premises is the Petrossian Delicacies Shop, which ships by mail all over the world.

RAINBOW ROOM, on the 65th floor of 30 Rockefeller Plaza. Tel. 632-5000.
Cuisine: CONTINENTAL. **Reservations:** Required.
$ **Prices:** Rainbow Room: Appetizers $8–$14; main courses $27–$35. Rainbow Promenade Bar: "Little meals" $9–$13; "feasts for sharing" $19.95. AE.
Open: Dinner Tues–Sat 6:30–10pm; pre-theater fixed-price dinner Tues–Sat, seatings at 5:30 and 6pm; supper Fri–Sat 10:30pm–midnight. Rainbow Promenade: Mon–Thurs 3pm–12:30am, Fri 3pm–1:30am, Sat–Sun 4pm–1:30am (bar); Sun brunch noon–2pm. **Bus:** Any Fifth Ave. bus to 50th St. **Subway:** B, D, F, or Q to 47–50 Sts./Rockefeller Center.

Bring your pot of gold when you visit the Rainbow Room—an evening here will be at least $100 per person. But who's counting? Here's a chance to step back into the glamorous prewar world of New York's cafe society, when socialites, celebrities, and star-struck lovers wined and dined at one of New York's most romantic and sophisticated supper clubs. The Rainbow Room has been restored to its original Art Deco luster, and the critics agree that "S'Wonderful."

Dining at the Rainbow Room is in every way a theatrical experience. Wraparound views of New York from the floor-to-ceiling windows, colored lights flickering across the domed ceiling, an enormous crystal chandelier over the revolving dance floor, waiters in pastel tails, cigarette girls in outfits from the Rockefeller Center past, and silver-lamé tablecloths are all part of the background. Don't come here if you're in a hurry; dinner will take several hours, the meal deliberately paced so that the women in sequined gowns and the men in black tie (not required but very evident) can merengue and rhumba and fox-trot between courses.

Dinner might begin with lobster bisque with whiskey, cake of wild mushrooms with herb sauce, or—appropriately—oysters Rockefeller. Well recommended among the main courses are lobster Thermidor, roast rack of lamb for two, and crispy roasted squab with pancetta and apples. For dessert, go all out and order Baked Alaska, flamed at your table. The pretheater dinner offers good value at $38.50, and after 10:30pm, you can have a stylish supper for slightly less than dinner prices.

If you don't spend an evening at the Rainbow Room, at least visit the **Rainbow Promenade.** Just a few steps from the Rainbow Room, it's a "little meals" restaurant and bar. The views are front-row center on the Statue of Liberty, the Empire State Building, the World Trade Center, and the rivers and their bridges. While you're soaking in the view, you can sip a Stork Club Cocktail or a Manhattan (both $6.50)—and treat yourself to some "little meals." They feature appetizer-size portions of such dishes as Maine crab salad and artichoke hearts, pizza with three cheeses, chilled shrimp, and seasonal oysters.

Rainbow & Stars, the complex's intimate nightclub, features its own menu and top cabaret performers like Tony Bennett, Rosemary Clooney, and Jerry Herman. (For details, see Chapter 10.)

MODERATE

AMERICAN FESTIVAL CAFE, 20 W. 50th St., at Rockefeller Center. Tel. 246-6699.

Cuisine: AMERICAN. **Reservations:** Recommended.

$ Prices: Appetizers $6.95–$10.95; main courses $12.95–$26; prix-fixe dinner $24.95; $18.95. AE, DC, MC, V.

Open: Mon–Fri 7:30am–midnight, Sat–Sun 9am–midnight.

Subway: B, D, F, or Q to 47–50 Sts./Rockefeller Center.

The most popular dining place for Rockefeller Center visitors is the American Festival Café, an exuberant celebration of Americana, with changing exhibits of primitive and folk art from the American Museum of Folk Art always on display. During the spring and summer, it has the largest number of tables available in the garden. And you don't have to be going to the theater to take advantage of their pretheater dinner; it's served all the way from 4 to 10pm on Monday to Saturday, and since it includes complimentary parking (after 5pm) at the Rockefeller Center Garage, it's one of the best buys in town. You have a choice of such appetizers as Texas Gulf shrimp cocktail, applejack onion soup, or a salad of mixed field greens, and such main courses as Baltimore crab cakes, chicken pot pie, certified Angus sirloin steak, or rib au jus. Desserts include Key lime pie, Mississippi mud pie, and bread pudding with Kentucky bourbon sauce.

You never know what special celebration you'll find going on here—it might be the cooking of California's missions, along with a gold-medal–winning California wine list, a Baltimore crab feast, or the cooking of Florida. Regional dishes, old American favorites, and lightly cooked main courses are all featured. Breakfasts are also intriguingly (and differently) themed and in summer, out in the garden, offer a wonderful way to begin a day in New York for under $10. A special section of the restaurant is called the Bar-Carvery, where trenchermen can fill up on sandwiches or platters of handcarved meat.

BECCO, 355 W. 46th St. Tel. 397-7597.

Cuisine: ITALIAN. **Reservations:** Recommended; required for pretheater dinner.

$ Prices: Antipasto and pasta dinner $19; three-course dinner $23.95–$29.95; main courses à la carte $16–$20. AE, CB, DC, DISC, MC, V.

Open: Lunch Tues–Sat noon–3pm; dinner Mon–Sat 5pm–midnight, Sun 5–10pm. **Subway:** C or E to 50th St.

★ Becco is a one-of-a-kind restaurant that New Yorkers are nuts about—and with good reason. Created by Italian food authority Lydia Bastianich (she's a cookbook author and lecturer as well as the owner of prestigious Felidia, see "Midtown East," below) and her son Joseph, Becco is a restaurant with a slightly different concept. The restaurant is modeled after the farmhouses (trattorie/pattorie) in the Italian countryside that open their doors, especially on weekends, and invite guests to share the local bounty; first there's usually an antipasto, followed by a pasta, then by a main course. At Becco, this means that you can order one of two menus. Menu I begins with waiters bearing two trays of *antipasti assortiti*—one of succulently grilled vegetables and fish, the other of luscious cold seafood tidbits—and serving them family style. Then the waiters return to offer samples of pastas and risottos (three different ones at each meal); you choose what you like and eat as much as you wish. If this is all you want (trust me, it's more than plenty)—the price is an amazing $19! However, should you feel really gluttonous, you can order Menu II (which includes the antipasti and the pastas but also features such main courses as delicious grilled chicken breast with arugula, osso buco, salmon or swordfish, and grilled portobello mushrooms with polenta. This adds only another $3 to $9 to the tab. Or you can order the main dishes à la carte, accompanied by a green salad. At lunchtime, Menu I is $3 less, and so are all the à la carte main dishes. No matter when or what you eat, however, plan on having dessert. Chocolate zabaglione cake with zabaglione sauce and amaretto semifreddo are as close to perfection as one can hope for. Wines are reasonably priced, all at $15 per bottle. The restaurant itself is a charmer, a two-story affair with a lively bar scene up front, still lifes of fruits and flowers on the walls. My favorite is the smaller back room with its graceful skylight.

B. SMITH'S, 771 Eighth Ave., at 47th Street. Tel. 247-2222.

Cuisine: CARIBBEAN. **Reservations:** Recommended.

$ Prices: Appetizers $5.95–$9.95; main courses $10.50–$19.95; Sun brunch $8–$12.50. AE, CB, DC, MC, V.

Open: Daily noon–11:30pm; brunch Sun noon–4pm. **Subway:** C or E to 50th St.; 1 or 9 to 50th St.

For pre- and post-theater dining, this dynamic up-tempo restaurant offers good down-home Caribbean cooking adapted to northern tastes. The glossy art deco building houses a lively bar where a sleek, stylish crowd of regulars unwinds nightly over drinks and conversation.

Begin your dinner here with a spicy "frico" whose crust of melted Gruyère cheese holds a mixture of diced onion, tomato, capers, olives, and Swiss chard under lemon vinaigrette; or sample the garlicky Gulf shrimp steeped in Chardonnay. The best-bet main course is the popular lobster ravioli with tarragon shellfish bisque and warm mascarpone cheese. Other items on the all à la carte menu include sandwiches, salads, and several Cajun specialties. There's a good selection of wine in the $25 range. Desserts are a joy, like the sweet-potato–pecan pie, spiced with nutmeg and topped with gobs of whipped cream, or the roast fresh pineapple, finished with a Caribbean coconut rum sauce and a tropical sorbet. Sunday brunch features a live jazz duo, with no extra music charge. B. Smith's Rooftop Café is a highly popular jazz and blues spot (see Chapter 10 for details).

CARMINE'S, 200 W. 44th St. Tel. 221-3800.
    Cuisine: SOUTHERN ITALIAN. **Reservations:** Recommended.
$ Prices: Appetizers $4.50–$18; main courses $13–$44. AE.
    Open: Mon 11:30am–11pm, Tues–Sat 11:30am–midnight, Sun 1–11pm.

Although Carmine's has been open at this location only since June 1992 (its sister restaurant at 2450 Broadway at 91st Street has been around a little longer), it has the comfortable feel of your favorite sweater: warm and familiar, with lots of elbow room. Carmine's is an ideal place for big groups, and when you see the portions, you'll understand why. A bustling, convivial after-work crowd gathers here under the quiet revolving wooden ceiling fans and big copper chandeliers. The walls are covered with enormous oil paintings, old photos, and bottles of wine. One caveat: It's packed on theater nights. Carmine's draws its fair share of celebrities, including the likes of Al Pacino, and with good reason—you'll notice there are a lot of happy people here as laughter rings and ripples continuously throughout the restaurant.

Everything is served family style. Carmine's fried calamari set a standard for the appetizers. They're thick and tender, and the sauce is perfect, warm and diligently replenished by the friendly wait staff. Although specials might be fusilli or other pastas, Carmine's serves three pasta mainstays: linguine, rigatoni, and spaghetti. Of them, the rigatoni country style is fabulous, served with white beans and savory sausage pieces. If you want a smaller main dish, order the veal chop or chicken marsala. For dessert, the tiramisù, topped with chocolate shavings, is pie-sized, rich and sweet, a heady treat soaked in Kahlúa and Marsala wine. The bread pudding and homemade tortoni are equally scrumptious and very popular.

CHRISTER'S, 145 W. 55th St., between Sixth and Seventh avenues. Tel. 974-7224.
    Cuisine: SCANDINAVIAN/SEAFOOD. **Reservations:** Recommended.
$ Prices: Appetizers $7–$11.50; main courses $15.50–$26. AE, DC, MC, V.
    Open: Lunch Mon–Fri noon–2:30; dinner Mon–Sat 5:30–10:30pm. **Subway:** B, D, or E to 7th Ave.; N or R to 57th St.

Although Christer's is cozily decorated with nets, flickering lanterns, wooden bird feeders, fish sculptures, and small trees made of pinecones, you might find yourself staring at the floor, wondering why your feet aren't getting wet. It's covered with colorful stencils of fish and ocean life, air bubbles, seaweed and all. The restaurant has a rustic yet comfortable feel, with wooden chairs in primary colors, banquettes upholstered in red-and-white–checkered cotton fabric and walls covered with fishing scenes. Large wooden beams and a fireplace in the second dining room and a skylight and sea-blue ceiling in the back room put the crowd, liberally peppered with literary agents, fashion and publishing people, and blue-suited business folk, at ease.

The mild-mannered wait staff are not shy about giving their opinions on selections from the menu. Executive chef and owner, the highly acclaimed Christer Larsson, who for six years was chef at the Scandinavian restaurant Aquavit, serves up perfectly sized portions of food that manage to be both no-nonsense and innovative. He integrates a number of ethnic cuisines, not only Scandinavian, with starters ranging from warm terrine of mushrooms, wild rice and hazelnuts to dill pancake with house-smoked char and horseradish, to light entrées like the savory veal fricadelles with plum compôte sauce and mashed potatoes. The beautiful presentation of one of the many salmon entrées is typical: long, slender corn chips are fashioned into a teepee above the seared Serrano marinated salmon with guacamole and black beans. The braised lamb shank with dill sauce and root vegetables is popular. And it's also great fun to sample the sumptuous smorgasbord bar, with its fantastic selection of herring, gravlax, and Swedish meatballs: It's available either as an appetizer ($11.50) or a main course ($19).

Desserts boast an intriguing mix of influences. There's lingonberry bread pudding and a warm Swedish blueberry compôte from Scandinavia; and from Australia (and my favorite), the national dessert, Pavlova: it's a decadent meringue with lingonberry sorbet and whipped cream. You might even feel as though you've been momentarily spirited to Stockholm when Larsson, clad in clogs, comes out to survey the dining area.

LA VIEILLE AUBERGE, 347 W. 46th St., between Eighth and Ninth avenues. Tel. 247-4284.

Cuisine: FRENCH. **Reservations:** Recommended.

$ Prices: Prix-fixe dinner $21.50–$32; prix-fixe lunch $16; lunch main courses $14.75–$19.75.

Open: Lunch Mon–Sat noon–2:30pm; dinner Mon–Thurs 5–9pm, Fri–Sat 5:30–10pm. **Subway:** A, C, E to 42nd St.

With its aura of quiet charm, La Vieille Auberge gives you the feeling of dining in a private home, and the dessert display will make you anxious to be seated and begin feasting. For the price of your dinner main course, you can enjoy a complete meal, and that includes either appetizers like duck pâté, quiche Lorraine, and stuffed mussels, or the soup du jour, vichyssoise, or lobster bisque. And wonderful home-made desserts—like *mousse au chocolat,* lemon sorbet, and cheesecake—are included as well. Well recommended among the main courses are salmon and scrod in lobster sauce, veal scallopine with wild mushrooms, and rack of lamb. Lunch offers similar value, with the main course including an appetizer or soup and a lovely dessert (coffee is extra).

LE BAR BAT, 311 W. 57th St. Tel. 307-7228.

Cuisine: AMERICAN. **Reservations:** Recommended.

$ Prices: Appetizers $7–$12; main courses $15–$23. AE, DC, MC, V.

Open: Lunch Mon–Fri 11:30am–3pm; dinner Mon–Sat 5:30pm–12:30am. **Subway:** A, B, C, D, 1, or 9 to 59th St./Columbus Circle.

Avoid Le Bar Bat at all costs if you have any phobia of winged creatures. Surrealistic bats—in stainless steel, copper, and glowing cobalt glass—populate this fantastic "environment" carved out of a former church. Everything about Le Bar Bat crackles with the same irreverence. Drinks bear monikers like Confucious Colada, Echolation Libation, and Bora Bora Tomorrow; a monstrous concoction called the Bat Bite, designed for two, spews a volcanolike geyser when it reaches your table. Chef Doug Vincent offers solid fare: roast chicken, shrimp risotto, and spaghetti with artichokes are all good. After dinner, hang out with the masses who've made Le Bar Bat an all-night after-work singles haven.

PIERRE AU TUNNEL, 250 W. 47th St. Tel. 575-1220.

Cuisine: FRENCH. **Reservations:** Recommended.

$ **Prices:** Prix-fixe dinner $28; surcharges $3–$7. AE, MC, V.

Open: Lunch Mon–Sat noon–3pm; dinner Mon 5:30–10pm, Tues and Thurs–Fri 5:30–11:30pm, Wed and Sat 4:30–11:30pm.

Subway: C or E to 50th St.; 1 or 9 to 50th St.

One of New York's oldest French bistros and still one of its most deservedly popular, Pierre au Tunnel charms everyone who passes through its doorway. So do Jacqueline and Jean-Claude Lincey, the daughter and son-in-law of Pierre and Jane Pujol, the original owners, who now run this family business. White napery, good wine, courteous waitresses, and flowers at the entrance set a convivial mood. You could begin with a plate of *hors d'oeuvres variés,* proceed to onion soup or *terrine de poisson,* then move on to a favorite like red snapper *à la croûte d'herbe* or pan-broiled baby chicken. If it's Friday, don't miss the *bouillabaisse à la Marseillaise.* My favorite dessert here is the *mousse au chocolat.* Lunchtime prices are lower, from $10 to $16 (à la carte) for dishes like calves' liver sauté, *tête de veau vinaigrette,* and broiled lamb chops.

RENE PUJOL, 321 W. 51st St., between Eighth and Ninth avenues. Tel. 246-3023.

Cuisine: FRENCH. **Reservations:** Recommended.

$ **Prices:** Appetizers $4–$12; main courses $18–$25; prix-fixe lunch $23; prix-fixe dinner $32. AE, DC, MC, V.

Open: Lunch Mon–Sat noon–3pm; dinner Mon–Thurs 5–10:30pm, Fri–Sat 5–11:30pm. **Subway:** 1 or 9 to 50th St.

Don't wait until you're going to the theater to have dinner here. The food is so outstanding and the atmosphere and service so convivial you really don't need entertainment afterward. But if you do want to make an 8 o'clock curtain, make an early reservation so you can enjoy the complete dinner. Two French country rooms (one with a working fireplace, the other with an antique grandfather clock) provide comfortable and attractive surroundings in which to savor a first-class meal. René Pujol has been popular for more than 24 years: René Pujol's son-in-law, Claude Franques, now does the honors as chef, and his creations are both light and sophisticated and wonderfully earthy. The complete dinner includes an appetizer— sliced sea scallops on a bed of Provençal vegetables and cold eggplant-and-tomato terrine with goat cheese are both wonderful— plus a choice of soup (lobster bisque, onion soup, or soup of the day) or a small green salad. After these two courses, you're ready for superb main courses like sautéed veal chop in its own juice, broiled lamb chops, or roasted salmon on a bed of braised leeks and mushrooms in red-wine sauce. Now for coffee and dessert: I wouldn't dream of missing the warm Valhrona chocolate cake or one of the fresh fruit tarts. A complete lunch is available with similar selections, and one may also order à la carte (main courses $15–$19). Dinner is à la carte only after 8pm. There's an extensive and well-priced wine list.

RUSSIAN TEA ROOM, 150 W. 57th St. Tel. 265-0947.

Cuisine: RUSSIAN. **Reservations:** Recommended.

$ Prices: Appetizers $6.95–$65.50 (for Beluga Malossol caviar); main courses $22.75–$34.50; prix-fixe pre-theater dinners $39.75, $45, and $62; prix-fixe lunch $25; prix-fixe brunch $25. AE, CB, DC, MC, V.

Open: Lunch Mon–Fri 11:30am–4:30pm; brunch Sat–Sun 11am–4pm; dinner daily 5–11pm. Cabaret Sun–Mon 8–10:30pm. **Subway:** B, D, or E to Seventh Ave.; N, or R to 57th St.

★ New York's most celebrated artistic "salon" is the venerable Russian Tea Room, located "slightly to the left of Carnegie Hall" and as famous for its loyal following of musicians, dancers, and performers as it is for its borscht, caviar, and blinis. It's an incredibly warm and cozy place, always heady with excitement and good talk and the aroma of those marvelous Russian favorites. Here's your chance to feast on steaming bowls of borscht (perfect on a cold New York winter day), delicate *blinchiki* (crêpes stuffed with cottage cheese and preserves and topped with sour cream), rich beef Stroganoff, *shashlik Caucasian, luli kebab* (Georgian lamb sausage), or chicken Kiev. Desserts are special, and I often have hot tea, served steaming in a glass, and some *kissel* (cranberry purée) or *kasha à la Gourieff* (warm farina with fruit baklava).

It's fun to arrive at the Russian Tea Room about 6 in the evening to see the people who make this place so special; or you can come after the performance and join them as they reminisce, over a glass of vodka or a bowl of borscht, about the high notes or the *grands jetés.* Sunday is cabaret night, with shows at 8 and 10pm and a special prix-fixe menu of $25.

SYMPHONY CAFE, 950 Eighth Ave., at 56th St. Tel. 397-9595.

Cuisine: NEW AMERICAN. **Reservations:** Recommended for pre-theater dinner.

$ Prices: Appetizers $6.50–$12; main courses $14.50–$24.50; prix-fixe pre-theater dinner $30; Sun brunch $9–$16. AE, DC, DISC, MC, V.

Open: Lunch Mon–Fri noon–3pm. Dinner Tues–Sat 5–11:30pm; Sun–Mon 5–10pm; brunch Sun 11:45am–3pm. **Subway:** 1, 9, D, B, A, C to 59th St./Columbus Circle.

The Symphony Café, just around the corner from Carnegie Hall, opened to bravos a few years ago and is continuing to reap warm applause from the theater- and concert-going crowd. Spacious and handsome, with mahogany walls, large glass windows, and an eye-catching mural of Carnegie Hall, this is just the kind of place where you can relax after the show, discuss the performance, and maybe spot a few celebrities at the next table. Theatrical memorabilia are all about, and the menu is worth your attention, too, as Chef Neil Murphy is being praised for his interpretations of New American cuisine.

You might begin with ricotta ravioli in sweet-basil broth; strudel-wrapped shrimp with shaved fennel, mesculun greens, and tomato niçoise; or iced oysters on the half shell. For a main course, choose the commendable sautéed Atlantic salmon, the grilled lamb T-bones with crisp Montrachet potatoes, or the chicken grilled with lemon thyme and olive oil, served with a soft potato tart and sautéed Swiss chard. The desserts are exquisite treats: torte of bittersweet-chocolate mousse with chocolate malted ice cream, Brazil nut and nutmeg ice cream sandwich with hot date beignets, and a chilled rhubarb and banana soup with caramelized banana gratin.

INEXPENSIVE

CENTURY CAFE, 132 W. 43rd St. Tel. 398-1988.
   Cuisine: CONTEMPORARY AMERICAN. **Reservations:** Recommended.
$ **Prices:** Appetizers $4.25–$6.95; main courses $12.95–$19.95. AE, DC, MC, V.
   Open: Lunch Mon–Sat 11:45am–3:30pm; dinner Mon–Sat 4–11:30pm. **Subway:** 1, 2, 3, 9, N, or R to Times Square.

An enormous Loews Theater sign glowing over the bar, large canvases of ballerinas gracing the walls, and red and white spotlights let you know you're in the heart of the Theater District. The atmosphere is open and unpretentious (and comfortable for dining alone), and chef Steven Myer's menu makes it fine for both pre-theater dining and for an evening where food is the main attraction. Myers uses seasonal foods for a contemporary American menu blended with subtle French influences that is best reflected in the seafood dishes. One of the most popular appetizers is the baked shrimp with crisp risotto cake and garlic-parsley butter. Salads are really special—notably the warm duck salad with bacon and warm cherry-vinegar mustard. The Fisher Island oysters with lemon-and-champagne vinaigrette are hand-picked especially for the restaurant. The butternut-squash ravioli, with diced carrots and shiitake mushrooms in a light broth, looks and tastes lovely, and the seared, peppered tuna is succulent and moist. Lunch specials range from braised osso buco leg of lamb with Swiss chard, roasted tomatoes, and white beans to misto-grilled eggplant and zucchini with roasted peppers, white-bean salad, and couscous. Superb desserts include a brilliant flourless chocolate cake with warm chocolate sauce and crème brûlée and raspberries. At lunchtime, Century Café is filled with writers and others who toil nearby at the *New York Times* and *The New Yorker*. Dinner attracts pre-theater patrons.

LA FONDUE, 43 W. 55th St., between Fifth and Sixth avenues. Tel. 581-0820.
   Cuisine: FONDUE. **Reservations:** Not necessary.
$ **Prices:** Appetizers $3.45–$4.95; main courses at lunch $6.50–$12.95, at dinner $6.50–$17.95. AE, CB, DC, DISC, JCB, MC, V.
   Open: Mon–Thurs noon–midnight, Fri–Sat noon–12:30am, Sun noon–11pm. Full dinners and snacks served until closing. **Subway:** E or F to Fifth Ave.

It's a cheese-lover's idea of paradise, and even if you don't know your Emmenthal from your Esrom, we think you'll still enjoy a visit here. Owned by one of the largest cheese importers and retailers in the city, La Fondue is a large French Provincial–looking place that handles hungry cheese-loving hordes very well at the busier times of the day. But if you come a bit late for lunch, on a weekday for dinner, or after the theater or concert, you'll really have the time and comfort for enjoying the quality food. There are five kinds of fondues—the classic Swiss-cheese fondue, the prime filet mignon fondue, a stuffed crab claws fondue, a prime filet mignon and stuffed crab claws fondue, and a heavenly Swiss-chocolate fondue (cubed banana bread and assorted fruits are used for dunking). There is also a variety of cheese and sausage boards, excellent quiches and croques, even le cheeseburger, all modestly priced à la carte. Pasta primavera with pesto, and fish and meat dishes are available for noncheese eaters. Lunch offers many à la carte choices, as well as several terrific complete lunches. Cider, beer, and wine, plus Swiss grape juice, are available, as well as cocktails.

PIATTI PRONTI, 1221 Avenue of the Americas, in the McGraw-Hill Building, between 48th and 49th streets. Tel. 391-7800.
   Cuisine: ITALIAN. **Reservations:** Not necessary.
$ **Prices:** Pizzas, pastas, sandwiches, $7.95–$10.95; main courses $10.95–$12.95. Pretheater dinner $12.95–$13.95. AE, DISC, MC, V.
   Open: Breakfast Mon–Fri 6:30–9:30am; lunch Mon–Fri 11am–4:30pm; dinner Mon–Sat 4:30–9pm; brunch Sat 10am–6pm. Pretheater dinner Mon–Fri 4:30–7:30pm. **Subway:** B, D, F, or Q to 47th–50th Sts./Rockefeller Center.

If you're touring Rockefeller Center or visiting Radio City Music Hall, this is a perfect place to stop in for wonderful pastas, pizzas, Italian sandwiches, and other Italian dishes, especially when the weather is fine and you can sit outdoors in the courtyard. Sandwiches like the Lucca—sliced roasted chicken breast and prosciutto with sun-dried tomatoes, arugula, and garlic-flavored oil on brick-oven Italian bread—are mighty crowd pleasers. Their gourmet pre-theater dinner includes appetizer and dessert, and main courses like pasta, salmon, grilled pork chops, and pan-roasted chicken: it's one of the better deals in the area.

PLANET HOLLYWOOD, 140 W. 57th St. Tel. 333-STAR (333-7827).
   Cuisine: AMERICAN. **Reservations:** Not accepted.
$ **Prices:** Appetizers $4.95–$6.95; main courses $7.50–$18.95. AE, MC, V.
   Open: Daily 11am–2am. **Subway:** N or R to 57th St; B, Q to 57th St.

Part restaurant, part movie museum, and part merchandising machine, the $15-million Planet Hollywood keeps drawing curious hordes anxious for a glimpse of investors Arnold Schwarzenegger, Sylvester Stallone, and Bruce Willis. Alas, Arnold, Sly, and Bruce seem to hang out elsewhere, so Planet Hollywood diners have to settle for a look at the *Terminator 2* cyborg, James Dean's motorcycle from *Rebel Without a Cause,* and Judy Garland's dress from *The Wizard of Oz,* plus a host of other memorabilia. But those artifacts alone, and the late Anton Furst's stunning design, make it worth a visit (and an interminable wait in line on weekends). A kind of Gotham City meets Malibu, the interior should keep the kids wide-eyed and occupied throughout a rather average meal; the menu offers wide-ranging "Californian cuisine"—from Chinese chicken salad to fajitas to grilled sirloin steak. But the food, obviously, isn't the point here.

TOUT VA BIEN, 311 W. 51st St. Tel. 974-9051.
   Cuisine: FRENCH. **Reservations:** Not necessary.
$ Prices: Appetizers $3–$7; main courses $9–$18. AE, MC, V.
   Open: Lunch Mon–Sat noon–2:30pm; dinner Mon–Sat 5–
   11:30pm, Sun 4–10pm. **Subway:** 1 or 9 to 50th St; C or E to
   50th St. **Bus:** M104 to 50th St.

A longtime French favorite, this small, one-room French bistro, complete with red-checkered tablecloths, is a family affair, and its faithful clients have come here for years for solid home cooking— none of that fancy nouvelle stuff here. The entrées are reasonably priced and about $1 cheaper at lunch—the likes of *coq au vin, boeuf bourguignon,* frogs' legs, *salade niçoise,* and Cornish game hen. The hors d'oeuvres are excellent, especially the *pâté maison* and the *haricots blancs avec oignons* (white beans with onions). Bouilla- baisse is available on Fridays in winter for about $18. Desserts include spumoni and tortoni, as well as the most expected French offerings like *pêche Melba* and *poire Hélène.*

**ZEN PALATE, 663 Ninth Ave. at 46th Street. Tel. 582-
1669.**
   Cuisine: VEGETARIAN. **Reservations:** Recommended.
$ Prices: Appetizers $3–$7.50; main courses $9–$16; prix-fixe
   lunch $7–$10.
   Open: Lunch Mon–Sat 11:30am–3pm, Sun noon–3pm; dinner
   Mon–Sat 3pm–10:45pm, Sun 3–10:30pm. **Subway:** C or E to
   50th St. **Bus:** 49th St. Crosstown.

Through Zen meditation, "one can attempt to enter the realm of a worry-free space from a chaotic environment," explains the menu. You might say the same about Zen Palate, a stylish oasis from frenzied Ninth Avenue. From its understated, angular entryway to its highly original vegetarian cuisine, this place leaves both belly and soul satisfied. The closest to nouvelle Chinese I've ever seen, the menu brings a light touch to familiar appetizers—like dumplings and hot-and-sour soup—and exotic main courses—like Vegetable Bun- dles (zucchini, basil, black mushrooms, bamboo shoots, and water chestnuts wrapped with vegetarian ham) or Sweet-and-Sour Divine (deep-fried pecan puffs sautéed with sweet-and-sour sauce and peppers). Among the desserts, fried jelly rolls and tofu cheesecake stand out; the service is impeccable, too. At lunch, main courses include special rice, spring rolls, and dessert. Zen Palate does not have a liquor license, but you may bring your own bottle.
   Note: Zen Palate now has a second location: 34 Union Square East (corner of 16th Street; tel. 614-9345).

---

10. MIDTOWN EAST

EXPENSIVE

**ADRIENNE, in the Peninsula Hotel, 700 Fifth Ave., at 55th
Street. Tel. 903-3918.**
   Cuisine: CONTEMPORARY AMERICAN. **Reservations:** Recommended.
$ Prices: Appetizers $7–$18; main courses $19.50–$29; two-
   course pre-theater dinner $32; three-course pre-theater dinner
   $32.

Open: Lunch Mon–Fri noon–2:30pm; dinner Tues–Sat 6–10pm; pre-theater dinner 6–7:30pm; Sun brunch 11:30am–2:30pm. **Subway:** E or F to Fifth Ave.

To maintain one's sense of balance in New York, it sometimes helps to retreat somewhere that lets you forget the outside world. In midtown, the place to escape is Adrienne, an art deco jewel featuring globe-hopping cuisine of Louisiana-born Nicholas Rabalais. A recent menu offered such appetizers as salmon with dill beggar's purse and crawfish étouffé in a puff pastry leaf with essence of crawfish; the succulent main courses included Amish chicken confit, grilled tuna with black pepper and oyster couscous, and a roulade of veal tenderloin. Crown dinner in style with a dessert such as the warm flourless chocolate cake with pistachio ice cream. The pre-theater dinners offer good value. Solicitous service complements the superb cuisine.

DANIEL, 20 E. 76th St., between Fifth and Madison Avenues. Tel. 288-0033.

Cuisine: FRENCH. **Reservations:** Required.

$ **Prices:** Appetizers $9.50–$22; main courses $26.50–$33. Prix-fixe dinner $55–$85; prix-fixe lunch $31. AE, DC, MC, V.

Open: Lunch Mon–Thurs noon–2:30pm; dinner Mon–Thurs 5:45–10:30pm, Fri–Sat 5:45–11pm. **Subway:** 6 to 77th St.

This new restaurant has garnered numerous culinary accolades for chef Daniel Boulud, formerly of Le Cirque; it's widely considered to be one of the best new restaurants in the country. Even the decor reflects the highest standards of taste: All fabrics are imported from France, the china is by Limoges, and the circular foyer is paved with authentic 18th-century clay tiles. Daniel is decked with splendid antique mirrors and paintings by contemporary artists in the style of the French impressionists.

Appetizers are intricate, perfectly balanced creations like nine-herb ravioli with pine nuts in a tomato coulis or curried tuna tartare with radishes, chive, and celery. Main courses include a succulent and delectable roasted rib-eye chop with stuffed marrow bone, tender root vegetables, thick fries, and a peppery sauce; and a marvelous grilled salmon with savory on a bed of minced spinach, mushrooms, sweet onion, and a black olive jus. Service is beyond compare. You're certain to be lavished with attention in a way that's unique to Daniel.

Desserts by pastry chef Francois Payard might be rhubarb soup with strawberries in season, or passion fruit sorbet, or millefeuille of chocolate and mascarpone "tiramisù" with espresso sauce. A selection of imported cheeses can substitute for dessert, and extraordinary ice creams and sorbets are available. Jackets are required for men, but we can't imagine that anyone would mind dressing up for a meal here.

FELIDIA, 243 E. 58th St. Tel. 758-1479.

Cuisine: ITALIAN. **Reservations:** Recommended several days in advance.

$ **Prices:** Appetizers $7–$12; main courses $25–$28. AE, CB, DC, DISC, MC, V.

Open: Lunch Mon–Fri noon–3pm; dinner Mon–Sat 5pm–midnight. **Subway:** 4, 5, 6 or N, R to 59th St.

Felidia is one of the great Northern Italian restaurants of New York. The dining experience is exemplary and expensive, but it's well worth it. And the place is lovely, with brick and whitewashed walls, lush vegetation, skylights that create almost a greenhouse ambience, brocade chairs, and terra-cotta floors. And the food can be awe-inspiring.

You might start with a superb appetizer such as heady wild-mushroom soup or hearty minestrone. (Or you can have mussels in a sauce of garlic and white wine or grilled polenta with fonduta cheese and wild mushrooms.) Then proceed to poached salmon in mustard sauce or Dover sole, both outstanding. The calves' liver balsamic here is fantasy-perfect, and several unusual pasta dishes are wonderful, too. Daily specials often include roasted breast of pheasant or other game. Rare, fresh white truffles are often served with pastas. Desserts—fudge cake, raspberry tart, and blueberry cheesecake—are worth breaking any diet. Finish with some cappuccino and anisette, perhaps, and leave feeling totally content with the world.

Felidia's owner, Lydia Bastianich, shares her recipes and her life story in a highly praised book, *La cucina di Lydia* (Doubleday), which you can pick up on your way out of the restaurant.

THE FOUR SEASONS, 99 E. 52nd St. Tel. 745-9494.

Cuisine: CONTINENTAL. **Reservations:** Required.

$ Prices: Appetizers $9.50–$25; main courses $30–$45. Prix-fixe dinner from $26.50–$37.50 served in Grill Room 5:30–9pm Mon–Fri, 5–10:30pm Sat. AE, CB, DC, DISC, JCB, MC, V.

Open: Lunch Mon–Fri noon–2:15pm; dinner in Pool Room Mon–Fri 5–9pm, Sat 5–11:15pm. **Subway:** 6 to 51st St. or E, F to Lexington Ave.

★ One of the great showplace restaurants of New York—and the only one ever to be designated a New York City Landmark—the Four Seasons is a place where the food, wine, decor, and service are artfully combined to catch the spirit of New York today. As seasons change, so do the menus and decor. The art collection is highlighted by the world's largest Picasso and a 24-foot-long James Rosenquist painting. The restaurant is really two-in-one. The Pool Room, with its marble reflecting pool and lavish use of space, offers elaborate, inventive fare and formal service. The Grill Room, where the space is just as lavish, does things on a simpler scale, but this is where the movers and shakers of New York congregate for lunch. The wine cellar is considered one of the most complete in America.

There are several menus at the Four Seasons. In the Pool Room, there's a special pre-theater dinner from 5 to 6:15pm and post-theater dinner from 10 to 11:15pm—these are your best bet. Main courses that appear frequently on the menu include soft-shell crabs with herbs, mustard, and fiddlehead ferns; or grilled loin of rabbit with lemongrass and peanut sauce. And you can also choose from the highly popular Spa Cuisine menu for the health-conscious, with appetizers like mussels in green-chile sauce and main courses like escalope of sturgeon with tomatillo sauce or breast of pigeon with grilled polenta and shiitake mushrooms. Desserts might include flamed strawberry crêpe or guava-and-macadamia soufflé. In the Grill Room, lunch and dinner are offered on Monday to Friday (Saturday dinner only). The new "Grill at Night" menu offers a prix-fixe menu all evening long, plus a wine list of 30 vintages, all under $30. Jackets are required, ties requested. Dress up for the Pool Room: *Le tout New York* will be there.

LA COTE BASQUE, 5 E. 55th St. Tel. 688-6525.

Cuisine: FRENCH. **Reservations:** Required.

$ **Prices:** Prix-fixe dinner $58; prix-fixe lunch $31. AE, CB, DC, JCB, MC, V.

Open: Lunch Mon–Sat noon–2:30pm; dinner Mon–Sat 6–10:30pm. **Subway:** E or F to Fifth Ave.

La Côte Basque has long been one of the great dining places for the beautiful people, and beautiful it is. The Bernard Lamotte murals of St. Jean-de-Luz make you feel you're dining by the seaside in a French cafe; the service is gracious and courtly (especially if you're known to the management), and the company is top-drawer. For three decades now, La Côte Basque has been a favorite with a well-heeled crowd (they usually arrive by limo), who favor the traditional classics of French cooking, in generous portions. Among the appetizers on the prix-fixe menu are very light *quenelles,* a hearty *vol au vent de St. Jacques* or foie gras; main courses like *noisettes de veau, steak au poivre, ragoût de homard,* sweetbreads, and Long Island bay scallops are always excellent. Game dishes are also well prepared. For dessert, there are heady temptations of sorbets and *pâtisseries,* and sinful delights like *mousse au chocolat* or *mousse au Grand Marnier.* Fruit tarts are memorable, and few desserts can compare with the frozen raspberry soufflé with fresh berries.

LE PERIGORD, 405 E. 52nd St., east of First Avenue. Tel. 755-6244.

Cuisine: CLASSIC FRENCH. **Reservations:** Recommended.

$ **Prices:** Prix-fixe lunch $29; prix-fixe dinner $49 (with selected dishes available at an additional $3–$15).

Open: Lunch Mon–Fri noon–3pm; dinner Mon–Sat 5:15–10:30pm. Open Sun for private parties of 35–100 only. Ties and jackets required at all times. **Subway:** E or F to Lexington–Third Aves.

One of New York's favorite French restaurants for almost 30 years, Le Périgord is named for the province in southwest France where, historically, luxuries like truffles and foie gras are as plentiful as fresh croissants in the morning. And, indeed, stepping into Le Périgord is like traveling back in time. The tone in the dining room evokes that found in a typical French château restaurant, where dulcet tones seem fitting. A soft din is punctuated only by the occasional tinkling of goblets. The considerate service could be described as *en famille,* if your warm yet slightly formal family happens to be landed gentry.

Chef Antoine Bouterin, born in Provence, creates food that is both earthy and sophisticated. The five-course prix-fixe lunch could include light asparagus or artichoke in vinaigrette, delicate crêpe of sweetbread, or tasty vegetable tart with lemon butter. A full-bodied lobster bisque, grilled salmon, and roast duck with seasonal fresh fruits are just a few of the specialties. The prix-fixe dinner will permit you such treats as melt-in-your-mouth marinated salmon, light but hearty smoked trout Napoléon, noodles bedecked with shrimp and smoked salmon, lush sautéed bay scallops, grilled Dover sole, or veal kidney with Burgundy sauce.

The array of desserts is dazzling—chocolate mousse, second-to-none chocolate cake, distinctive "floating islands" of meringue and caramel, and unforgettable chocolate soufflé. All are perfect finales for your exquisite and leisurely meal at Le Périgord.

LESPINASSE, in the St. Regis Hotel, 7 East 85th St. Tel. 339-6719.
Cuisine: EUROPEAN/ASIAN. **Reservations:** Required.
$ Prices: Lunch: Prix fixe $39.50; dinner: Appetizers $14 to $26, main courses $27–$35; Vegetarian Tasting Menu $51; Prix fixe $67. AE, CB, DC, DISC, JCB, MC, V.
Open: Breakfast 7–10:30am daily; lunch noon–2pm Mon–Sat; dinner 6–10pm Mon–Sat. **Subway:** 4, 5, or 6 to 86th St.

★ Since it was recently awarded a coveted 4-star rating from the *New York Times,* the telephones at Lespinasse have been ringing off the hook. You may have to wait up to a month for a weekend dinner reservation, maybe two weeks for a weeknight reservation, a week to book lunch—or, you may luck out and pick up a cancellation or a less-than-prime-time reservation at the last minute. Whatever you have to do to sample the spectacular food that Chef Gray Kunz has created, do it and thank your lucky stars you can. This is not just good cooking, not just great cooking, it is superlative cooking, among the best to be found in New York. It doesn't get much better.

The dining room, a study in Louis XV gilded elegance, is spacious and lovely, with a Waterford crystal chandelier, striking flowers, Limoges china, and deep armchairs to sink into. But what really dazzles here is the food. Chef Kunz, classically trained in the French kitchens of Switzerland, spent the first 10 years of his life in Singapore, where he developed a lifelong feel for the exotic tastes of Asia, especially those of India, Malaysia, and Thailand. He puts these elements together in ways that are shockingly tasty. One of his signature main courses, steamed black bass, is served with a fragrant lovage broth. Another, braised salmon—the most tender I've ever tasted—arrives on a bed of crisped artichokes with a Shyra (red wine) reduction, mysteriously tasting of just a hint of kokum (lotus seed) and thyme. A mushroom fricassée spooned over herbed risotto flavored with a truffle-infused oil is a wonderful beginning to your meal; so is the salad of shrimp with a kaffir remoulade, or chilled cucumber soup flavored with dill and lemon balm. The menu changes seasonally, but whatever you have will be special. So, too, are the desserts: A ginger-chocolate mousse with passion fruit and mango and a crêpe of sour cherries with vanilla rice pudding are unforgettable. The wine list is well thought out and not overly pricey. Considering the quality of the fare, the prix-fixe lunch of $39.50 (with no supplementary charges) is eminently fair. Vegetarians will know they've reached nirvana when they sample the $51 Vegetarian Tasting Menu in the evening (crisped zucchini blossoms, marinated vegetables with kaffir remoulade, and popcorn sprouts, and the like). The four-course tasting menu is another good offering at $67, and there is an ample à la carte menu as well. Service is elegant and unobtrusive.

LUTECE, 249 E. 50th St. Tel. 752-2225.
Cuisine: FRENCH. **Reservations:** Required—accepted up to one month in advance.
$ Prices: Prix-fixe dinner $60; prix-fixe lunch $38. AE, CB, DC, MC, V.
Open: Lunch Tues–Fri noon–2pm, dinner Mon–Sat 6–10pm.
Closed: Sun and major holidays, Sat in summer, the entire month of August. **Subway:** 6 to 51st St.; E or F to Lexington Ave.

⭐ One of the ultimate French restaurants in New York must surely be Lutèce, where André Soltner serves what many consider the finest haute cuisine in the city. You can sit in a greenhouse setting where the city landscape is reflected hazily under a Mylar dome or, in colder weather, upstairs in the elegant dining room typical of a private town house. The food can be as unreal as this gracious setting. The prix-fixe menus are good value for a New York restaurant of this caliber. Among the appetizers at lunch, the fish pâté and all the *pâtés en croûte* are superbly flavored. For your main course, ask what the chef has dreamed up for the day. Good lunch menu choices are *poulet en croûte, escalopes de veau,* and delicate filet of sole amandine. Everything is prepared in the grand manner and served with flair. For dessert, you can't surpass the rich *mousse au chocolat au rhum* or the light and lovely *tarte tatin.*

The dinner menu is much more extensive, with a variety of amazing appetizers (salmon, mousse of duckling with juniper berries, sauté of lobster); and main courses like the house specialty, the *mignon de boeuf en feuilleté Lutèce* (a variation of beef Wellington), filet of lamb with peppercorns, and sweetbreads with capers. Rabbit is often available and especially well prepared here. The desserts are classics: *crêpes flambées* Alsatian style, frozen raspberry soufflé, and a warm soufflé, which you must remember to order at the beginning of your meal.

MARCH, 408 E. 58th St. Tel. 838-9393.
Cuisine: AMERICAN. **Reservations:** Recommended.
$ Prices: $40, $55, $100, $175 prix-fixe dinners. AE, DC, MC, V.
Open: Dinner only, Mon–Thurs 6–10pm, Fri–Sat 6–10:30pm.
Bus: Any First Ave. bus. **Subway:** 4, 5, 6 or N, R to 59th St./Lexington Ave.

⭐ A veteran of the venerable Quilted Giraffe and La Colombe d'Or, chef Wayne Nish (along with co-owner/host Joseph Scalice) struck out on his own with this small, sumptuous spot in a swank Sutton Place town house, especially nice when the garden is open in warm weather. With a "cosmopolitan" cuisine that sometimes combines seemingly discordant elements, Nish spins gold from strange bedfellows like jumbo shrimp tempura with pomegranate and spicy carrot sauces; five-spice North Atlantic salmon with sherry vinegar and roast chicken sauce; and winter vegetable ravioli in game broth with fresh herbs. Nish's desserts boast equal artistry and attention to detail: Don't miss the crispy pancake with vanilla ice cream, mango, and berries; the warm Valrhona chocolate cake with whipped cream; and March's signature dessert: grapefruit sorbet and grapefruit sections in gin syrup with coriander seed. Three-course prix-fixe menus start at $40; a seasonal menu is $55; a tasting menu without wine is $70; with four glasses of selected wines, $100; and a nine-course gourmand menu is $175. Scalice has designed a room as inspired as the cooking, with a graceful Chinese tapestry on one wall; turn-of-the-century chandeliers; reproduction Biedermeier furnishings; and, in colder months, a roaring fireplace. His wine list has won the *Wine Spectator*'s "Award of Excellence."

MODERATE

AMARCORD, 7 E. 59th St. Tel. 935-3535.
Cuisine: CONTEMPORARY ITALIAN. **Reservations:** Recommended.

$ Prices: Appetizers $7–$9.50; main courses $15–$28. AE, DC, MC, V.
Open: Lunch daily noon–3pm; dinner daily 5:30–11:30pm.
Subway: 4, 5, 6 or N, R to 59th St./Lexington Ave.

Some of the best contemporary Italian fare in the city is not in Little Italy but only a heartbeat away from Central Park. With its low ceilings, blond wood chairs upholstered in muted hues, and a well-heeled crowd, Amarcord offers a stylish setting and an outstanding menu. Amid huge displays of flowers, models bat their eyelashes at their dates, and diners have a difficult time restraining themselves from sampling their dinner companions as well.

Amarcord means "I remember" in Italian dialect, and the exquisite Italian fare with a modern twist celebrates the Emilia-Romagna region of Italy, the birthplace of balsamic vinegar and tortellini. Of the main courses, the seafood ravioli with artichokes are sublime, delicately blended and loaded with shrimp, and the braised turkey leg with white wine, spinach, leeks, herb, cognac, and polenta is equally tempting.

Even the breadsticks are artfully presented, with prosciutto and a careful splash of olive oil. Those ordering tuna tartare will find the tasty appetizer anointed at tableside with a few drops of authentic balsamic vinegar—from a dropper, no less. You can also choose from other tempting starters, including radicchio and quail-egg salad in a warm bacon dressing and sweetbreads sautéed with mushrooms and cabbage. The personable Italian staff with classic good looks right out of a Botticelli painting graciously attend to your needs.

You'll think you're dreaming when you taste the warm chocolate cake with its petal of crisp chocolate wafer, hazelnut ganache with sugar sprinkled like snow on the plate. Or try the Sabbiosa, a very light poundcake with mascarpone cream and fresh berries that's also special.

MAD. 61, 10 E. 61st St. Tel. 833-2200.

Cuisine: AMERICAN. **Reservations:** Recommended.
$ Prices: Appetizers $6.50–$8.50; main courses $16–$27. AE, MC, V.
Open: Lunch Mon–Sat 11:30am–3:30pm; Sun 12:30–3:30pm; dinner Mon–Sat 5:30–10:45pm, Sun 5:30–10pm. **Subway:** N or R to Fifth Ave.

In the heart of one of Manhattan's toniest shopping districts is one of Manhattan's toniest stores, Barney's; and in the basement of Barney's is Mad. 61, a magnet for everyone from tourists in T-shirts to power brokers and shopaholics, sleek Barney's bags in tow. A fountain dominates the center of the dining area and a blue-and-white–striped awning covers the partially open ceiling, allowing diners to glimpse the legions of ecstatic shoppers upstairs. Pleasant pop music at low decibel level, soft lighting, and low, cushy, stylish chairs make this the perfect spot to recuperate after a hard day of shopping.

You're sure to get a kick out of the fresh, sprightly presentation of dishes here. Of the appetizers, one of the best is the asparagus salad with beets, leeks, and drops of vinaigrette dressing sprinkled on the plate with utmost care and topped with Roquefort cheese. The warm goat-cheese-and-artichoke salad is also popular. Luckily, in case you forget your manners, each plate is decorated with an image of a fork on the left and a knife on the right. Entrées will not leave you feeling overstuffed; smoked grilled salmon with Savoy cabbage and roasted turnips is perfection, and Amish chicken with a light garlic glaze, garnished with shoestring potatoes, could not be more satisfying. Valrhona chocolate cake served warm with crème fraîche ice cream looks like an unassuming little piece of cake, but it is extraordinary. You'll also find "cheeses for meditation" and other superb desserts, including warm apple tart with caramel ice cream and banana sorbet fudge sundae with pralines and whipped cream.

Mad. 61 also carries an impressive selection of beers from everywhere from Brooklyn to Thailand and features a market dining area, a wine bar with 34 selections to choose from, an espresso bar, and a retail counter offering prepared foods and gourmet packaged foods.

DOCKS OYSTER BAR & SEAFOOD GRILL, 633 Third Ave., at 40th Street. Tel. 986-8080.

Cuisine: SEAFOOD. **Reservations:** Recommended.

$ Prices: Appetizers $4.50–$40; main courses $8.75–$27. AE, DC, MC, V.

Open: Lunch Mon–Fri 11:30am–3pm; dinner Sun–Thurs 5–11pm, Sat–Sun 5pm–midnight; brunch Sun 11:30am–3pm. **Subway:** 4, 5, 6, 7, or Times Square Shuttle to Grand Central.

Looking for the quintessential American seafood restaurant in New York? Look no farther than Docks. Hardwood floors, brass-and-mahogany rails, and tiled columns make for an updated deco-nautical setting. Docks is popular with businesspeople, as midtown professionals crowd the bar after work, but it also makes for an ideal family restaurant.

Chef Stanley Kramer uses a light touch with sauces and seasoning to bring out the true flavor of Docks's seafood, bought fresh every day. Kramer's philosophy is unusual seafood served simply. For an appetizer adventure, try the chilled Maine sea urchins. Those brave enough to dig their spoons into the orange-colored lobes inside these spiny creatures will be rewarded with a unique, sweet, and oceany taste experience. For a more traditional appetizer, the mussels in rich tomato broth are extra large and not overwhelmed by garlic.

For a killer main course, order the blackened medallions of Block Island swordfish in a light barbecue sauce with white wine and spices. The swordfish is complimented by sweet-potato purée with a hint of nutmeg. The Alaskan white salmon, when available, is rich and buttery and highly recommended. Also excellent is the halibut in tomato-and-rosemary vinaigrette. Docks's amazing Key lime pie is made on the premises. The mud-fudge cake, complete with an ice-cream sundae, is the ultimate rich and gooey treat—very appropriate for birthdays. Be forewarned: You'll have to split it; it's enormous. Docks's also offers a reasonable wine list and a bountiful Sunday brunch at $11.50 per person.

ROSA MEXICANO, 1063 First Ave., at 58th Street. Tel. 753-7407.

Cuisine: MEXICAN. **Reservations:** Recommended.

$ Prices: Appetizers $5.75–$11; main courses $15.50–$24. AE, CB, DC, MC, V.

Open: Dinner only, daily 5pm–midnight. **Subway:** 4, 5, 6 or N, R to 59th St./Lexington Ave.

Don't expect the usual Tex-Mex food and ambience here. Instead, join the delighted throngs who come here (and keep coming back) for the classic regional Mexican cuisine, served in a warm and inviting house-party atmosphere. My favorite Mexican restaurant in New York is the creation of Josefina Howard, who is credited for leading much of the current "Mexican Revolution" in the city. Rosa Mexicano is a study in pinks and mauves, with tall Mexican-colonial wooden chairs and tables flanking the long tile bar and an open grill, or *parilla*. Choose the first room for bustle and sparkle; opt for the back room for quiet conversation in a setting of tropical plantings.

Start your dinner with a margarita made tangy with fresh pomegranate juice, then sit back and study the menu. Someone in your party should have the knockout guacamole, prepared right at your table, and someone else should order the cold seafood platter, the better to sample the superb ceviche, shrimp, oysters, and more. The main courses offer delightful choices: unusual enchiladas filled with chicken and topped with a mole sauce that includes chocolate as well as 19 other spices; *crêpes camarones,* filled with chopped shrimp and served with a chile pasilla sauce; and *pescado en cilantro,* baked filet of fish with fresh coriander, tomato, and onion. Desserts, too, are wondrous: flan with a sauce of cactus pears or fresh pineapple sautéed with coconut and pecans. The service is gracious and friendly.

SNAPS, 230 Park Ave., at 46th Street. Tel. 949-7878.
  Cuisine: SCANDINAVIAN. **Reservations:** Recommended.
$ Prices: Appetizers $7–$9; main courses $18–$22; prix-fixe dinner $19.95. AE, DC, MC, V.
  Open: Breakfast Mon–Fri 7:30–10am; lunch Mon–Fri noon–2:30pm; dinner Mon–Sat 5:30–10:30pm; prix-fixe dinner 5:30–6:30pm. **Subway:** 4, 5, 6, 7, or Times Square Shuttle to Grand Central.

Smart, sophisticated, Scandinavian—Snaps is *rara avis* in New York. There's only one other top-notch Scandinavian restaurant in Manhattan, Snaps's more expensive sister restaurant, Aquavit (see "Midtown West," above). Here at Snaps, in a spacious room with bright yellow walls, large windows, and oversize ceilings from which a boat is suspended, you dine more reasonably (especially if you opt for lunch and have one of the open-face *smorrebrod* sandwiches, for around $8, or if you have the prix-fixe or pre-theater menu at dinner). Whether it's lunch or dinner, you'll want to start off with one of the bracing *aquavits* (potato-based vodkas), laced with a hint of citron, or berries, or fennel and caraway seeds. Appetizers are marvelous: You can choose from a variety of herrings (this is Scandinavian food, after all) or go with the wonderful warm potato cake (julienned potatoes baked and topped with gravlax); or try the equally delicious Jansson's Temptation, julienned potatoes in a casserole, with crème fraîche and Swedish anchovies. The house specialty is grilled seafood, so you can't go wrong with main courses like salmon in wild-mushroom sauce and trout roe or a wonderful dish of sea scallops with warm purple potato salad and herb sauce; venison ragout with mushrooms and grilled mallard duck with sundried-cranberry and Port sauce are good choices for game lovers. Desserts are ethereal: The warm chocolate cake with espresso sauce and hazelnut is the stuff that sweet dreams are made of. Stop by at breakfast time, too, and feast on yummy Swedish pancakes or a traditional Scandinavian breakfast plate, complete with smoked salmon and herring.

TRUMPETS, in the Grand Hyatt New York, Park Avenue at 42nd Street. Tel. 850-5999.
  Cuisine: REGIONAL AMERICAN. **Reservations:** Recommended.
$ **Prices:** Appetizers $6–$8; appetizer plates for sharing $14–$18; main courses $15–$24.
  Open: Dinner only, Mon–Sat 5:30–10:30pm. **Subway:** 4, 5, 6, 7, or Times Square Shuttle to Grand Central.

Candlelight and quiet, a sheltered oasis away from the busy world outside—it's hardly what one expects but exactly what one finds at Trumpets, in the midst of the glamorous, glittering lobby of the Grand Hyatt. In this traditional setting done in tones of beige, brown, and rust, with burled elm and beveled-mirror panels, the tables are comfortably placed for conversation. The chef presents a superb menu. He will come to your table to discuss your selections and honor any special requests (if you're on any special diet regime, call him a day before and he'll whip up something heart-healthy or macrobiotic or whatever you like). Warm appetizers are a delight: Try the earthy Oregon State shiitakes sautéed with garlic, chives, and white-wine reduction; skilled-seared shrimp with red Fresno chiles and egg noodles; wonderfully crisp calamari with baby lettuce and sesame-ginger vinaigrette. Fish is done very nicely here, especially the Dover sole sautéed with almonds, lemon, and Chardonnay, and the crispy gulf snapper with egg noodles and cilantro with lime broth. Wisconsin veal scaloppine with spinach and capers and Sonoma lamb are other good choices. Desserts are the best of the best—at least one person in your party should order one of the irresistible hot soufflés (Grand Marnier, chocolate, hazelnut, and more), and somebody should definitely have the double chocolate torte with brandied cherries or the delectable lemon chiffon with fresh raspberries and blackberries.

VONG, 200 E. 54th St. Tel. 486-9592.
  Cuisine: THAI-FRENCH. **Reservations:** Recommended.
$ **Prices:** Appetizers $8–$14; main courses $16–$22. AE, MC, V.
  Open: Lunch Mon–Fri noon–2:30pm; dinner Mon–Fri 6–11pm, Sat 5:30–11pm; Sun 5:30–10pm. **Subway:** 4, 5, or 6 to 51st St, E or F to Lexington Ave.

⭐ You've tried Thai food and French food; now try a new taste thrill: Thai-French cuisine, as interpreted by one of New York's wünderkind chefs, Jean-Georges Vongerichten, also wooing the crowds at Jo-Jo's (see "Upper East Side," below). It's not hard to see why New York foodies consider it the most exciting new kitchen in town. The staid marble exterior of the Revlon building gives no hint of the dramatic, Southeast Asian feel of the restaurant inside, done in striking tones of salmon and burnt orange, with curving teak walls, a handsome collage of golden leaves, bits of maps, and Thai letters on a wall up front. A geometric pagoda dominates the dining room, which boasts floral banquettes, slate tables, and blown-glass pink-tulip lights hanging from the ceiling. In some places the ceilings are gold, reflected in the woven-brass trays in which your food arrives.

Don't miss the irresistible appetizers: The delicate crab spring roll with tamarind dipping sauce is perfectly blended, and you'll marvel over the fabulous raw tuna and vegetables in rice paper. The egg-noodle soup with shredded duck and preserved lime is miraculously not greasy. The soup of chicken in coconut milk and galanga is delicious, and the shrimp with lemongrass-and-bergamot-leaf broth is tangy and wonderful.

Main courses like rabbit curry bask in the chef's signature contrasting sauces made without butter or cream. The black bass with wok-fried napa cabbage is smooth and lightly buttery, and the boneless sliced duck Oriental is delightfully easy to eat. Side orders of rice and vegetables, like grilled Asian eggplant and pineapple fried rice, are yours for the asking. Desserts are the very definition of exotic: Consider the banana-and-passion-fruit salad with white-pepper ice cream or the roast Asian pear with licorice ice cream and ginger sableuse.

Vong attracts a chic Madison Avenue crowd with dashes of Hollywood flash. With its white-rimmed pastel plates, very cool feel, and delicate yet satisfying food, it gives the impression that a catastrophe at Vong would be defined as nothing worse than a busboy dropping a plate or someone's Chanel bag falling to the floor. Perhaps the bowl of goldfish in the men's room best embodies the mod Zen demeanor. Fortunately, you don't have to meditate to achieve a state of bliss here; you simply have to order.

Lipstick Café, 855 Third Ave., at 53rd Street (tel. 486-8664), Vong's neighboring glass-walled offshoot, is proof positive that lunch in midtown can be pleasant, intriguing, and inexpensive. Lipstick's varied yet compact lunchtime menu features substantial salads, like roast leg of lamb with artichokes and salad of mixed beans and marinated wild mushrooms; there also are daily galettes, including potato gorgonzola and fromage blanc, onion, and bacon. Even the sandwiches are exceptional, served with vegetable chips and mesclun salad. You might have roast veal on a baguette with arugula emulsion or egg salad with asparagus and homemade ketchup. For dessert, you can choose from luscious out-of-the-ordinary offerings like the banana dome with rum anglaise or pineapple soup with coconut sorbet. Lipstick Café is open Monday through Friday from 7:30am to 4pm. Appetizers and main courses range from $5.50 to $12; there is a $5 minimum per person.

11. LINCOLN CENTER/ UPPER WEST SIDE

A sophisticated dinner on the Upper West Side used to mean Szechuan Chinese. But over the last decade, gentrification and yuppification have altered the landscape. Today, this part of town boasts some of New York's quirkiest, coziest places—plus some of its best values. I recommend the following, in addition to those given full descriptions below: **Sfuzzi,** 58 W. 65th St. (tel. 873-3700), near Lincoln Center, serves moderately priced Italian bistro fare, featuring pizza, pasta, and delectable desserts in a Romelike setting with faux architectural ruins and friezes. Check out the prix-fixe pre-theater special at $29.95 from 5 to 7pm. Capacious **Carmine's,** 2450 Broadway at 91st St. (tel. 362-2200), offers gargantuan "family-style" portions of old-fashioned Italian food. Dark, bustling **Docks,** 2427 Broadway at 90th Street (tel. 724-5588), prides itself on impeccably fresh fish and seafood; and the chic, clubby **Poiret,** 474 Columbus Ave. at 83rd Street (tel. 724-6880), is lauded by locals for fine French fare.

For the health conscious, both **Mana,** 2444 Broadway at 90th Street (tel. 787-1110), and **Ozu,** 566 Amsterdam Ave. at 87th Street (tel. 787-8316), provide macrobiotic and natural Japanese cooking in simple, spare settings; **Mary Ann's,** 2452 Broadway at 91st Street (tel. 877-0132), offers inexpensive Mexican fare in a sprightly setting. **Josie's,** 300 Amsterdam Ave. at 74th Street (tel. 769-1212), packs in a neighborhood and Lincoln Center crowd for very fresh, superbly prepared seafood at very fair prices; and **Trattoria Sambuca** (tel. 787-5656), 20 W. 72nd St., just off Central Park West, dishes out tasty, generous portions of old-fashioned Italian food, family style. And they have a terrific Sunday brunch buffet.

On the homey front, join the neighbors at the warm, welcoming **Popover Café,** 551 Amsterdam Ave. at 87th Street (tel. 595-8555), for satisfying soups, sandwiches, and luscious popovers. On weekends, neither rain nor snow nor sleet deters crowds from **Sarabeth's Kitchen,** 423 Amsterdam Ave. at 81st Street (tel. 496-6280), or its younger rival **Good Enough to Eat,** 483 Amsterdam Ave. at 83rd Street (tel. 496-0163); the sublime comfort food and hearty brunches make the long waits worthwhile. On Sunday, the masses also flock to **Barney Greengrass,** "The Sturgeon King," 541 Amsterdam Ave. at 86th Street (tel. 724-4707)—a classic, 1908 New York deli—where lox and bagels become high art. Don't miss the scrambled eggs with Nova Scotia salmon. Even more down to earth—with prices to match—is **EJ's Luncheonette,** 433 Amsterdam Ave. at 81st Street (tel. 873-3444), which cleans up classic diner food in a whimsical 1950s setting. For dessert, the crowded **Café Lalo,** 201 W. 83rd Street (tel. 496-6031), a favorite for sinful sweets, is about as close as you'll get to Paris in New York.

EXPENSIVE

CAFE DES ARTISTES, 1 W. 67th St. Tel. 877-3500.
   Cuisine: FRENCH. **Reservations:** Recommended a week or two in advance.
$ **Prices:** Appetizers $6–$15; main courses $17–$29; three-course prix-fixe dinner $32.50; three-course prix-fixe lunch $19.50; Great Dessert Plate $19.50; Sun brunch main courses $10–$23.
   Open: Lunch Mon–Sat noon–3pm; dinner Mon–Sat 5:30pm–midnight, Sun 5:30–11pm; brunch Sun 10am–3pm. **Bus:** M104 to 68th St. and Broadway. **Subway:** 1 or 9 to 66th St.

Many of its regular customers like to think of Café des Artistes as their neighborhood restaurant—and when the neighborhood happens to be Lincoln Center, this means that the regulars are apt to be celebrities: For example, James Levine of the Metropolitan Opera or Barbara Walters of ABC. But long before there was a Lincoln Center, artistic-minded New Yorkers were enjoying the fine art of eating good food in this stylish, European cafe atmosphere. The restored Howard Chandler Christy murals of nude wood nymphs can provide a lively topic of conversation if you happen to sit up in the bustling front dining room (a quieter, less formal dining room near the bar in back offers no murals but more privacy for conversation).

The menu is huge and eclectic. You might start with a plate of cold salmon in four variations or a dish of sweetbread headcheese with cucumber from the charcuterie. The menu changes daily and may include lusty *pot au feu,* paillard of swordfish with mustard-and-butter sauce, and stuffed breast of veal. You might, however, wish to eat lightly here and save your strength: For the true glutton there is the "Great Dessert Plate"—a piece of every pie, cake, and pastry on the changing menu—and the hazelnut gianduia, toasted-orange pound cake, macadamia-nut pie, and homemade sherbets are worth the wait. Café des Artistes is also fine for Sunday brunch, which features cold buffet plates and an extensive choice of favorite egg dishes. Jackets are required for men after 5pm.

CAFE LUXEMBOURG, 200 W. 70th St. Tel. 873-7411.

Cuisine: FRENCH/AMERICAN. **Reservations:** Required on weekends and for pre-theater dinner (5:30–6:30pm).

$ **Prices:** Appetizers $6.75–$10; main courses $16–$28.00; prix-fixe dinner $28.50 (5:30–6:30pm and after 10:30pm); Sun brunch $8.50–$17.

Open: Lunch Tues–Sat noon–3pm; brunch Sun 11am–3pm; dinner Mon–Sat 5:30pm–12:30am, Sun 10–11:30pm. **Subway:** 1, 2, 3, or 9 to 72nd St.

Café Luxembourg has won itself a reputation as an oasis of outstanding cooking on New York's trendy Upper West Side and as a haven for glitterati—Steve Martin, Barbra Streisand, Mick Jagger, and the entire cast of "Saturday Night Live" have been patrons. Were it not for the high noise level, it would be just about perfect. The decor—yellow and blue tile, mirrored center columns, tile floors, and colorful wicker chairs—is cheery and cozy. The wide-ranging à la carte menu is a masterful combination of French modern and American fresh; it changes seasonally. To start your meal, either the baby artichokes or country salad come highly recommended. Follow these with roast leg of lamb, cassoulet (in winter), grilled salmon or wild-mushroom risotto. Pasta du jour is $16.50 and fish du jour is market priced. Desserts are uniformly delicious, with special kudos for the chocolate mousse, crème brûlée, and lemon tart.

FISHIN' EDDIE, 73 W. 71st St. Tel. 874-3474.

Cuisine: ITALIAN-ACCENTED SEAFOOD. **Reservations:** Recommended.

$ **Prices:** Appetizers $5.50–$9.95; main courses $12–$19.95; three-course pre- and post-theater menu $24.95. AE, DC, MC, V.

Open: Dinner Mon–Fri 5pm–midnight, Sun 5–11pm. **Subway:** 1, 2, 3, or 9 to 72nd Street.

Owner Vince Orgera calls Fishin' Eddie "a neighborhood restaurant that goes beyond the neighborhood"—and he's right. However, it's not so neighborhood that you feel out of place while enjoying some of the most soul-satisfying seafood dishes to be found anywhere in Manhattan. Big solid-oak tables topped with Fiestaware and high-backed rope-weave chairs dominate the dining room; little brass lamps glow on each table. With its weather-beaten rustic furniture, Fishin' Eddie seems so authentic you'd almost expect the room to tilt with the waves. A lot of couples meet after work for dinner, and it's easy to see why—it's the perfect setting for a rainy-weather tête-à-tête.

Chef Scott Campbell has an amazing way with beans, often used to complement the splendid seafood. For an unbelievably tantalizing appetizer, try the grilled shrimp with white beans. The smoky flavor and smoothness are simply mesmerizing. The salads present an arresting and imaginative array of greens: The endive, pear, gorgonzola, and walnut salad is excellent. For a main course, specials like sautéed striped bass with warm lentil salad show off Campbell's expertise and finely tuned sense of proportion, as does the blackened mahimahi with perfect mashed potatoes.

For dessert, the chocolate-walnut cake is deliciously moist and nutty, and the pecan pie will surprise you with a rich cache of nuts. The wait staff are genuinely nice and accommodating.

Fishin' Eddie features a pre-theater menu Monday to Saturday before 6:30pm and after 10:30pm.

GABRIEL'S, 11 W. 60th St., between Broadway and Columbus Avenue. Tel. 956-4600.
   Cuisine: NORTHERN ITALIAN. **Reservations:** Recommended.
$ Prices: Appetizers $6.50–$9; main courses $14–$28. AE, MC, V.
   Open: Lunch Mon–Fri noon–3pm; dinner Mon–Thurs 5:30–11pm, Fri–Sat 5:30pm–midnight. Closed Sun. **Subway:** 1, 9, A, B, C, D to 59th Street/Columbus Circle.

With its warm, ochre walls, well-spaced tables and large, curved bar in front, Gabriel's plays host to a potpourri of fascinating people, from glitzy high-profile types from the entertainment industry to downtown artists and a sizable pretheater crowd.

Gabriel's is known for its wood-grilled dishes, including appetizers like grilled portobello mushrooms and a tremendously popular grilled tuna sausage. It's also known for its homemade pastas, among them the pappardelle, a broad noodle, served with rabbit, chanterelle mushrooms, and prunes; a fabulous artichoke lasagna; and homemade gnocchi served with fresh baby herbs.

Entrées get high marks too; the grilled young chicken marinated with buttermilk is exquisitely tender, and the sea bass baked in terra cotta with artichoke hearts and potatoes is seafood as it was meant to be. Of the desserts, try the heady and sweet chocolate and bourbon pound cake with mascarpone ice cream or the amazing ricotta cheesecake with fresh strawberry compote. You can also choose from a selection of homemade gelati, with flavors like hazelnut and blood orange.

IRIDIUM, 44 W. 63rd St. Tel. 582-2121.
   Cuisine: AMERICAN REGIONAL. **Reservations:** Recommended.
$ Prices: Appetizers $6–$11; main courses $16–$23. AE, CB, DC, DISC, MC, V.
   Open: Lunch Mon–Thurs 11:30am–3pm; dinner Sun–Thurs 5pm–midnight, Fri–Sat 5pm–12:30am; brunch Sat 11:30am–3pm, Sun 11:30am–4pm. **Subway:** 1, 9, A, B, C, D to 59th St./Columbus Circle.

With furniture and fixtures that appear to be in motion, evoking Bedrock if it were designed by Salvador Dalí, Iridium is a one-of-a-kind place. It's a playful blur of color and shapes that will put your imagination into overdrive as you take in the prehistoric-meets-surreal surroundings. Mosaic tile floors in brilliant colors and mohair upholstered furniture in eccentric shapes compete for attention, while cabinets and shelves lean and twist and seem to be melting.

Despite it all, it's easy to focus on the food, as it shows just as much imagination.

Innovative appetizers include stone-oven roasted quail or mussel chowder with red onion, potato, and herbs. Entrées are created to intrigue the palate as well and include a hearty stone-oven roasted breast of chicken with confit of leg, chayote, pearl onion, and roasted apple sauce; pan-roasted cod on potato purée with niçoise and picholine olives, dried tomato and roasted garlic butter. Desserts include an eye-catching chocolate mousse with grillatine cherries served in a tall glass and a mouth-watering coconut parfait within an intricate cage of chocolate.

Brunch dishes will woo you with selections like a luscious chocolate-and-banana French toast and either apple-smoked sausage or bacon, while the lunch menu includes venison chili served with Brooklyn brown beer. There is a minimum food charge at tables of $15 per person.

MICKEY MANTLE'S RESTAURANT AND SPORTS BAR, 42 Central Park South, between Fifth and Sixth avenues. Tel. 688-7777.

Cuisine: CONTEMPORARY AMERICAN. **Reservations:** Recommended.

$ Prices: Appetizers $4.95–$7.95; main courses $9.95–$19.95; Little League Menu (children's portions) $6.95–$7.95. AE, CB, DC, DISC, JCB, MC, V.

Open: Mon–Sat noon–1am, Sun noon–midnight; same menu served continuously. **Bus:** M5, M6, or M7. **Subway:** N or R to Fifth Ave.

Here's a place that will please both you and the kids. Named for the legendary New York Yankees slugger, Mickey Mantle's gets top ratings for its display of museum-quality memorabilia as well as for its something-for-everyone menu. A commemorative plaque from Yankee Stadium's centerfield, on the restaurant's front door, shares billing with vintage photographs, paintings, and lithographs (many for sale, along with souvenirs). The Mick himself frequently stops by and is, I am told, very gracious about autographing baseballs and the like. Other pro athletes and celebrities also tend to hang out here. A sidewalk cafe facing Central Park across the street is a plus in summer.

The cuisine is Mickey Mantle's selection of "home-cooking" Oklahoma delights, starting with such appetizers as fried calamari with spicy tomato sauce, blue-corn nachos with guacamole and salsa, and southern-fried chicken fingers. The main courses are home-run caliber: sublime chef's salad prepared with grilled sirloin, roast chicken, and fresh mozzarella; linguine with seared shrimp; and chicken-fried steak with mashed potatoes and cream gravy. As side dishes, try Texas onion rings; smoky baked-bean stew; and fried waffle potatoes, a house specialty. "Spring Training Specials" include grilled and roasted vegetables and wild mushrooms with vegetable lasagne and red-pepper marmalade, a vegetarian's delight. Non-calorie counters can indulge in such desserts as chocolate chunk rice pudding; fresh berry crumb cobbler à la mode; and hot-fudge-and-brownie sundae, to name a heavenly few.

SHUN LEE WEST, 43 W. 65th St. Tel. 595-8895.

Cuisine: CHINESE. **Reservations:** Recommended.

$ Prices: Appetizers $4.50–$14.95; main courses $12.95–$35. AE, CB, DC, MC, V.
Open: Mon–Sat noon–midnight, Sun noon–10pm. **Subway:** 1 or 9 to 66th St./Lincoln Center.

Long a darling of the food critics, Shun Lee West, half a block from Lincoln Center, is a large, sleek establishment where Chinese food takes on a new meaning. No chow mein or egg foo yung is served here. Rather, there is the delicate Neptune's Net—fresh-sliced shrimp, scallops, sea bass, and lobster sautéed in wine sauce and served in a potato basket; chan-do-chicken—chicken nuggets marinated in spices and sautéed with ginger and hot pepper; and leg of lamb Hunan style. Peking duck is a specialty (a $35 order can serve about four), and it need not be ordered in advance.

The ambience is as exciting as the food. The bar's white monkey and dragon sculptures, with their tiny flashing eyes, lead the way to the boldly elegant dining area. Tall booths ring an open central dining area; high banquettes offer total privacy. Each table is set with pink linen and black tableware. Down a couple of steps are the open tables, also laid with the dramatic pink-and-black settings. Surrounding the entire ceiling is a continuous white dragon. All in all, it's an impressive sight.

In addition, **Shun Lee Café,** adjacent to Shun Lee but with its own 65th Street entrance, serves dim sum, the traditional Chinese tea lunch, and Chinese street foods from rolling carts. It is open weekdays from 5:30pm to midnight and Saturday and Sunday from noon to 2:30pm, with dim sum available at all times.

TAVERN ON THE GREEN, in Central Park, at West 67th Street. Tel. 873-3200.

Cuisine: CONTINENTAL. **Reservations:** Advised, well in advance.
$ Prices: Appetizers $5.95–$17.25; main courses $12.75–$32.50; three-course pre-theater dinner $21.50–$25.50; three-course prix-fixe lunch $17.50–$19.95; Sat–Sun brunch main courses $11–$26.50. AE, DC, MC, V.
Open: Lunch Mon–Fri 11:30am–3:30pm; dinner Sun–Fri 5pm–11pm, Sat 5pm–1am; brunch Sat–Sun 10am–3:30pm. Pretheater dinner served Mon–Fri 5:30–6:45pm. **Subway:** 1 or 9 to 66th St./Lincoln Center, then walk east to the park.

New York's venerable Tavern on the Green, right in Central Park, is a fantasyland come to life. Rooms of crystal and frosted mirrors, of sparkling lights reflected from the trees in the park, of dazzling chandeliers and Tiffany-style lamps, create a kind of modern rococo setting. When you call for reservations, ask to be seated in the Crystal Room; with its three walls of glass and ornate chandeliers, you'll feel as if you're inside a huge transparent wedding cake. And the mood is as festive as that of a wedding, too, with masses of flowers everywhere and all kinds of festivities and celebrations going on at neighboring tables. Of all the restaurants in New York, it seems that the Tavern is most perfectly suited for celebrations. Service is deft and professional, and you will be well taken care of by a friendly crew.

The food is first-rate: Chef Marc Poidevin's style is basically French, with Northern Italian accents. Caesar salad or trio-smoked gravlax and cold poached salmon are both good ways to start dinner. Two or three pastas are available (I especially like the fetuccine with spring vegetables), along with half a dozen seafood choices (chef Marc does an excellent grilled swordfish steak with lime sauce and vegetables). Other grills and main courses include roast rack of lamb with spring vegetables; flavorful sautéed quail with rosemary and polenta; and roasted half chicken with apricot-cumin sausage, mashed potatoes, and thyme sauce. Save room for a dessert like the "red, sweet, cold and crisp" concoction of raspberries and strawberries in phyllo pastry with vanilla ice cream. Lunch and brunch have similar menus and are somewhat less expensive.

Tavern on the Green offers outdoor seating in a lovely garden in fair weather. There's dancing on summer evenings only, to both live and taped music. The mood is pure magic. Tuesday through Saturday, the Chestnut Room features top jazz and other music groups in another spectacular setting.

VINCE & EDDIE'S, 70 W. 68th St. Tel. 721-0068.

Cuisine: AMERICAN. **Reservations:** Recommended a week in advance; try for cancellations.

$ **Prices:** Appetizers $4.50–$12; main courses $14.95–$19.95.
Open: Lunch Mon–Sat noon–3pm; dinner Mon–Sat 5pm–midnight, Sun 5–11pm; brunch Sun 11am–3pm. **Subway:** 1 or 9 to 66th St./Lincoln Center.

One is almost tempted to say, "Welcome Home to Vince and Eddie's." Ensconced in a cozy brownstone, with a lovely back garden for warm-weather dining, this warm and tasteful yet unpretentious place serves the kind of food your grandmother used to make—and if your grandmother happened to be a simple yet superb cook with a light touch, you'll definitely feel at home. In cool weather, a fire roars in the hearth just opposite the bar.

Checkered table linens, handsome antiques, and warmly attentive service underscore the innlike ambience. The selection of dishes includes melt-in-your-mouth charcoal-grilled salmon, which arrives resting atop a bed of tender young steamed asparagus au beurre and makes you wonder why anyone would even consider eating plain old meat and potatoes again—that is, until you taste Vince & Eddie's grilled shell steak with peppercorn sauce and french fries. Red snapper with pecans and pan-fried quail with sweet-potato fries are slightly whimsical—and delicious—variations on a theme. The rather short menu rotates, so don't expect to find everything I've described, but whatever is on the menu will be excellent. Desserts, too, are winners.

INEXPENSIVE

DALLAS BBQ, 27 W. 72nd St., just off Central Park West. Tel. 873-2004.

Cuisine: AMERICAN. **Reservations:** Not accepted.

$ **Prices:** Appetizers $2.95–$7.95; main courses $3.95–$8.95; Early Bird special $7.95 for two, Mon–Fri noon–6pm.
Open: Sun–Thurs noon–midnight. Fri–Sat noon–1am. **Subway:** 1, 2, 3, or 9 to 72nd St., then walk east.

One of the Upper West Side's busiest thoroughfares, West 72nd Street, boasts one of the best bargains in town. If your taste runs to barbecued chicken and ribs, then Dallas BBQ is a must. Arrive early, or you'll have to wait in line. The crowds are drawn by the combination of the attractive room—a two-level space with modern art on the walls—and the incredibly reasonable prices on the chicken and ribs. Side orders of fresh vegetable tempura and a loaf of onion rings, huge enough for several famished eaters, should not be missed. Burgers, Texas-style chili, chicken salad, and fried Texas-style chicken wings are also crowd pleasers. The best buy of all is the Early Bird special, on Monday to Friday from noon to 6pm, which includes chicken-vegetable soup, half a barbecued chicken, cornbread, and potatoes. This place is crowded, noisy, and lots of fun. And their margaritas are first-rate.

Note: Dallas BBQ has spread its wings all over town, including two tremendously popular outlets in Greenwich Village: at 21 University Place (tel. 674-4450) and 132 Second Ave. at 8th Street (tel. 777-5574); on the Upper East Side (tel. 772-9393), a chrome-and-neon version is at 1265 Third Ave., between 72nd and 73rd streets. All feature the same menu, and prices rarely vary by more than a dollar or two.

JOSEPHINA, 1900 Broadway, between 63rd and 64th streets. Tel. 799-1000.
  Cuisine: CONTEMPORARY ITALIAN/SEAFOOD/VEGETARIAN. **Reservations:** Required.
$ **Prices:** Appetizers $4.75–$7; main courses $10.75–$15.75. AE, MC, V.
  Open: Lunch Tues–Fri noon–3pm; dinner daily 5:30–midnight; brunch Sat noon–3pm, Sun noon–4pm. Bar open noon–1am, light food available in between lunch and dinner. **Subway:** 1 or 9 to 66th St./Lincoln Center.

Fifty years ago, people ate healthy without knowing it, claims Louis Lanza, owner/chef at this smashing grand cafe directly across from Lincoln Center. High-ceilinged and with a casual-yet-sophisticated Mediterranean/Caribbean mood, Josephina boasts two outdoor dining areas, one on the sidewalk facing Lincoln Center, the other in a private garden out back. Lanza's grandmother, Josephina, for whom the restaurant is named and from whom he learned to cook, used olive oil instead of butter and plenty of mineral-filled greens like broccoli rabe, and arugula. Louis has adapted her ideas and come up with a winning menu, emphasizing food that's high in taste but low in fat—and at good prices. Poached shrimp and sea scallops in lemongrass-vegetable broth with sweet-potato-and-cashew dumplings and julienne vegetables, pasta pesto, and horseradish-crusted salmon are among his signature main courses; Thai shrimp on cool Asian noodles and flavorful grilled portobello mushrooms are among the appetizers. Free-range chicken, organic greens when available, and organic quinoa grain underscore the kitchen's commitment. They cater to the Lincoln Center crowd; come before 6:30pm and they guarantee to get you into your seat by curtain time. You can—and should—come back after for the dessert sampler ($5 per person); heavenly lemon-ribbon ice-cream pie, macadamia-and-oat apple crisp with vanilla-bean ice cream, and chocolate ovation bring the crowds to their feet.

JOSIE'S, 300 Amsterdam Ave., at 74th Street. Tel. 769-1212.
  Cuisine: NATURAL GOURMET. **Reservations:** Recommended.
$ **Prices:** Appetizers $4.50–$7.50; main courses $8–$15.

Open: Lunch Mon–Fri noon–3pm; dinner daily 5:30pm–midnight; brunch Sat–Sun noon–3pm. **Subway:** 1, 2, or 3 to 72nd St.

⭐ Josie's, New York's stellar natural gourmet restaurant, has been packing in the crowds night and day since its opening last year. If ever there was a restaurant for the '90s, an ecologically sound one for those who believe dining should be both delicious and healthful, this is it. The room is smart and sophisticated, with modern woods and curving lines: an enormous zinc-topped zebra-striped wood bar undulates across a wall. Service is snappy and knowledgeable. Don't be surprised if you see a few celebrity faces here: Rob Morrow (Joel Fleischman of "Northern Exposure") is a high-school buddy of owner/chef Louis Lanza, and one of the investors.

And the menu is amazing. Everything on it, save for one or two desserts, is dairy-free; all grains, beans, flours, and most produce is organic; chicken and meat are organically raised and naturally fed; water is filtered; taste combinations are exquisite. It's a bit like having the kitchen of a famed spa move to the Upper West Side. In addition to the usual range of alcoholic beverages, one has the choice of starting a meal with freshly squeezed vegetable or fruit juice; most wines are either organic or naturally farmed (no pesticides or fertilizers are used in growing the grapes).

Fabulous appetizers include ginger-grilled calamari with pineapple–red pepper salsa; steamed three-potato dumpling with tomato, chipotle and truffle coulis; spicy Thai chicken satay over arugula and radicchio; and Josie's Almost Caesar Salad, made with seaweed instead of anchovies, and no eggs. Earth-friendly, all-vegetarian dishes include a three-grain vegetable burger, marinated portobello mushroom fajita with tomato avocado salsa and whole-wheat tortillas. There are half a dozen pasta choices, including ravioli: my favorites are the sweet potato ravioli with Gulf shrimp, sweet corn and roasted peppers in a white wine–leek sauce and wild mushroom ravioli with sautéed chicken tenders, capers, and sun-dried tomatoes. Of the seafood selections, grilled Louisiana redfish and seared St. Peter's fish (tiliapa) are organically farm raised. Or go for a grilled breast of chicken on mesclun greens with tomato basil concasse, or marinated steak fajitas with tomato avocado salsa and whole-wheat tortillas. Desserts should not be missed: the lemon ribbon ice cream pie, light as a dream, is perhaps my all-time favorite dessert; also delectable is the triple chocolate mousse, rich and fudgy, with vanilla crème anglaise. Fresh fruit pies and the carrot cake with "cream cheese" frosting are dairy-free and fruit juice–sweetened.

Lanza, also in charge at Josephina (above) calls his new place "funky healthy." I call it terrific.

PATZO, 2330 Broadway, corner of 85th Street. Tel. 496-9240.

Cuisine: NORTHERN ITALIAN. **Reservations:** Recommended.

$ Prices: Appetizers $2.95–$4.95; main courses $6.95–$14.95; weekday lunch special $4.95; weekend brunch from $4.95. AE, CB, DC, MC, V.

Open: Mon–Thurs 11:30am–midnight, Fri 11:30am–1am, Sat 11am–1am, Sun 11am–midnight. Bar open until 2am. **Subway:** 1 or 9 to 86th St.

★ This pleasant, casually stylish Upper West Side cafe emphasizes light Northern Italian cooking. Patzo is a two-story space with an atrium stairway and a huge bar on one side of the first floor. The other side of the ground floor has banquettes and tables, and upstairs is a large seating area, my favorite section, with large windows looking out on the bustling street life. The decor is understated, but the color is all there in the delicious food.

There are beautiful antipasti misti plates to start, or maybe you'll have the steamed mussels, fragrant in a broth of garlic, white wine, parsley, and basil. Then try a bowl of hearty minestrone or a Caesar salad. Recommended among the main courses are fresh salmon steak topped with basil and fresh plum tomatoes; penne primavera with vegetables, garlic, and light tomato-cream sauce; and baked chicken breast, stuffed with fresh mozzarella, sun-dried tomatoes, and fresh basil. Don't miss the desserts: The tiramisù could easily be the best in New York, and the almond bread pudding and homemade cheesecake are also fine. You can enjoy Saturday or Sunday brunch to the tune of a live jazz combo.

PEPINA, 434 Amsterdam Ave., at 81st Street. Tel. 721-9141.
   Cuisine: ITALIAN. **Reservations:** Recommended.
$ **Prices:** Appetizers $3.75–$7.50; main courses $9.95–$15.95. DISC, MC, V.
   Open: Lunch Mon–Fri noon–4pm; dinner Sun–Thurs 4pm–midnight; Fri–Sat 4pm–1am; brunch Sat 11am–4pm; Sun 10:30am–4pm. **Subway:** 1 or 9 to 79th St.

With its European posters on the wall, Victorian sconces, tiled floors, and animated atmosphere, this could be a trattoria in Rome or Florence; instead, it's on the corner of Amsterdam and 81st, in the heart of the Upper West Side and not far from Lincoln Center, a neighborhood restaurant with better-than-neighborhood food and very neighborly prices. No wonder it's always packed! Its outdoor deck puts you in the middle of the Amsterdam Avenue action, although the indoor setting is much cozier. Start your meal with a big bowl of yummy Prince Edward Island mussels in a white wine, shallot, and parsley sauce; or try the roasted marinated eggplant and red peppers with mozzarella. There are more than a dozen pastas plus specials every night; on the regular menu, the fettuccine Livornese—a blend of marinara and clam sauces, with scallops, shrimps, clams, and mussels—covers all bases. They also do perfectly grilled lamb chops and a nice roast duck with a wild sour-cherry sauce. Best among the desserts is the house's own tiramisù. Lunch has sandwiches, salads, pastas, and good entrées in the $6.95 to $11.95 range. Saturday and Sunday brunches draw the neighborhood folks for the likes of poached eggs and smoked salmon, penne with chicken and red peppers, even buckwheat pasta with fresh veggies.

RUPPERT'S, 269 Columbus Ave., between 72nd and 73rd streets. Tel. 873-9400.
   Cuisine: AMERICAN. **Reservations:** Recommended.
$ **Prices:** Appetizers $.95–$2.95–$3.25; most main courses $3.95–$6.95; Sat and Sun brunch $5.95–$10.95. AE, MC, V.
   Open: Lunch daily 11am–4pm; dinner Sun–Thurs 5pm–12:45am, Fri–Sat 5pm–1:45am; brunch Sat–Sun 10:30am–4pm. **Subway:** 1, 2, or 3 to 72nd St.

It's not hard to figure out why Ruppert's is one of the most popular restaurants in the Columbus Avenue–Lincoln Center neighborhood: It promises and delivers "today's menu at yesterday's prices." When was the last time you sat down in a full-service restaurant and had an appetizer like stuffed potato skins for $2.95 or main courses like sautéed chicken livers or a steamed vegetable plate for $3.95? It's a handsome, stylish spot whose 40-seat glassed-in sidewalk cafe allows you a prime vantage point from which to watch the people parade on Columbus Avenue. Indoors, the mood is that of an 1877 saloon restored to its turn-of-the-century Victorian atmosphere, with mirrors and a big mahogany bar. The food is always satisfying and imaginatively seasoned, without being pretentious. Salad, pasta, burgers, sandwiches, and main courses are available all day. Among favorite main courses are the fresh fish of the day, grilled Santa Fe chicken breast with tequila salsa, and New York sirloin steak (topping the menu at $11.95). Saturday and Sunday brunch are always fun.

There's another Ruppert's, also refreshingly inexpensive, over on the Upper East Side, 1662 Third Ave. at 93rd Street (tel. 831-1900).

STEVE MCGRAW'S, 158 W. 72nd St. Tel. 362-2590.
  Cuisine: CONTINENTAL. **Reservations:** Recommended.
$ Prices: Appetizers $3.95–$5.75; main courses $9.95–$16.95; Sun brunch $6.25–$8.95. AE, DC, MC, V.
  Open: Dinner Sun–Thurs 5pm–midnight, Fri–Sat 5pm–1am; brunch Sun noon–4pm. Piano bar open til midnight; regular til 2am. **Subway:** 1, 2, or 3 to 72nd St.

Most New Yorkers know Steve McGraw's as a supper club with top-notch cabaret revues. But people may not know that Steve McGraw's is also an excellent restaurant; you can have a very good meal in the attractive little dining room downstairs whether or not you attend the upstairs entertainment afterward. There's a piano player from 9pm to midnight. Lots of Broadway casts come here after their own shows are finished, and they often take the mike and do some of their numbers. Don't forget Sunday brunch (the eggs Benedict are outrageous!). Chef Marc Rosen's menu is Contemporary American, featuring fresh and natural ingredients, herb-infused oil, and vinaigrettes as healthful flavor sources. Grilled vegetables and goat cheese terrine, with mesclun lettuce and saffron aïoli, and a rosemary-marinated chicken and sea scallop kebob make excellent starters. Signature main courses include the grilled rack of lamb with a roasted hazelnut sauce and a roasted garlic-and-thyme custard; lime-marinated pan-seared breast of chicken with a tequila-ginger-lime beurre blanc, served with spiced couscous; and the jumbo shrimp marinated in caramelized shallots—all delicious. Desserts are on the irresistible side: hot chocolate soufflé with candied orange sauce, vanilla bread pudding, and apple crisp tart with raw maple syrup are perfect endings to a sophisticated meal at a refreshingly low price.

TEACHERS TOO, 2271 Broadway, between 81st and 82nd streets. Tel. 362-4900.
  Cuisine: CONTEMPORARY AMERICAN. **Reservations:** Recommended.
$ Prices: Appetizers $3.95–$7.95; main courses $6.50–$17.95; Sun brunch $4.95–$8.95. AE, DC, MC, V.

Open: Daily 11am–1am; brunch Sat–Sun 11am–4pm. **Subway:** 1 or 9 to 79th St.

⭐ There's a very relaxed feeling at Teachers Too, a hangout for many of the city's artists, writers, and other members of the intelligentsia who live on the West Side. Since it's just about 15 blocks (one subway stop, or a pleasant stroll) from Lincoln Center, it makes sense to enjoy a delicious, reasonably priced meal here before or after a Lincoln Center event. Walk past the big mahogany bar up front and you'll find a dining room with natural-wood walls, butcher-block tables, and an intimate yet lively atmosphere. All the paintings and photographs on the walls were done by customers or by the aspiring artists and performers who wait tables with good cheer and courteous attention.

The food is the work of its artistic Thai cook, who is known for his lightly spiced chicken gai yung and traditional pad thai, as well as other inspirations, like Santa Fe chicken fajitas, Indonesian chicken satay, and Roumanian steak smothered in caramelized onions. Blackboard specials always include at least five broiled fresh (never frozen) fish dishes every night. Teachers Too is also known for its tasty spinach-and-bacon salad (if you find sand in it, your meal is on the house!); great appetizers like fresh Maine mussels, fried Cajun rock shrimp, and a nacho platter with guacamole; and luscious desserts, of which the praline ice-cream cake and the orange pound cake are standouts. Come on Saturday or Sunday and indulge in one of the liveliest brunches in town—eggs Benedict, eggs rancheros, caviar and sour cream, and the like, with a cocktail thrown in for good measure. In warm weather, it's fun to sit at the sidewalk cafe.

THE SALOON, 1920 Broadway, at 64th Street. Tel. 874-1500.
   Cuisine: AMERICAN/CONTINENTAL. **Reservations:** Recommended, especially for pretheater dinner.
$ **Prices:** Appetizers $4.25–$7.95; main courses $7.50–$18.95. AE, CB, DC, MC, V.
   Open: Sun–Thurs 11:30am–midnight for food, bar until 2am; Fri–Sat 11:30am–2am for food, bar until 3am. **Subway:** 1 or 9 to 66th St./Lincoln Center.

One of the most enjoyable restaurants at Lincoln Center is this bustling and attractive place, with an invitingly spacious sidewalk cafe open in nice weather. The menu has something for just about everyone—burgers, omelets, a hot salad of wild mushrooms and fresh salmon, and roast chicken with black olives. They'll see that you get to your Lincoln Center event promptly if you tell them you have a curtain to make. And after the curtain falls, plenty of luscious desserts; a variety of coffees, teas, and mineral waters; and an extensive wine list make this a perfect place for discussing the niceties of the performance. Yes, they do have roller-skating waiters.

12. UPPER EAST SIDE

EXPENSIVE

LE CIRQUE, 58 E. 65th St. Tel. 794-9292.

Cuisine: FRENCH. **Reservations:** Required one to two weeks in advance.

$ Prices: Appetizers $11–$18; main courses $26–$31; dégustation dinner menu $70 and $90; prix-fixe lunch $29. AE, DC, MC, V, and more.

Open: Lunch Mon–Sat 11:45am–2:45pm; dinner Mon–Sat 5:45–10:30pm. **Closed:** Sun and the month of July. **Subway:** 6 to 68th St./Hunter College.

⭐ There's no other restaurant quite like Le Cirque for glamour, prestige, and the meal of a lifetime, served in elegant continental splendor. Awarded four stars by the *New York Times* and the only U.S. restaurant rated 19 out of 20 toques by Gault Millau, it is the place to see and be seen—unique, memorable, and expensive. Credit much of Le Cirque's success to dedicated owner Sirio Maccioni and chef Sylvain Portay, who comes up with a menu of impressive scope and variety. Note the interior's soft French blue color scheme and the witty murals of costumed monkeys in chefs' toques. Cheerful lighting and bouquets of fresh flowers complement the romantic baroque interior.

A relatively "inexpensive" way to visit Le Cirque is to opt for the three-course prix-fixe luncheon at $29, not including wine. Start with stuffed artichokes or the warm medallion of salmon with crispy vegetable salad. Roasted saddle and braised leg of rabbit is an eminently worthwhile main course, as is the lobster risotto with shredded green cabbage and lobster sauce with rosemary. Desserts are first-rate—the heavenly brûlée "Le Cirque" is considered the best in town, and a crisp, thin disc of chocolate alternating with layers of raspberry mousse is superb.

Dinner, à la carte, usually runs about $55 to $60, excluding wine, tax, and tip. (The exceptionally broad international wine list has won awards for excellence.) Appetizers include a baked potato in sea salt stuffed with fresh black or white truffles. Among the main courses is black bass wrapped in red potatoes and treated to red-wine sauce. Yet another suggestion is roasted saddle of rabbit with garlic and carrot purée. Dinner shares the same *"cartes des desserts"* as lunch, but an extra finishing touch is *"l'inspiration du chef pâtissier,"* an offering of three or four of the day's pastries to round out your four-star meal.

MARK'S, in The Mark Hotel, 25 E. 77th St. Tel. 879-1864.
Cuisine: FRENCH CUISINE BOURGEOISE/AMERICAN. **Reservations:** Recommended.

$ Prices: Appetizers $7.50–$14.50; main courses $18–$32, prix-fixe dinner $45–$65; lunch main courses $14–$18; three-course prix-fixe lunch $19.95; Sun brunch three-course prix-fixe $28 (also à la carte). AE, CB, DC, MC, V.

Open: Breakfast daily 6:30–10am; lunch Mon–Sat 11:30am–2:30pm; dinner daily 6:30–10:30pm; afternoon tea daily 2:30–5:30pm. Brunch Sun 11:30am–2:30pm. **Subway:** 6 to 77th St.

⭐ Sublime food, an exquisite setting, and the air of a romantic retreat are winning high praise for Mark's, a perfect place for lunch or dinner if you're museum- or gallery-hopping uptown. Arranged in tiers and dimly lit, Mark's is an intimate, clublike oasis appointed in velvet, silk, and mahogany and dotted with potted orchids and palms, antique prints, marble columns, brocaded pillows, and tufted, heavily fringed, English-style banquettes. Mark's tables are set with Villeroy & Boch china and engraved silver—a perfect background for exquisite food.

Chef Erik Maillard learned and refined his art in his native France. Many of his selections change seasonally. At dinner, you might begin with ragoût of snails and sweet garlic custard, New York goat-cheese parfait, or napoleon of asparagus. Roasted free-range chicken for two, served with mashed potatoes, is a simple yet excellent entrée, matched but not outdone by such selections as crisp roast breast of guinea fowl with calvados and baby turnip sauce, sautéed sweetbreads with ragoût of chanterelles, and grilled dry-aged sirloin steak with peppercorn sauce. A monthly rotating "Vintner's Dinner," available every evening, pairs the personal selection of a notable winemaker with a three-course dégustation menu created by chef Maillard. And desserts are lovely—perhaps the Gourmandise of chocolate, fruit soup flavored with lemongrass, or crème brûlée with nougatine crust.

Lunch is fun, too, with two-course and three-course prix-fixe meals, plus à la carte selections. Whether it be Louisiana prawns on lentil salad with parsley vinaigrette or a deli sandwich—turkey, ham, and Swiss cheese on farm rye—it will be executed to perfection. And many lunchtime salads are available as either an appetizer or a main course. Afternoon tea is à la carte or $15 prix-fixe. And brunch is a Sunday favorite.

THE SIGN OF THE DOVE, 1110 Third Ave., at 65th Street. Tel. 861-8080.
Cuisine: CONTEMPORARY AMERICAN. **Reservations:** Recommended.
$ Prices: Appetizers $8–$14; main courses $20–$32; prix-fixe dinner $48; prix-fixe lunch $20. Pre-theater menu $30. At the Café Bar, appetizers $8–$12; main courses $12–$18. AE, CB, DC, DISC, MC, V.
Open: Lunch Tues–Fri noon–2:30pm; dinner Mon–Fri 6–11pm, Sat 5:30–11:30pm, Sun 6–10pm. Pretheater menu Mon–Fri 6pm; brunch Sat–Sun 11:30am–2:30pm. Café Bar open until the "wee hours." **Subway:** 6 to 68th St./Hunter College.

★ This is perhaps New York's most unabashedly romantic restaurant, and one of those rare few whose cooking lives up to the splendor of its setting. Chef Andrew D'Amico's menu, twice awarded three stars by the *New York Times*, perfectly complements the old-world Mediterranean-style decor. The dining areas are separated by brick walls with wrought-iron filigree; the skylight admits sunlight by day and soft lights by night; the decor features glorious flowers, antiques, mirrors, and tables well spaced for privacy. In such a setting, every dining experience is a celebration. Start with the butternut and Parmesan ravioli with homemade ricotta and sage butter or the crisp pomegranate-cured quail with apple butter, dates, and walnuts. Main courses are similarly imaginative: Grilled salmon is served with saffron onions and basil-mashed potatoes and pea shoots; prunes and apples with parsnip purée and red wine sauce accompany the venison loin; and oriental greens and dried shiitake mushrooms combine with pan-seared tuna in a green curry broth. Portions are not large, but you'll probably be pleasantly full by the time they arrive, since the wine list is outstanding and the bread basket—filled with double-walnut bread, pepper brioches, or dark sourdough—is one of the marvels of New York! (All breads are baked at their own bread shop, Ecce Panis, three doors away, and are for sale at the shop.) The desserts, like warm chocolate-caramel soufflé tart and fig pudding with buttermilk sorbet, dazzle.

To sample the fare for a less exalted bill, come for lunch, when main courses like the focaccia sandwich of roasted chicken, marinated peppers, and oven-dried tomato and the warm lobster salad with papaya and avocado in lime vinaigrette are in a comfortable $14 to $20 range. Brunch (most main dishes $14 to $18) is splendid, or you can have your meal in the oh-so-cozy Café/Bar, a very "in" East Side scene. While the bass and piano purr in the background, couples sip and share the likes of grilled Moroccan-spiced salmon, crispy pan-fried oysters, or Niçoise salad with pan-seared tuna. You can have a meal for under $18, and the food is extraordinarily good. Dress in this part of the restaurant can be anything from blue jeans to black tie—and often is. Tuesday to Friday there's a jazz group and vocalist every night in the café.

MODERATE

ARIZONA 206, 206 E. 60th St. Tel. 838-0440.
   Cuisine: NOUVELLE SOUTHWESTERN. **Reservations:** Recommended.
   $ Prices: Appetizers $7–$12; main courses $20–$29. AE, DC, MC, V.
   Open: Lunch Mon–Sat noon–3pm; dinner Mon–Thurs 5:30–11pm, Fri–Sat 5:30–10pm, Sun 5:30–10:30pm. **Subway:** 4, 5, 6 or N, R to 59th St./Lexington Ave.

⭐ Some of the best nouvelle southwestern cuisine anywhere can be found right here in New York at Arizona 206, one of the liveliest and most talked about restaurants in town. The long, narrow, cavelike setting, with its faux-adobe plaster walls, papier-mâché animals, and cowbells, is noisy and animated, hardly conducive to a quiet tête-à-tête; what you come here for is the brilliant, complex, imaginative menu that has New York foodies raving (it has received a coveted three-star rating from the *New York Times*). Its new wunderkind chef is 28-year-old David Walzog. He surprises with such combinations as green chile corn cakes with tequila-cured salmon, salmon roe and a shot of iced tequila, and an earthy black-bean terrine with pear-tomato salad and grilled bread, to begin the meal. Main courses present a variety of temptations: grilled rabbit loin in fragrant cilantro oil; grilled Atlantic salmon with tangerine-jicama salsa, salmon roe and potato galette; and charred venison loin, venison picadillo, huckleberries, and caramelized parsnips. Desserts are similar miracles: End your meal with the *cajeta* banana sundae (caramelized goat's milk atop cinnamon ice cream) or the chocolate-hazelnut flan with honey-glazed shredded wheat—cool winds after the spicy fires.

Note: See below for information on **Arizona Café**, offering similar great food, in smaller portions and prices.

COCO PAZZO, 23 E. 74th St. Tel. 794-0205.
   Cuisine: ITALIAN. **Reservations:** Necessary.
   $ Prices: Appetizers $6–$9.50; main courses $16–$28. AE, MC, V.
   Open: Lunch daily noon–3pm; dinner Mon–Sat 6pm–midnight, Sun 5:30–11:30pm. **Closed:** Major holidays.

⭐ The name means "crazy chef," but the cook here seems about as crazy as a fox. Raves—and crowds—have poured in since this white-hot Upper East Sider opened in 1991. The secret: simplicity, from the bright interior to the generous portions of solid Italian fare, with an emphasis on the flavors of Tuscany. Executive Chef Cesare Cella, formerly of the highly acclaimed restaurant Vipore in Lucca, Italy, is the man behind the magic: he combines seasonal offerings with the freshest herbs to create simple and delicious dishes. Roasting and grilling make familiar favorites fresh: start with a grilled bread and polenta squares with assorted toppings, light but satisfying grilled vegetables, or the *ribollita,* the classic Tuscan bean, cabbage, and bread stew. Don't miss main courses like the spaghetti with lobster, basil, and chopped tomato; the large shrimp grilled with pancetta, or the breast of guinea hen roasted with mushrooms. Lunch features similar offerings at slightly lower prices.

CONTRAPUNTO, 200 E. 60th St. Tel. 751-8616.
   Cuisine: NOUVELLE ITALIAN. **Reservations:** Not accepted.
$ **Prices:** Appetizers $7–$9.50; main courses $12.50–$22. AE, DC, MC, V.
   Open: Mon–Sat noon–midnight, Sun 3–11pm. **Subway:** 4, 5, 6, or N, R to 59th St./Lexington Ave.

⭐ Contrapunto has to be the best thing that's happened to Third Avenue since Bloomingdale's. Located on the corner right across from that famed shopping emporium, Contrapunto is also the best thing to happen to the noodle since Marco Polo came back from China. Two sides of this stylish second-story trattoria are totally glass, so your view is of Third Avenue, just above Cinema Row. Everything in the room, which seats 60, is snow white—walls, napery (under glass)—and there is sparkling track lighting.

Contrapunto's theme is to serve as "counterpoint" to other restaurants serving pasta, and they carry it off with class. The menu lists 17 creations of either fresh or imported pasta; and since they're all so good, you might do best to come here with a group and try a little bit of several. I like the *capelli bergino* (angel-hair pasta enlivened with sun-dried tomatoes and artichokes); *pappardelle boscaiola* (a wide ribbon pasta with wild mushrooms); and best of all, either fettuccine aragosta (with Maine lobster and sage) or rigatini pollo (small pasta tubes with braised chicken breast). Other specialties include a very good broiled veal chop served with braised escarole, tomatoes, and garlic; and a whole Cornish hen, roasted with white wine and bay leaves. Let your group also share some flavorful appetizers, like the grilled Portobello mushrooms with arugula. And when it comes to dessert, no one should have to choose between creamy homemade gelati of praline or white chocolate (the flavors change every day) or chocolate raspberry crème brûlée tarte or espresso mascarpone cake, so don't—share them all.

ETATS UNIS, 242 E. 81st St., at Second Avenue. Tel. 517-8826.
   Cuisine: CONTEMPORARY AMERICAN. **Reservations:** Required.
$ **Prices:** Appetizers $8.50–$12; main courses $18–$32. AE, DC, MC, V.
   Open: Dinner only Mon–Fri 6–11pm. **Subway:** 4, 5, or 6 to 86th St.

"Etats Unis" means United States in French and the concept behind Etats Unis is that of a true family-owned and operated American restaurant, with the owners—Tom Rapp and his children Emily and Jonathan—cooking and in control of the menu, which they change often. The experience is meant to be similar to coming to someone's house for a very good dinner party. The decor at this diminutive restaurant is casually elegant, modern, and minimal, with hues of beige and gray and high ceilings.

Combinations are unusual, flavors assertive—and the results are almost always first-class. You might start with lobster roll with cabbage and asparagus or wonderful pastas of all shapes and varieties, made fresh on the premises. Of the entrées, the charcoal-grilled veal chop with asparagus and morrel sauce is most delicious; and the shrimp in a Thai red curry sauce with coriander, green onion, and Southeast Asian sticky rice is tangy and filling. There are fabulous fish dishes to choose from, like flounder braised with chives, white wine, and butter, served with asparagus and crisp bacon.

The dessert menu almost always features a rich chocolate soufflé and a luscious crème caramel that changes flavors, including mocha, ginger, and mint. Etats Unis has no bar, but beer and wine are served, and the wines are thoughtfully chosen.

JO-JO'S, 160 E. 64th St. Tel. 223-5656.

Cuisine: FRENCH LOW FAT. **Reservations:** Required.

$ **Prices:** Appetizers $8–$12; main courses $18–$24. AE, MC, V.
Open: Lunch Mon–Fri noon–2pm; dinner Mon–Sat 6–11pm.
Subway: 4, 5, or 6 to 59th St./Lexington Ave.

Jean-Georges Vongerichten—Jo-Jo to his friends and fans—is the young Frenchman who virtually singlehandedly adapted the classic cuisine of France to contemporary tastes. Jean-Georges favors cooking with vegetable juices and flavored oils instead of rich sauces. Now his imitators are everywhere, but he is the original. His intimate restaurant, on two levels of a lovely East Side town house, is noisy and cheery. On the main level, red banquettes, beveled gold-leaf mirrors, and pink Venetian glass sconces set the warmly elegant mood. Paper tablecloths and purple, yellow, and orange plastic napkin rings let you know things are a bit tongue-in-cheek. Upstairs, oil lamps, bold cartoonlike oil paintings, and mahogany bentwood chairs with black-leather seats are a bit more serious. And there's an irresistible back room with a fireplace, a fringed Victorian lamp, regal Queen Anne chairs, and a large faux-leopard divan. It looks good enough to move into. The food is even better.

The simple and deliberately clear menu offers just eight choices for each course. You could start, for example, with terrine of goat cheese and potatoes with arugula juice, rabbit ravioli with Swiss chard and tomato oil, or shrimp in a spiced carrot juice with Thai lime leaves. Then move on, perhaps, to lobster with sautéed mushrooms flavored with asparagus juice. Refreshing salmon with citrus vinaigrette is wrapped in rice paper. Lamb cutlet and shoulder confit with basil oil is served with eggplant pancake. Desserts, created by colleague Eric Hubert, include light and cool champagne sorbet with berries; chocolate Valrhona cake; and apple confit.

For food of this caliber, Jo-Jo's is not expensive. Even the wine list includes 10 wines under $20. Jean-Georges wanted to give people a sophisticated neighborhood place they would feel comfortable coming back to again and again.

LE REFUGE, 166 E. 82nd St., between Lexington and Third avenues. Tel. 861-4505.
    Cuisine: FRENCH. **Reservations:** Recommended.
$ Prices: Appetizers $5.50–$10.50; main courses $16.50–$23.50. AE.
    Open: Lunch Mon–Sat noon–3pm; dinner Mon–Sat 5:30–11pm, Sun 5–9:30pm; brunch Sun noon–4pm. **Subway:** 4, 5, or 6 to 86th St.

If it were in the French countryside instead of on Manhattan's East Side, Le Refuge would probably have a rating of three stars in the French guidebooks. And it wins several stars from me, too. Visiting this enchanting bistro, now in its 19th year, is the next best thing to being in France. The atmosphere is relaxed and romantic; the service by the young, friendly staff is impeccable; and the food is traditional French country fare of the highest order.

Of the several dining rooms, my favorites are in the rear: One, with a 17th-century French tapestry, overlooks a small garden; another has a fireplace, and there are beamed ceilings and brick walls all about. A meal could start with a mild, extremely tasty and creamy potato-leek soup; snails in puff pastry; or a commendable ravioli stuffed with langoustines and a warm goat-cheese salad. Of the main courses, the filet of beef with green peppers, loin of lamb stuffed with spinach, poached salmon, and bouillabaisse are highly recommended. Desserts are not to be missed, especially the chocolate-soufflé cake. The extensive French wine list is personally overseen by chef/owner Pierre Saint-Denis and has several moderately priced selections.

Since Le Refuge is within walking distance of the Metropolitan Museum of Art and the rest of Fifth Avenue's Museum Mile, it's an excellent lunch stop for light fare like omelets and salads.

LE VEAU D'OR, 129 E. 60th St., between Park and Lexington avenues. Tel. 838-8133.
    Cuisine: FRENCH. **Reservations:** Recommended.
$ Prices: Prix-fixe dinner $24–$30; prix-fixe lunch $16–$22. AE, MC, V.
    Open: Lunch Mon–Sat noon–3pm; dinner Mon–Sat 5:30–10pm. **Closed:** Sat in July–Aug. **Subway:** 4, 5, 6 or N, R to 59th St./Lexington Ave.

Le Veau d'Or has long been hailed as one of New York's best French bistros. Its robust, hearty bourgeois fare is responsible for drawing almost unmanageable crowds night in, night out. And no wonder: The food and service are impeccable, and you can have a complete meal, from pâté to fromage, for the price of a main course. Rarely have I been disappointed in any of the house specials—and that includes the filet of sole amandine, veal kidneys in mustard sauce, roast duck with cherry sauce and wild rice, and veal scaloppine with mushrooms. You may begin with an appetizer like artichoke vinaigrette or pâté, have onion soup or soup of the day, and end with a lovely dessert like crème caramel or *pêche Melba*. This is not the place for a quiet, hand-holding dinner—it's too crowded and tends to get noisy. For more relaxation, come at lunchtime, when it's not quite as frantic.

MAY WE, 1022 Lexington Ave., at 73rd Street. Tel. 249-0200.
   Cuisine: SOUTHERN FRENCH/NORTHERN ITALIAN. **Reservations:** Recommended.
$ **Prices:** Appetizers $6.50–$11.50; main courses $16–$21.50. AE, DC, MC, V.
   Open: Dinner Mon–Thurs 5:30–10:30pm, Fri–Sat 5:30–11pm.
   Subway: 6 to 68th St.

After stints in Monaco and at prestigious Le Colombe d'Or in New York, chef Mark May has opened his own little restaurant, and his combination of southern French and northern Italian cooking, with a bit of Moroccan spicing thrown in for good measure, has the posh neighborhood folks cheering. The two-story restaurant is an old-fashioned Mom-and-Pop affair: Host Nini May greets customers, seating them either downstairs at the bar (where they thoughtfully serve complete meals) or upstairs via a spiral staircase in an elongated dining room overlooking the street, its walls painted with a floral motif. In the summer, one can dine on a sidewalk terrace. Appetizers steal the show: On no account miss the ethereal bouillabaisse ravioli in saffron fumet or prickly shrimp with garlic flan and vegetable broth. The ragoût of pig's feet and sweetbreads with cèpes, morels, and creamy polenta is another marvel of the chef's art; and his *socca roulade,* a chickpea pancake fried and stuffed with warm ratatouille and goat cheese, is a unique creation. As for main courses, semicured cod with blended celery root and white beans; seared tuna with pickled radish salad, sesame vinaigrette, and infused oils; and sautéed halibut with Swiss chard, red wine vinaigrette, and tomato/apple sauce suggest May's innovative way with fish; calf's liver with a pistachio-nut crust and sweet onion plus grilled breast and confit of duck are other stars. Desserts are wondrous, especially the signature apple tart topped with cinnamon ice cream and the extravagantly rich chocolate fondant. The wine list is decently priced and well thought out. Do I like this place? *Mais oui.*

INEXPENSIVE

ARIZONA CAFE, 206 E. 60th St. Tel. 838-0440.
   Cuisine: NOUVELLE SOUTHWESTERN. **Reservations:** Not accepted.
$ **Prices:** Appetizers $6–$10; main courses $12–$17. AE, DC, MC, V.
   Open: Mon–Sat noon–midnight, Sun 11:30am–11pm; Sun brunch 11:30–4pm. **Subway:** 4, 5, 6, or N, R to 59th St./Lexington Ave.

To sample the delicious—and expensive—nouvelle southwestern cuisine of Arizona 206 (see this section, above) at budget prices, come right into the main restaurant at 206 E. 60th St. and walk through the archway to the right of the reservations desk to the Arizona Café, where scrumptious small-portioned goodies from the chef's brilliant menu await you. The beamed ceiling, natural-wood tables and chairs, and handmade Mexican floor tiles suggest a southwestern interior. At the center of it all is a fabulous white-tiled open kitchen displaying a myriad of foodstuffs to stimulate the senses. The menu, which changes to accommodate market specials, offers a limited but exciting selection of the day's specialties priced by category; two diners would find four plates perfect for sharing. How about chicken quesadilla with green chiles and smoked chile cream, or roasted lamb wrapped in scallion flatbread with pumpkin seed–buttermilk dressing and vegetable slaw? For dessert, there's a warm chocolate cake filled with orange truffle and served with black pepper syrup, and a banana pastry basket filled with banana cream and peanuts and served with a caramel sauce. The cafe, like the main restaurant, tends to be noisy—all part of the fun.

BLUE MOON MEXICAN CAFE, 1444 First Ave., at 75th Street. Tel. 288-9811.

Cuisine: MEXICAN. **Reservations:** Not accepted.

$ **Prices:** Appetizers $3.50–$6.95; main courses $8–$12.95; brunch $6.95–$9.95. AE, DISC, MC, TR, V.

Open: Lunch Tues–Sun noon–4pm; dinner Sun–Thurs 5pm–midnight, Fri–Sat 5pm–1am; brunch Sat–Sun 11:30am–4pm.

Subway: 6 to 77th St.

Although the Blue Moon doesn't offer the most authentic south-of-the-border fare, the atmosphere is fun and prices are reasonable. Upper East Siders trickle in around 6:30pm, dressed in everything from dark suits to T-shirts and shorts. The decor is Navajo desert white with neon accents.

Your table will be set with a bunch of flowers and a brimming bowl of chips with salsa. If the chips aren't appetizer enough, try the chicken taquitos, jalapeño cheese fries, or the special Blue Moon prime sirloin chili. The quarter-moon chili is mild, while the full moon is a hotter variety of the same. Dinner main dishes include chimichangas, enchiladas, fajitas, tostadas, and other Mexican specialties. All include refried beans and rice. There are even a couple of burger selections for those of you who refuse to get into the Mexican mode.

The Blue Moon also serves a $9.95 Saturday and Sunday brunch with unlimited champagne or one Bloody Mary, screwdriver, or margarita.

There are two other Blue Moons in Manhattan. One is located at 150 Eighth Avenue, between 17th and 18th streets (tel. 463-0560). The other is located at 287 Columbus Avenue, between 73rd and 74th streets (tel. 721-2701). Both serve the same good food as the Blue Moon on the Upper East Side.

SARANAC, 1350 Madison Ave., between 94th and 95th Streets. Tel. 289-9600.

Cuisine: CLASSIC AMERICAN. **Reservations:** Recommended for large parties.

$ **Prices:** Appetizers $4.75–$7.75; main courses $7.75–$16.50; sandwiches and burgers $6.75–$8.75; Kid's Corner (daily noon–7:30pm) $7.50 including beverage.

Open: Lunch Mon–Fri noon–5:30pm; dinner Sun–Thurs 5:30–11pm, Fri–Sat 5:30pm–11pm; brunch Sat–Sun 11am–3:30pm.

Subway: 6 to 96th St.

Just the ticket for jaded city sophisticates, this restaurant makes you think you're up at Saranac, a picturesque lake in the Adirondacks. The owners seem to have unearthed treasures from the family attic, and these fill every available cranny—old fishing nets, snowshoes, a pair of hand-carved cuckoo clocks, and vintage watercolors and photos. An entire Native American canoe is suspended from the ceiling, and an antlered chandelier is the room's centerpiece. The many artists and writers and other folks who live in this neighborhood find this setting a perfect retreat. The atmosphere is convivial yet low-key, and the food is very good indeed.

The menu is basically the same all day, with the addition of specials at lunch and dinner. Conjure up the waterfront with Point Jude fried calamari or smoked Adirondack trout. Try the Cobb salad or the pear Roquefort and pine-nut salad over mixed greens. The Saranac burger is like none other: It shares bun space with Black Forest ham, Swiss cheese, grilled onions and mushrooms, and horseradish dressing. Perennial favorites are the chicken potpie, the cold meatloaf sandwich, and the Kansas City fried chicken with onion mashers. There are also great crabcakes with corn and white beans, and grilled tuna and salmon. Bring the kids. There's a special menu for the pint-sized from noon to 7:30pm, and the stroller set is welcome.

SERENDIPITY 3, 225 E. 60th St. Tel. 838-3531.
   Cuisine: CONTEMPORARY AMERICAN/NATURAL FOODS.
   Reservations: Recommended.
$ **Prices:** Main courses and sandwiches $6.95–$14.95. AE, CB, DC, MC, V.
   Open: Sun–Thurs 11:30am–12:30am, Fri 11:30am–1am, Sat 11:30am–2am. **Subway:** 4, 5, 6, or N, R to 59th St./Lexington Ave.

I doubt if there's another place in New York—or anywhere else, for that matter—quite like Serendipity 3, a block east of Bloomingdale's. It's a way-out country store that has been selling Tiffany shades and cinnamon toast, Hebrew eye charts and Zen hash, frivolous hats and frozen hot-chocolate drinks, for more than 40 years.

The prettiest people lunch at marble-topped coffeetables and meet here for afternoon tea and after theater; and while the food is on the whimsical side, there are times when fantasy is more fun than meat and potatoes. Personally, I have long found Serendipity 3 to be one of the city's happier happenings. The "serious food" side of the menu features comfy foods like very good casseroles served with a salad; salmon; shrimp and vegetable brochette; country meatloaf; lemon chicken, a foot-long chili hot dog, hamburgers, and the enticing Ftatateeta's toast. Zen hash and a variety of open-faced vegetable sandwiches are there for those on natural-food trips. But don't dream of coming here without indulging in the desserts: perhaps the heavenly apricot smush, the frozen mochaccino, the lemon ice-box pie, or the dark double devil mousse . . . not to mention the glorious espressos and hot chocolates and spicy teas and chocolaccinos—but come and see for yourself.

SEVENTH REGIMENT MESS RESTAURANT & BAR, Seventh Regiment Armory, 643 Park Ave., at 67th Street. Tel. 744-4107.
   Cuisine: AMERICAN. **Reservations:** Not required.
$ **Prices:** Appetizers $3.75–$8; complete dinners $8–$17. AE, MC, V.
   Open: Dinner only, Tues–Sat 5–9:30pm. **Closed:** June 30–July 7. **Subway:** 6 to 68th St.

⭐ ⓢ This is one of New York's best-kept restaurant secrets. Housed on the fourth floor of the Seventh Regiment Armory, a historic building completed in 1880 as headquarters for the volunteer militia unit of "gentlemen soldiers" that became a precursor of the National Guard, the dining room, with its superb windows and fine wrought iron, was designed by no less than Louis Comfort Tiffany. In this spacious Victorian setting you can dine on good food at some of the most amazing prices in New York. Where else can you sit down in such comfort, order a drink from the popular bar, and be served such main courses as fresh fish of the day, baked manicotti, lasagne, chicken cacciatore, fresh roast turkey, broiled lamb chops or roast prime rib of beef au jus, accompanied not only by soup and salad, but also by vegetables, potatoes, and coffee for prices that begin at $8? Should you feel the need of dessert, fresh pastries and cakes are also available, for another $3.50. The service is friendly and efficient. And happily, because this place is still much of a secret, the huge dining room is almost never crowded; it's a great place to come with friends when you want to really relax. There's a good wine list as well.

Note: For those interested in architecture, tours of the building can be arranged upon request (tel. 744-2968 in advance). The remarkable collection of furnishings, objets d'art, and regimental memorabilia have caused the Armory to be designated as both a New York City and a National Historic Landmark.

VASATA, 339 E. 75th St., between Second and First Avenues. Tel. 988-7166.

Cuisine: CZECHOSLOVAK. **Reservations:** Recommended.
$ **Prices:** Appetizers $3.50–$5.95; main courses $12.95–$18.95. AE, MC, V.
Open: Tues–Sat 5–10:45pm, Sun noon–9:45pm. **Closed:** Three weeks in July. **Subway:** 6 to 77th St.

⭐ Although New York's Yorkville, once the home to thousands of Germans, Hungarians, Czechs, and Ukrainians, has changed, there are still plenty of Central European beer halls and cafes, intriguing butcher shops, and fragrant spice and cookery emporiums. (**Paprikas Weiss,** one of the best, at 81st Street and Second Avenue, stays open until 6pm for pre-dinner browsers.) Almost all restaurants are good here, and Vasata is one of the best. The setting is very comfortable, something right out of the old country—as are many guests—Vasata has been popular with a Central European crowd for many years. Whitewashed-brick walls are decorated with ceramic plates, and crisp white cloths cover the tables.

Traditional Czech appetizers—marinated herring, homemade duck-liver pâté with pistachios, and headcheese with onions—are all here. Main courses include side dishes, like dumplings, potato salad, and sauerkraut, and might feature three kinds of veal schnitzel, pork chops, shish kebab, fresh-breaded calves' brains, and, of course, the ever-popular roast duckling. During the winter you can feast on roast goose (no need to wait for Christmas!) and on winter Thursdays you can usually get some form of game. Now for the desserts! Chocolate-mousse cake, poppyseed cake, and wonderful *palačinky* (here stuffed with either apricot preserves or chocolate sauce) are hard to resist.

YELLOWFINGERS DI NUOVO, 200 E. 60th St., corner of Third Avenue. Tel. 751-8615.
   Cuisine: CALIFORNIA/ITALIAN. **Reservations:** Not accepted.
$ **Prices:** Appetizers $4.50–$6.50; main courses $7–$16. AE, DC, MC, V.
   Open: Sun–Thurs 11:30am–11:45pm, Fri–Sat 11:30am–12:45am. **Subway:** 4, 5, 6 or N, R to 59th St./Lexington Ave.

Take the freshest natural ingredients (produce, herbs, and spices), add a dash of daring, cook everything to order, and you have the latest California-style cuisine. Accent it with an Italian flair and you have Yellowfingers di Nuovo, a well-priced restaurant with an ingenious menu. The spacious dining area features a fascinating open kitchen, a stainless-steel ceiling and, at the far end, a bar that jumps with activity. Sometimes noisy (I like to request the quieter, glass-enclosed cafe), often crowded, but very New York, Yellowfingers is both casual and upbeat.

One diversified à la carte menu covers both lunch, dinner, and everything in between. A neat starter might be the seasonal field lettuces with sherry vinaigrette, or the basket of focaccia sprinkled with slivers of roasted peppers and onion. Among the appealing entrées are the pepper-seared tuna, served rare, and the mixed grill of cornish hen, potatoes, and marinated vegetables with basil oil. By all means, try "fa'vecchia," a wonderful crusty pizza done with various toppings (my favorite is the melted mozzarella and sliced tomatoes) and the club nuovo—grilled boneless breast of chicken, pancetta (bacon), and arugula served on focaccia. Some 32 wines are all $15 per bottle, with many selections available by the glass. Taking advantage of the best seasonal fruits, the pastry chef dreams up such scrumptious desserts as banana praline tarte and hazelnut-chocolate cheesecake.

ZUCCHINI, 1336 First Ave., at 72nd Street. Tel. 249-0559.
   Cuisine: NATURAL FOODS. **Reservations:** Recommended for three or more.
$ **Prices:** Appetizers $5.50–$8.95; main courses $10.95–$15.95; specials $17.95. Early Bird dinner daily 4–7pm $9.95; Sat–Sun brunch $8.95. AE, MC, V.
   Open: Lunch Mon–Fri 11am–4pm; dinner daily 5–10:30pm; brunch Sat–Sun 11am–4pm. **Subway:** 6 to 68th St.

A gourmet natural-foods restaurant, a cut above the usual, this spot offers lots more than zucchini: Dinner in three attractively decorated little rooms with oak tables and antiques, plants, changing art exhibits, and (praise be) classical music in the background, is quite special. They use organically grown fruits and vegetables when available in the market. In addition to imaginative daily specials, there are a dozen salads every day, giant bowls of pasta and sauce, tossed with steamed garden vegetables, an array of fresh fish daily from the mixed-wood grill, as well as any number of fresh fish and seafood specials, including a lusty bouillabaisse. There are many low-fat vegetarian main courses, plus homemade vegiburgers and whole-wheat crust California-style pan pizza. Salad, bread, brown rice, veggies, and tofu or melted cheese accompany most main courses. Soups are homemade and fresh (cream of zucchini is excellent), and their double-chocolate velvet cake, with its subtle almond flavor and a slice of lemon on the side, is truly something to shout about. Lunch is a wonderful buy at $6.95 to $8.95, with choices of pasta, fish, chicken, wood-grilled kabobs, soups, salads, pita pocket sandwiches, and more. There's also a delicious weekend brunch. In short, here's an ideal menu for health-conscious gourmets who are also watching the pocketbook. And all eat-in patrons get free astrology horoscopes every day!

---

13. HARLEM

INEXPENSIVE

SYLVIA'S, 328 Lenox Ave. Tel. 996-0660.
   Cuisine: SOUL FOOD. **Reservations:** Recommended for Sun brunch.
$ Prices: Appetizers $4–$6; main courses $6–$16. AE.
   Open: Mon–Sat 7:30am–10:30pm, Sun 1–7pm. **Subway:** 2 or 3 to 125th St. **Bus:** 7.

★ Sylvia's is so fabulous it's not necessary for the menu to remind you that Sylvia has been the Queen of Soul Food since 1962, when this legendary Harlem restaurant opened. The walls are covered with movie posters, plaques, records, and autographed photos of the famous—but here you'll find no pricey pseudo-Southern cooking. At Sylvia's, it's the real deal. During Sunday brunch, the tuxedoed Gospel Brothers perform, strolling through the dining room, singing and shaking tambourines for the delight of the after-church crowd. Part of the movie *Jungle Fever* was filmed here. Those in the know come in droves from lower Manhattan and other various and sundry hinterlands for the best fried chicken in New York.

Southerners will be mesmerized by the familiar fantastic aroma of real down-home country cooking, and they'll swear they're in grandma's kitchen. Solo diners can eat at the bustling counter, but for larger parties there are two dining rooms. The iced tea is served sweet, as it should be, and the biscuits are incredibly fluffy and buttery. For a main course, the smothered chicken is delicious and tender, or perhaps you'll want to try Sylvia's world-famous barbecued ribs. Naturally, side orders of cow peas and rice, string beans, and collard greens are available. Desserts are Southern classics: sweet-potato pie, peach cobbler (served only on Thursdays), and Yumie-Yumie Rum Cake.

WILSON'S BAKERY & RESTAURANT, 1980 Amsterdam Ave., near 158th Street. Tel. 923-9821.
   Cuisine: SOUL FOOD. **Reservations:** Not required.
$ Prices: No appetizers, but no charge for side dishes; main courses $6–$24. No credit cards.
   Open: Daily 6am–9pm. **Subway:** 1 to 157th St. B to 115th St. and St. Nicholas Ave.
Since 1947, the Wilson family has delighted Harlem residents with unbeatable down-home country cooking at this down-to-earth restaurant. Celebrities like Wesley Snipes, Sugar Ray Leonard, Melba Moore, and Phyllis Hyman have all dined here, as do members of the Black Rodeo when they're in town.

You'll be immediately drawn to the sweet-laden cake counter to the right, but the dining area, with photos of celebrities lining the cozy wooden walls, is equally inviting. Sunday brunch is packed with regulars who happily stand in line for entrées like barbecued ribs, ham hocks, homemade meatloaf, chicken wings stewed in their own juice, and Southern-style smothered chicken. There's no extra charge for side dishes, which change daily; select whatever suits your fancy, whether it be collard greens, lima beans, mashed sweet potatoes, pickled beets, spinach, potato salad, or good old-fashioned macaroni.

The seemingly endless dessert menu offers a heavenly assortment of baked goods, including peach cobbler, sweet potato pie, carrot cake, rum-flavored cake, lemon meringue pie plus banana pudding. As the original Mr. Wilson hailed from North Carolina, you can be certain that, in addition to offering a mouth-watering menu of authentic soul food, Wilson's brews its own thirst-quenching iced tea right on the premises.

---

14. SPECIALTY DINING

KOSHER GOURMET

There was a time when the typical kosher restaurant in New York served either blintzes and gefilte fish or chicken soup with matzo balls and beef flanken—in other words, Jewish Eastern European–style food. These restaurants are still around, of course, but with large numbers of well-educated, affluent, and cosmopolitan New York Jews beginning to observe dietary laws, a whole new breed of kosher restaurants has risen on the scene. They're continental, Moroccan, Chinese, and Israeli. And they're very sophisticated. And you needn't be kosher—or even Jewish—to enjoy them. Herewith a sampling of the best of the new breed. *Note:* Hours vary, but most are closed on Friday; some reopen late on Saturday night, after the Sabbath. Call to confirm hours.

As for kosher Chinese restaurants, they just keep proliferating. On the East Side, try **Vege-Vege,** 544 Third Ave., between 36th and 37th streets (tel. 679-4710); in addition to being kosher, everything here is vegetarian as well! **Yoffe Chai,** 210 W. 14th St., between Seventh and Eighth avenues (tel. 627-1923) is your best bet in the Village. On the Upper West Side, go to **China Shalom,** 696 Columbus Ave., between 93rd and 94th streets (tel. 662-9676). You should also know that on the Upper West Side, **Whole Foods Uptown,** 2421 Broadway at 89th St. (tel. 874-4000), an enormous natural foods supermarket, has a section for take-out foods that are kosher, vegetarian, and organic as well. It's two short blocks to lovely Riverside Park and picnic possibilities.

MODERATE

LA KASBAH, 70 W. 71st St. Tel. 769-1690.
   Cuisine: KOSHER MOROCCAN/MEDITERRANEAN. **Reservations:** Recommended.
$ Prices: Appetizers $3.75–$6.50; main courses $13.50–$20. AE, CB, DC, MC, V.
   Open: Mon–Thurs 5–11pm; Sat (Oct–May) sundown–1am. Sun

2–11pm. **Closed:** Every Fri–Sat (June–Sept); call for exact dates. **Subway:** 1, 2, 3, or 9 to 72nd St.

How about kosher Moroccan food? You can get outstanding couscous, with vegetables, chicken, or lamb, at this attractive restaurant serving Moroccan and Mediterranean cuisine. The available main courses are shish kebab, Moroccan *koufta,* baby lamb chops, and salmon on the grill; appetizers include falafel, hummus, tahini, and other Middle Eastern standbys.

LEVANA, 141 W. 69th St. Tel. 877-8457.
Cuisine: CONTINENTAL/GLATT KOSHER. **Reservations:** Recommended.
$ **Prices:** Appetizers $5–$12.50; main courses $17.95–$36.95 ($44 for buffalo venison); prix-fixe dinner $19.95 and $37.95. AE, MC, V.
Open: Lunch Mon–Thurs 11:30am–2:30pm; dinner Sun–Thurs 5–11pm, Sat 7:30pm–1am (fall and winter only). **Subway:** 1 or 9 to 66th St./Lincoln Center.

Levana is the innovative leader of the genre. Beautiful, romantic, very European, with a unique, mostly nouvelle menu—it's the only Glatt kosher restaurant in the world, they claim, to serve bison and venison! Lamb canneloni with rosemary glace d'agneau is a unique appetizer; main courses include baby rack of lamb, prime meats (they're noted for their 12-ounce steaks and 2-inch-thick veal chops), fresh Dover sole and other fish, wonderful pastas, and extraordinary desserts, like chocolate-truffle torte with mint crème anglaise. *Note:* Almost anything can be cooked plain, with or without sauce.

VA BENE, 1589 Second Ave. (between 82nd and 83rd streets). Tel. 517-4448.
Cuisine: ITALIAN KOSHER. **Reservations:** Recommended.
$ **Prices:** Appetizers $6.95–$10.95; main courses $16.95–$23.95. AE.
Open: Dinner Mon–Thurs 5–11pm. **Subway:** 4, 5, or 6 to 86th St.

If you think kosher Italian means tomato sauce on a bagel, you're in for a pleasant surprise. Va Bene is Italian for "going well," and a meal here should go very well, indeed. In an upscale, classic Italian setting, Va Bene serves a host of tantalizing appetizers, including melanzane—baked eggplant with tomato and mozzarella, and tuna carpaccio. Entrées could be red snapper or tortelloni with mushrooms, or any number of popular pastas. There's an excellent wine list. As for desserts, they pride themselves on one of the best Napoleons in town; and you won't be disappointed by the tiramisù, either.

INEXPENSIVE

DELI KASBAH, 251 W. 85th St. Tel. 496-1500.
Cuisine: KOSHER ISRAELI. **Reservations:** Not accepted.
$ **Prices:** Appetizers $3–$9.50; main courses $6.50–$17.50; lunch main courses $4.95–$11.50. MC, V.
Open: Sun–Thurs 12:30–11:30pm; Sat sundown–1am (winter only). **Closed:** Every Fri–Sat in summer. **Subway:** 1 or 9 to 86th St.

Israeli grills abound, and Deli Kasbah is very popular on the Upper West Side, with a moderately priced menu featuring salads and deli sandwiches. A daily lunch special might be a fresh turkey sandwich barbecued on the grill, served with french fries and a salad.

DELIS

New York has long been famous for its Jewish (but not kosher) delicatessens, but the genuine article is no longer so easy to find in Manhattan. True mavens advise that you avoid all imitations and head directly for any of these four places, where the traditions of succulent corned beef and spicy pastrami, greasy gribenes, and caloric chopped liver (with chicken fat) are still honored.

CARNEGIE DELICATESSEN, 854 Seventh Ave., near 55th Street. Tel. 757-2245.

Cuisine: JEWISH DELI. **Reservations:** Not accepted.

$ Prices: Appetizers $6.45–$9.45; main courses and sandwiches $9.95–$14.95. No credit cards.

Open: Daily 6:30am–4am. **Subway:** B, D, E to Seventh Ave., N or R to 57th St./Carnegie Hall.

On the West Side, the shrine for deli lovers is near the shrine for music lovers: The Carnegie Deli has practiced and practiced for years to turn out some of the juiciest and most flavorful corned beef on ryes in New York. Main courses are also tasty, and prices are affordable. Widely known as a celebrity hangout, Carnegie Delicatessen was used for some of the scenes in *Broadway Danny Rose.*

KAPLAN'S AT THE DELMONICO, in the Delmonico Hotel, 59 E. 59th St. Tel. 755-5959.

Cuisine: JEWISH DELI. **Reservations:** Not required.

$ Prices: Appetizers $3.95–$8.75; main courses $8.95–$14.95. AE, DC, MC, V.

Open: Mon–Sat 7am–10pm, Sun 8am–10pm; same menu all day. **Subway:** N or R to Fifth Ave.

On the East Side, this is the classiest of the lot. High marks go to the deli sandwiches, as well as to such old-time favorites as chicken or beef in the pot, Roumanian tenderloin, stuffed cabbage, and potato latkes.

SECOND AVENUE DELICATESSEN, 156 Second Ave., at the corner of 10th Street. Tel. 677-0606.

Cuisine: JEWISH DELI. **Reservations:** Not required.

$ Prices: Appetizers $2.50–$5.50; main courses $10.95–$16.95.

Open: Sun–Thurs 7am–midnight, Fri–Sat 7am–2am. **Subway:** 6 to Astor Place, N or R to 8th St.

The best prices for this kind of food can be found downtown at the long-beloved spot where you may have to stand in line to sample the superlative chopped liver. A cafe room, named after Molly Picon and decorated with memorabilia from her career, adjoins the plain main dining room. The meat is kosher, with generous portions.

STAGE DELICATESSEN, 834 Seventh Ave., off 53rd Street. Tel. 245-7850.

Cuisine: JEWISH DELI. **Reservations:** Not required.

$ Prices: Appetizers $8.95–$20; main courses and sandwiches $8.50–$16.75. AE, MC, V.

Open: Daily 6am–2am; breakfast menu until 11am. **Subway:** B, D, E to Seventh Ave.; N or R to 57th St./Carnegie Hall; 1 or 9 to 50th St.

Begun in 1937 by the almost legendary deli man, Max Asnas, this is probably the oldest continuous deli in New York. The Stage is bright and cheerful and adorned with photos of the many show-biz personalities who have had a knish or a kasha varnishka for an appetizer, then gone on to one of the famous Stage Specialty sandwiches, 36 at the last count (most around $13), all named after famous people. The Dolly Parton, for example, is corned beef and pastrami on twin rolls. They also now offer a menu in Japanese, since Japanese tour groups seem to revel in such exotica as pastrami and cream cheese with lox on bagels.

DINING WITH A VIEW

New York's waterways and skyscrapers afford some of the most extraordinary views in any city. A handful of restaurants show them to full advantage. In addition to those reviewed below, glorious views are also available at **Hudson River Club** in downtown Manhattan and at the **Rainbow Room** in midtown, both covered earlier in this chapter.

EXPENSIVE

THE RIVER CAFE, 1 Water St., Brooklyn. Tel. 718/522-5200.
   Cuisine: AMERICAN NOUVELLE. **Reservations:** Recommended.
$ **Prices:** Prix fixe dinner $58; tasting menu $78; appetizers at lunch $8–$16; main courses at lunch $19–$24.
   Open: Lunch Mon–Sat noon–2:30pm; dinner daily 6–11pm, with seatings almost every half-hour; brunch Sun 11:30am–2pm. Bar open daily until 1am, outdoor deck Fri–Sat until 2am in summer. **Subway:** 2, 3, or A.
A bastion of American nouvelle cuisine exists in exotic Brooklyn, at the River Café. One of the city's see-and-be-seen restaurants, the Café is built on a barge underneath the Brooklyn Bridge and commands a truly spectacular view of lower Manhattan and New York Harbor. Perfect for a romantic night rendezvous, it has a special daytime appeal, too, as you watch the river busy with waterborne traffic. Beautifully appointed in pale tones, with each table sporting a tiny shaded lamp evocative of a 1930s supper club, the River Café is movie-star glamorous. But the food—a unique style of American cooking concentrating on seasonal changes and the finest, freshest products available—is not to be ignored. The prix-fixe dinner may include appetizers such as sea scallop en croûte with asparagus butter, sautéed salmon with grilled vegetarian lasagne, quesadillas, or Moroccan glazed and grilled prawns. Main courses such as grilled swordfish with bacon, potato cake, and shiitake hash or mustard-crusted rack of lamb are impressive. Desserts are wickedly wonderful, on the order of chocolate marquis and caramel mousse tarte or peanut-butter crème caramel with banana ice cream.

MODERATE

WATER'S EDGE, 44th Drive at the East River, East River Yacht Club, Long Island City. Tel. 718/482-0033.
   Cuisine: AMERICAN/CONTINENTAL. **Reservations:** Recommended.

$ Prices: Dinner: Appetizers $7.50–$12; main courses $19–$29. Appetizers at lunch $4–$10.50; main courses at lunch $10–$16. AE, DC, MC, V.

Open: Lunch Mon–Fri noon–3pm; dinner Mon–Sat 6–11pm.
Subway: E or F to 23rd St. & Ely; walk down 44th Dr. to river.

⭐ The restaurant with the best views of the Manhattan skyline is not in Manhattan at all—it's in Long Island City. Surely, there can be few more glamorous evenings in New York than one that begins at the restaurant's own Riverboat, which shuttles guests from 34th Street across the East River (champagne is available during the 10-minute crossing) to the glass-enclosed restaurant, where every table affords a view of sailboats, sunsets, and the fabled Manhattan skyline. The restaurant itself (whose upstairs dining room is one of the city's "in" spots for weddings), is attractive, with a sophisticated French country decor and a working fireplace. The menu has an international flair. Choice appetizers include grilled shrimp tostada, venison carpaccio with mixed-grain salad, and minestrone with lobster and smoked sweetbreads. For a main dish, try grilled swordfish with sweet-corn waffles, mesquite-grilled duck breast, or pan-seared veal chop with vegetable purée and cranberry-noodle kugel. Seasonal specialties might include smoked foie gras or grilled sea scallops with polenta and Swiss chard. Save room for dessert—maybe the chocolate truffle with white-chocolate mousse.

In warm weather, sit outdoors on the garden deck and enjoy light fare on the café menu, which features such choices as warm oysters with champagne, leeks, cream, and caviar, and a salad of fresh tomatoes and mozzarella, along with rotating dessert selections, exotic coffees, and wines by the glass.

The Riverboat shuttle operates from 34th Street at the East River, weather permitting, between 6 and 11pm on Tuesday to Saturday, with return trips leaving the restaurant on the half-hour from 6 to 11:30pm. Reservations are required only for groups of six or more. If you plan to drive from Manhattan, phone the restaurant for directions; you go via the 59th Street Bridge or the Midtown Tunnel.

THE VIEW, in the New York Marriott Marquis, 1535 Broadway, between 45th and 46th streets. Tel. 704-8900.

Cuisine: AMERICAN. **Reservations:** Recommended.

$ Prices: Appetizers $6.50–$14.50; main courses $24.50–$32.95; pre- and post-theater menu $39.95; Sun brunch $29.95. AE, CB, DC, DISC, JCB, MC, V.

Open: Dinner Sun–Thurs 5:30–11pm, Fri–Sat 5–12pm; brunch Sun 10:30am–2pm. Theater dinners daily 5–closing. **Subway:** 1, 2, 3, 9 or N, R to 42nd St./Times Square; N, R to 49th St.

There's no chance you can get bored with the view here: It changes constantly. New York's only rooftop restaurant revolves slowly, moving a full 360 degrees in the space of an hour. It's a splendid way to see the major vistas of the city and have a pretty good meal at the same time. Start with the New England crabcakes or the napoleon of escargots, then move onto such main courses as swordfish Louisiana, veal piccata, or a whole Maine lobster. The dessert cart is a special treat.

After dinner, amble over to The View lounge, one of the most romantic spots in the city; there's live entertainment and dancing Tuesday to Saturday nights ($5 cover charge per person).

WORLD YACHT CRUISES, Pier 81, West 41st Street, at the Hudson River. Tel. 630-8100.
   Cuisine: CONTINENTAL. **Reservations:** Essential.
$ **Prices:** Sun–Fri dinner cruise $62; Sat cruise $75; Liberty Luncheon cruise $27.50 adults, $16 children; Sun brunch cruise $39.95 adults, $25 children. AE, MC, V.
   Open: Weeknight cruise 7–10pm; Liberty Luncheon cruise noon–2pm; Sun brunch cruise 12:30–2:30pm. All cruises can be boarded one hour before sailing time. **Bus:** M106.

The whole of New York Harbor becomes your view when you dine aboard one of the five luxury restaurant yachts operated by World Yacht Cruises. Every night, some 2,000 people board the glamorous yachts to embark on an evening of gourmet dining, dancing to live music, and watching some of the most spectacular views New York has to offer. Between the appetizers and the coffee, the sun sets over the water and the boat steams around the tip of the island, cruises halfway up the East River, and then cruises down again. By the time dessert is on the table, it's dark and the thousand lights of the city are ablaze.

The state-of-the-art ships sport glassed-in and climate-controlled dining rooms surrounded by large windows that provide panoramic views. Full restaurant galleys enable all food to be prepared on board by an executive chef and staff. Menu selections are not large but are choice. I began one meal with a complimentary "Amuse," a seasonal pre-appetizer. Among the appetizers, bow-tie pasta with a garlic sauce is excellent; so is the brie en croûte. Main courses include rack of lamb, roasted chicken with green and black olives in couscous, and filet mignon. Menus change with the season. The dessert course is unlimited pastries, fresh fruit, cheeses, and vanilla ice cream. There's an excellent wine list and a variety of champagnes for a celebration.

Beverages and gratuities are not included in the quoted prices. Inquire about special evening cruises and afternoon theme cruises. On-site parking is available at a nominal fee.

SUNDAY BRUNCH

Sunday brunch is a favorite New York institution. After sleeping late and reading the *Times,* many a New Yorker heads for a restaurant close to home or farther afield, to meet friends and relax over eggs Benedict or waffles or lox and bagels or the like. The choice of brunch spots is enormous, everything from the grand hotel and restaurant buffets to more modest meals at neighborhood places where two courses plus champagne or a cocktail costs under $10.

I'll start with some of the most sumptuous buffets, particularly enjoyable for the visitor because each gives you a chance to dine in posh surroundings and sample wonderful food for much less than the cost of dinner. One of my all-time favorites is the enormous spread in **Peacock Alley** at the Waldorf-Astoria, where the cost is $42 for adults and $19.75 for children. The **Ambassador Grill** at the United Nations Plaza Hotel, 1 United Nations Plaza (tel. 355-3400), has a Sunday Champagne Brunch (lobster, smoked salmon, omelets made to order, boudin blanc with lentils, and unlimited bubbly) at $38 ($40 on special holidays) for adults and $17.50 for children. Its mirrored-glass ceiling of prisms within prisms creates an extraordinary effect. The **Crystal Fountain** at the Grand Hyatt New York, Park Avenue at Grand Central Terminal (tel. 850-5998), offers a luxurious spread at $30 for adults and $15 for children 12 and under, including a cocktail, seafood, steaks, breakfast specialties, and many desserts. One of the best. There's a nifty Jazz Brunch every Sunday at **Cecil's** in the Tudor Hotel, 304 E. 42nd St. (tel. 297-3456). Cecil's is an authentic carvery restaurant, and the $19.95 spread includes a buffet of appetizers, salads, seafood, a carvery roast, a cocktail, and a dessert buffet.

For brunch with a view, ascend to the 54th floor of the **Rhiga Royal Hotel,** 151 W. 54th St. (tel. 468-8888), where you enjoy vistas of Central Park, the Hudson River, and the Manhattan skyline as well as an extraordinary Marketplace Brunch. It reflects classical cuisine from the neighborhoods of New York City: The "Seafood Market" has especially delicious selections of cold and smoked fish. The buffet extends into the Marketplace kitchens, where omelets and frittatas are prepared to order. Price is $28.50 for adults and $14 children under 12 (free for those under 7). Nearby, on the 65th floor of Rockefeller Center, the posh art deco **Rainbow Room,** 30 Rockefeller Plaza (tel. 632-5000), offers à la carte meals (approximately $35 to $40 per person) enhanced by views of the skyscrapers of Manhattan and the rivers bordering them.

Reserve a table in the Crystal Room of **Tavern on the Green** in Central Park (tel. 873-3200) and enjoy a varied brunch menu in a sparkling crystal-and-glass room that's as pretty as a wedding cake and meant for celebrations. Brunch main courses cost between $12 and $32.50.

If you're visiting the American Museum of Natural History (even if you're not), Saturday or Sunday Brunch at **Main Street,** 446 Columbus Ave., between 81st and 82nd streets (tel. 873-5025), is a smart idea. The large, open space, with gigantic ceilings and a skylight, gives you the feeling of being in a sunny courtyard. Everything is served family style, and it's all delicious. For $8, you're treated to beverages, homemade breads, bowls of fresh fruit, yogurt, and granola. If you need more, there are nine-egg omelets, French toast, wonderful blueberry pancakes, and the like, from $8 to $18. And don't pass up the great desserts, especially the peanut-butter pie.

For sheer variety, venture over to Times Square and **Samplings Bar** at the Holiday Inn–Crowne Plaza, 1605 Broadway (tel. 315-6000), before a matinee. Sunday from 11am to 3pm, the sweeping bar carries breakfast food from smoked salmon and whitefish to waffles, omelets, pâtés, and hot main courses for $20, $10 for children under 12. One of the best buys and most delicious spreads in town!

Lola, 30 W. 22nd St. (tel. 675-6700), presents a spirited Gospel Brunch every Sunday, with performances by gospel musicians free with the cost of the meal; these meals are so popular that reservations must be made at least two weeks in advance.

DINING COMPLEXES

SOUTH STREET SEAPORT & MARKETPLACE, between Fulton and South streets at the East River.

This "museum without walls" celebrates the days of the tall ships. The South Street Seaport is one of New York's top visitor attractions (see Chapter 7). It also has 14 bonafide restaurants, 21 quick-stop eateries, and 7 gourmet take-out stores—all of which makes it a good place to repair to for a meal when you're touring downtown Manhattan. Here are some of my favorites at the Seaport:

Roebling's, on the Mezzanine Level of the Fulton Market Building (tel. 608-3980), is a great place to sit and watch all the busy goings-on at the ground-level shops and stalls. The atmosphere is casual, and the 70-foot corner bar always attracts a lively crowd, especially on Friday afternoon when Wall Street folks quit for the week. The food is elegant and imaginative, with a daunting selection of fresh fish and seafood dishes. In addition, the menu, the same for lunch and dinner, boasts a wide variety of South American favorites, and lush, rich desserts on the order of Mississippi mud pie and Georgia pecan pie. Most main courses are below $14.95.

Gianni's, in the Cannon Walk block (tel. 608-7300), is a sophisticated glass-enclosed people-watching restaurant serving regional Italian-American cuisine. Its active outdoor cafe overlooks the South Street Seaport's cobblestone walk. Featured are home-baked focaccia, an antipasto sampling plate, fresh fish, prime sirloin, a variety of desserts baked on the premises, and an extensive wine and port list. Discount parking is available. Most checks run $25 and up per person.

Liberty Café and Oyster Bar, atop Pier 17 (tel. 406-1111), provides direct waterfront views from anywhere in its dining room or private outdoor terrace. The 100-foot bar contains a working replica of a cross-country train. Featured are seasonal seafood as well as a variety of pasta dishes, pizzas from the woodburning oven, steaks, and chops. Most main courses are below $18.95. Sunday brunch is especially enjoyable. The Oyster Bar features fresh clams and oysters served at a bar surrounding a unique shark aquarium.

Pedro O'Hara's at Pier 17 (tel. 227-6735) sports a 50-foot bar for those who would like to sip a margarita, a daiquiri, or some other "frozen fantasies and tropical delights" before indulging in great Mexican and American regional specialties. Burgers, sandwiches, "overstuffed salads," and main courses range from about $6.95 to $13.95 per person.

To get a good meal for $5 or $6 or less at the Seaport, repair to the food court on the third floor of Pier 17 and help yourself to dishes from such places as **Pizza on the Pier, Salad Bowl, Seaport Fries,** and **Acropolis;** try to get a seat on the deck outside, where you can watch the busy harbor traffic on the river below. There's a similar food court (but without the sensational view and breezes) at the Fulton Market Building: **Burger Boys of Brooklyn** and **Kam Wan Foods** are some of the possibilities.

A&S PLAZA'S TASTE OF THE TOWN, Sixth Avenue at 33rd Street.

Should you find yourself in the Herald Square area, perhaps shopping at Macy's or A&S Plaza and want a quick lunch or snack, a good choice is the Taste of the Town food court on the seventh level at A&S Plaza. A huge central dining area provides seating for a number of imaginative fast-food stands: Possibilities include **Sbarro** for pizza and pasta; **Wok 'n Roll** for Chinese food; **Flamers** for chicken or burgers charbroiled over an open flame; **Amir's Kitchen** for Middle Eastern foods; and **The Salad Bowl** and the **Great Steak and Fry Company,** whose names say it all. Try to get a table near the windows and watch the crowds go by.

Note: The seventh level also contains the A&S Plaza Visitors Center, with helpful information on attractions, transportation, restaurant and theater reservations, car services, and more.

THE MARKET at **Citicorp Center, 53rd Street, between Lexington and Third avenues.**
Midtown on the East Side, this handsome skylit atrium has three levels of shops and restaurants surrounding a graceful central cafe. One of my favorite Greek restaurants, **Avgerinos,** is there, and so are such attractive other sit-down restaurants as **Alfredo, The Original of Rome** (tel. 371-3367) serving Italian cuisine; and **La Brochette** (tel. 223-0919), an upscale French bistro with an open rotisserie. Or pick up a snack from **Nyborg & Nelson** (Swedish delicacies and deli food), **The Market Coffee Shop, Au Bon Pain,** or **Alfredo to Go** and take it to one of the courtyard tables. You might be able to enjoy a free concert or show while you munch.

STREET FOOD & PIZZA

Many people don't realize that even New York executives often eat their lunch at one of the hundred or more hot-dog wagons seen on corners all over midtown and at other high-traffic locations—near train stations, outside museums, and elsewhere. New Yorkers are people in a hurry, and when you're in a hurry, street food fills the bill. It's cheap and often surprisingly good.

Ice cream and hot dogs—stadium fare—are still the most abundant. **Häagen-Dazs** and **Ben and Jerry's** wagons and **Good Humor** and **Mr. Softy** trucks are everywhere, and so are **Sabretts.** But ethnic food also finds its way into New York's thoroughfares. Italian sausages, Jewish knishes, Chinese dumplings, and Japanese tempura are appetizing more for their aroma than the way in which they are displayed, but people wolf them down anyway. Pita-wrapped falafel sandwiches, burritos, vegetarian food, and fried fish are all very popular. There are even gourmet soup wagons— they're called **Soup's On**—and if you spot one of their red-and-white-checkered carts (at 54th and 56th streets on Madison Avenue and at 50th and 55th streets on Sixth Avenue), you're in for a treat. Everything is natural, and no preservatives are used.

Other roadside snacks include orange juice squeezed on the spot, honey-roasted peanuts, and Italian ices. Fruit vendors offer whatever's in season at bargain prices. In winter, you can buy wonderful roasted chestnuts. Great New York–style soft pretzels, bagels, donuts, and coffee are dispensed from carts parked anywhere people seem to be hurrying to work.

Pizza is the only popular New York food that hasn't found its way onto the street, but you will see hole-in-the-wall outlets where you can grab a slice on the run as well as larger places. Most of New York's pizza parlors offer certainly passable, and rarely inedible slices and pies, but here are some favorites. **John's Pizzeria,** 278 Bleecker St. in Greenwich Village (tel. 243-1680), sells its outstanding brick-oven pizza only by the pie and has sit-down service. The place is so packed in the evenings and on weekends with Village regulars, college kids, and visitors to the neighborhood that there's often a line. They also have two northern outposts—one near Lincoln Center at 48 W. 65th St., another on the Upper East Side at 408 E. 64th St. **Arturo's,** 106 W. Houston (tel. 677-3820), boasts brick-oven pizza that is quite good and also has live jazz. **Goodfellas Pizza,** Seventh Ave. at 14th Street is a sleek-looking spot that serves up gourmet pizzas with very fresh ingredients; I particularly like the margherita (plum tomatoes, fresh mozzarrela, and fresh basil) and the grilled chicken and avocado. They have good focaccia sandwiches, too, and a small pasta menu. On the Upper East Side, **Goldberg's Pizzeria,** if you can believe it, has fantastic pies. It's at 996 Second Ave., between 52nd and 53rd streets (tel. 593-2172). **Mimi's Pizza** at 1248 Lexington Ave., at the corner of 84th Street, is practically an institution, having been in the same spot for over 30 years. The pizza is very good, and if you want a real treat, order a hero on "homemade" bread, baked with pizza dough. This fantastic bread is also available by the loaf for $2.

TEA TIME

Although New York is surely not London, it does have its share of tearooms (some independent establishments, some in the more elegant hotels). These do a lovely job of celebrating the time-honored English tradition known as afternoon tea. Most places serve a multicourse tea featuring scones with jam and Devonshire cream (or a Devonshire cream taste-alike). Finger sandwiches and pastry are pretty much universal. And most, too, have a copious selection of traditional teas, herbals, and heady aromatics (fruit-infused teas). Many also serve tea dainties à la carte and make a glass of sherry, port, champagne, or whatever available. Not all places below take reservations, but it's best to call ahead.

INDEPENDENT ESTABLISHMENTS

Anglers & Writers, 420 Hudson St., at St. Luke's Place (tel. 675-0810), serves a splendid tea with all the fixings each afternoon from 3 to 7pm for a modest $12.50 amid a decor of antiques and fishing paraphernalia.

Book-Friends Café, 16 W. 18th St., between Fifth and Sixth avenues (tel. 255-7407), serves tea from 3 to 5:30pm; tea dances, with live music and ballroom dancing, are held every other Wednesday from 7 to 10pm. A unique salon, Book-Friends also serves lunch daily and dinner on weekdays; it boasts an enthralling assortment of antique books (from 1840 to 1940: Victorians, old New York, Paris in the 1920s). Books can be perused, but if you want to skim one as you sip, you'll have to purchase it before sitting down. Tea is $12.95. Call for a schedule of literary events, tea dances, and special theme dinners.

Danal, 90 E. 10th St., between Third and Fourth avenues (tel. 982-6930), serves its tea, with aplomb, from 3:30 to 5:30pm. There are 40 teas to choose from, and all can be purchased loose for your home teapot for $5 to $7 per quarter pound; the meal is $12. You may sit at one of the antique tables or love seats or at one of the garden tables in back. Up front is Danal Provisions, which offers fine foods and gifts and serves both lunch and dinner. Scones are baked on the premises, and lemon tartlets and meringue often comprise dessert. *Note:* Closed on Monday and Tuesday; reservations are required.

✪ T Salon Café Emporium, beneath the SoHo Guggenheim Museum, 142 Mercer St. (tel. 925-3700), is the place to mend your frazzled nerves after a day of gallery hopping and shopping in SoHo. This stunning, 6,500-square-foot restaurant and retail shop with its curvy copper bar (a scene of many glamorous "happenings") offers three tea services, in addition to an à la carte menu, a juice bar, an herbal elixir bar, and a rare port and wine bar. A proper English afternoon tea is served from 3 to 5pm; the $18.50 tab includes the traditional three-tier cake stand with such delicacies as blueberry walnut whole wheat scones with Vermont crème fraîche; sandwiches of green tea chicken with peanut dressing and smoked salmon; luscious tea pastries. A similar "New Yorker's Tea" is served at 6pm, and a "Champagne Tea" at midnight, both at the same prices. Any time of day one can sample and taste hundreds of exotic teas and dine on foods inspired by and compatible with tea.

You'd be hard-pressed to find a more authentic tea than the daily service at **Tea & Sympathy,** 108 Greenwich Ave. (tel. 807-8329), a whimsical West Village salon. Owner Nikki Perry, a London native, loads a three-tiered cake stand with tea sandwiches, cakes, scones with clotted cream, and jam; her unusual tea selections, strained and served "the proper way," range from Ty-Phoo (a popular British variety) to Mango to Licorice. Tea, offered from noon to 6pm, is $10.95 per person. For lunch and dinner, Tea & Sympathy also serves such British treats as bangers and mash (sausages and mashed potatoes), Welsh rarebit, and ploughman's lunch.

Tea Box Cafe, housed in Manhattan's exclusive Takashima department store at 693 Fifth Ave. near 54th Street (tel. 350-0100), is a graceful, spare room, that boasts one of the finest selections of teas from around the world, a luncheon menu featuring New American cuisine with a Japanese flair, and an afternoon tea service from 3 to 5pm daily with a selection of tea savories and sweets including finger sandwiches, pastries, Japanese butter cookies, and chocolates from Lyons ($14.50). At the specialty shop next door you can purchase the same 37 teas that are offered on the menu, as well as an array of antique Japanese teapots and tea accessories. A very relaxing stop.

HOTEL TEAROOMS

The **Carlyle,** 35 E. 76th St. (tel. 744-1600), serves tea in its intimate Gallery. The decor, modeled on that found in Istanbul's famed Topkapi Palace, is similar to the "Turkish room" found in many 18th- and 19th-century European country homes. Italian hand-painted paper has been painstakingly applied to screens and walls in an intricate mosaic pattern, and the burgundy-velvet sofas have been appliquéd with antique kilims. A soft paisley carpet completes the effect. Tea, served from 3 to 5:30pm, is $18 for three ample courses.

The **New York Palace,** 455 Madison Ave. (tel. 888-7000), offers tea in the aptly named Gold Room each afternoon from 2 to 5pm. The atmosphere is regal-rococo: frescoes and gilding everywhere, silk-brocade Louis XIV chairs, and a harpist playing in the gallery above. The tea is up to snuff, and the atmosphere, rather formal, is geared to aristocrats, would-be aristocrats, and those who simply appreciate elegant service. The price is $24 for a three-course tea service.

The **Lowell,** 28 E. 63rd St. (tel. 838-1400), pours its tea from a samovar and features silver service. Ladylike charm and manners reign supreme in the small, second-floor Pembroke Room, where English chintz abounds. F. Scott and Zelda Fitzgerald, Noël Coward, Dorothy Parker, and other literary lights all roamed these premises at one time. All this history and tea, too, for just $21.50, from 3:30 to 6:30pm.

Mayfair Hotel, 610 Park Ave., at 65th Street (tel. 288-0800), serves tea in its engaging balconied lobby lounge every day from 3 to

5:30pm. There are settees as far as the eye can see. Sconces and chandeliers light the room, and columns are interspersed with flowers and palms. People-watching is recommended and eavesdropping advised, if at all possible. The waitresses dress English-style in long skirts for the occasion. The staff is courteously warm and the mood contagiously celebratory. The tea is $18.

The Pierre, Fifth Avenue at 61st Street (tel. 838-8000), serves tea from 3 to 5:30pm in its elegant rotunda, where guests lounge on silk settees surrounded by dramatic frescoes of ladies and gentlemen strolling in gardens and languishing outdoors. As the menu points out, "the romantic setting is enhanced by celestial blue skies, marble pillars and ornate candelabras." The price for all this atmosphere, not to mention the tea, scones, sandwiches, and pastries, is $18.

The Palm Court at **The Plaza,** Fifth Avenue at 59th Street (tel. 759-3000), is legendary for its foliage and for violinist Sandu Marcu and pianist Sasha Aloni, who have been serenading guests from what could be termed time immemorial. Native New Yorkers, not impressed by much, fondly remember being taken to tea at the Plaza as the first grown-up activity of their childhoods and await the day when they can initiate the next generation. The decor has been spruced up since then and the bygone tattered charm has been replaced by a little dazzle—a few pre-divorce Ivana Trump–esque touches: The space is now punctuated by gold columns. Live palms cast flattering shadows, and the tea is $20, served from 3:45 to 6pm.

DESSERT & COFFEE

New York has always been a great place to indulge a sweet tooth. Now that the West Coast coffee bar trend is catching on, more and more dessert and coffeehouses are springing up all over town. They are some of the most enjoyable places to perk up after a hard day of shopping or sightseeing, and the city is covered with them.

THE VILLAGE & SOHO

Café Rafaella, 134 Seventh Ave. South (at 10th Street; tel. 929-7247), is a real pleasure with high silver ceilings, assorted antique wooden chairs, marble tables, and classical music resonating wonderfully throughout. It's easily the best place to people-watch in the West Village. The tiramisù is nothing short of fabulous. Don't just read the menu; give yourself the pleasure of choosing your dessert from the exquisite dessert case. Café Rafaella is home to coffees galore, or perhaps you'll order steamed milk with honey to soothe your stressed-out soul.

At **Café Sha Sha,** 510 Hudson St. (tel. 242-3021), you can enjoy the outdoor patio during warm weather or relax at tables on the sidewalk and watch the parade of personalities down Hudson Street while you indulge in cheesecake, chocolate mousse, or any one of the multitude of stars in Sha Sha's dessert spectrum.

At **Dean & Deluca,** 560 Broadway at Prince Street (tel. 431-1691), a grand emporium of gourmet food, the incredibly popular espresso bar up front is a magnet for gallery-goers and other arty SoHo types. You'll find other Dean & Deluca espresso bars around town, including ones at 75 University Place, One Wall Street Court (tel. 514-7775), Rockefeller Center (between Fifth and Sixth avenues; tel. 664-1363), and in the Paramount Hotel at 235 W. 46th St. (tel. 869-6890). These guys are purveyors of the chunkiest brownies in New York, as well as other sublime sweet treats.

Limbo, 47 Avenue A (between Third and Fourth streets; tel. 477-5271), is a colorful East Village coffeehouse that was designed by Aldo Rossi's *studio di architettura* with glorious high ceilings and wonderful light. It's furnished with vintage-1950s dinette tables and comfy old chairs, so it's easy to see why friendly East Village bohemians come here to read, drink a variety of teas and coffees, peruse magazines, and talk. The chocolate-chip cookies are highly recommended, but there are plenty of other great desserts, as well as cheeses, to choose from. Limbo was opened by Sarah Goodman, whose great-grandfather was Edwin Goodman, founder of Bergdorf Goodman.

New World Coffee, 449 Ave. of the Americas (between 10th and 11th streets), is one of those places whose wonderful aroma is guaranteed to pull you in. With a specially developed roast flown in from Seattle every week, New World serves freshly brewed coffee, espresso, cappuccino, caffè latte, caffè mocha, Belgian hot chocolate, tea, fresh-squeezed juices, and light food items; it also offers a selection of freshly roasted coffee beans from around the world. Its second shop is at 1159 Third Ave. (between 67th and 68th streets; no phone) and more openings are planned around town.

Rumbul's, 20 Christopher St. (tel. 924-8900), is a cozy dessert haven that serves up great American and Italian cakes, coffee, and cappuccino, as well as lasagne and quiches. With its brick walls and fireplace in back, it's a perfect stopping place on a brisk fall day; there are others at 128 E. Seventh St. (tel. 473-8696) and 559 Hudson St. (tel. 929-8783).

CHELSEA

Newsbar, 2 W. 19th St. (tel. 255-3996), is where the media-addicted TV generation snacks—and with good reasons. Newsbar sells over 300 magazine titles and newspapers, as well as gourmet coffees, natural juices, sodas, and light foods. You can watch MTV or CNN on three TV monitors suspended above or read glossy magazines while you munch on muffins and scones. Another location has opened at 366 West Broadway in SoHo.

Michael's Muffins, 158 Seventh Ave. (between 19th and 20th streets; tel. 366-5505), is a tiny but great muffin shop with whimsical animal murals. Owner Michael Venetucci created all the recipes for his 15 varieties, including fat- and sugar-free treats. Michael's also serves lunch, fresh-baked bread, and homemade soups and salads. There's another store at 144 Chambers St., at West Broadway in Soho.

MIDTOWN

Au Café, 1700 Broadway, near 53rd Street (tel. 757-2233) has everything a New York cafe should have, and then some: gorgeous 16-foot glass windows, palm trees, a private terrace and sidewalk cafe, and a full menu—and it's open 24 hours a day. Beignets are the house specialty, served plain with powdered sugar, or with fruit, savory, or cheese. Splendid European coffees are served here; café au lait comes in a bowl, French country style.

Oh La La, 229 W. 45th St. (tel. 704-8932), is located in the heart of the Theater District, on the ground floor of the sparkling Marriott Marquis. This Eurostyle coffee bar serves numerous types of regular and decaffeinated coffee: gourmet filtered coffee, caffè latte, café au lait, caffè mocha, espresso, and a sensational cappuccino. Oh La La also has delicious pastries, breads, and an assortment of cookies and brownies, baked fresh daily. Lo La La is the name of their special variety of tasty low-cal, low- and no-fat, and low- and no-cholesterol baked goods.

Philip's, 155 W. 56th St., in the Carnegie Hall Towers Building (tel. 582-7347), is a full cafe with some seating; the other Philip's, at 14 E. 33rd St., inside King Office Supply (tel. 686-6000), offers all to-go service. These nifty espresso bars sell espresso drinks, wonderful coffee beans, and assorted pastries and sandwiches. An incredible caffè latte is Philip's specialty.

Simon Sips Coffee Bar, located in the lobby of the Wiley Building, 605 Third Ave. (at 39th Street; tel. 986-7537), and in an outdoor kiosk with seating at the entrance to Bryant Park (42nd Street and Sixth Avenue, behind the New York Public Library), serves all types of coffee, espresso-based coffee drinks, and assorted baked goods.

UPPER EAST SIDE

At **Caffè Bianco,** 1486 Second Ave. (at 77th Street; tel. 988-2655), take a seat by the fountain in the lovely garden to escape instantly from urban chaos. This charming European-style cafe is perfect for cooling off on a hot summer day with one of their popular frozen ice cream or blended fruit drinks. Caffè Bianco's espresso-mousse pie will put you into orbit; they also feature a full menu with superb main courses.

UPPER WEST SIDE

The best literary cafe on the Upper West Side is on the balcony of the **Barnes & Noble** superstore at 2289 Broadway (at 82nd Street; tel. 362-8835). Photo murals of famous authors line the walls as neighborhood artists and writers (as well as mommies and kids and just about everyone else) sip Starbucks' coffees, espressos, and cappuccino; juices, spritzers, and Italian sodas. The cafe also serves fragrant teas from Republic of Tea—ginger peach and cinnamon plum are wonderful, especially iced. And they have sandwiches, soups, summer salads, and, of course, all kinds of scones, tea breads, cakes, and delectable pastries.

Coopers Coffee and Espresso Bar, 2151 Broadway (at 75th Street; tel. 496-0300), 159 Columbus Ave. (at 67th Street; tel. 362-0100), and at 2315 Broadway (at 82nd St.; tel. 724-0300) are not far from Lincoln Center. These upscale, European style coffee bars serve Italian coffee fare, morning pastries and breads, homemade soups, sandwiches, and desserts. All coffees are roasted and fresh brewed within seven days. Cooper's also offers a thirst-slaking host of Italian sodas, granitas, herbal teas, egg creams, and fresh-squeezed juices.

The hip staff of **Joe Bar,** 2459 Broadway (at 91st Street; tel. 787-3684), have named Jimi Hendrix patron saint of this coffee stop, with a framed photo of the pop star on the wall. The modern coffee bar specializes in high-end specialty coffees, espressos, and tea, but can also whip up some pretty tasty casual cafe meals, including sandwiches, pasta salads, and soups. Joe Bar's luscious hot chocolate is the real thing, made with ground Ghiradelli chocolate.

Starbucks, the immensely popular Seattle chain, has come to New York, with its first store at 2379 Broadway (at 87th Street; tel. 875-8470). Here, in the biggest Starbucks in the United States, one can enjoy a full range of coffee and espresso drinks, prepared by Starbucks's professional baristas (coffee bartenders). This is a comfortable place to hang out, attracting all ages and types, from hipsters to executives. There's another Starbucks coffee bar at the Barnes & Noble superstore in Chelsea, at Sixth Avenue and 21st Street, and many more to follow around Manhattan.

The very cool yet dramatic postmodern gothic decor at **Edgar's,** 255 W. 84th St. (just west of Broadway; tel. 496-6126), is the setting for an excellent assortment of desserts, including profiteroles, ganache, Edgar's own tiramisù, and unusual Italian cakes, plus light foods like focaccia and bruschetta.

LATE-NIGHT/24-HOUR

BRASSERIE, 100 E. 53rd St., between Park and Lexington avenues, in the Seagram Building. Tel. 751-4840.

Cuisine: ALSATIAN FRENCH. **Reservations:** Recommended.

$ Prices: Appetizers $4.95–$7.95; main courses $9.50–$19.75; prix-fixe dinner $19.95. AE, CB, DC, MC, V.

Open: Daily 24 hrs. Breakfast 6–11am; lunch 11am–5pm; dinner 5–10pm; supper 10pm–6am; brunch Sat–Sun 11am–4pm. **Subway:** E or F to Lexington Ave.; 6 to 51st St.

⭐ It's always open, it's always fun, and the food does not disappoint here at one of midtown's most popular informal restaurants. The decor is brightly French provincial, the menu a combination of French and Alsatian dishes, plus some French-American hybrids, like fromage burgers. *Le déjeuner, le dîner,* and *le souper* menus feature the likes of *omelette Lorraine, choucroûte à l'alsacienne* (a house specialty), and onion soup. Prix-fixe dinners are also available, with a changing menu that features duck, fish, and steak items for $19.95, served with hors d'oeuvres or soup, vegetables, and dessert. Lunch, with main courses like quiche of the day and eggs Benedict, goes from about $9.95 to $17.95. The late supper is perfect after an evening's entertainment, and the Brasserie is also the scene of many a "power" breakfast.

FRENCH ROAST, 458 Sixth Ave., at 11th Street. Tel. 533-2233.

Cuisine: FRENCH/AMERICAN. **Reservations:** Recommended on weekends.

$ Prices: Appetizers $3.50–$6.75; main courses $7.50–$13.

Open: 7 days, 24 hours. **Subway:** F to 14th St.

This casual, Parisian-style cafe with antique Parisian signs and a coffee bar is usually packed with a lively Village crowd, everyone from NYU students who stop in for hamburgers to older longtime neighborhood residents enjoying an energizing cup of coffee to tourists in animated conversation over dinner. The menu is very accessible French/American and guaranteed to offer something to please every palate. Of the appetizers, the crab cakes are in big demand, and the leek-and-onion tart is excellent, as is the artichoke vinaigrette. My favorite main course is the pan-seared skate served over wild rice with vegetables; the couscous—with vegetables or

chicken—gets high marks, too. All desserts are r
premises by French Roast's own pastry chef. Don't d
dense and delicious chocolate mousse cake or the rich b
pudding.

PICNIC FARE & WHERE TO EAT IT

When the weather is fair, New York is picnic country. The parks, the
plazas, and the atriums around town are all fine places for holding an
impromptu picnic. If you're attending one of the free entertainments
in Central Park (perhaps the New York Philharmonic or the New
York Shakespeare Festival), a picnic is essential. And you need never
look far to find provisions.

Starting with the most exalted picnic fare, there's lofty **Fraser
Morris** at 1264 Third Ave., between 72nd and 73rd streets (tel.
288-2727), where an epicurean's basket of caviar, foie gras, cheese,
fruit, pâté, and whatever could easily cost between $400 and $500,
although most of their picnics for two are competitively priced
between $45 and $50. You should also consider the appetizing stores
discussed in Chapter 9 under "Gourmet Food Stores." All of them
dispense incredible selections of imported cheese, breads, smoked
fish, sausages, baked goods, homemade salads, and spreads—all
mouth-watering and well priced. **Fairway,** 2127 Broadway, at 74th
Street (tel. 595-1888), has delectable picnic possibilities in the rear,
and some of the freshest and most beautiful produce up front—at
just about the lowest prices for food of this caliber.

A specialty gourmet shop with an Italian theme, **Platti Pronti,**
34 W. 56th St. (tel. 315-4800), also at 1221 6th Ave., at 48th Street
(tel. 391-7882), 10 E. 44th St. (tel. 922-0808), and 8 Maiden Lane
downtown (tel. 233-1500), is the place to pick up wonderful gourmet
sandwiches, Italian sandwiches and cold dishes, unusual pizzas, and
pastas for elegant picnicking.

You'll see the name **Burke & Burke** at various outlets around
town, including one at 2 E. 23rd St. (tel. 505-2020); it offers
wonderful muffins and croissants as well as striking salads, sandwiches, and desserts. Trust **Zaro's Bread Basket,** too, which
specializes in bakery items, sandwiches, topped baked potatoes, and
more, all moderately priced. There are branches at the South Street
Seaport, Grand Central Terminal, Penn Station, Port Authority, and
elsewhere.

Most of the major supermarkets—such as **Food Emporium,
D'Agostino,** and **Gristede's,** found all over town—have deli
counters that could well be called delicacy counters, where you can
arrange the elements of quite a gracious meal. And year-round on
Wednesday, Friday, and Saturday, weather permitting, you can pop
over to the farmer's market at **Union Square** (14th to 17th streets
near Park Avenue South) to pick up homemade pies, cakes and
muffins, bagels, breads, preserves, fresh-off-the-farm fruits and vegetables, and even an occasional New York State wine.

But wherever you are you'll find good food to go. Delis are on
almost every corner, as are Korean groceries with their amazing
salad-buffet bars, often with quite an extensive selection of hot and
cold dishes and salad fixings. And the price is right.

Remember that, with one or two exceptions, you can purchase a
bottle of wine only at a licensed liquor store and never on Sunday,
but beer is available in any grocery store.

CIALTY DINING • 195

made fresh on the
ny yourself the
rioche bread

PTER 7

TO SEE &
NEW YORK

N ew York tourists generally fall into one of two categories. The first are the compulsive sightseers who feel that if they don't get to the top of the World Trade Center, visit the United Nations, have a meal in Chinatown, and take the boat to the Statue of Liberty, they might as well have stayed home. The second are the more easygoing tourists who like to know that the World Trade Center is there if they really want to see it, but are perfectly happy just walking around the city, absorbing the sights, sounds, and sensations as they find them.

Both have a point: The major sights of New York are exciting and important, and you should see as many of them as you comfortably can; but you should also allow yourself plenty of time to let New York sink in by osmosis: to rummage through Village antiques stores or watch lovers stroll through Central Park or sip a martini at a cocktail lounge in the sky as the city shimmers below. A holiday in New York, I think, ought to be made up of equal parts of doing and dreaming—with enough leisure for both.

Fitting everything in can be quite complicated, especially if you're here for just a short time. So have a look at the following listings of the city's attractions, decide what you want to see, and get started. After you've seen the main sights, you may also want to take some walking tours covering historical and architectural highlights of the city (see Chapter 8). Note that you'll be doing plenty of walking, so be sure to wear comfortable shoes. You should also carry with you bus and subway maps, available on buses, at subway stations, and at the New York Convention and Visitors Bureau, 2 Columbus Circle.

SUGGESTED ITINERARIES

IF YOU HAVE 1 DAY

Get up early and take the ferry to the Statue of Liberty and Ellis Island before the crowds get too big. If you visit both places, you will have

DID YOU KNOW . . . ?

- The Duke of York, the naval hero after whom the city is named, became James II of England.
- The Dakota apartment house at 72nd Street and Central Park West probably received its name because in 1881 it was considered so far north as to be in Dakota Territory.
- Mah Jong was introduced to Americans in 1902 when Abercrombie & Fitch bought up all the sets they could find in China.
- For 130 years, November 25 was a New York holiday celebrating the day in 1783 when British troops sailed home.
- Tammany Hall, the Democratic Party political machine, was named after an earlier local sachem, Chief Tammany of the Lenni-Lenape.

spent most of the day. Repair to Chinatown for late afternoon and early evening.

IF YOU HAVE 2 DAYS

Day 1 Spend day one as outlined above.

Day 2 Visit the Metropolitan Museum of Art in the morning, then spend the afternoon and early evening downtown at the South Street Seaport.

IF YOU HAVE 3 DAYS

Days 1–2 Spend days one and two as outlined above.

Day 3 On day three, visit the Empire State Building, Rockefeller Center, and the Museum of Modern Art. Spend the late afternoon and early evening wandering around Greenwich Village and SoHo.

IF YOU HAVE 4 DAYS

Days 1–3 Spend days one to three as outlined above.

Day 4 On the fourth day, visit the Observation Deck at the World Trade Center, tour downtown Manhattan, and relax in the afternoon on a Circle Line boat trip around Manhattan.

IF YOU HAVE 5 DAYS

Days 1–4 Spend days one to four as outlined above.

Day 5 On the fifth day, spend the morning at the United Nations and, depending on the weather, the afternoon in Central Park or shopping New York's major department stores—Saks Fifth Avenue, Bloomingdale's, Lord & Taylor, Macy's, and A&S.

1. THE TOP ATTRACTIONS

DOWNTOWN

STATUE OF LIBERTY, in New York Harbor.
   The Statue of Liberty is one sight in New York that no one, not even the most blasé, should miss. You'll enjoy your visit more if you come early on a weekday, since the crowds are large in the afternoon

and particularly on weekends and holidays. (Tel. for general information, 363-3200; for ferry, 269-5755.)

Every American schoolchild, of course, knows the story of the statue: of how it was given to the United States by the people of France in 1886 to commemorate the alliance of the two countries during the American Revolution. Its construction became the ruling passion of French sculptor Frédéric-Auguste Bartholdi, who raised funds in France and then designed the monument (Alexandre-Gustave Eiffel, who built the famous tower in Paris, did the supporting framework); and the people of the United States, reluctant to match the one-million-franc contribution of the French people, had to be prodded into it by an intensive campaign led by the *New York World*'s Joseph Pulitzer. Finally, the money was raised, and now it seems as if the statue has always been there, so magnificently does it blend into its site in Upper Bay, so splendidly does it typify the ideals and dreams on which the nation was built. Stepping from her chains, Liberty, a tablet commemorating the date of July 4, 1776, in her left hand, the torch of freedom held high in her right, has become the symbol of a new life to thousands of immigrants and exiles from all over the world.

When you actually get to the statue, the statistics—the figure is 152 feet high, the pedestal another 150 feet, the arm 42 feet long, the head large enough for a couple of people to stand in—become an awesome reality. The 21-foot-high bronze doors through which you enter the statue recount, in bas-relief panels, the history of Lady Liberty's construction and her restoration, a massive 2½-year, almost

---

FROMMER'S FAVORITE NEW YORK EXPERIENCES

A Morning or Afternoon in Central Park   Row on a surprisingly rural lake, ride a bike, sail a model boat, visit the zoo, hear the street musicians and the sound of birds, and watch the incredible people parade.

Late Afternoon and Early Evening at the South Street Seaport   Soak up the ocean breezes, board the old ships, shop at a bevy of intriguing stores, dine, and maybe even take a cruise around New York Harbor. There are often free concerts on the pier in early evening.

English Tea   Try Danal, 90 E. 10th St., or Little Nell's Tea Room, 343 E. 85th St., for a proper English tea in enchanting surroundings.

A Visit to Ellis Island   An incredibly moving journey back to the early years of the century when over 12 million immigrants passed through this portal to the new world.

The Metropolitan Museum of Art by Night   On Friday and Saturday night the museum stays open late. Leisurely browse through the galleries, then dine at the museum's own restaurant, or have drinks on the balcony and listen to live chamber music.

$70-million project that was completed in time for the gala centennial celebration on July 4, 1986. Although the statue still looks on the outside as it always did, major changes were made in the landscaping of Liberty Island; in the American Museum of Immigration at the base; and in the entrance to and the interior of the statue, which has been opened up to expose the "bones" of Eiffel's original structure and create an amazing indoor space. The former flame (it was also replaced in the restoration) is mounted in the center of the lobby floor. There's an elevator to the top of the pedestal, and from there, a 12-story (146-step) circular stairway to the crown's viewing platform. All in all, this is an unforgettable experience of what many consider to be America's greatest piece of monumental sculpture.

Open: Daily 9am–5pm (subject to change, so call first); admission to the statue is free, though donations are gratefully accepted.

Ferry Take the number 1 subway to South Ferry and head for the Castle Clinton National Monument in Battery Park, where you will buy your ticket for the Statue of Liberty ferry. Ferries leave every half hour from 9:30am to 3:30pm every day. They will deposit you, in about 20 minutes, on Liberty Island, a short distance from the statue. A stop at Ellis Island (see below) is included in the fare.

Prices: Fares—$6 adults, $5 seniors, $3 children 3–17, under 3 free.

Car & Ferry An alternate way to reach the Statue of Liberty is now available to those driving to New York via the New Jersey Turnpike and from New York through the Holland Tunnel. In both cases take Exit 14B to Liberty State Park (parking and park admission are free). The advantage here is that lines are generally shorter and parking is free. Incidentally, Liberty State Park is the scene of frequent concerts and events. Circle Line ferries depart every half hour from 9:30am to 3:30pm daily (except November 27 to early spring) for the Statue.

Prices: Fares—$6 adults, $5 seniors, $3 children 3–17, under 3 free; same as from Battery Park.

ELLIS ISLAND, in New York Harbor.

One of New York's newest—and most moving—sights, which

opened in the fall of 1990, is the restored Ellis Island, a few hundred yards north of the Statue of Liberty. Ellis Island was the portal through which more than 12 million immigrants entered the United States between 1892 and 1954. More than 100 million living Americans—40% of the nation's population—trace their roots to an ancestor who came through Ellis Island. The focal point of the restoration is the Ellis Island Immigration Museum, which does a masterful job of telling the immigrant's story in a series of innovative displays that feature historic artifacts and photos, interactive devices, and taped reminiscences of the immigrants themselves. Don't miss the superb documentary film shown free throughout the day. Also powerful is the American Immigrant Wall of Honor, which includes the names of nearly 200,000 American immigrants who have been commemorated by their descendants. Overlooking both the Statue of Liberty and the Manhattan skyline, it is the longest wall of names in the world.

Circle Line Tours runs daily ferries to Ellis Island both from Battery Park and from Liberty State Park at frequent intervals. (For details, see "Statue of Liberty" above.)

SOUTH STREET SEAPORT & SOUTH STREET SEAPORT MUSEUM, at the southeastern tip of Manhattan.

To see what a very practical group of dreamers and visionaries are doing to preserve the old days when South Street was the "street of ships" in the 19th century, visit the South Street Seaport Museum (tel. 669-9400). The museum is located in the 11-block South Street Seaport that stretches from Piers 15 and 16 all the way over to Fulton Street. Stroll out on the piers to see the magnificent ships of the museum's collection, or better still, take a museum walking tour to discover the history of the ships and the people of the old port. Museum admission of $5 for adults, $4 for senior citizens, $3 for students, and $2 for children under 12 allows you to visit museum galleries on Water and John streets; see museum films; board the original lightship *Ambrose*, which guarded the approach to the Port of New York for more than two decades; and climb aboard the *Peking*, a barque that is longer than a football field, with four masts 17 stories high! Your ticket also allows you to join the basic guided tour of the ships and the historic district, plus a tour behind the scenes of the restoration of the great ship *Wavertree* (built in 1885) and a tour of the unrestored district.

If you'd like to get out on the water yourself, that's also possible. In spring, summer, and early fall, you can take a one-hour **cruise** aboard a Circle Line boat around the southern tip of New York harbor. Tickets cost $12 for adults, $6 for children 12 and under. For more information, call 563-3200. Even more fun for those who like to sail is a cruise aboard the 100-year-old schooner *Pioneer*. Its specific destination depends on winds and tides; passengers are limited to 40, and those who wish to do so are invited to help sail the vessel. For a two-hour sail, the cost is $16 for adults, $13 for seniors, $12 for students with valid ID, and $5 for children 12 and under. For reservations or information, call 669-9417.

Another attraction is **Bowne & Co., Stationers,** at 211 Water St., a re-creation of a 19th-century stationery shop whose antique letterpresses are used daily. Bowne sells fine paper products, many printed in the shop itself. Other stores include the **Edmund M. Blunt Book & Chart Store** (nautical books and materials); the

Museum Shop (museum merchandise); **Staple & Fancy Goods** (antique gifts and decorative items); and the **Container Store** at Pier 16, in season (children's toys and accessories).

There's always plenty of activity going on at the South Street Seaport Museum, including concerts, films, readings, nautical events, classes, workshops, and special events.

The museum's ships and piers and its architectural focal point, the 1811 countinghouses called **Schermerhorn Row,** are part and parcel of the South Street Seaport area; it may remind you of Boston's Faneuil Hall Marketplace and Baltimore's Harborplace. It's great fun to shop at dozens of specialty shops, eat from exotic food stalls or at fancy restaurants, or just enjoy the street life; there are always street musicians and entertainers performing.

The **Fulton Fish Market building,** once the site of the Fulton Fish Market (which now operates weeknights from midnight to 8am right next door), is devoted exclusively to food—provisions on the first floor, fine restaurants and international "fast-food" menus from all over the world on the upper floors. Some of my favorite shops in this area include **Brookstone** for one-of-a-kind gadgets; **Captain Hook's** for nifty marine antiques; and **Caswell-Massey** for George Washington's favorite cologne, Sarah Bernhardt's cucumber cream, and other authentic old-time apothecary items.

Be sure to visit **Pier 17,** a huge three-story pavilion that juts out into the East River, housing more restaurants, bars, clothing stores, and food and specialty shops. There's another fast-food court here, and while the food is not exciting, it's fun to pick up a drink or a snack and take it out to the second-floor balcony to enjoy the tangy sea air and the splendid views of the river and the Brooklyn Bridge. From the third floor you get good views of the Statue of Liberty. As for the shopping here, it's pricey but very entertaining. My favorites are the **Sharper Image,** the catalog store to end all catalog stores, where there's always a line waiting to try out such wonderful adult playthings as electronic massage tables, talking scales, or indoor rowing machines; and **A2Z,** which also has nifty gadgets, like a solar-powered baseball cap with a built-in brow fan!

STATEN ISLAND FERRY, plying New York Harbor between South Ferry terminal in Manhattan and St. George terminal in Staten Island.

The cost is 50¢ (payable on the Staten Island side) for an enthralling hour-long excursion (round-trip) into the world's biggest harbor. Ferries run every 20 to 30 minutes (less often late nights). Most of the Staten Island commuters will be sitting inside reading papers, but do join the sightseers out on the deck, where you can view the busy harbor traffic. You'll pass close to the Statue of Liberty. When the boat arrives at St. George, Staten Island, debark, walk through the terminal, and, before you catch another boat going back to Manhattan, have a look at the Staten Island Ferry Collection of the Staten Island Institute of Arts and Sciences. In addition to a display of ferry artifacts such as ships' wheels and whistles, scale models, and historic photographs and postcards, the Ferry Collection also features a museum store with gifts and souvenirs. (Suggested admission is $1, 25¢ for children 12 and under.) If you have some time, you might want to walk two short blocks from the terminal to the Staten Island Institute of Arts and Sciences itself; changing exhibitions offer a glimpse of the more than two million artifacts in the collections, which explore the region's art, natural science, and history. There's an attractive museum store, too. (Suggested admission is $2.50 adults, $1.50 students and seniors.) The boat ride going back to Manhattan is really the best part of the trip, for now you can catch sight of the fabled New York skyline looming ahead of you. If you have time, try a ferry ride at night, when the skyline is even more dazzling. (To get to the ferry, take the number 1 subway to South Ferry, and make sure you are in one of the first four cars.)

EMPIRE STATE BUILDING, Fifth Avenue and 34th Street. Tel. 736-3100.

No visitor should leave New York without a visit to the top of the Empire State Building (completed 1931). You'll have plenty of company; over 2½ million visitors a year, from all over the world, make the pilgrimage to the world's once-highest building: At 1,454 feet above sea level, 102 stories high, this sleek, modernistic monument typifies the skyscraper city in its boldness, daring, and dominance. The real excitement starts when you reach the 86th-floor **Observatory;** from the outdoor promenade deck, it's a 360-degree view, and if the day is clear, you can see as far as 80 miles into the distance. But the big show lies below you—Manhattan, an island of steel and concrete and glass rising out of the sea, looking from this height like a Lilliputian landscape. For a view from an even higher vantage, you can go up another 16 stories, to the 102nd floor and its spaceship environment. After dark, the city becomes a fantasy of sparkling lights and stars against a panoramic background of darkness.

Admission: $3.75 adults, $1.75 seniors and children under 12.
Open: Daily 9:30am–midnight. Tickets sold until 11:20pm.
Subway: B, D, F or N, R to 34th St.

While you're here, stop in at the **Guinness World Record Exhibit Hall** on the concourse level (right next to the Observatory ticket office) to see who and what broke all the records. This multimedia display brings the world-famous *Guinness Book of Records* to life in an entertaining and lively fashion and is great fun for kids and adults alike. **Open:** Daily 9am–10pm. Admission is $6.95 for adults and $3.50 for ages 3–11 (tel. 947-2335).

MUSEUM OF MODERN ART, 11 W. 53rd St. Tel. 708-9480.

The Museum of Modern Art (MoMA) has been controversial since it was founded in 1929. The Modern's early shows—of fur-lined teacups, Dadaesque landscapes of the mind, cubism, and abstractions—were considered shocking by the staid art establishment of the time; now there are some who declare MoMA to be too old hat! Whichever side you're on, MoMA is a great, lively, wonderfully exciting museum that takes all of modern art and design as its province—and that includes photography, film, prints, illustrated books, furniture, and architecture, as well as paintings and sculpture. It presents the world's most comprehensive survey of 20th-century art. The Modern's notable building was opened in 1939.

Of course, you must see the Picassos, Chagalls, Kandinskys, Mondrians, and Matisses on permanent display, as well as the Rodin and Calder and Moore and Maillols in the splendid outdoor Abby Aldrich Rockefeller Sculpture Garden. Film buffs practically make the museum's theaters a second home; it's the place to catch an early

Garbo classic, a Flaherty masterpiece, your favorite Bogart flick, recent films you might have missed at the box office, as well as the work of new filmmakers. Because there is usually a heavy demand for movie tickets, get there as early as possible to commandeer a reservation. Summer garden is a popular series of free musical evenings held in the Sculpture Garden during July and August. Free jazz concerts are held every Friday from 5:30 to 8pm at the Garden Café.

Dining possibilities here include chic **Sette MoMA,** a northern Italian cafe on the second floor, whose outdoor terrace overlooks the garden; it's the members' dining room, but open to the public, space permitting. Reservations are a must. **The Garden Café,** under the same management, is a cafeteria for the public on the ground floor, overlooking the sculpture garden.

Admission (including entrance to movie): $7.50 adults, $4.50 students with valid ID and senior citizens, members, and children under 16 accompanied by an adult free; Thurs–Fri 5:30–8pm, "Pay What You Wish."

Open: Sat, Sun, Mon, Tues 11am–6pm; Thurs, Fri 12 noon–8:30pm. **Subway:** E or F to Fifth Ave.

RADIO CITY MUSIC HALL, Avenue of the Americas at 50th Street. Tel. 247-4777.

The world's biggest theater is, of course, the famed Radio City Music Hall Entertainment Center. Restored to its 1932 art deco elegance, the 5,875-seat theater is an architectural wonder, and its shows—concerts, spectacular presentations, and special events (rarely movies)—run the gamut from family entertainment like the magnificent Christmas Spectacular starring the Rockettes (America's most famous chorus girls) to pop acts such as Bette Midler and Tina Turner.

Tickets, priced according to the attraction, are available at the box office or can be charged through any **Ticketmaster** outlet (tel. 307-7171). Even if you don't see a show at Radio City, take a guided tour viewing the grand foyer, the orchestra, back and below stage, and the Wurlitzer. For information, call 632-4041.

Tours: Hour-long tours usually given Mon–Sat 10:15am–4:45pm, Sun 11am–4:45pm, for $9. **Subway:** B, D, F, or Q to 47–50th Sts./Rockefeller Center.

ROCKEFELLER CENTER, 47th Street to 52nd Street, just west of Fifth Avenue.

It's noted as one of the architectural marvels of New York—and of the United States—a high-water mark of urban design. Although it is one of the busiest, most heavily trafficked areas in the city, this 24-acre, 19-skyscraper complex gives the feeling of old-world gentility and beauty, thanks to its masterful use of open space. You'll appreciate this as you approach the Center from the best vantage point, the Channel Gardens, which begin between 49th and 50th streets, across Fifth Avenue from St. Patrick's Cathedral and Saks Fifth Avenue. Depending on the season, the gardens will be abloom with chrysanthemums, lilies, roses, or tropical plants, and you'll see scores of people stopping to sit on the benches and maybe munch a lunchtime sandwich. On either side of the walk is an array of shops and services. Continue down the promenade to the central sunken plaza, the focal point of the complex. In winter, the plaza is an ice-skating rink, a Breughel canvas in the heart of the city; in summer, it's an open-air restaurant. Directly behind the plaza is the golden statue of *Prometheus* (1934) by Paul Manship, with its fountain in back; behind that the GE Building soars skyward.

Subway: B, D, F, or Q to 47–50th Sts./Rockefeller Center.

THE UNITED NATIONS, on the East River between 42nd Street and 48th Street. Tel. 963-7713.

At the United Nations, world history happens almost every day. An international enclave on the East River, it is headquarters for almost 6,000 men and women from all over the world who carry on the work of the Secretariat and the General Assembly. Most of the U.N. complex was built from 1947 to 1953.

Just *being* at the United Nations will give you an excitement that you'll find nowhere else. You could have a lovely visit just walking around, observing the sculptures and artworks donated by the member nations (in the garden, for example, a massive sculpture of a Soviet worker beats a sword into a plowshare), shopping in the downstairs stores (more about these later), and observing the lively international crowd; but do take time to attend one of the General Assembly or other meetings and/or to take a guided tour. The guided tours, a wonderful introduction to the history and activities of the U.N., give you a chance to explore the varied collections of art and sculpture. There are also tours for non–English-speaking guests.

Free tickets to the meetings are given out in the lobby of the General Assembly building just before they start, on a first-come, first-served basis. To find out in advance what meetings will be held, phone 963-1234 after 9:30am on the day you wish to attend. Once you gain admission, you can plug in your earphones and listen to the debates—sometimes quite heated—in English or French or Chinese or Spanish or Russian or Arabic—the official languages of the U.N.

You could easily browse away a few hours downstairs at the United Nations. My favorite spot here is the **Gift Center,** where beautiful and tasteful handcrafts from many of the member nations are sold. On one visit, for example, I found pewterware from Norway, beautifully painted nesting dolls from Russia, silk scarves from India, brassware from Iran, and carved figures from Nigeria. The collection of ethnic dolls is enough to win the heart of any little girl on your list. Stamp buffs should stop in at the **United Nations Postal Administration Sales Counter,** the only spot on the globe (besides the United Nations offices in Geneva and Vienna) where you can mail cards and letters bearing U.N. postage stamps.

If you arrive early enough, have lunch at the United Nations in the **Delegates Dining Room.** It's open to the public Monday to Friday between 11:30am and 2:30pm. You may see a few of the delegates, and the view of the East River and the United Nations gardens is one of the best in town. Call 963-7625 for reservations.

Tours: Guided English-language tours about every half hour, from 9:15am–4:15pm; they cost $6.50 adults, $4.50 seniors, $4.50 college and high school students, $3.50 for children grades 1–8 (children under 5 not permitted on tours). For information on tours in other languages, phone 963-7539 on the day of your visit. **Bus:** M104, 42nd St. crosstown bus, M15 uptown. **Subway:** 4, 5, 6, 7 or the Times Square Shuttle to Grand Central.

UPPER WEST SIDE

LINCOLN CENTER FOR THE PERFORMING ARTS, 70 Lincoln Center Plaza. Tel. 875-5350 for tour information; 875-5400 for events hotline.

Whether or not you see any performances at Lincoln Center (more details in Chapter 10), take a tour of this impressive complex of theaters and concert halls. Just to see the art and sculpture on the grounds is an experience in itself: Alexander Calder's *Le Guichet* in front of the New York Public Library for the Performing Arts; Richard Lippold's *Orpheus and Apollo* in Avery Fisher Hall; Henry Moore's gigantic *Reclining Figure* in the reflecting pool in front of the Vivian Beaumont Theater; and Marc Chagall's lilting paintings for the Metropolitan Opera House. The buildings themselves—the Metropolitan Opera House, the New York State Theater, the Vivian Beaumont Theater, Avery Fisher Hall, Alice Tully Hall, The Juilliard School, the Walter Reade Theater, and the New York Public Library for the Performing Arts—have been criticized and praised: Take a look and reach your own conclusion. You'll probably see all the buildings and may even get to watch rehearsals of the New York City Ballet or the New York City Opera Company. But if you have your heart set on seeing the interiors of the theaters, do not come on a Saturday afternoon; that's matinee time, and the doors are closed to tour takers.

Tours: Hour-long tours daily 10am–5pm; cost is $7.75 adults, $4.50 children 6–12; $6.75 senior citizens and students. Backstage tours of the Metropolitan Opera House alone are held during the Met's season (usually October to June at 3:45pm weekdays and 10am Saturday morning). Admission is $8 adults, $4 students. Phone 769-7020 for reservations. **Subway:** 1 or 9 to 66th St.

THE AMERICAN MUSEUM OF NATURAL HISTORY, Central Park West at 79th Street. Tel. 769-5100.

One of the great scientific museums of the world, the American Museum brings the natural history of the earth and the cultural diversity of humans to vivid life for visitors of all ages. Through the end of 1995, the museum will be celebrating its 125th anniversary, with a year-long program of special events and exhibitions, including the recent opening of the Lila Acheson Wallace Wing of Mammals and Their Extinct Relatives, the greatest collection of fossil mammals in the world. Added to that and such perennial crowd-pleasing (and kid-pleasing) exhibitions as the Hall of Minerals and Gems, the Hall of African Peoples, the Hall of Reptiles and Amphibians, and the Hall of Ocean Life (with its 94-foot whale suspended from the ceiling) is the exciting Arthur Ross Hall of Meteorites, whose centerpiece is the largest meteorite ever retrieved. The Barosaurus exhibit—not to be missed—is the largest free-standing dinosaur display in the world. Another winner is the Hall of Asian Peoples, which explores the complex cultures of the Asian continent. The new Hall of Human Biology and Evolution is noteworthy. Children over five will enjoy the learning games in the Discovery Room. You could spend days—no, weeks—here, enjoying ethnological and anthropological collections, seeing the dioramas of animals in their natural habitats, and watching the dance, music, and crafts programs shown live at the Frederick H. Leonhardt People Center. And you won't want to miss seeing the exciting films shown daily in the Naturemax

Theater on New York's largest screen (separate admission of $5 adults, $2.50 children.

Admission: Suggested admission $5 adults; $4 seniors and students; $2.50 children.

Open: Sun–Thurs 10am–5:45pm, Fri–Sat 10am–8:45pm. **Closed:** Christmas and Thanksgiving. **Subway:** C to 81st St.; 1 or 9 to 79th St.

UPPER EAST SIDE

THE FRICK COLLECTION, 1 East 70th St., at Fifth Avenue. Tel. 288-0700.

One of the most beautiful small museums in the world, this former home of industrialist magnate Henry Clay Frick is filled with treasures: Rembrandts, Turners, Vermeers, El Grecos, 18th-century French furniture, Chinese vases, and Limoges enamels. Its central courtyard, with greenery and a fountain, is an oasis in the city. The home was built in 1914 and was transformed into a museum in 1935. An audio-visual show, "The Frick Collection: An Introduction," is presented daily at regular intervals. Concerts and lectures are held throughout the year. Phone for details.

Admission: $5 adults; $3 students and seniors. Children under 10 not admitted; those under 16 must be accompanied by an adult.

Open: Tues–Sat 10am–6pm, Sun and minor holidays 1–6pm. **Closed:** Major holidays. **Subway:** 6 to 68th St.

SOLOMON R. GUGGENHEIM MUSEUM, 1071 Fifth Ave., near 88th Street. Tel. 423-3500.

Completely restored and expanded with the addition of a 10-story tower, Frank Lloyd Wright's 1959 creation, considered to be one of the greatest buildings of the 20th century, reopened in June 1992 after a two-year hiatus: Wright's landmark building is now more exciting and dramatic than ever. From the outside, it looks something like a gigantic wedding cake tilted to one side; on the inside, it's a superb showcase for art—a large spiral ramp on which you walk downward, viewing art set in bays along the curved walls. Many exciting shows complement Solomon Guggenheim's collection of 20th-century art, which focuses mainly on abstract expressionist and nonobjective masters. The Justin K. Thannhauser Wing permanently displays works by great artists like Picasso, Degas, and Cézanne. A full-service cafe run by Dean & Deluca and based on Wright's original design offers excellent refreshments.

The Guggenheim Museum has also expanded downtown: The **Guggenheim Museum SoHo** is located in a 19th-century landmark building at 575 Broadway (tel. 423-3500), in the SoHo Cast-Iron Historic District. **T,** a stylish tearoom and cafe, is located on the lower level.

Admission: For adults, $7 Guggenheim Museum, $5 Guggenheim Museum SoHo, $10 both locations. For students and senior citizens, $4 Guggenheim Museum, $3 Guggenheim Museum SoHo, $6 both locations. Children under 12 free with an adult.

Open: Guggenheim Museum: Sun–Wed 10am–6pm; Fri–Sat 10am–8pm; closed Thursday. Guggenheim Museum SoHo: Sun, Wed, Thurs, Fri 11am–6pm; Sat 11am–8pm; closed Mon–Thurs. **Subway:** B, D, F, Q to Broadway-Lafayette St.; N, R to Prince St.

THE JEWISH MUSEUM, 1109 Fifth Ave., at 92nd Street. Tel. 423-3200; information recording 423-3230.

★ This world-class museum dedicated to presenting the remarkable scope and diversity of Jewish art, history, and culture reopened in 1993 after a 2½-year expansion and renovation program, designed by AIA Gold Medal winner Kevin Roche. From the outside, the original 1908 Warburg Mansion gives the appearance of a late French Gothic château; inside, the museum's outstanding collection of some 27,000 works of art, antiquities, ceremonial objects, and electronic-media materials are showcased in various temporary exhibits. There's a stunning two-floor centerpiece permanent exhibition, "Culture and Continuity: The Jewish Journey," which traces over 4,000 years of Jewish experience. A wide variety of educational, cultural, and artistic programs take place here on a regular basis. The cafe serves light kosher fare. Be sure to visit the outstanding bookstore with many gift ideas, including children's items, and the unique Design Store, which features one-of-a-kind handcrafted pieces.

Admission: $6 adults, $4 students and senior citizens; children under 12 free. Free Tues after 5pm.

Open: Mon, Wed, Thurs, and Sun 11am–5:45pm, Tues 11am–8pm. **Closed:** Major legal and Jewish holidays. **Subway:** 4, 5, or 6 to 86th St.

METROPOLITAN MUSEUM OF ART, Fifth Avenue at 82nd Street. Tel. 535-7710 for recorded information, 879-5512 for news of concerts and lectures.

Whether you're interested in Egyptian artifacts or Roman armor or Chinese porcelain or Renaissance or impressionist painting, the Metropolitan is the place. You could spend weeks studying the collection of European and American painting, a masterful group of Raphaels, Titians, El Grecos, Rembrandts, Picassos, Pollocks, and Braques—enough to make your head swim. You'll surely want to visit the 18 new galleries devoted to the art of South and Southeast Asia, some 1,300 magnificent works from India, Nepal, Cambodia, and nine other countries in that region. Then there's the spectacular wing devoted to the art of Africa, the Pacific Islands, and Pre-Columbian and Native America. You must not miss the American wing, which has brought some of Central Park indoors in a 70-foot-tall glass-enclosed garden that leads to three floors of American paintings, furniture, sculpture, silver, glass, textiles, and decorative arts. Also high on your agenda should be the splendid 19th-century European Painting Galleries, with particular emphasis on the impressionist and post-impressionist painters and a large collection of Rodin sculptures. If your interest is 20th-century art, visit the Lila Acheson Wallace Wing; during the summer, its roof garden is a showplace for large-scale sculpture. The Chinese Scholars garden court and the superb Asian collection are a must. The 32 dramatic Egyptian galleries, including the incredible Temple of Dendur, are considered a triumph of art and scholarship, one of the most distinguished collections of its kind anywhere. The exhibit is absorbing for everyone, and the kids, especially, will love the mummy cases! The kids—and grown-ups, too—will also be enthralled by the Arms and Armor galleries, displaying an encyclopedic collection of the art of the armorer, swordsman, and gunmaker, from the 5th to the 19th century. There is a particularly large collection of Japanese arms and armor, as well as works from Europe, America, the Near East, and elsewhere in Asia.

Admission (including same-day admission to the Cloisters, detailed under "More Attractions," below): Suggested charge $7 adults; $3.50 students and seniors.

Open: Sun and Tues–Thurs 9:30am–5:15pm, Fri–Sat 9:30am–8:45pm. Visitors should be aware that some galleries are closed for portions of the day on Tues–Thurs and Sun, so it is best to call before your visit. The Metropolitan now stays open late on Friday and Saturday nights, when the museum restaurant is open for cocktails and/or dinner until 10pm. Visitors can dine leisurely (and very reasonably), then browse through the museum's collection or special exhibitions. **Closed:** New Year's Day, Thanksgiving, and Christmas. **Subway:** 4, 5, or 6 to 86th St.

WHITNEY MUSEUM OF AMERICAN ART, 945 Madison Ave., at 75th Street. Tel. 570-3600, 570-3676 for recorded information.

What many consider the very best collection of 20th-century American art is housed in Marcel Breuer's superb modernistic building (1966), an inverted wedding cake to which you gain entrance by crossing a bridge. Founded by Gertrude Vanderbilt Whitney, the museum opened in Greenwich Village in 1931 and is now in its third home. At least two major exhibitions are on view at all times, often (though not always) including a good sampling from the permanent collection by such artists as Alexander Calder, Edward Hopper, Jasper Johns, Roy Lichtenstein, Reginald Marsh, Louise Nevelson, and Georgia O'Keeffe. The noted Whitney Biennial exhibit is due again in 1995.

Sarabeth's at the Whitney offers lunch daily and brunch on weekends.

Note: The **Whitney Museum of American Art at Philip Morris,** Park Avenue and 42nd Street, across from Grand Central Terminal, features a sculpture court and garden, with an adjacent gallery for changing exhibitions. The sculpture court is open Monday to Saturday from 7:30am to 9:30pm and Sunday and holidays from 11am to 7pm; gallery is open Monday to Friday from 11am to 6pm and Thursday to 7:30pm. Admission is free (tel. 878-2550).

Admission (including programs in the New American Film and Video Series): $6 adults, $5 senior citizens and college students with valid ID; children under 12 with an adult free. Thurs 6–8pm free.

Open: Wed 11am–6pm; Thurs 1–8pm, Fri–Sun 11am–6pm. **Closed:** National holidays. **Subway:** 6 to 77th St.

CENTRAL PARK, between Central Park West and Fifth Avenue from Central Park South (59th Street) to Central Park North (110th Street). Tel. 360-8111, or 360-3456 for recorded information.

What Tivoli is to Copenhagen and Chapultepec is to Mexico City, Central Park is to New York: the great public playground. A magnificent garden in the midst of concrete canyons, it offers city-jaded New Yorkers a breath of the country, a chance to wander among country landscapes, climb rocks, listen to the song of birds, and stare at the sky. It also gives them the chance to stare at one another: Frederick Law Olmsted and Calvert Vaux's 19th-century greensward is one of the most popular places in town. Three visitor centers—The Charles A. Dana Discovery Center, the Dairy, and Belvedere Castle provide free visitor information. To see the park in

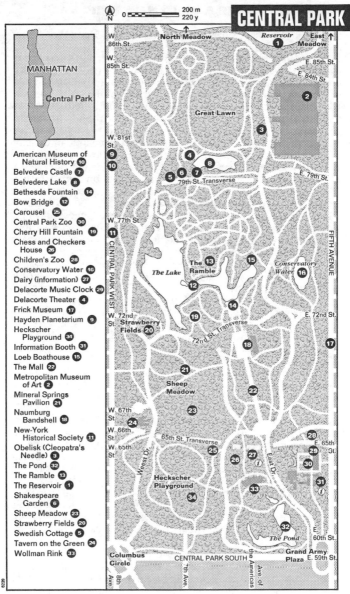

CENTRAL PARK

0 — 200 m
0 — 220 y

North Meadow
Reservoir ❶
East Meadow

W. 86th St.
W. 85th St.
E. 85th St.
E. 84th St.

Great Lawn ❷

❸

W. 81st St.
❹
❾
❿
❻ ❼ ❽
❺
79th St. Transverse
E. 79th St.

W. 77th St.
⓫
The Lake
The Ramble ⓭
⓯
Conservatory Water
⓰
⓬
⓮
W. 72nd St.
Strawberry Fields ⓴
⓳
E. 72nd St.
72nd St. Transverse
⓲
⓱

㉑
Sheep Meadow
㉒
㉓

W. 67th St.
㉔
W. 66th St.
65th St. Transverse
㉘
E. 65th St.
W. 65th St.
㉕
㉖ ㉗ ⓘ
㉙
㉚
㉛ ⓘ
Heckscher Playground
㉞
㉝
㉜ The Pond

Columbus Circle
CENTRAL PARK SOUTH
Grand Army Plaza
E. 59th St.
8th Ave.
7th Ave.
Ave. of the Americas
Ave. of the Americas

FIFTH AVENUE
CENTRAL PARK WEST
West Dr.
East Dr.

style, board the Central Park Trolley for a 90-minute tour: The Trolley traverses the park from end to end and includes stops at key points. It leaves from the kiosk at Grand Army Plaza, Fifth Avenue at 60th Street, Mon–Fri at 10:30am, 1 and 3pm; the cost is $12 adults, $10 seniors.

The park offers many recreational and cultural outlets. During summer, there's the New York Shakespeare Festival, plus concerts by the Metropolitan Opera, the New York Philharmonic, and many others—most of them free. To find out about a multitude of events sponsored by the Department of Parks and Recreation, phone 360-3456.

Kids adore the park, but with or without them, don't miss taking a rowboat out on **Conservatory Lake** (north of 72nd Street), an unexpectedly rural spot for New York. (You can rent boats just north of the 72nd Street transverse on the east side of the lake.) And when you've finished, join the throngs strolling around the beautiful **Bethesda Fountain** area, which is really the focal point of the park. The setting—with the fountain, the lake, and the towers of New York in the background—is one of the most romantic in the city.

A particularly romantic way to see Central Park is in a **horsedrawn carriage** ($34 for the first 20-minute ride; $10 for each additional 15 minutes; pick up a carriage on 59th Street; tel. 246-0520). The energetic can join the local jogging set or rent a horse from the **Claremont Riding Academy,** 175 W. 89th St. (tel. 724-5100; about $33 an hour; you must be experienced in English riding at walk, trot, and canter) and trot through miles of lovely bridle paths. Or you can rent a bike from the **bicycle concession** near the boathouse on the east side of the lake just north of 72nd Street and join the throngs of New Yorkers—families, kids, and singles looking for other singles—who've discovered the joy of life on wheels. During the summer, the park is closed to traffic from 10am to 3pm and again from 7 to 10pm on weekdays, as well as all day on the weekends, so bikers, riders, and kids reign supreme. Tennis buffs can also find a home in Central Park; the courts at 93rd Street are insanely popular. **Tennis permits** cost $50 for adults, $20 for senior citizens, and $10 for juniors, and they entitle you to an hour of play every day. Good news for short-term visitors: Single-play tickets, good for an hour, are available for $5 and can be purchased right at the courts. There are also several bubbled courts that stay open during the winter. For information on permits and what courts are open, phone the **Permit Office,** 830 Fifth Ave. (tel. 360-8133). Skaters can enjoy ice-skating in winter or roller-skating in summer at the Lasker Rink (tel. 996-1184), mid-park at 106th Street, or at the more centrally located Wollman Rink (tel. 517-4800); enter the park at 59th Street. Just to the north on the other side of the northbound Park Drive at 64th Street is the Central Park Zoo (see below under "Parks and Gardens") and the Carousel (open daily from St. Patrick's Day to Thanksgiving; only on weekends the rest of the year). More sedentary types can enjoy browsing through the **book stalls** (New York's modest answer to the Left Bank quais of Paris) along the outer wall of the park, at Fifth Avenue and 60th Street. (There are also some great little kiosks serving all sorts of international snacks.)

A living memorial to John Lennon grows in Central Park, in a hilly 2½-acre area across the street from the Dakota Apartments, Central Park West and 72nd Street, where Lennon was slain in 1980. Five years after the event, his widow, Yoko Ono, who donated $1 million to the project, joined in an opening ceremony for **Strawberry Fields** with an array of international diplomats, many of whose countries had sent gifts to this "International Garden of Peace." There are river birches from the former Soviet Union, maples from Canada, cedars from Israel, daffodils from Holland, and dogwoods from the late Princess Grace of Monaco. Most poignant, perhaps, is Italy's gift, a black-and-white mosaic starburst with the word *Imagine* inscribed in its center. For those who remember John Lennon, this is a very special bit of New York.

Subway: B, D, A, C, 1, or 9 to 59th St./Columbus Circle; or N, R to Fifth Ave., depending upon which entrance you wish to use.

2. MORE ATTRACTIONS

New York City's possibilities are endless. I haven't attempted to cover everything, since this is a guidebook, not an encyclopedia. Listed below are some major and minor sights of the city, chosen either for their importance or their special, if offbeat, charm.

ARCHITECTURAL HIGHLIGHTS

SONY BUILDING, 550 Madison Ave., between 55th and 56th streets.

Designed by Philip Johnson and John Burgee, the former AT&T corporate headquarters was hailed as the first major office structure in the post-modern style when it opened in 1984. The facade is pink granite, the inside walls are marble. Its distinctive top resembles a notched piece of 18th-century Chippendale furniture. Sony Plaza, which provides a walkway between 55th and 56th streets, has public seating, a cafe and bakery, retail shops, and the fascinating new science museum, Sony Wonder Technology Lab.

CHRYSLER BUILDING, 405 Lexington Ave., at 42nd Street.

One of the best examples of the art deco period in New York, the Chrysler Building was completed in 1930 and was the world's tallest building for a few months. Its lobby is considered one of the city's most splendid art deco interiors. The upper tower is clad in stainless steel. The lower masonry portion features designs that recall automobile hubcaps.

FORD FOUNDATION BUILDING, 320 E. 43rd St., just east of Second Avenue. Tel. 573-5000.

The Ford Foundation Building (1967), designed by Kevin Roche, is considered one of the rare modern architectural masterpieces of New York, a structure built with humanistic concerns for its employees and environment. It is especially notable for its splendid indoor garden—a glorious 12-story, 160-foot-high hothouse. The former architecture critic of the *New York Times,* Ada Louise Huxtable, called the building "a splendid, shimmering Crystal Palace" and its garden "probably one of the most romantic environments ever devised by corporate man." Don't miss a quiet few moments here.

Open: Garden, Mon–Fri 9am–5pm.

GRAND CENTRAL TERMINAL, 42nd Street at Park Avenue.

A symbol of the power of New York City, Grand Central Terminal is a magnificent beaux arts structure built in 1903–13. Its architectural focus is the main concourse, one of the great interiors of New York City, topped by a ceiling painted with the constellations of the zodiac.

WOOLWORTH BUILDING, 233 Broadway, at Park Place in the Financial District.

Until the coming of the Chrysler Building and the Empire State Building, this was the world's tallest—60 stories, pretty good for 1913. It's a lovely, lacy, Gothic froufrou. Walk in to see the lobby with its walls of golden marble.

ART GALLERIES

Art is "hot" in New York City. At last official count, there were something like 560 art galleries in town—and the number keeps growing, almost weekly. New York is still the acknowledged center of the international art scene, and for art-happy New Yorkers, gallery-going is a favorite pastime. The uptown scene of the action is still 57th Street and up Madison Avenue into the East 70s and 80s. Also, many prestigious East Side galleries have relocated to SoHo. Saturday is the big browsing and shopping day. If your interest in art is more than casual, come join the crowd.

Since there is no admission fee to galleries (unless there is a special charity benefit), you can come and go as you please. Where you go will be determined by what you're interested in: the moderns, the traditionalists, or the Old Masters. The quickest way to find out who's showing where is to consult the art pages in the "Arts & Leisure" section of Sunday's *New York Times* or *New York* magazine. The following are some of the big names among the galleries showing the moderns: **Holly Solomon**, 172 Mercer St., in SoHo; **Marlborough**, 40 W. 57th St.; **André Emmerich**, 41 E. 57th St.; **Tibor de Nagy**, 41 W. 57th St.; **Saidenberg**, 1018 Madison Ave.; **Stark**, 594 Broadway, Suite 301, in SoHo; **Cordier & Ekstrom**, 417 E. 75th St.; **Forum**, 745 Fifth Ave. at 57th St.; **Terry Dintenfass**, 50 W. 57th St.; and **Pace**, 32 E. 57th St.

Should your taste run more to the impressionists and French masters, visit **Hammer Galleries**, 33 W. 57th St., or **Wally Findlay Galleries**, 17 E. 57th St. (which also shows contemporary Europeans and Americans). **Spanierman**, 45 E. 58th St., specializes in 19th- and 20th-century American paintings and sculpture, with an emphasis on American impressionism. **Hirschl & Adler**, 21 E. 70th St., specializes in American paintings from the 18th century to the present, as well as French and European paintings from the early 19th to the early 20th century (during August, open by appointment only). Old Masters? Get out your checkbook and head for the hallowed and haughty temples of **Wildenstein**, 19 E. 64th St. (where you could also pick up an impressionist, Postimpressionist, or 20th-century master). **Knoedler & Co.**, 19 E. 70th St., is noted for contemporary American and European paintings and sculpture.

CEMETERIES

Should you want to pay your respects to some notable New Yorkers, you can visit these four famous cemeteries.

MANHATTAN

TRINITY CHURCH, 74 Trinity Place. Tel. 602-0800.

The churchyard that surrounds the historic church on three sides contains the graves of some noted parishioners—among them, Alexander Hamilton, Robert Fulton, and Albert Gallatin.

Open: Daily 9am–5pm. **Subway:** 4 or 5 to Wall St.; N or R to Rector St.

TRINITY CHURCH CEMETERY, 770 Riverside Drive, at 153rd to 155th streets. Tel. 368-1600.

This is the largest cemetery in Manhattan. You'll spot names of historic New York families, among them the Astors, the Van Burens, and the Schermerhorns. Clement C. Moore, the author of the poem "'Twas the Night Before Christmas," is also buried here.
Open: Daily 9am–4:30pm. **Subway:** 1 to 157th St.

BROOKLYN

GREEN-WOOD CEMETERY, Fifth Avenue and 25th Street. Tel. 718/783-8776.

Some half-a-million people are interred here: Famous names include De Witt Clinton, Horace Greeley, Samuel F. B. Morse, and Rev. Henry Ward Beecher.
Open: Daily 8am–4pm. **Subway:** R to 25th St.

THE BRONX

WOODLAWN CEMETERY, East 233rd Street and Webster Avenue. Tel. 920-0500.

This enormous park dates back to 1863. It contains the mausoleums of such tycoons as Jay Gould, F. W. Woolworth, and O. H. P. Belmont. Famous literary, newspaper, and entertainment figures buried here include Herman Melville, Joseph Pulitzer, Charles Scribner, George M. Cohan, and Duke Ellington. An on-going schedule of free events takes place on a monthly basis—concerts, tours, musical theater, and the like.
Open: Daily 9am–4:30pm. **Subway:** 4 to Woodlawn.

CHURCHES & SYNAGOGUES

ST. PATRICK'S CATHEDRAL, Fifth Avenue between 50th and 51st streets. Tel. 753-2261.

"St. Pat's" is New York's foremost Roman Catholic church and the seat of the Archdiocese of New York. Designed by James Renwick and built in 1878–88, it is a majestic structure, one of the finest Gothic churches in the United States.
Admission: Free.
Open: Daily 8:30am–8pm. **Subway:** B, D, F, or Q to 47–50th Sts./Rockefeller Center.

MARBLE COLLEGIATE CHURCH, Fifth Avenue at 29th Street. Tel. 686-2770.

The church that Norman Vincent Peale made famous, this Gothic Revival structure was built in 1854. Its elegant facade is made of marble. This is the oldest Reformed Church in New York City.
Admission: Free.
Open: Services at 10:30am in summer, 11:15am in fall and winter. **Bus:** Fifth Ave. southbound. **Subway:** 6 to 28th St.; R and N to 28th St.

TRINITY CHURCH, Broadway at Wall Street. Tel. 602-0800.

Consecrated in 1846, and the church of such famous people as Alexander Hamilton and Robert Fulton, Trinity Church is still a vital center for the downtown community. Featured are tours, organ recitals, and museum.
Admission: Free; $2 suggested donation to recitals.

Open: Sun–Fri 7am–6pm; Sat 8am–4pm. **Subway:** 4 or 5 to Wall St.; N or R to Rector St.

ST. PAUL'S CHAPEL, Broadway between Fulton and Vesey streets. Tel. 602-0874.

The oldest public building in continual use in Manhattan, St. Paul's dates back to 1764; George Washington's pew is still here. There are noontime concerts and exhibits.

Admission: Free; $2 suggested donation to concerts.

Open: Mon–Fri 9am–3pm; Sun 7am–3pm. Closed Sat. **Subway:** 4 or 5 to Fulton St.

CENTRAL SYNAGOGUE, 123 E. 55th St., at Lexington Avenue. Tel. 838-5122.

This New York City and National Historic Landmark, built in 1872, is perhaps the finest example of Moorish Revival architecture in New York.

Admission: Free.

Open: Services (Reform Jewish) Friday night and Saturday; open Mon–Thurs 12–2pm for meditation and prayer (except on holidays). **Subway:** 6 to 51st St./E or F to Lexington Ave./53rd St.

TEMPLE EMANU-EL, Fifth Avenue and 65th Street. Tel. 744-1400.

The city's most famous synagogue—its congregations have always included some of New York's most prominent and wealthy Jewish families—Temple Emanu-El is the largest Reform synagogue in the world. Its magnificent building (1929) is largely Romanesque in design, with Byzantine ornamentation.

Admission: Free.

Open: Services Sun–Thurs at 5:30pm, Fri at 5:15pm, and Sat at 10:30am. **Subway:** 6 to 68th St.

CONGREGATION SHEARITH ISRAEL (THE SPANISH AND PORTUGUESE SYNAGOGUE), 2 W. 70th St. Tel. 873-0300.

This Orthodox Sephardic synagogue was erected in 1897 by the oldest Jewish congregation (founded in 1654) in North America. It was established by descendants of Spanish and Portuguese Jews persecuted by the Inquisition who had found refuge first in Brazil, later in New York. Louis Comfort Tiffany designed the windows of this landmark structure.

Open: Services every morning and evening. Call synagogue office for a schedule. Tours by appointment. **Subway:** C to 72nd St.; 1, 2, 3, or 9 to 72nd St.

ST. PETER'S LUTHERAN CHURCH, Lexington Avenue at 54th Street. Tel. 935-2200.

This modern church (1977), part of Citicorp Center, boasts a chapel designed by Louise Nevelson, the External Pomodoro Cross, and three art galleries.

Admission: Free.

Open: The church is noted for its Jazz Vespers, held Sunday at 5pm. Traditional masses are held Sun at 8:45am, and sung mass at 11am Sun. There are weekday concerts at noon; call for a detailed schedule. **Subway:** 6 to 51st St.; E or F to Lexington Ave./53rd St.

CATHEDRAL CHURCH OF ST. JOHN THE DIVINE, 1047 Amsterdam Ave. at 112th Street. Tel. 316-7540.

The largest Gothic cathedral in the world, St. John the Divine is still not finished—and construction began in 1892! One of the major cultural and spiritual forces of New York, the cathedral is known for presenting outstanding musical events and important speakers. The free New Year's Eve concert at St. John's draws thousands of New Yorkers—so, too, does its annual "Blessing of the Animals."

Admission: Suggested donation, $2.

Open: Daily 7am–5pm. **Tours:** Tues–Sat 11am, Sun 1pm. "Vertical Tours"—a hike up the 11-flight circular staircase to the top—can be booked by appointment at 932-7347. For information on group tours—Tues–Sat 9am–3pm, call the same number. **Subway:** 1 or 9 to 110th St.

RIVERSIDE CHURCH, 490 Riverside Drive, between 120th and 122nd streets. Tel. 222-5900.

Built in 1930 and funded by John D. Rockefeller, Jr., Riverside Church was modeled on the Cathedral at Chartres. Noted for its commitment to major social issues, it attracts a diverse, interracial, and cosmopolitan group of congregants. Be sure to visit the Laura Spelman Rockefeller Memorial Carillon, the world's largest, with 74 bells; its observation platform affords a splendid view of the city (Sundays only, 12:30–4pm).

Admission: $1.

Open: Services: Sun 10:45am, with carillon recitals before and after. Summer organ recitals Tues 7pm in July ($7). **Subway:** 1 or 9 to 116th St./Columbia University.

HISTORIC BUILDINGS & MONUMENTS

CITY HALL, City Hall Park, between Broadway and Park Row.

Head for City Hall and the mayor will be out to greet you if you're an astronaut, a prime minister, or a beauty queen, but you may not get to see him if you're just an ordinary mortal. You can, however, see the splendid place in which he works, an early 19th-century Federal building considered to be one of New York's prime architectural treasures. Walk up the majestic marble staircase to the Governor's Room, a museum with historic furniture (the desk George Washington used as president is here) and Trumbull portraits of Washington, Alexander Hamilton, and others.

A lot of history was made at City Hall Park out front, which, in the early days of New York, was a kind of village square: Political riots, hangings, police wars, and one of the first readings, in 1776, of the Declaration of Independence to a group of New York revolutionaries, all took place here.

Admission: Free.

Open: Mon–Fri 10am–3:30pm. Groups of more than five by appointment only. **Subway:** 4, 5, or 6 to Brooklyn Bridge/City Hall/Centre St.

MORRIS-JUMEL MANSION, in Roger Morris Park, 65 Jumel Terr., between West 160th and 162nd streets, one block east of St. Nicholas Avenue. Tel. 923-8008.

One of New York's most important landmarks, this Palladian country villa was built in 1765 by Roger Morris and was headquarters for Gen. George Washington in 1776. It is Manhattan's oldest remaining residence. Aaron Burr married Eliza Jumel here in 1833. For elegance and sweep of historic significance, no house in New York outshines this.

Admission: $3 adults, $2 students and senior citizens; children under 10 with adult free.

Open: Wed–Sun 10am–4pm. **Subway:** Weekdays B to 163rd St.; weekends A to 163rd St.

OLD MERCHANT'S HOUSE, 29 E. 4th St. Tel. 777-1089.

This landmark house, home to prosperous merchant Seabury Tredwell and his family from 1835 to 1933, is among the finest surviving examples of late Federal and Greek Revival architecture of the period. Its original textiles, furniture, and decorative art reflect the lifestyle of a typical New York City upper-middle-class family of the 19th century.

Admission: $3 adults, $2 senior citizens and students; children under 12 free with adult.

Open: Sun–Thurs 1–4pm; group tours by appointment. Call for free museum calendar of events. **Subway:** 6 to Astor Place; N or R to 8th St.

THEODORE ROOSEVELT BIRTHPLACE, 28 E. 20th St. Tel. 260-1616.

Teddy Roosevelt, the 26th president, was born on the site in 1858 and lived here until he was 15 years old. The original home, built in 1848, was later demolished. Five rooms of this reconstructed (1923) Victorian brownstone, now a National Historic Site, have been restored to look as they did during Teddy's boyhood. The house also contains a museum of Roosevelt memorabilia.

Admission: $2 adults; children under 17 and seniors free.

Open: Wed–Sun 9am–5pm. **Closed:** Federal holidays. **Subway:** 6 to 23rd St.; N or R to Broadway and 23rd St.

NEW YORK VIETNAM VETERANS MEMORIAL, Vietnam Veterans Plaza, next to 55 Water St.

Sixteen feet high and 66 feet long, this memorial (1985) not far from the South Street Seaport contains excerpts from news dispatches, letters, diaries, and personal and public observations on the war.

Subway: 2 or 3 to Wall St.

LIBRARIES

NEW YORK PUBLIC LIBRARY, Fifth Avenue at 42nd Street. Tel. 930-0800.

One of the finest examples of beaux arts architecture in the country, the majestic New York Public Library is a true "people's palace." Outside, office workers, shoppers, strollers, and street musicians frequent the broad stone steps presided over by two majestic lions. Inside, you'll find classical grandeur, modern technology, and changing exhibits. From May 1995 through April 1996, the library will be celebrating its centennial with many special exhibits and programs.

Behind the library, Bryant Park is a great place for sunbathing and people-watching. Restrooms have baby-changing tables.

Tours: Free tours Tues–Sat 11am and 2pm.

Open: Main Reading Room, Tues–Wed 10am–7:30pm, Thurs–Sat 10am–6pm. **Subway:** B, D, F, or Q to 42nd St.

NEW YORK PUBLIC LIBRARY FOR THE PERFORMING ARTS, at Lincoln Center, 40 Lincoln Center Plaza, at 65th Street. Tel. 870-1600 or 870-1630 for information during open hours.

A division of the New York Public Library based at Lincoln Center, the Library for the Performing Arts is an entity unto itself and one of the liveliest places in town. Everything is dedicated to the performing arts here, and you can do a lot more than just borrow a book. You can sit in a comfortable chair and listen to a recording of an opera or a musical (while studying the score at the same time); see excellent exhibits; and catch concerts, plays, and dance performances.

Admission: Free.

Open: Days and hours vary, call for details. Free guided tours are held each Wednesday at 2pm. **Subway:** 1 or 9 to 66th St.

PIERPONT MORGAN LIBRARY, 29 E. 36th St., at Madison Avenue. Tel. 685-0610.

One of New York's most elegant and intimate museums, the Pierpont Morgan Library is a Renaissance gem in the heart of midtown Manhattan. Built to house the princely collections of rare books, manuscripts, and drawings amassed by financier J. Pierpont Morgan, it is today one of the nation's most distinguished museums. There is a continuing program of special exhibitions, lectures, and concerts, as well as selections from the full range of the collections permanently displayed in the library's sumptuous period rooms. The newest addition is a sunlit garden conservatory and cafe.

Admission: Suggested contribution $5 adults, $3 seniors and students.

Open: Tues–Fri 10:30am–5pm; Sat 10:30am–6pm; Sun noon–6pm. **Subway:** 6 to 33rd St.

MUSEUMS & GALLERIES
DOWNTOWN

NEW YORK CITY FIRE MUSEUM, 278 Spring St., between Varick and Hudson streets. Tel. 691-1303.

This combined collection of the old Fire Department Museum and the Firefighting Museum of the Home Insurance Company makes up one of the most comprehensive assemblages of firefighting memorabilia anywhere, with items dating from 1765 to the present.

Admission: Suggested donation $3 adults, 50¢ children.

Open: Tues–Sat 10am–4pm. **Closed:** Holidays. **Subway:** C or E to Spring St.; 1 or 9 to Houston St.

POLICE ACADEMY MUSEUM, 235 E. 20th St., between Second and Third avenues. Tel. 477-9753.

You've heard about "New York's Finest"—now see their collection of police memorabilia, one of the largest in the world.

Admission: Free.

Open: Mon–Fri 9am–2pm, but call in advance to make sure they are open on the day you wish to visit. Groups by prior appointment only. **Subway:** 6 to 23 St.; N or R to 23rd St.

FORBES MAGAZINE GALLERIES, 62 Fifth Ave., at 12th Street. Tel. 206-5548.

Kids will be intrigued by the permanent exhibit of 12,000 toy soldiers, 500 toy boats, and 300 trophies. Adults can admire the Imperial Easter Eggs created by Peter Carl Fabergé, jeweler to the czars, and the rotating exhibits of historical paintings and presidential papers.

Admission: Free.

Open: Tues–Sat 10am–4pm. Group tours on Thurs, by reservation. **Closed:** Major holidays. **Subway:** 4, 5, 6, N, or R to 14th St./Union Square.

MIDTOWN

INTERNATIONAL CENTER OF PHOTOGRAPHY MIDTOWN, 1133 Ave. of the Americas, at 43rd Street. Tel. 768-4680.

Twice the size of its parent gallery (see "Upper East Side," below) the International Center of Photography Midtown features exhibits, lectures, and a unique photography bookstore.

Admission: $4 adults, $2.50 students and senior citizens.

Open: Tues 11am–8pm; Wed–Sun 11am–6pm. **Subway:** B, D, F, or Q to 42nd St.

INTREPID SEA-AIR-SPACE MUSEUM, at Pier 86, Hudson River and the foot of West 46th Street. Tel. 245-2533 for reservations or 245-0072 for recorded information.

One of New York's most popular attractions, the aircraft carrier USS *Intrepid*, now a National Historic Landmark, is a fascinating floating museum of naval history, space and undersea exploration, and early aviation. The museum complex features more than 40 craft: The famed Lockheed A-12 *Blackbird*, the destroyer USS *Edson*, the submarine USS *Growler*, and the lightship *Nantucket*.

Admission: $7 adults, $6 seniors, $4 children 6–11. Discount packages with nearby attractions available.

Open: Summer, daily 10am–4pm; winter, Wed–Sun 10am–4pm. **Bus:** Crosstown 42nd St. or 49th St.

JAPAN SOCIETY, 333 E. 47th St. Tel. 832-1155.

This stunning example of contemporary Japanese architecture, with its beautiful gallery, extensive library, Toyota Language Center, the Lila Acheson Wallace Auditorium, and outdoor garden, is headquarters of the Japan Society. Contemporary and traditional performing arts, lectures, and special exhibits are held year-round. There are regular series of contemporary and classic Japanese films as well. Call for a program schedule.

Admission: $7 admission to films; $2.50 suggested donation for gallery.

Open: Mon–Fri 9:30am–5pm. **Subway:** 6 to 51st St.

MUSEUM OF TELEVISION & RADIO, 25 W. 52nd St. Tel. 621-6800.

Want to catch up on the Ed Sullivan shows of the 1950s or the Jack Benny broadcasts of the 1930s? You can watch Uncle Milty cavort, hear FDR's campaign speeches, and lots more at this enormously popular museum. Its collection includes just about everything that's ever gone out on the airwaves, yours to watch or hear at your own private console. Selected programs are also presented on large exhibit screens.

Admission: Suggested donation $6 adults, $4 students, $4 senior citizens, $3 children under 13.

Open: Tues, Wed, Sat, and Sun noon–6pm; Thurs noon–8pm; Fri noon–9pm. **Subway:** B, D, F, or Q to 47–50 streets; E or F to 53rd St./Fifth Ave.

SONY WONDER TECHNOLOGY LAB, Sony Plaza, 550 Madison Ave., at 56th St. Tel. 833-8100.

Kids and adults alike will love this one: this interactive science and technology center exploring communications and information technology allows visitors to experiment with robotics, explore the human body through medical imaging, edit a music video, mix a hit song, and design a video game; the lab also features the first high-definition interactive theater in the United States.

Admission: Free.

Open: Tues and Fri 10am–9pm; Wed, Thurs, Sat 10am–6pm; Sun noon–6pm. **Subway:** 4, 5, 6 or N, R to 59th St./Lexington Ave.

UPPER EAST SIDE

ASIA SOCIETY GALLERIES, 725 Park Ave., at 70th Street. Tel. 288-6400.

A splendid building houses one of the most well known private collections of Asian art in the world, the Mr. and Mrs. John D. Rockefeller III collections of sculpture, ceramics, and paintings from India, Southeast Asia, China, Korea, and Japan. Special exhibitions of the greatest art of Asia, both traditional and contemporary, are presented throughout the year. Outstanding cultural and performing art events are also presented each season.

Admission: $3 adults, $1 seniors and students with ID; children under 12 free with parent.

Open: Tues–Thurs and Sat 11am–6pm, Fri 11am–8pm, Sun noon–5pm. **Subway:** 6 to 68th St.

COOPER-HEWITT, National Museum of Design, Smithsonian Institution, 2 E. 91st St., at Fifth Avenue. Tel. 860-6868.

The Cooper-Hewitt is an exquisite gem of a museum, housed in the restored Neo-Georgian Andrew Carnegie mansion. Cooper-Hewitt's collection of design and decorative arts approaches 250,000 objects in such fields as drawing and printing, rare books, textiles, wallcoverings, furniture, porcelains, glass, metalwork, and jewelry. The museum's areas of interest include graphic design, industrial design, and architecture. There are changing exhibitions.

Admission: $3 adults, $1.50 senior citizens and students; children under 12 free. Free Tues after 5pm.

Open: Tues 10am–9pm, Wed–Sat 10am–5pm, Sun noon–5pm. **Closed:** Monday and major holidays. **Subway:** 4, 5, or 6 to 86th St.

INTERNATIONAL CENTER OF PHOTOGRAPHY, 1130 Fifth Ave. at 94th Street. Tel. 860-1777.

Housed in a superb Georgian building, this is the city's only museum devoted to photography, offering a great variety of changing exhibitions, workshops, and educational programs. A branch is in midtown (see above).

Admission: $4 adults, $2.50 students and senior citizens.

Open: Tues noon–8pm, Wed–Fri noon–5pm, Sat–Sun 11am–6pm. **Subway:** 6 to 96th St.

MUSEUM OF THE CITY OF NEW YORK, 1220 Fifth Ave., at 103rd Street. Tel. 534-1672.

For a capsule look at New York history, this is the place—especially before beginning your historical tour of downtown Manhattan. Special and permanent exhibits trace the city's history from Native American days to the present, through costumes, photographs, prints, ship models, fire engines, maps, furnishings, theatrical memorabilia, and toys. "The Big Apple," an exciting film exhibition, tells the story of the city from 1624 to today. Programs for both children and adults, including concerts, lectures, and panel discussions, are presented throughout the year; many are free, while others involve a nominal fee.

Special note: The museum has long been known for its outstanding walking tours, which explore various city neighborhoods in depth, focusing on architecture and social history. The cost is $15; call for a free brochure and information.

Admission: Suggested donation $5 adults; $3 children, senior citizens, and students; $8 for families.

Open: Wed–Sat 10am–5pm; Tues 10am–2pm (for preregistered school group tours only); Sun 1–5pm. **Closed:** Monday and legal holidays. **Subway:** 6 to 103rd St.

UPPER WEST SIDE

AMERICAN MUSEUM—HAYDEN PLANETARIUM, 81st St. at Central Park West. Tel. 769-5100 for general information, Sky Show information, and Laser Show information.

This is one of the most exciting shows in town—for children, for adults, for anyone who ponders the mystery of the stars and of the great drama of outer space. Through the magic of the Zeiss VI star projector and hundreds of special effects, audiences can be shown the wonders of the night sky and be taken to other worlds and even beyond. Show topics range from black holes to the search for life beyond our galaxy. Sky shows, included in the price of admission, are given every day except Thanksgiving and Christmas. Dazzling 3-D laser light shows are performed to popular rock music on Friday and Saturday evenings. On Saturday mornings, there are often special programs for children and preschoolers.

Admission: $5 those 13 and over, $4 senior citizens and students with ID, $2.50 children. **Laser shows:** $8.50. (Prices subject to change.)

Open: Oct–Jun, Mon–Fri 12:30–4:45pm, Sat 10am–5:45pm, Sun noon–5:45pm; July–Sept, Mon–Fri 12:30–4:45pm, Sat–Sun noon–4:45pm. **Subway:** C or B to 81st St.; 1 or 9 to 79th St.

MUSEUM OF AMERICAN FOLK ART, 2 Lincoln Square at Columbus Avenue, between 65th and 66th streets. Tel. 977-7298.

Until it settles into its permanent home on West 53rd Street late in 1996, the Museum of American Folk Art is temporarily ensconced in handsome galleries across the street from Lincoln Center. On display are some of the outstanding pieces from its permanent collection of some 3,000 objects—quilts, toys, furniture, pottery, paintings, sculpture, decorative objects, and a giant Indian chief weathervane at its central point. Next door is an engaging shop with many handmade objects in the folk tradition.

Admission: Free.

Open: Tues–Sun 11:30am–7:30pm. **Closed:** Legal holidays. **Subway:** 1 or 9 to 66th St.

WASHINGTON HEIGHTS

THE CLOISTERS, in Fort Tryon Park. Tel. 923-3700.

This is one of the high points of New York, artistically and geographically. The Cloisters is a bit of medieval Europe transplanted to a cliff overlooking the Hudson. The Metropolitan Museum of Art, of which this is the main medieval branch, brought intact from Europe a 12th-century chapter house, parts of five cloisters from medieval monasteries, a Romanesque chapel, and a 12th-century Spanish apse. Smaller treasures include rare tapestries like the 15th-century *Hunt of the Unicorn,* paintings, frescoes, stained glass, precious metalwork. All this is set in tranquil gardens overlooking the Hudson; note the herb garden in the Bonnefont Cloister and the garden in the Trie Cloister, planted with flora depicted in the Unicorn tapestries. Recorded concerts of medieval music are played over speakers at 12:45 and 3:15pm every day. Since this extraordinary collection is one of the most popular in the city, especially in fine weather, try to schedule your visit during the week, rather than on a crowded Saturday or Sunday afternoon.

Admission (including same-day admission to Metropolitan Museum of Art): Suggested admission $7 adults, $3.50 students and seniors.

Open: Mar–Oct, Tues–Sun 9:30am–5:15pm. Nov–Feb, Tues–Sun 9:30am–4:45pm. **Closed:** Thanksgiving, Christmas, and New Year's Day. **Bus:** No. 4 bus up Madison Ave., marked "Fort Tryon Park—The Cloisters" takes about an hour and a half from midtown. **Subway:** A to 190th St. Overlook Terrace (about a 45-minute trip), then about a five-minute walk.

ROOSEVELT ISLAND

ROOSEVELT ISLAND AERIAL TRAMWAY, Tramplaza, 59th St. and Second Avenue Tel. 832-4543.

Here's a chance to soar above the East River at a height of 250 feet, get spectacular views (and photos) of Manhattan, and visit Roosevelt Island, a model planned community that has plenty of attractions—all for $1.40 round trip! ($1.25 seniors and disabled, free for students with ID). The tram's jaunty twin red cabins make the four-minute run every 15 minutes from 6am to the wee hours. A red minibus meets the tram and takes you through the island for 10¢. Four spacious parks feature historical landmarks, recreational areas, and sports fields, and barbecues and picnic sites. Two additional cultural attractions, the Noguchi Foundation art exhibit (tel. 718/204-7088) and the outdoor Socrates Sculpture Park (tel. 718/956-1819) are both a short walk over the Roosevelt Island Bridge to Long Island City. Take the 4, 5, 6 or N, R subway lines and walk east on 59th Street to get to Tramplaza.

NEIGHBORHOODS

CHINATOWN & LITTLE ITALY Chinatown and Little Italy are all about street life, sometimes strident and overwhelming but always vibrating with an energy unmistakably their own. Although there are few architectural landmarks and most housing is tenement style, these tiny neighborhoods offer a real glimpse of New York's cultural diversity at its lively best. In Chinatown, shopkeepers hawk their produce from open-fronted stores along Canal Street each day, while behind them lies a warren of streets and alleyways filled with restaurants and shops. Little Italy bustles with animated cafes and restaurants, and every September it is transformed into a carnival-like atmosphere with lights and banners for the festival of San Gennaro.

Located south of Canal Street, Chinatown centers on Mott and Pell streets. It now expands in all directions, owing to new immigration from Hong Kong and other Asian locales. On the north side of Canal Street is Little Italy, just east of Broadway; the heart of this enclave is Mulberry Street.

SOHO   Until the late 1840s what we now call SoHo (an acronym for *So*uth of *Ho*uston Street) was a quiet residential quarter at the northern edge of town. Around 1850, a commercial building boom (petering out finally in the 1890s) totally transformed the place into a neighborhood of swank retail stores and loft buildings for light manufacturing. All this activity coincided with the development of cast iron as a building material. Columns, arches, pediments, brackets, keystones, and everything else that once had to be carved in stone could now be mass-produced at lower cost in iron. The result was a commercial building spree that gave free rein to the opulent architectural styles of the day.

After the spree came long generations of neglect. But by the late 1960s the area began attracting artists. By the early 1970s the real estate boom was on. Today the area is literally lined with rarified boutiques, avant-garde galleries, and trendy restaurants. SoHo lofts now appear in the pages of *Architectural Digest*.

Centered around West Broadway, Spring, and Greene streets between Houston and Canal streets (just west of Little Italy), SoHo is home to the world's largest collection of cast-iron commercial architecture and is one of New York's most vital artists' colonies.

ATRIUMS & PLAZAS

Not all the green space in New York is found in the city's parks. A recent trend in years has been for builders to include atriums and courtyards on the ground floors of new buildings, many of them rich with flowers, plantings, trees, waterfalls, art galleries, and exhibits. They're all free and all fine places for sightseers, shoppers, and local office workers to have a rest, have a bite, and watch the passing parade. Here are some to look for as you wend your way around town. **The Market at Citicorp,** 53rd and 54th streets, between Third and Lexington avenues: Three levels of entertaining shops and restaurants surround a graceful central cafe area, the scene of numerous free entertainments and concerts; adjoining it is St. Peter's Church, with its Louise Nevelson sculptures. . . . **ChemCourt,** 277 Park Ave., at 47th Street: A handsome greenhouse in the center of town, featuring flowers, trees, pools, and sculpture. . . . **IBM Garden Plaza,** 56th St. at Madison Avenue: Visit the New York Botanical Garden shop and the IBM Gallery of Science and Art, then relax at tables and chairs amid the tall bamboo trees. Free concerts are held on Wednesdays at 12:30pm. . . . **Trump Tower,** 56th Street and Fifth Avenue: An indoor street paved with pink marble and bronze leads to five stories of pricey shops and restaurants. Crowned by a transparent skylight in a bronze frame, the atrium is graced by terraced walkways, hanging gardens, and a spectacular 80-foot waterfall that cascades into a series of pools on the garden level. . . . **Crystal Pavilion,** 50th Street at Third Avenue, one of New York's most glamorous arcades: Neon flashing lights and disco music set the tone for this ultramodern space. . . . **Olympic Towers Arcade,** 51st Street and Fifth Avenue: A more tranquil oasis, with a reflecting waterfall, street benches and chairs, and a Japanese restaurant. . . . **Sony Plaza Public Arcade,** Madison Avenue between 55th and 56th streets is a grand space for sitting, eating, and getting out of the midtown crush. There are shops, a cafe and bakery, and best of all, the new Sony Wonder Technology Lab, a fascinating interactive science and technology center, free to visitors. . . . **Whitney Museum at Philip Morris,** Park Avenue at 42nd Street. The museum features an indoor garden with ficus trees and flowers, a gallery and sculpture court, and free tours and entertainment. . . . Downtown, the World Financial Center (directly across from the World Trade Center) boasts the **Winter Garden,** a glass-enclosed atrium with palm trees and benches. The Courtyard houses shops and restaurants, and outdoors there's the Esplanade, a wonderful waterfront park.

PARKS & GARDENS

BROOKLYN BOTANIC GARDEN, 1000 Washington Ave., at Eastern Parkway. Tel. 718/622-4433.

Next door to the Brooklyn Museum and a major destination in its own right, the Brooklyn Botanic Garden is a glorious 52 acres' worth of flowers, trees, and exotic plants. If you are in town in May, make a pilgrimage here to see the flowering of the cherry trees; they are even more beautiful than the ones in Washington, D.C. (Phone the garden to check on blossoming time.) The Japanese mood also prevails in the traditional Japanese Garden, considered one of the finest outside of Japan. Other special treats include the Cranford Rose Garden, the Fragrance Garden for the Blind, and the Shakespeare Garden. You can browse through the greenhouses with their exotic tropical, desert, and temperate plants and be convinced that you are light-years away from Brooklyn. The Bonsai Museum houses the most outstanding collection in the western world, and the Trail of Evolution offers a unique look at 3½ billion years of plant life. Free tours of the Garden's highlights are held every Saturday and Sunday (except certain holidays) at 1pm. The Garden's Terrace Café serves a delightful lunch.

Admission: General admission free; Sat–Sun and holidays 25¢ admission to Japanese Hill-and-Pond Garden.

Open: Hours change with seasons, so call for exact times. Summer, Tues–Fri 8am–6pm, Sat–Sun 10am–6pm. **Subway:** 2 or 3 to Eastern Pkwy.

THE NEW YORK BOTANICAL GARDEN, Bronx Park. Tel. 718/817-8700

New York's oldest and largest public garden and one of New York City's unique attractions, this National Historic Landmark contains 250 acres of natural and landscaped grounds that include 27 outdoor gardens and plant collections. The Garden offers a wide array of programs and activities. Take an audio tour of the T. H. Everett Rock Garden and Native Plant Garden. Enjoy a narrated tram ride. Tour the 40-acre NYBG Forest dating from prerevolutionary times, and visit the magnificent collection of rhododendrons, daffodils, azaleas, day lilies, and chrysanthemums.

Stop in the gift shop of unusual objets d'art and plants, then have lunch at the Tulip Tree Café on Museum Mall or at the romantic Snuff Mill River Café, on a terrace overlooking the Bronx River, which looks positively rural at this point.

Admission: Grounds admission $3 adults, $2 children 6–16, students, and seniors; children under 6 free. Combination tickets are available.

Open: Apr–Oct, 10am–6pm, Tues–Sun and Mon holidays; Nov–Mar, 10am–4pm., Tues–Sun and Mon holidays. **Shuttle:** Visitors can reserve a seat on the Garden Shuttle minibus from Manhattan on weekends: for schedule and reservations, call 718/ 817-8700. **Train:** Metro North's Harlem Line to the Botanical Garden Station (20 minutes from Grand Central). **Subway:** D or 4 to Bedford Park station or 200th St.; then walk eight blocks east or take the Bx26 to the Botanical Garden stop. **Directions:** The Garden is at Exit 7W on the Bronx River Parkway, half-a-mile north of Fordham Road and the Bronx Zoo. Parking is $4.

BRONX ZOO/WILDLIFE CONSERVATION PARK, Bronx River Parkway and Fordham Road. Tel. 718/367-1010.

The Bronx Zoo/Wildlife Conservation Park—open every day of the year—is, at 265 acres, the largest metropolitan wildlife park in the United States. One of the best zoos in the world, the park is home to over 4,000 animals exhibited in naturalistic habitats. African Market, a plaza area, links **Baboon Reserve,** featuring gelada baboons and ibex, with the **African Plains,** where lions, gazelles, giraffes, and zebras can be seen. **Wild Asia** (open April to October) offers a guided 25-minute safari via monorail (the Bengali Express) through 38 densely forested acres where elephants, tigers, and other animals roam free ($1.50). **Jungle World,** another segment of Wild Asia, re-creates a Southeast Asian rain forest, mangrove swamp, and scrub forest. **Himalayan Highlands Habitat** features snow leopards, the world's most beautiful and elusive cats, along with cunning red pandas, white-naped cranes, and tragopans. In the **World of Birds,** visitors walk through a rain forest and into jungles while birds swoop around their heads.

A big one for kids! Take the moppets to the world-famous **Children's Zoo** (open Apr–Oct), where they can climb on a spider's web, try on a turtle's shell, and crawl through a prairie dog tunnel ($1.50). They'll also love a ride in **Skyfari,** a four-seater cable car ($1.50).

Admission: Apr–Oct; $5.75 adults, $2 children and seniors, children under 2 free. Wed, by donation. Nov–Mar, $2.50 adults, $1 children and seniors.

Open: Mon–Fri 10am–4:30 or 5pm, depending on time of year, Sat–Sun 10am–4:30 or 5:30pm. **Bus** (most convenient): Liberty Line Express Bus service from midtown Manhattan. Phone 718/652-8400 weekdays 9am–5pm for schedules and timetable; fare is $3.75. **Train:** From Grand Central in Manhattan via Metro North; phone 532-4900. **Subway:** 2 to Pelham Pkwy.; walk west to Bronxdale entrance. **Car:** Take Exit 6 off Bronx River Pkwy. Parking is $5.

CENTRAL PARK ZOO/WILDLIFE CONSERVATION CENTER, near the park entrance at Fifth Avenue and East 64th Street. Tel. 861-6030.

After a $35-million renovation, the Central Park Zoo emerged as one of the most endearing small zoos anywhere. The joyful 5½-acre "animal garden" is state of the art, designed to make both its inhabitants and its visitors very happy. A beautifully landscaped Central Garden and **Sea Lion Pool** is flanked on three sides by a glass-roofed colonnade (no need to stay away if it rains), which leads to three polar ecological areas. Inside the skylighted octagonal building called the **Tropic Zone** is a misty rain forest inhabited by the likes of red-bellied piranhas, caiman, and a python or two. The **Temperate Territory** is open to the skies and provides realistic outdoor habitats for, among others, Asian red pandas and North American river otters. Most fun of all is the **Polar Circle,** an indoor-outdoor environment whose glass walls provide views of frolicking penguins and polar bears both above and below water. The cafeteria and gift shop are great fun.

Admission: $2.50 adults, $1.25 seniors, 50¢ children 3–12, toddlers free.

Open: Mon–Fri 10am–5pm; Sat–Sun and holidays 10am–5:30pm.

CONSERVATORY GARDEN, 105th Street and Fifth Avenue. Tel. 860-1382.

Like a bit of fairyland in the midst of the urban jungle, Conservatory Garden is Central Park's only formal garden. Magnificent plantings reflect the seasons: two separate gardens, each with reflecting pools, surround the massive central lawn, lovely with its crabapple trees and iron pergola covered by wisteria vines. Concerts and lectures are occasionally held during the warm months. Conservatory Garden is a favorite site for summer wedding ceremonies. The iron gates are open every day from 8am to dusk.

AND IN BROOKLYN & QUEENS

BROOKLYN

BROOKLYN MUSEUM, 200 Eastern Parkway at Prospect Park. Tel. 718/638-5000.

One of the best reasons for leaving Manhattan is to see the Brooklyn Museum, among the best museums in the country. One of the largest fine art museums in the United States, it is more exciting than ever, now that its new Ancient Egyptian galleries are open; they feature more than 500 objects from the museum's world-renowned Egyptian collection, some of them never before on public view. It also has superb collections of Asian, American, and European art, as well as a fine primitive collection, 27 period rooms, and Japanese and Korean galleries. Be sure to see the outstanding collection of American painting and sculpture (with works by Winslow Homer and John Singer Sargent), as well as the Frieda Schiff Warburg Sculpture Gallery, a repository of some of the architectural relics of old New York.

Don't miss a visit to the museum shop, with its wonderful handcrafts from Mexico, Japan, South America, and Scandinavia—all authentic, beautifully made, and well priced. The kids can stock up here on slews of inexpensive presents to bring their friends back home. Brunch and lunch are available at reasonable prices at the Museum Café.

Admission: Suggested contribution, $4 adults, $2 students with valid ID, $1.50 seniors; free for children under 12 with adult.

Open: Wed–Sun 10am–5pm. **Closed:** Thanksgiving, Christmas, and New Year's Day. **Subway:** 2 or 3 to Eastern Pkwy.

THE BROOKLYN HISTORICAL SOCIETY, 128 Pierrepont St. Tel. 718/624-0890.

The Coney Island of old, the legendary Brooklyn Dodgers, the Brooklyn Bridge, the Brooklyn Navy Yard, and the diverse peoples of the borough come alive in the society's museum; a research library contains the largest collection of materials on Brooklyn in existence. Public programs include walking tours, concerts, food festivals, lectures, readings, and workshops for children. All of the above make a visit to this lovely Victorian-era landmark building in Brooklyn Heights worthwhile. Tie your trip in with an exploration of the charming shops and restaurants of Montague Street around the corner, ending with a stop at the Brooklyn Promenade, known for its sweeping view of the Manhattan skyline and the Statue of Liberty.

Admission: $2.50 adults, $1 children under 12 and seniors for museum; $5 for museum and library; free Wed. **Subway:** 2, 3, 4 or 5 to Borough Hall; A or F to Jay St.; M, N, or R to Court St.

Open: Tues–Sat 10am–5pm.

QUEENS

AMERICAN MUSEUM OF THE MOVING IMAGE, 35th Avenue at 36th Street, Astoria. Tel. 718/784-0077.

Opened in the fall of 1988 on the site of the East Coast facility of Paramount Pictures in the 1920s, this is the first museum in the United States dedicated exclusively to film, television, and video. Through exhibitions, screenings, and collections, visitors explore the art, history, technique, and technology of the moving image media and their influence on 20th-century American life.

Admission: $5 adults, $4 senior citizens, $2.50 children and students with valid ID.

Open: Tues–Fri noon–4pm, Sat–Sun noon–6pm. **Subway:** R or G to Steinway St.

3. COOL FOR KIDS

For kids worn out by too much sightseeing, an hour or so in **Central Park** is the perfect antidote. There's so much for them to do here, however, that you may want to schedule it for an entire morning or afternoon. First, everybody must see the wonderfully renovated **Central Park Zoo;** really small kids will also enjoy the Central Park **Children's Zoo.** Then take them for a ride on the **Carousel,** opposite 65th Street in the center of the park. The whole family will enjoy rowboating on the picturesque lake: Boats can be rented at Loeb Boathouse (near the 72nd Street and Fifth Avenue entrance); they cost $7 for a minimum of one hour and require a $20 deposit. Or let the kids sail their model boats at **Conservatory Water** near

72nd Street and Fifth, join the local youngsters flying kites, or work off some excess energy at any of the inspired **Adventure Playgrounds** (there are at least nine of them in the park; two locations are at 86th Street and Central Park West and 67th Street and Fifth Avenue). Summer Saturdays between 11am and noon, they can listen to stories at the charming **Hans Christian Andersen statue,** near the model boathouse. Check in, too, at **The Belvedere,** a castle at 79th Street, south of the Great Lawn, which has frequent exhibits and special programs for parents and children (tel. 772-0210).

BROOKLYN CHILDREN'S MUSEUM, 145 Brooklyn Ave., at St. Marks Avenue. Tel. 718/735-4400.

This is one museum that children will want to visit again and again; here they can touch and play with the exhibits. BCM has focused on "interactive play or learning" since its opening in 1899 as the world's first children's museum. The semiunderground structure is a high-tech, learning/looking/growing environment, with its own greenhouse, running-water stream, boneyard, workshops, and library. Call for a listing of weekly performances and education workshops.

Admission: Suggested contribution, $3 per person.

Open: Wed–Fri 2–5pm, Sat–Sun and school holidays noon–5pm. **Subway:** 3 to Kingston Ave.

CHILDREN'S MUSEUM OF MANHATTAN, Tisch Building, 212 W. 83rd St., between Broadway and Amsterdam Avenue. Tel. 721-1234.

The Children's Museum of Manhattan is such a magical, mind-boggling place for kids 2 to 12 that there is only one problem about bringing them here: They may not want to leave and see the rest of New York! One of the most technologically and conceptually sophisticated children's museums in the world, the museum's theme is self-discovery, which it fosters through a series of brilliant interactive exhibits and activity centers. At the Time Warner Center for Media, children can learn animation techniques and produce their own videotapes; they can also work as engineers, writers, newscasters, and camera operators in a full-size television studio and control room. Performances by children's theater groups, dancers, musicians, puppeteers, and storytellers are held every weekend. Participatory creative arts workshops are offered throughout the year.

Admission: $5.

Open: Mon, Wed, and Thurs 1:30–5:30pm, Fri–Sat 10am–5pm. **Closed:** Major holidays. **Subway:** 1 or 9 to 86th St.

OTHER ATTRACTIONS FOR KIDS

The following attractions of special interest to children have already been described in this chapter.

American Museum—Hayden Planetarium (see p. 220). Kids love the sky and laser shows.

American Museum of Natural History (see p. 205). There are hours of absorbing interest here for the kids. Those over five will enjoy the learning games in the Discovery Room.

Bronx Zoo (see p. 224). Simply the best. Really small kids will adore the Children's Zoo (open April through October), which allows them to experience what it feels like to be a particular animal. They can even ride a real camel.

Central Park Zoo (see p. 224). Another must. Small, beautiful, and enchanting, it's for kids of all ages.

Ellis Island (see p. 199). A marvelous history lesson for older children.

Empire State Building (see p. 202). Youngsters love the view from the top.

***Forbes* Magazine Galleries** (see p. 217). Youngsters will admire the display of 12,000 toy soldiers, 500 toy boats, and 300 trophies.

***Intrepid* Sea-Air-Space Museum** (see p. 218). Kids of all ages find this one exciting.

Lincoln Center for the Performing Arts (see p. 205). Older children will enjoy the backstage tours.

Metropolitan Museum of Art (see p. 207). The mummies in the Egyptian galleries and the "Arms and Armor" exhibit are all-time kid-pleasers.

Museum of the City of New York (see p. 220). New York history comes to life here. There are many special shows for children, including puppet shows.

Museum of Television and Radio (see p. 218). Here's a chance to catch the old shows.

New York City Fire Museum (see p. 217). Guaranteed to fascinate anyone who dreams of growing up to be a firefighter.

New York Public Library for the Performing Arts (see p. 217). Free story hours, puppet shows, concerts, dance presentations, films, and more are presented in the Hecksher Oval.

Sony Wonder Technology Lab (see p. 219). Science-minded older kids can explore the current and future worlds of communications and high technology.

Statue of Liberty (see p. 197). A must. Kids are enthralled by the whole experience, from the ferryboat ride and the first sight of the Lady, up to the 12-story climb to the viewing platform in the crown (parents, be warned).

4. SPECIAL-INTEREST SIGHTSEEING

FOR LITERARY BUFFS New York City is full of hallowed spots for literary buffs. There's the **Chelsea Hotel** (222 W. 23rd St.), for example, where Thomas Wolfe wrote *You Can't Go Home Again,* Arthur Miller penned *After the Fall,* and William Burroughs worked on *Naked Lunch.* Dylan Thomas and Brendan Behan are among the many who found solace and inspiration here. Thomas's favorite drinking spot, by the way, was the **White Horse Tavern** in Greenwich Village (corner of Hudson and 11th streets), where such American literary lights as Norman Mailer, Louis Auchincloss, and Calder Willingham were once regulars.

Greenwich Village, of course, has long been home to writers and assorted Bohemians. In the 1920s and 1930s, **137 Bleecker**

Street was the site of the old Liberal Club, a hotbed for anarchists and free-thinkers of all stripes. Among these were John Reed, who wrote *Ten Days That Shook the World* and whose story was told in the film *Reds*. Next door, in what is still the **Provincetown Playhouse,** George Cram Cook and his wife, Susan Glaspell, founded the Provincetown Players; in tow they had a promising young playwright named Eugene O'Neill and a young actress from Maine named Edna St. Vincent Millay. On Commerce Street in the Village is the still active **Cherry Lane Theater,** which Edna St. Vincent Millay founded. "Vincent," one of the most authentic of the Village Bohemians, made her home at **75½ Bedford Street,** still known as the "narrowest house in the Village."

In another part of the Village, at Fifth Avenue and Waverly Place, is Washington Square. Project yourself back into the world of the 19th-century New York aristocracy as you study the elegant Greek Revival houses of **Washington Square North.** Henry James's novel *Washington Square* took place here, and James, Edith Wharton, William Dean Howells, John Dos Passos, and painter Edward Hopper have all lived on this block at one time or another. Poet e. e. cummings lived on Patchin Place.

In midtown, the **Algonquin Hotel** (49 W. 44th St.) is something of a literary shrine, for it was here that the celebrated wits of the Round Table, including Robert Benchley, James Thurber, H. L. Mencken, and Dorothy Parker, traded *bons mots*. Of course, the Algonquin is not far from the offices of *The New Yorker* (20 W. 43rd St.), where many of their pieces were published over the years.

Uptown on the East Side, the **Poetry Center of the YM-YWHA** (part of the Tisch Center for the Arts), 92nd Street and Lexington Avenue, is the place where Dylan Thomas, W. H. Auden, and T. S. Eliot enthralled admiring crowds.

5. ORGANIZED TOURS

GRAND TOURS

CIRCLE LINE SIGHTSEEING CRUISES, with departures from Pier 83, at the foot of West 43rd Street and Twelfth Avenue. Tel. 563-3200.

The Circle Line sightseeing boat makes a three-hour around-the-island tour of Manhattan, and it is one of the most popular attractions in town—and one of the best. The trip will give you an unusual perspective on Manhattan; the buildings that you've already seen at close range suddenly look quite different when viewed from the sea. Your orbit around the island begins at Pier 83, at the foot of West 42nd Street; takes you down into Upper Bay past the Statue of Liberty and Ellis Island; then continues up along the East River, as the Brooklyn Bridge, the Manhattan Bridge, and the former Brooklyn Navy Yard come into view. As you go along the East River you'll view the splendor of the United Nations from the sea, and farther along, Gracie Mansion, the home of the mayor. The East River merges into the Harlem River at Hell Gate, then on northward through Spuyten Duyvil and exits into the Hudson River. The giant lacework of the George Washington Bridge emerges now, and you go down the Hudson, joining slews of tiny pleasure craft, work boats, perhaps even an oil tanker or freighter coming down from the upper Hudson. To your left is Riverside Park. You'll spot Grant's Tomb as you come down along 122nd Street. As you approach midtown, the docks of the great shipping companies come into view. When your sightseeing yacht docks, you may be lucky enough to see a slew of tugs nudge a beauty like the *QE II* into its berth!

The sightseeing boat comes equipped with a refreshment stand and a narrator who is likely to tell some very ancient jokes; but you will emerge rested, cool, and well informed about New York. *Parents' note:* Children about eight and over love this trip, but young ones can get awfully wriggly; remember, it takes three hours, and you can't get off!

Prices: $18 adults, $9 children under 12. Prices subject to change. **Departures:** Summer trips scheduled daily every 45 minutes, from 9:30am to 4:30pm, less frequently at other times of year (season runs from late March to December 24). Harbor Lights cruises are held every night at 7pm from May 8 to October 3. On weekends only, cruises are held March 27 to May 1 and October 4 to December 24. **Bus:** 42nd St. (no. 106), 49th St., or 34th St. westbound crosstown buses all stop within a few feet of the ticket booth.

SEMI-CIRCLE LINE CRUISES, with departures from Pier 16 at the South Street Seaport. Tel. 563-3200.

Those opting for a shorter sightseeing cruise should try this one, which sails around the southern end of Manhattan from Battery Park City on the Hudson River, past the Statue of Liberty and Ellis Island to the Williamsburg Bridge on the East River in a total of 90 minutes.

Prices: $12 adults, $6 children under 12. Combination tickets for the South Street Seaport Museum and Semi-Circle Line cruises are $17 adults, $14 seniors, $8 children under 12. **Departures:** Four cruises are offered daily, at 10am, 12 noon, 2 and 4pm. Two-hour "Harbor Lights" cruises sail from Pier 16 Monday and Tuesday at 7pm.

GRAY LINE NEW YORK TOURS, 900 Eighth Ave., between 53rd and 54th Streets. Tel. 397-2600.

By land, sea, and air, this venerable tour company conducts some 33 different sightseeing trips. Tours last from two to about nine hours, and are conducted in English, French, German, Spanish, and Italian.

OTHER TOURS

INSIDER'S NEW YORK   This joint venture of the Municipal Art Society and Gray Line New York offers Saturday afternoon bus tours that emphasize the city's cultural and geographic diversity. Tours visit waterfront, artists' studios, churches, planned neighborhoods, skyscrapers, gardens, cemeteries, public and private monuments, and more. Recent tours have included visits to Historic Staten Island and Brooklyn's Industrial Waterfront Warehouses. The cost ranges from $15 to $30. For information, phone 439-1049.

NYC/DOWNTOWN   offers a series of avant-garde bus tours for "sophisticated, globe-trotting visitors." Tours explore the lofts and galleries of the downtown art scene in SoHo, downtown nightlife and theater, and include a taste tour with a stop at downtown's own micro-brewery. Prices range from $34 per person for "The Best of

NYC Downtown" to $99 per person for an evening on the town, featuring visits to out-of-the-way bars and clubs, a Prohibition speakeasy, and the watering holes of downtown's past and present literary legends. For information, phone 932-2744.

SINGER'S BROOKLYN According to the U.S. Census Bureau, one out of seven families in the United States has roots in Brooklyn. Perhaps this is what makes Lou Singer's tours so popular. Singer, a self-taught historian who must know more about Brooklyn than anybody, conducts absorbing tours focusing on Revolutionary, Dutch, ethnic, and architectural Brooklyn, via bus or private car. Evening tours, which always start with a sunset view of the city from the Promenade in Brooklyn Heights, usually wind up with dinner and dancing at one of the lively Russian nightclubs in Brighton Beach. Private tours for special interests can be arranged.

Singer offers some 16 different adventures; all are eminently worthwhile and enjoyable excursions. For individuals, costs should run about $25 per person, plus food (group rates are also available). Phone **Lou Singer** at 718/875-9084 after 7pm or write to him at 18 Henry St., Brooklyn, N.Y. 11201.

WHOLESALE SHOPPING So you'd like to shop the wholesale houses of New York's Garment District but don't know how? Sara Gardner of **Fashion Update** (tel. 718/377-8873) will take you by the hand and arrange a highly personalized tour to designers' showrooms, where you can save from 50% to 90% off retail prices, on men's, women's, and children's clothing; bridal attire; furs; leather; cosmetics; shoes; and accessories. Cost of the tour is $50. Group rates are available also.

WALKING TOURS A number of individuals and organizations offer exemplary walking tours around the streets of New York. Contact any of the following when you're in town to check schedules and make reservations. For news of specific tours held each week, consult the "Other Events" section of *New York* magazine.

Adventure on a Shoestring (tel. 265-2663) offers members of this 32-year-old organization a variety of unusual excursions—perhaps a visit to an orchestra rehearsal or the studio of a noted portrait painter. If you're in the city for an extended stay, it's worthwhile to pay the $40 membership fee and join. However, even if you're not a member, you can still participate in their walking tours held year-round, rain or shine, for a fee of just $5. Excursions have taken visitors to historic Gramercy Park; to Chinatown; and to the "Little Odessa" section of Brooklyn to visit a lively Russian Jewish community. Tours are usually accompanied by ethnic eating adventures. Phone the number above or write Howard Goldberg, Shoestring, 300 W. 53rd St., New York, NY 10019.

Big Onion Tours (tel. 439-1090) offers a variety of engaging tours on such subjects as "Burial Grounds of Lower Manhattan," "New York at War and Peace," and "From Naples to Bialystock to Beijing: A Multi-Ethnic Eating Tour." They are the only company that runs tours to Governor's Island. Cost is $9 for adults and $7 for students and seniors.

The Brooklyn Historical Society (tel. 718/624-0890) features spring and summer walking tours that highlight various neighborhoods in Brooklyn. Some tours focus on particular ethnic groups; others feature famous places like Coney Island and Green-

Wood Cemetery. Call for information. The cost is $10 for adults with reservations, $12 at the door, and $5 for children.

City Walks (tel. 989-2456) are offered three weekends a month by John Wilson, a 38-year-resident of New York and a sometime guide for the Municipal Art Society, who leads small groups on informal, "homey," tours of Greenwich Village, midtown, downtown, and the Lower East Side. Private tours are available on request. Two-hour tours cost $12.

Joyce Gold (tel. 242-5762) has a major goal—making tourists out of New Yorkers and New Yorkers out of tourists. To that end, she leads Sunday public walking tours that focus in-depth on the historical, architectural, and cultural backgrounds of various neighborhoods, from the Financial District to Harlem. Gold is considered a master Manhattan historian; other tour guides come to the classes she teaches at local colleges. Tours can last anywhere from 2½ to 4½ hours and cost $12. If no public tour is scheduled, private tours are available. Phone the number above or write Joyce Gold, 141 W. 17th St., New York, NY 10011, to receive schedules of her tours.

Lower East Side Tenement Museum Tours (tel. 431-0233) covers the Lower East Side, the place the immigrants often went *after* they left Ellis Island. In honor of these "urban pioneers," a dedicated group is preserving an 1863 tenement and offering an exciting program of walking tours, dramas, "urban explorations," children's programs, and exhibitions from their storefront gallery. Year-round, they offer a Sunday tour at 12:30pm called "The Streets Where We Lived," a multiethnic look at past and present on the Lower East Side, Chinatown, and Little Italy. During the spring and summer months, there is usually another tour at 2:30pm, an "Ethnic Heritage Walk," exploring the Italian, Irish, Jewish, and Chinese neighborhoods, among others. Be sure to call first to find out which tours are scheduled. All tours begin at the museum's Gallery 90 at 90 Orchard Street, last two hours, and cost $12 for adults, $10 for seniors and students. Admission to the gallery alone is $3; to the gallery and the original tenement building, $5.

The Municipal Art Society, a century-old organization dedicated to beautifying New York through public art has a series of weekday walking tours—most other tours are held on weekends. Knowledgeable guides lead explorations of the city's most fascinating neighborhoods, and architectural sites, including SoHo, Ladies' Mile, lobbies, TriBeCa, Park Avenue South, Carnegie Hill, the new mosque, Roosevelt Island, Rockefeller Center, and more. Tours cost $10 for adults, $8 for students and seniors, and last 90 minutes. For information, call 439-1049.

The 92nd Street YM-YWHA (tel. 996-1100), one of the city's leading cultural institutions, offers a series of Sunday walking tours that are a bit different. "Tour and Tea at the Algonquin Hotel," for example, is a behind-the-scenes exploration of the Algonquin, followed by an authentic English afternoon tea. Other topics include "Jewish Williamsburg," "Edith Wharton's New York," "The Chelsea Hotel," "Manhattan's New Mosque," and even a "Moonlit Walk in Central Park," a stroll at dusk with a naturalist. Tours vary from about $15 to $25 and should be reserved in advance by calling the number above; call them also for a brochure, or write to the 92nd Street YM-YWHA, 1395 Lexington Ave., New York, NY 10128.

Radical Walking Tours (tel. 718/492-0069) are way left of the beaten path. Self-proclaimed anarchist Bruce Kayton explores the Wall Street, Greenwich Village, and Chelsea haunts of such folk as Leon Trotsky, Abbie Hoffman, John Reed, Emma Goldman, Margaret Sanger, and—yes—Madonna. Tours last about three hours and cost a proletarian $6.

Sidewalks of New York (tel. 517-0201) offers a large number of unusual walking tours every weekend. Favorite topics include "A Writer's Walk Through Greenwich Village," "Hollywood on the Hudson," "Screen Scenes," and "Secrets of Central Park." Most tours cost $10. Private tours are available by appointment. For a calendar, write to P.O. Box 1660, Cathedral Station, New York, NY 10025.

Urban Explorations (tel. 718/721-5254), the creation of Patricia Olmstead, has a roster of engaging tours in which Ms. Olmstead combines her extensive knowledge of architecture, history, and landscaping, revealing the city as a "museum" in itself, full of such treasures as landmark architecture and multiethnic neighborhoods. Favorite tours include "Chinatown" (focusing on history and architecture), the food of Chinatown (followed by a dim sum luncheon), Islamic architecture and the 96th Street Mosque, a literary tour of Greenwich Village, a gay and lesbian history tour of the Village, and a tour of Brooklyn Heights. Tours, which run 2½ to 3 hours, are intimate, since groups are limited to 15 people; the cost is $12, $10 for students and seniors. Private tours are available; call for rates.

Wild Food Tours (tel. 718/291-6825) has some of the most unusual and enjoyable walking tours, taking place not on the city streets but in its parks, with "Wildman" Steven Brill, a naturalist-ecologist-author-artist who is a self-made authority on the wild edible fruits, vegetables, roots, nuts, seeds, and mushrooms that grow in New York City's parks, backyards, and vacant lots. Although it's illegal (and dangerous) to forage on your own, it's safe when you do so on one of Wildman's tours, because he supervises very carefully. Brill's commentaries are highly informative and enjoyable, interspersed with cooking information, folklore, and "plenty of bad jokes." Four-hour fieldwalks are held in parks throughout the New York Metropolitan area every Saturday and Sunday from March through December. Central Park is the locale about once every four weeks. Reservations must be made in advance by phoning the number above; or send a stamped, self-addressed envelope to **"Wildman" Steve Brill,** 143-25 84th Drive, Apt. 6-C, Jamaica, NY 11435, for a free yearly schedule of field walks. The tour is $10 or whatever you can afford. No smoking on walks.

6. SPORTS & RECREATION

SPORTS Baseball New York baseball fans are incurable fanatics who root for either the **New York Mets** or the **New York Yankees.** The Mets play at Shea Stadium in Queens from April through October. For ticket information, phone 718/507-TIXX. The New York Yankees, a.k.a. the Bronx Bombers, play at Yankee Stadium; call 718/293-6000.

Basketball The local basketball season runs from November to spring. Madison Square Garden is the home of the **New York Knickerbockers (the Knicks)** (tel. 212/465-MSG1). Just a short bus trip from Manhattan is the Brendan Byrne Arena at the Meadowlands Sports Complex in East Rutherford, N.J., home of the **New Jersey Nets** (tel. 201/935-8888).

Football Both New York teams now play in New Jersey! The **New York Jets** (tel. 201/935-8888) and the **New York Giants** (tel. 201/935-8222) play from September through December at Giants Stadium at the Meadowlands Sports Complex. The best way to get to see a game is to know someone who's holding a season ticket; almost all the seats are sold out.

Horse Racing New Yorkers love the races. They bet on them constantly at numbers of Off Track Betting parlors (OTBs) throughout the city. But, of course, it's much more enjoyable to get out to the track. Consider these: **Aqueduct Racetrack** in Ozone Park, Queens (tel. 718/641-4700), which presents thoroughbred racing from mid-October through May; **Belmont Park** in Elmont, on the Queens/Nassau County border (tel. 718/641-4700), where thoroughbred racing goes on from May through July and September through October. Then there's **Meadowlands Racetrack** in East Rutherford, N.J. (tel. 201/935-8500), which offers thoroughbred racing from September through mid-December and trotters from late December through August. There's trotters racing all year long at **Yonkers Raceway** in Yonkers, N.Y. (tel. 914/968-4200).

The tracks are easily reachable by buses from the Port Authority Bus Terminal; the A train goes to Aqueduct/North Conduit Ave.

Ice Hockey The 1994 World Champion **Rangers** and the **Islanders** and **Devils** are New York–area NHL teams. Home base for the Rangers is Madison Square Garden (tel. 465-MSG1); the Islanders are at the Nassau Coliseum, Hempstead Turnpike, Uniondale, N.Y. (tel. 516/587-9222), not difficult to get to by the Long Island Rail Road; and the Devils play at Brendan Byrne Arena at the Meadowlands Sports Complex in East Rutherford, N.J. (tel. 201/935-3900).

Tennis Flushing Meadow, Queens, is the scene in late summer (end of August to early September) of the **U.S. Open Tennis Championships,** featuring some of the world's top-seeded players (tel. 718/271-5100). Top women players compete in the **Virginia Slims Championship** at Madison Square Garden in mid-November (tel. 212/465-6000).

RECREATION In addition to **Central Park** (see "The Top Attractions" at the beginning of this chapter), New Yorkers also have **Riverside Park,** a lovely stretch on the Upper West Side, which contains the 79th Street Boat Basin and the Soldiers and Sailors Monument at 89th Street and Riverside Drive. **Carl Schurz Park,** which lies between the East River and East End Avenue in the upper 80s is another popular spot; at its northern end is Gracie Mansion, the residence of the mayor of New York. (Schurz, incidentally, was a German revolutionary who became a close friend and advisor of Abraham Lincoln.)

Bicycling The best place in the city to bike is Central Park. Bikes can be rented at the **Loeb Boathouse,** Park Drive North at 72nd Street (tel. 861-4137) and at **West Side Bicycle Store,** 231 W.

96th St. (tel. 663-7531), just a few blocks from the entrance to the park on the West Side. **Metro Bicycles,** 1311 Lexington Ave., at the corner of 88th Street (tel. 427-4450), is convenient to the park on the East Side; and **Midtown Bicycles,** 360 W. 47th St., at the corner of Ninth Avenue (tel. 581-4506) caters to the midtown hotel crowd.

Horseback Riding   **Claremont Riding Academy,** 175 W. 89th St. (tel. 724-5100), will rent you a horse for about $33 an hour; you must be experienced in English riding, walk, trot, and canter. If not, take a lesson; they have expert instructors.

Running   All of the parks are popular places to run. Several of the luxury hotels now provide personal trainers who will run with you if you feel uneasy venturing out into the streets and parks on your own. The **New York Road Runners Club,** 6 E. 89th St. (tel. 860-4455, ext. 219), is the place to contact concerning group runs and races. They are the sponsors of the annual New York City Marathon, held each November.

Swimming   Several city hotels now have pools (see Chapter 5). In summer, you can get to some of Long Island's best beaches from Pennsylvania Station, courtesy of the Long Island Rail Road. Special Beach Package tickets are available to Jones Beach ($10.50 round-trip), Long Beach ($12), Robert Moses State Park ($12), and Watch Hill on Fire Island ($16). For information, telephone 718/217-LIRR.

Tennis   Central Park's tennis courts at 93rd Street welcome visitors; you can purchase tickets for single play, good any hour, for $5. For information, phone the **Permit Office** at 360-8133.

CHAPTER 8

STROLLING AROUND NEW YORK CITY

1. **LOWER MANHATTAN**
2. **GREENWICH VILLAGE**
3. **UPPER WEST SIDE**

To me, one of the most fascinating free activities in Manhattan is a simple walk through several of its fabled neighborhoods, soaking up the architecture, learning a bit about the history, absorbing the sights and sounds.

The financial district with its winding, narrow streets is New York's oldest area. Greenwich Village offers picturesque variety. And don't neglect the Upper East Side with its elegant ambience or the lively, trendy Upper West Side.

Put on a pair of comfortable shoes and take off.

Note: For more information on some tour stops, see Chapter 7.

WALKING TOUR 1 — LOWER MANHATTAN

Start: Broadway and Wall Street.
Finish: South Street Seaport.
Time: About two hours.
Best Time: Weekdays, when New York Stock Exchange is open.

If you are interested in history—or money or architecture or the sea—you will have to visit Lower Manhattan. Haunted with ghosts of the city's past, booming with the construction and commerce of the present, an area rich in classic architecture and sleek, new futuristic office buildings, ringed by the sea that made its wealth possible, this oldest area of the city is so richly textured that you could spend days here.

More than anything else, New York is a marketplace, today the greatest on earth. It has always been a marketplace. It was settled, back in 1626, not as a haven for political or religious freedom but as a fur-trading post. Peter Minuit technically "bought" the island from Native Americans for $24 worth of baubles. The fledgling revolutionary government of the United States of America established its capital and inaugurated its first president here. And through the years its ideal deep-water harbor attracted the commerce of many nations. The temples of finance and commerce grew up along the water's edge, and this is where they still are. A modest stock exchange had already been set up—under a buttonwood tree in 1792—but it was not until the New York financiers had been able to underwrite the Civil War that Wall Street took its place as the financial power of the nation—and, indirectly, of much of the world. Residential New York grew up and moved north, but the citadel of money and power remains. And this is where you begin your downtown tour.

Take subway line 4, 5, or 6 to the Wall Street station at Broadway and Wall Street. Upon emerging from the station, you'll spot:

1. **Trinity Church,** a graceful English Gothic beauty that was built by Richard Upjohn and completed in 1846. This National Historic Landmark was once the tallest building in Lower Manhattan. In its tranquil churchyard lie buried a few parishioners who once lived in this area: Robert Fulton, Alexander Hamilton, and other early leading Americans. You can visit both church and churchyard weekdays from 7am to 6pm, weekends to 4pm. Guided tours are given daily at 2pm. The Trinity Museum is open daily.

After paying your respects to these early New Yorkers, proceed down Wall Street (there really was once a wall here made of tree trunks by the Dutch settlers to protect their city from the wilderness) and stop at the corner of Wall and Nassau streets, at the:

2. **Federal Hall National Memorial.** This place is full of ghosts: It was on this site that John Peter Zenger won the case that helped establish the right of freedom of the press, and it was here that General Washington took the oath of office as the first U.S. president, in 1789. A statue of Washington commemorates the event. The first American Congress met here and adopted the Bill of Rights. First a Customs House, later a Sub-Treasury, now a museum of the Colonial and Early Federal periods, it is considered perhaps the finest example of Greek Revival architecture in the city (built 1834–42). It is open Monday to Friday from 9am to 5pm.

Double back along Wall Street and on the other side at the corner of Broad you'll see the:

3. **New York Stock Exchange.** If Federal Hall is the shrine to history on Wall Street, the New York Stock Exchange, at the corner of Wall and Broad streets, is the temple to the gods of money. Appropriately, the 1903 building is done in "Renaissance-temple" architecture. Inside, in the Great Hall of the Exchange, the member brokers, acting for clients all over the world, buy and sell millions of dollars' worth of securities in an atmosphere that, to the uninitiated, looks like pandemonium. To understand the subtle inner workings of the whole scheme, go to the two-tiered Visitors' Gallery, entrance at 20 Broad St. (tel. 656-5167), open Monday to Friday from 9:15am to 4pm (closed on major holidays); the activities are described by automatic narration in four languages. Only a certain number of tickets are given out each day, so it's wise to get yours as early as possible; they become available at 9am. For more information and reservations for groups of ten or more, phone 656-5168. The Exchange is the second most popular tourist attraction in New York.

Continue back to Broadway and turn right. Walk north a few blocks and turn right on Liberty Street, where you'll find the:

4. **Federal Reserve Bank of New York** at 33 Liberty St. Modeled after a Renaissance palace, this formidable 1924 building contains the world's largest known accumulation of

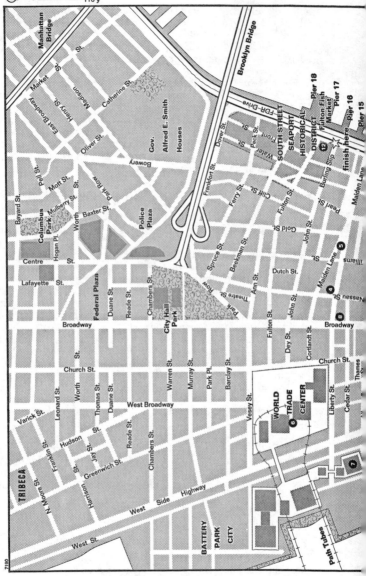

monetary gold. Take a guided tour through the gold vault and view an exhibit on cash processing, which includes many examples of old currency and coins. Tours are given at 10:30 and 11:30am, 1:30 and 2:30pm during banking days, and reservations must be made at least one day to one week in advance. Family groups may include children. (Large groups should make reservations several months in advance.) You may write to the Public Information Department at the bank (the zip code is 10045), or phone 720-6130 to request a reservation.

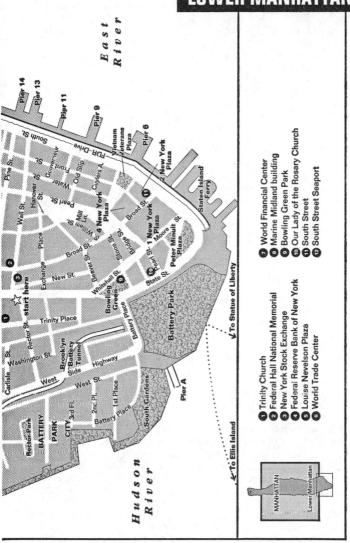

East River

Pier 14
Pier 13
Pier 11
Pier 9
Pier 6

South St.
FDR Drive
Vietnams Veterans Plaza
2 New York Plaza

Pine St.
Gouverneur La.
Front St.
Old Slip
Water St.
Cuylers A.
Wall St.
Hanover St.
Pearl St.
Mill St.
William St.
Exchange Place
Broad St.
Stone St.
3 New York Plaza
4 New York Plaza
Broad St.
1 New York Plaza
New St.
Beaver St.
Bridge St.
Pearl St.
Peter Minuit Plaza
Whitehall St.
Bowling Green
State St.
Staten Island Ferry
Trinity Place
Battery Place
Battery Park

start here

Rector St.
Carlisle St.
Washington St.
Brooklyn Battery Tunnel
West Side Highway
West St.
3rd Pl.
2nd Pl.
1st Place
Battery Place
South Gardens
Pier A

↓ To Statue of Liberty

↓ To Ellis Island

BATTERY PARK CITY
Rector Park

Hudson River

① Trinity Church
② Federal Hall National Memorial
③ New York Stock Exchange
④ Federal Reserve Bank of New York
⑤ Louise Nevelson Plaza
⑥ World Trade Center
⑦ World Financial Center
⑧ Marine Midland building
⑨ Bowling Green Park
⑩ Our Lady of the Rosary Church
⑪ South Street
⑫ South Street Seaport

MANHATTAN
Lower Manhattan

Continue east on Liberty Street to:

5. Louise Nevelson Plaza, where William Street, Liberty Street, and Maiden Lane meet at a tiny vestpocket park (1978) fitted with trees, benches, and seven vertical sculptures by Nevelson called *Shadows and Flags.*

Head back to Broadway now and continue walking west one block for the highlight of your downtown excursion, the:

6. World Trade Center. A less-than-a-minute ride will take you zooming to the top of the world's almost-tallest building. Here, at the glass-enclosed Observation Deck on the 107th floor of the **South Tower (Tower Two)**—more than a quarter mile in the sky—you'll see one of the most spectacular views on earth. Below you is all of New York, its bridges, its monuments, its maze of streets, its rivers and their toy ships, and, on a clear day, a view that extends 50 miles in all directions. At dusk, when the lights are just beginning to come up on the darkening city, it is particularly enchanting. If you also go up to the promenade on the roof above the 110th floor, you'll be on the highest outdoor observation platform in the world. Since anywhere from 6,000 to 9,000 people visit the Observation Deck on fine summer and holiday weekends, try to plan your visit for a weekday, when there will be only a few thousand. It's open from 9:30am to 9:30pm daily, with an admission charge of $4.75 for adults, $2.75 for seniors, $2.50 for children 6 to 12, and free for those under 6 (tel. 435-7377).

Now come down to earth and inspect some of the monumental art at the World Trade Center, including a gigantic **Joan Miró tapestry** (considered one of his masterworks), hung against a 50-foot-high marble wall in the mezzanine of 2 World Trade Center (1972); Alexander Calder's **World Trade Center Stabile,** resembling three giant sails, at Church and Vesey streets; and Louise Nevelson's sculpture **Sky-Gate New York,** which hangs in the mezzanine of 1 World Trade Center (1973). In the Austin J. Tobin Plaza, note Fritz Koenig's **Sphere for Plaza Fountain** (1972) in bronze, James Rosati's **Ideogram** (1974), in stainless steel, and Masayuki Nagare's **World Trade Center Sculpture** (1975), in Swedish black granite. You can also have a peek at the changing exhibits at the **United States Customs House** or stop in at the free visitors' gallery of the **Commodity Exchange,** on the ninth floor of 4 World Trade Center (1977), to watch some fast and furious trading (open weekdays from 10:30am to 3pm).

If you're planning to see a Broadway or Off-Broadway show at night, stop in at the branch of **TKTS** on the mezzanine level of 2 World Trade Center for half-price day-of-performance tickets. Hours are Monday to Friday from 11am to 5:30pm and Saturday from 11am to 3:30pm.

A block west of the World Trade Center, across the North Pedestrian Bridge to Battery Park City is the:

7. **World Financial Center,** whose four soaring granite-and-glass towers designed (mid-1980s) by architect Cesar Pelli house corporate headquarters for large international firms. When you cross the bridge, you'll find yourself in the splendid indoor **Winter Garden** (1988), a crystal palace atrium with a 120-foot vaulted glass ceiling, a magnificent marble-and-granite staircase, live palm trees, changing art exhibits, and glorious views out to the Hudson, the Statue of Liberty, and lower New York Harbor. It's one of New York's great indoor spaces. There are many shops and services here, plus almost a dozen restaurants and outdoor cafes. It's a choice place for:

REFUELING STOPS Both **Pipeline** (tel. 945-2755) and **Edward Moran Bar & Grill** (tel. 945-2255) are big, casual eating places with outdoor tables overlooking the waterfront; it's difficult to tear oneself away on a fine day. Indoors, under the palms in the Winter Garden, stylish **Sfuzzi** (tel. 385-8080) offers pastas, pizzas, and other Italian favorites.

The World Financial Center will probably have some form of free entertainment going on in good weather, everything from sunset dancing to live bands to puppet shows for the kids. Ogle the splendid boats in the yacht harbor at the North and South coves. You could then stroll along the **Hudson River Esplanade,** admiring the waterfront views and the parks and sculptures and flower gardens that make **Battery Park City,** which was built on 92 acres of landfill from the World Trade Center, one of the most graceful residential/commercial areas in New York. You can follow the esplanade all the way around to the tip of the island, until you arrive at Battery Park. From here, you can take a ferry to the Statue of Liberty and Ellis Island. (If you're coming to the World Trade Center or World Financial Center from midtown, take the 1, R, or N train to the World Trade Center; or the E train to Chambers Street/World Trade Center. Cross West Street to the bridge.) For more information on activities and events at the Winter Garden, phone 945-0505.

Alternatively, if you've decided to skip the World Financial Center on this particular excursion, return to Broadway after visiting the World Trade Center and proceed south. You'll see the:

8. **Marine Midland** building (1967) at 140 Broadway, with Isamu Noguchi's enormous rectangular *Cube* (1973) precariously balanced on one corner in front of it. This is one of the few new buildings in the area that has made any attempt at public art or sculpture.

Continue down Broadway to:

9. **Bowling Green Park.** Where the Dutch burghers actually used to bowl is ahead of you (it has been restored to look the way it did a century ago with London plane trees, wooden benches, and old-time lamp posts), and so is the massive beaux arts former **Custom House** (1907), with its imposing sculptures of Asia, America, Africa, and Europe, done by Daniel Chester French of Lincoln Memorial fame. Inside, in the Rotunda Room, are Reginald Marsh's famed WPA murals.

Bear left, following the other side of the street from Bowling Green and Battery Park, until you come to the building at 7 State Street:

10. **Our Lady of the Rosary Church,** one of the few remaining examples of Early Federal architecture in New York. Built by John McComb as a private town house around 1800, Watson House is noted for the colonnade that curves with the line of the street. As Our Lady of the Rosary Church, it is the shrine of Saint Elizabeth Bayley Seton.

Right behind State Street is Pearl Street, which you should follow west to the corner of Broad Street to see one of New York's most famous historical houses:

REFUELING STOP **Fraunces Tavern.** Built originally in 1719, Fraunces Tavern became part of American history when George Washington bade farewell to his officers in the Long

Room on December 4, 1783, after the American Revolution. Reconstructed in 1907, Fraunces Tavern is now owned and maintained by the Sons of the Revolution in the State of New York as a museum with permanent and changing exhibits of the Revolutionary War and 18th-century American history and culture. You might catch the museum's audiovisual presentation of the early history of New York City or attend some of their lectures and concerts (open Monday to Friday from 10am to 4:45pm, Saturday noon to 4pm; adults $2.50, seniors, students, and children under 12 with adult, $1; tel. 425-1778 for information). On the ground floor is one of the oldest continuously operated restaurants in America (tel. 269-0144), where the food is excellent.

Now make your way to the waterfront on Broad Street and begin walking up:

11. South Street, once dotted with ship chandlers' stores and other establishments having to do with sailing and the sea. Those who mourn the old days on the waterfront have mixed emotions about the steel-and-glass monsters, but there is no denying that some are handsome. If you're interested in architecture, have a look yourself at the soaring columns of **2 New York Plaza** or **55 Water Street,** which I find the most impressive building here. Next to it is the moving **New York Vietnam Veterans Memorial.** I especially like the plaza at 55 Water Street on its northern side that overlooks the highway. Here you can join the local office workers eating lunch at the chairs and tables outside or just sit and watch the tugs and the whirlybirds and the harbor traffic, catch the marvelous ocean breezes, and dream a little bit about the vanished days of the tall ships, the giant clippers that came from all over the world to drop anchor at the port of New York, arching their bowsprits across South Street. Continue walking until you reach the:

12. South Street Seaport, which you can explore now or save for a later day.

To get back to midtown, walk west from the South Street Seaport on Fulton Street and make connections to all major subway lines.

WALKING TOUR 2 —— GREENWICH VILLAGE

Start: Sixth Avenue and Waverly Place, near the West 4th Street subway station.
Finish: Same as start.
Time: Approximately 1 hour and 10 minutes.

The original Greenwich Village, the separate town that once lay beyond the boundaries of New York, is located in the region between Greenwich Avenue and the Hudson River, bounded on the south by West Houston Street. That Greenwich Village was one of the earliest settlements on Manhattan, a bucolic hamlet until the 1820s. Its

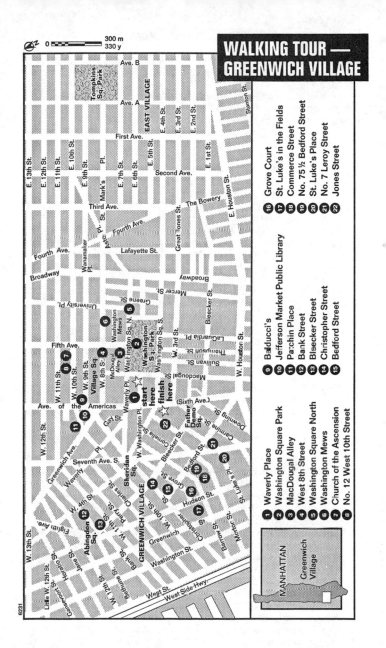

WALKING TOUR — GREENWICH VILLAGE

0 — 300 m / 330 y

16 Grove Court
17 St. Luke's in the Fields
18 Commerce Street
19 No. 75½ Bedford Street
20 St. Luke's Place
21 No. 7 Leroy Street
22 Jones Street

9 Balducci's
10 Jefferson Market Public Library
11 Patchin Place
12 Bank Street
13 Bleecker Street
14 Christopher Street
15 Bedford Street

1 Waverly Place
2 Washington Square Park
3 MacDougal Alley
4 West 8th Street
5 Washington Square North
6 Washington Mews
7 Church of the Ascension
8 No. 12 West 10th Street

MANHATTAN
Greenwich Village

---

sudden prosperity was largely a function of the poor quality of the drinking water in the neighboring city of New York. In those days epidemics of typhoid and smallpox were almost annual affairs. As soon as the new season's plague struck New York, everyone who could afford to decamped immediately to healthful semirural and nearby Greenwich.

Greenwich possessed its own bewildering network of built-up

streets well before burgeoning New York City engulfed it. They still exist, and even native New Yorkers can get lost in the Village, at least without a map.

This tour starts at Sixth Avenue and Waverly Place, an intersection located one block south of 8th Street and quite near the uptown exits from the Washington Square–West 4th Street subway stop. Proceed east from Sixth Avenue toward Washington Square Park on:

1. **Waverly Place,** a typical Village street lined with well-used brick town houses from the early 19th century as well as buildings of more recent vintage. At the end of one block you arrive at Macdougal Street and:

2. **Washington Square Park.** In 1789, the park was designated a pauper's burial ground. But by 1826 fashion was on the march. The paupers were unceremoniously removed, and the former graveyard became a parade ground. Soon fine Greek Revival houses began to appear along the southern boundary. All of these have disappeared, victims of time and the encroaching building programs of New York University's campus.

    Now make a short detour. Turn to your left (north) and head away from Washington Square Park up MacDougal Street. After a few steps you'll see:

3. **MacDougal Alley** on your right. This little street, lined with former carriage houses, is typical of the sort of small enclave that makes the Village such an appealing place to live. You might stroll up to the end of MacDougal Street (the Alley is private) and have a look at:

4. **West 8th Street** while you're here. It's a wilderness of shoe stores, clothing stores, poster shops, and copy centers. It's hard to believe that its mutilated buildings were ever aristocratic private houses.

    Now return to Washington Square, turn left (east), and walk along:

5. **Washington Square North.** Collectively known as The Row, the brick houses that still stand on the park's northern boundary give a vivid idea of what the whole square once looked like. They enjoyed their day (in the 1830s) as the homes of New York's elite. Henry James and Edith Wharton both lived and worked at **1 Washington Square North.** Today many of these old mansions are only facades masking new apartments inside, but a few have survived almost intact. Note the double house at **no. 20,** built in 1828 as a freestanding suburban mansion for one George P. Rogers. The very air on this block is redolent with the gentility of the past. You can almost imagine the clip-clop of horses and the creak of carriage springs as ladies lift their skirts while climbing out to make their calls. At Fifth Avenue, turn left (uptown). On the east side of the avenue you'll see:

6. **Washington Mews,** another alley lined with former carriage houses that are now converted to residences. Although the original town houses along this stretch of Fifth were long ago replaced with apartment houses, the Mews preserves a dignified residential air.

    Three blocks north of Washington Square at 10th Street is the:

7. **Church of the Ascension,** a pleasant old place set back from

the street behind an antique iron fence. It's been here since 1841, although the interior dates from a renovation in the 1880s by the celebrated McKim, Mead & White! Turn left off Fifth Avenue onto West 10th Street, one of the nicest blocks in the Village, lined with fine city houses. Note:

8. **No. 12,** a particularly capacious old manse once owned by Bruce Price, the architect of Tuxedo Park and the father of etiquette expert Emily Post.

   At the end of the block you'll reach the corner of Sixth Avenue. Turn left on Sixth and down the block is:

9. **Balducci's,** the famous Italian gourmet emporium.

   Across Sixth is the:

10. **Jefferson Market Public Library.** This exuberant Victorian castle, dating from the 1870s, was once considered one of the half dozen most beautiful buildings in the United States. Subsequent generations considered it a horror. Concerned Villagers saved it from demolition in the late 1960s after it had stood vacant for over 20 years. When built, it was part of an innovative multiple-use complex that included a jail, a market, a courthouse, and a prison.

    Across 10th Street from the Jefferson Library is another little enclave of the sort that so typifies Greenwich Village. Called:

11. **Patchin Place,** it contains but ten modest brick houses facing one another across a leafy cul-de-sac. Theodore Dreiser, Jane Bowles, and e. e. cummings were among Patchin Place's illustrious residents in the days when the Village was America's "Bohemia."

    Now continue walking west on 10th Street away from Sixth Avenue, across Greenwich Avenue, and keep walking west on 10th Street. The modest-looking tenements that line the street contain apartments as pricey as those on the elegant block between Fifth and Sixth. Why? Because they're on West 10th Street, a premium New York address. Continue straight across the intersection of 10th Street and Waverly Place (the excellent **Three Lives & Company** bookstore, a haven for literary types, is at the corner), turn left and walk two short blocks to a perfect place for lunch:

REFUELING STOP   Gus's Place, 149 Waverly Place (tel. 645-8511). This charming, Mediterranean-Greek bistro is cool and breezy, with huge windows and several tables almost out on the street. It's fun for two or three diners to make a meal of their "small plates"—steamed mussels and garlic, grilled portobello mushrooms and root-vegetable chips and the like—all modestly priced. From Gus's, you might, alternatively, go west to Christopher Street, cross it, and have some American fare or a drink at the **Lion's Head,** 59 Christopher St. (tel. 929-0670), a popular village tavern with an imaginative menu and brick walls lined with covers of books by its many literary patrons.

To the west is Seventh Avenue South. Cross the avenue and go just a few steps to the intersection of West 10th and West 4th streets (one of those conceptually bizarre intersections for which the Village is famous). On the corner, you'll pass **La Métairie,** "reservé aux gourmets"; marvelous garlicky aromas waft from its open windows in warm weather. (Main lunch courses under $10.) Then turn right and start walking northwest up West 4th. Now you're getting into the real Greenwich Village. The next couple of intersecting streets—Charles, Perry, West 11th, and Bank—are filled with old brick houses, shady trees, a smattering of tasteful shops, galleries, small restaurants and cafes, and a great feeling of calm. Note the brick house at the corner of West 11th and West 4th. It must have looked just as it does now for over 100 years, which is no mean feat in New York.

Turn left (west) when you reach:

12. **Bank Street,** where during a particularly virulent smallpox epidemic in the 1820s, so many New York banking institutions set up temporary offices on this street that the Village of Greenwich named it after them. Note the ancient wisteria growing on no. 60. This is the sort of tenement house that invaded the Village as it became less fashionable in the latter part of the 19th century. Today even the tenements have an appealing patina of age. Many fine old Greek Revival houses remain on this block of Bank, making it one of the Village's nicest. At the end of the block, at Abingdon Square, turn left onto:

13. **Bleecker Street.** This is a street of antiques shops, occasional boutiques, interesting bookstores, cracked sidewalks, and some blowsy-looking modernish buildings. The narrow tree-lined side streets, however, are delightful. Continue south on Bleecker for five blocks to:

14. **Christopher Street** and turn right (west toward the Hudson). Ahead in the distance you can see New Jersey across the river. On the street around you, you'll see gay New York in full flower, as Christopher Street is more or less its spiritual center.

Stay on Christopher one short block to:

15. **Bedford Street** and turn left (south). At the end of the block, on the corner of Grove Street, is a nest of particularly pictur-esque wooden houses. No. 17 Grove Street, on the corner of Bedford and Grove, was built by a Village sash-maker in the 1820s. It sags wonderfully and evokes the past quite vividly. No. 100 Bedford St., around the corner, is a Grimm's fairy-tale concoction of stucco, timbers, and crazy angles called Twin Peaks. Cross the street at the end of the block, make a right on Grove Street in the direction of the Hudson. The road makes a dogleg turn just a few steps from Bedford. Right at the angle of the turn you'll see a little gate set into a brick wall. Although it's private beyond, you can step up to the gate and look over it into:

16. **Grove Court.** Built for blue-collar tenants about 1830 and originally called Mixed Ale Alley, this tree-shaded enclave of little brick houses is the sort of Village spot many New Yorkers would kill to live in. After you've admired the Federal houses here, continue another half block to the end of Grove at Hudson Street. The old church across Hudson is:

17. **St. Luke's in the Fields,** built in the 1820s when so much of this part of the Village was going up. The original St. Luke's was destroyed by fire, but the restoration preserves its rural look, despite the enormous Victorian-era warehouses looming behind it. As you leave Grove Street, turn left (south) on Hudson for one block to Barrow Street, and turn left again. The first corner you'll come to is called:

18. **Commerce Street.** Note the interesting pair of identical

houses, no. 39 and no. 41 Commerce St., which were built in the 1830s and "modernized" in the 1870s with matching mansard roofs. This crooked little thoroughfare used to be called Cherry Lane (because of the many cherry trees in the area: the Cherry Lane Theater, a popular off-Broadway house, recalls those days) until the big smallpox scare of 1822 sent so many businesses up here from New York that the name was changed. When you reach the end of the block, you'll be back on Bedford Street. Turn right (south) again and then look to your right for:

19. No. 75½ Bedford St. This 9½-foot-wide house holds the distinction of being the narrowest house in Greenwich Village, as well as the one-time residence of poet Edna St. Vincent Millay. Sadly, it is now smeared with graffiti. Keep walking south on Bedford for two blocks to Seventh Avenue and then walk another block to the right to:

20. St. Luke's Place, where you should turn right. Although the south side of St. Luke's Place is occupied by a modern playground, the north side preserves a terrific old row of houses from the 1850s. No. 6 St. Luke's Place was the residence of a former mayor of New York, the popular James J. ("Gentleman Jimmy") Walker, and more recently Robert De Niro. Although a crook and a scoundrel, Walker managed to epitomize the glamour of the 1920s. Incredibly enough, he is remembered quite fondly to this day.

Return to Seventh Avenue and continue straight across it on the line of St. Luke's Place. Once across Seventh you'll note that St. Luke's becomes Leroy Street. Stay on Leroy, past the continuation of Bedford Street for one block to the corner of Bleecker Street. Just before this intersection, note:

21. No. 7 Leroy St., a nearly perfect circa-1810 house, complete with alley entrance and original dormers. When you get to Bleecker, note the local shops, then turn left for two very short blocks to:

22. Jones Street. Turn right onto Jones and take a quick look at no. 17 to see what usually happens to old houses like the one at no. 7 Leroy. A pity, no? At the end of the block, you'll be back on West 4th Street. Turn right for another short block and presto, here you are again back on Sixth Avenue, a mere two blocks south of Waverly Place, where the tour began.

WALKING TOUR 3 — UPPER
WEST SIDE

Start: Lincoln Center for the Performing Arts.
Finish: Northeast corner of 73rd and Broadway.
Time: 2 to 4 hours, depending on stops.
Best Times: Tuesday to Sunday, when museums are open.

Begin your tour at:

1. Lincoln Center for the Performing Arts, Broadway to Amsterdam Avenue, from 62nd to 66th streets. An energetic revitalization of the Upper West Side really began full force with the completion of the city's controversial multicultural facility at

Lincoln Center; some criticize the architecture as too conservative, others fault it for being too daring. The complex includes Avery Fisher Hall, formerly Philharmonic Hall (1962); the New York State Theater (1964); the Vivian Beaumont Theater (1965); the New York Public Library for the Performing Arts (1965); the Metropolitan Opera House (1966); and across 65th Street, Alice Tully Hall, the Juilliard School of Music (1968), and the Walter Reade Theater (1991). Three of the buildings face the central plaza—the Metropolitan Opera House in the middle, Avery Fisher Hall to the right, and the New York State Theater to the left. The plaza itself is dominated by a handsome fountain and, on summer evenings, by cafe tables that spill out from Avery Fisher Hall.

Looking east across the plaza, notice the rooftop replica of the:

2. **Statue of Liberty,** 43 W. 64th St. Her torch is gone and her spiral staircase is now closed permanently, but this 1902 lady is an exact duplicate of her larger, more famous counterpart.

In front of the plaza, in an island where Broadway and Columbus Avenue meet, is the tiny:

3. **Dante Park.** The bronze statue of the Italian poet Dante Alighieri by Ettore Ximenes was erected here in 1921 to commemorate the 600th anniversary of his death. He holds a copy of the *Divine Comedy,* in good company with the artistic offerings of Lincoln Center.

Cross Broadway and walk north to the:

4. **Museum of American Folk Art,** 2 Lincoln Square. The museum also has a charming shop filled with such treasures as ceramics, mobiles, toys, doll houses, and miniature Pennsylvania Dutch blanket chests—all handmade, naturally.

Recrossing (west) Broadway at 66th Street, you'll pass:

5. **Tucker Park.** A bronze bust honors Richard Tucker, the operatic tenor who, during his 21-year career with the Metropolitan Opera, sang almost 500 performances.

A branch of:

6. **Tower Records,** 1965 Broadway at 66th Street, contains two floors of records, tapes, CDs, and videos, both domestic and imported, often at discount prices.

Cross Broadway again and head east on 67th Street toward Central Park. The block between Columbus Avenue and the park is a delightful enclave of older buildings designed originally as artists' studios. Concealed behind their facades are double-height studio spaces.

7. **The Atelier,** no. 33, dates from 1902 and has a handsome stone-arched facade.

8. **No. 15** is notable for its Gothic Revival lobby resembling a chapel. And finally, the:

9. **Hotel des Artistes,** No. 1, is one of New York's treasures. Completed in 1918, this splendid building actually shows balconied artists' spaces behind its buoyant Elizabethan facade. A list of past residents reads like a who's who of entertainment and the arts: Noël Coward, Norman Rockwell, Isadora Duncan, and Edna Ferber, among others. The noted Café des Artistes (see Chapter 6) is on the hotel's first floor. Just across Central Park West and slightly into the park, trees strung with tiny lights identify:

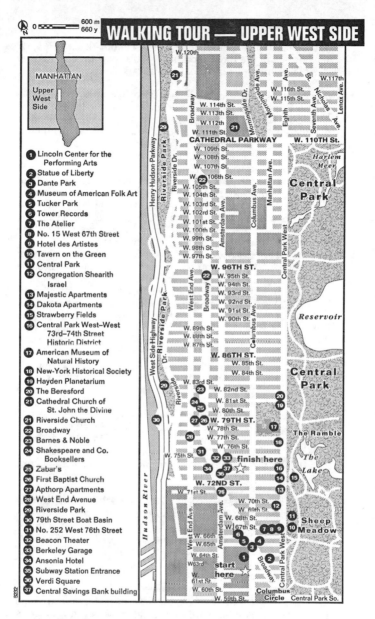

MANHATTAN

Upper
West
Side

1 Lincoln Center for the
   Performing Arts
2 Statue of Liberty
3 Dante Park
4 Museum of American Folk Art
5 Tucker Park
6 Tower Records
7 The Atelier
8 No. 15 West 67th Street
9 Hotel des Artistes
10 Tavern on the Green
11 Central Park
12 Congregation Shearith
   Israel
13 Majestic Apartments
14 Dakota Apartments
15 Strawberry Fields
16 Central Park West–West
   73rd–74th Street
   Historic District
17 American Museum of
   Natural History
18 New-York Historical Society
19 Hayden Planetarium
20 The Beresford
21 Cathedral Church of
   St. John the Divine
21 Riverside Church
22 Broadway
23 Barnes & Noble
24 Shakespeare and Co.
   Booksellers
25 Zabar's
26 First Baptist Church
27 Apthorp Apartments
28 West End Avenue
29 Riverside Park
30 79th Street Boat Basin
31 No. 252 West 76th Street
32 Beacon Theater
33 Berkeley Garage
34 Ansonia Hotel
35 Subway Station Entrance
36 Verdi Square
37 Central Savings Bank building

10. Tavern on the Green, 67th Street near Central Park West,
one of the most romantic dining/dancing spots in town (See
Chapter 6).

11. Central Park, 59th to 110th streets, Fifth Avenue to Central
Park West, a splendid 840 acres of landscaped lakes, hills,
meadows, footpaths, bridges, bridle paths, secluded glens, a bird
sanctuary, two skating rinks, a first-rate zoo, multiple recreational facilities, and an impressive collection of sculpture. The park

was designated a National Historic Landmark in 1965. It remains one of the most successful landscaped areas anywhere.

At the southwest corner of Central Park West and 70th Street is:

12. Congregation Shearith Israel (the Spanish and Portuguese Synagogue), 2 W. 70th St. This is the fifth home of the oldest Jewish congregation in the United States—Spanish and Portuguese refugees from the Inquisition in Brazil who built their first house of worship in 1730. After four successive moves uptown, this Classic Revival building was erected in 1897.

Continuing north, you reach the:

13. Majestic Apartments, 115 Central Park West, 71st to 72nd streets. Built in 1930, this is a fine example of the art deco style of the late 1920s and '30s. One of four twin-towered apartment houses that enliven the Central Park skyline, the attractive, much-imitated brickwork was designed by French sculptor René Chanbellan. Continuing north, you'll come to the:

14. Dakota Apartments, 1 W. 72nd St., northwest corner of Central Park West. Legend has it that this building got its name for its location in what was in 1884 the boondocks of Manhattan, so remote from the city center that it might as well have been in Dakota. It was designed by Henry J. Hardenbergh (also architect of the Plaza Hotel) in German Renaissance style, part fortress (it's surrounded by a dry moat), part château, with dormers, gables, arches, balconies, finials, and ornate stonework. Despite its status then and now as one of New York's most exclusive apartment houses, the Dakota has a moody atmosphere—it was the setting for the film *Rosemary's Baby* and the site of the tragic 1980 murder of former rock star and Beatle John Lennon, in whose memory his widow, Yoko Ono, has created the touching memorial directly across the street:

15. Strawberry Fields, Central Park at 72nd Street.

After you've paid your respects, cross Central Park West, walk to 73rd Street, and turn left, noticing the ornamental iron gate and dry moat of the Dakota. Clark and Hardenbergh joined forces in another project after the Dakota, the development of what is now the:

16. Central Park West—West 73rd—74th Street Historic District, animated by a series of rental row houses in polychrome, a departure from the relentless rows of brownstones that lined the city streets during the 1870s and '80s. Note especially nos. 15A–19 and 41–65, built between 1882 and 1885.

Continue west to:

REFUELING STOPS Columbus Avenue, which from 72nd to 81st streets is dotted with good eating places in a range of prices. **Ruppert's** (72nd and 73rd streets) and the **Museum Café** (77th Street) are well established and popular for leisurely lunches and dinners (they can get crowded, so best arrive at off hours). More casual is the branch of **Pizzeria Uno** at 81st Street.

As a diversion from sightseeing, explore some of the shops along Columbus Avenue. Eileen Fisher (no. 341), French Connection (no. 304), and Express Ltd. (no. 321) are among the better stores selling women's fashions. Putumayo (no. 339) specializes in sophisticated ethnic clothing and accessories. Along Columbus Avenue to Central Park West, from 77th to 81st streets, is the spectacular:

17. **American Museum of Natural History,** which houses one of the world's most important scientific collections and is among the most frequently visited museums in town. The original entrance is on the 77th Street side, a massive Romanesque Revival edifice in pink Vermont granite built from 1892 to 1899, with a carriage entrance, arcaded porch, towers and turrets, and a grand staircase. The Central Park West facade is dominated by an equestrian statue of Theodore Roosevelt sculpted by J. E. Fraser in 1939.

    Though overshadowed by the Natural History Museum, the:

18. **New-York Historical Society,** 170 Central Park West, on the southwest corner of 77th Street, is a pleasing, understated classical palace begun in 1908, with wings added in 1938. It's a major research venue for students of American history, though financial difficulties in 1993 led to reduced access. Walk north, rounding the corner at 81st Street to the:

19. **Hayden Planetarium,** 81st Street and Central Park West, where "cosmic laser concerts" are featured along with other heavenly explorations. The building is a 1935 adjunct to the American Museum of Natural History. Before heading west, glance at:

20. **The Beresford,** 211 Central Park West, on the northwest corner of 81st, built in 1929 during Central Park West's glory days. It's a luxury apartment house topped by a baroque tower that gives it a decidedly romantic aura, not easy for a structure as large as this.

    Walking west on 81st Street to Broadway, you'll pass the typical turn-of-the-century residential brownstones that characterize the side streets of the Upper West Side. At Broadway, the foot-weary can hop an M7 or M104 bus north to visit the:

21. **Cathedral Church of St. John the Divine** (Amsterdam Avenue and 112th Street) and/or **Riverside Church** (Riverside Drive and 122nd Street).

    The hardy can continue along:

22. **Broadway,** the main thoroughfare of the Upper West Side and the only major artery that runs on the diagonal in New York's grid system of streets. Seedy though it may be in parts, it's a monumental avenue edged by monumental buildings and centered by a wide grassy mall. At Broadway and 82nd Street is:

23. **Barnes & Noble,** a mega-bookstore with plenty of chairs for reading and browsing, plus a delightful espresso cafe. Booklovers should continue south to Broadway and 81st Street for:

24. **Shakespeare and Co. Booksellers,** another great place to browse. And just south is:

25. **Zabar's,** 2245 Broadway, between 80th and 81st streets. New York would be unimaginable without the gourmet food emporium whose variety of temptations defies categorizing. Known throughout the city, frequented by the cognoscenti in all boroughs, Zabar's is a landmark, an institution, an absolute

must for anyone interested in the New York food lover's state of mind. Continue south to:

26. **First Baptist Church,** Broadway at 79th Street, an austere Romanesque Revival structure dating from 1891, with curious asymmetrical twin towers.

   The entire block, Broadway to West End Avenue, and West 79th to West 78th streets, is taken up by the:

27. **Apthorp Apartments,** a dignified luxury building that still retains its old-world elegance. Built for William Waldorf Astor in 1908, the limestone structure surrounds a central courtyard with fountain beyond high vaulted passageways. Except for ground-floor shops on Broadway, the building remains intact and original. It is named for Charles Apthorp, who bought the land in 1763. It remained in the family until 1879, when Astor purchased it. Walk west on 77th Street to:

28. **West End Avenue,** until the early 20th century, a "millionaire's row" of stylish town houses. The wealthy moved a block west when Riverside Drive opened, but after World War I a plethora of apartment houses were built to lure tenants back.

   Continue west down the hill to:

29. **Riverside Park,** designed in 1875 by Central Park architect Frederick Law Olmsted and completed around 1910. A flight of steps to the left leads to a tunnel that in turn takes you down more steps, along a path, and through a rotunda to the:

30. **79th Street Boat Basin,** an unexpected and delightful marina where many New Yorkers tie up or live permanently on their houseboats.

   Return to Riverside Park and relax on a bench for a few minutes before taking the curved stairway at the basketball court up to Riverside Drive. Head east on 76th Street to:

31. **No. 252 W. 76th St.** and view it from the opposite side to appreciate the recently restored and quite splendid eclectic Classical facade.

   Turn right at Broadway. On the east side, near 75th Street is the:

32. **Beacon Theater** (1928), 2124 Broadway. No matter what's playing, don't miss the magnificent art deco interior, a designated city landmark. Walk around the theater to the:

33. **Berkeley Garage,** 201 W. 75th St., a wonderful 1890 Romanesque Revival building that once housed the stables of the New York Cab Company. The three arches provided a broad entrance for horses and carriages in the 1880s and '90s. Return to the west side of Broadway and continue south to one of New York's architectural masterpieces, the French beaux arts:

34. **Ansonia Hotel,** 2109 Broadway, on the northwest corner of 73rd Street. The Ansonia was a grande dame among apartment hotels when it opened in 1904. Opulent and richly ornamental, it meant to imitate the French resort hotels along the Riviera. Over the years the Ansonia became the bastion of the music profession: Among its illustrious tenants were Enrico Caruso, Ezio Pinza, Lily Pons, Igor Stravinsky, Arturo Toscanini, and Yehudi Menuhin. The building is striking for its mansard roof and rounded towers.

   If you're hungry, continue north on Broadway and between 81st and 82nd streets you'll find:

REFUELING STOP **Teachers Too,** 2271 Broadway (tel. 362-4900), a block north of Zabar's. This ever-popular neighborhood spot offers wonderful American food and a few Thai dishes at reasonable prices—fish selections are especially good. Sidewalk tables in good weather.

Returning to the intersection of Broadway and West 72nd Street, the:

35. Subway Station Entrance is one of the few remaining art nouveau structures of its kind, dating from 1904, when the underground railway was first built. The intersection is divided into Verdi Square to the north and Sherman Square to the south.

36. Verdi Square honors the Italian opera composer, whose statue in marble stands on a granite pedestal above four life-size figures of characters from his operas *Aïda*, *Falstaff*, *Otello*, and *La Forza del Destino*.

Dominating the north side of Verdi Square is the former:

37. Central Savings Bank building (now the Apple Bank for Savings), 2100 Broadway, at the northeast corner of 73rd Street. This massive Palladian palace gives an impression of financial security—obviously the intention of its builders. The wrought-iron window grilles and lanterns (by Samuel Yellin) embellish the facade, while two lions flanking a large clock decorate the 73rd Street entrance.

CHAPTER 9

NEW YORK SHOPPING A TO Z

Quite a lot of people come to New York for only one reason: to go shopping. For them, the greatest show in town begins right on Fifth Avenue. One woman I know flies in regularly from Detroit, checks into her hotel, grabs a cab, and heads immediately for Saks. "Then," she says, "I know I'm in New York."

What my friend senses, of course, is that New York is one of the great fashion capitals of the world, a city where *W* sits on the best coffee tables, where the fashion business provides a living, a *raison d'être*, or, at the very least, a subject of conversation for thousands of people. As a result of this high-keyed fashion consciousness, the New York woman, regardless of her income, is one of the best, most individually dressed women in the world. Close at hand she has the great department and specialty stores like Lord & Taylor, Saks Fifth Avenue, Bergdorf Goodman, Galeries Lafayette, Bloomingdale's, A&S, and Macy's. She also has hundreds of small boutiques and shops where she can buy anything from a Paris ball gown whose price tag runs into or even over four figures to a Mickey Mouse T-shirt for $12. She can suit her flights of fancy with a pair of fine Italian boots, a silk sari from India, a peasant jacket from Guatemala, or the latest from a trendy Japanese designer. She can also rummage through old capes and costumes in the Village and emerge with a vintage look. It's a wide-open, exciting scene, and one that any woman (or man, for that matter, since men's boutiques are proliferating almost as widely as women's) with an ounce of fashion curiosity will find absorbing.

Most stores are open Monday to Saturday from 9am to 6pm and on Sunday afternoon.

Note: New York City has a hefty **sales tax** of 8.25%.

INSIDE INFORMATION   In any one month, there are 100 to 150 sales in the private showrooms of New York's designers and manufacturers. Not only samples, but overstocks and cancellations—in women's, men's, and children's clothing; accessories; furs; furniture; and household goods. And if you were an insider in these businesses, you'd know, via the grapevine, when and where those sales, which are never advertised, were being held. Well, now you can get inside information, thanks to two publications sold by subscription to thousands of avid New York shoppers who wouldn't dream of paying retail, not when they can realize spectacular savings—anywhere from 50% to 90% on top brand-name and designer labels. If you'd like to join in the fun and buy, say, a $700 man's designer suit from Italy for $200, a woman's $2,000 mink coat for $895, a $350 leather bomber jacket for $60, or a child's $50 outfit from $5 to $10, here's how you do it.

Fashion Update, which comes out quarterly, costs $65 a year, with single copies $30. A hotline phone number is provided to subscribers for late-breaking sales. Publisher Sara Gardner also leads highly enjoyable personalized three-hour shopping tours for $50.

Phone 718/377-8873 or write *Fashion Update,* 1274 49th St., Suite 209, Brooklyn, NY 11219.

The other sales-and-bargain guide is *The S&B Report,* which is published monthly. It costs $49 for a yearly subscription, or $8.60 for a single copy; get one or both by phoning 212/679-5400 or writing *The S&B Report,* 112 E. 36th St., 4th floor, New York, NY 10016. Elyse Lazar, the publisher, advises that the most spectacular bargains are often in costume jewelry and accessories. "Stores mark these up as much as 400%," she says.

Lazar also puts out four other valuable publications. *Kids Report* ($29 a year for 12 issues) covers children's showroom sales, factory outlets, discounters, and mail-order companies. It also lists free educational, cultural, and recreational services for children in New York. *Home Report* ($39 a year) is a monthly listing of auctions, antiques shows and fairs, furniture and household showroom sales, and warehouse sales in New York, New Jersey, Pennsylvania, Massachusetts, and Connecticut. *Outlet Shopper's Guide* ($12.95) is a directory of all major outlet centers and individual outlet stores in the country; and *Shop By Mail* ($12.95) is a directory of 1,000 mail-order companies.

ANTIQUES & FLEA MARKETS

AMERICA HURRAH ANTIQUES, third floor of 766 Madison Ave., at 66th Street. Tel. 535-1930.

Hung up on patchwork quilts? America Hurrah Antiques has a superb collection of antique American quilts, most made between 1830 and 1930 in New York and Pennsylvania (many are Amish) at prices averaging $800 to $3,000, but many exceptional examples can run as high as $25,000. They are familiar with European bed sizes and can advise Europeans precisely which quilts will be suitable. Also beautiful are folk art and Americana, such as antique Native American art, hooked rugs, paintings, pottery, handmade antique weathervanes, baskets, and country accessories.

ANNEX ANTIQUES FAIR AND FLEA MARKET, Sixth Avenue, at 25th St. Tel. 243-5343.

This is a favorite weekend activity for New York's antique hunters. Prices here are lower than those in the stores, and there's something for everyone, most of it of fairly modern vintage: glass, pottery, china, jewelry, furniture, you-name-it. Over 300 vendors offer their wares. **Open:** Sat–Sun 9am–5pm year-round.

ARES RARE, 605 Madison Ave., between 57th and 58th streets, 4th floor. Tel. 758-5340.

The collection of jewels here spans 4,000 years—from ancient Greek and Egyptian to dazzling art deco designs. The gallery also offers fine jewelry repairs, appraisals, and an extensive book department. Special exhibitions are held throughout the year.

GREENWICH VILLAGE FLEA MARKET, P.S. 41, Greenwich Avenue, at Charles Street. Tel. 722-4068.

A favorite with village folk, this one has everything from furniture to clothing to jewelry—and then some. **Open:** Sat–Sun 10am–6pm.

I.S. 44, Columbus Avenue, at 76th Street.

Sharing space with a popular Greenmarket, this one is known as the "Greenflea." You'll find antique and estate jewelry, objets d'art, furniture, clothing, and lots more. **Open:** Sun 10am–6pm.

MANHATTAN ART & ANTIQUES CENTER, 1050 Second Ave., at 56th Street. Tel. 355-4400.

The Manhattan Art & Antiques Center is a handsome enclosed mall where over 100 antiques dealers have gathered their wares. The range goes from country furniture to rare Chinese porcelains, from African masks to temple hangings from Tibet. Collect a print or a Persian carpet, a music box or an old master, depending on what the budget will bear. **Open:** Mon–Sat 10:30am–6pm, Sun noon–6pm.

SOHO ANTIQUES FAIR AND FLEA MARKET, corner of Broadway and Grand Street. Tel. 682-2000.

This popular outdoor antiques and collectibles market is located in the heart of the vibrant SoHo gallery and shopping scene. Over 100 vendors offer American and European antiques, furniture, fine and decorative objects, vintage clothing, silver, china, glassware, jewelry, coins, original paintings, American Indian artifacts, folk art, and memorabilia. **Open:** Sat–Sun 9am–5pm.

AUCTIONS

Scores of New Yorkers have become auction addicts. When they need to furnish an apartment, buy a painting, or get a high chair for the baby, they wouldn't consider buying anything new or price-tagged. For them, the game is in the bidding, the adventure in seeing who gets what. You can visit New York auction houses and bid for anything from sewing machines to silverware, from lamps to lorgnettes, from baubles to barbells.

When you're out for big game (or just spectator sport), the most exciting place is **Sotheby's,** 1334 York Ave., at 72nd Street (tel. 606-7000), where the cognoscenti vie for Rembrandts, pedigreed furniture, decorative arts, and precious jewelry. Many items, however, are not exorbitant, so don't be afraid to participate, especially at the frequent "Arcade Auctions," which feature sales of "affordable antiques." Illustrated catalogs with estimated values are published for each auction. Sotheby's is really like a wonderful museum with an intimacy that museums can never achieve, in that prospective bidders are allowed to touch and handle the objects for sale in the pre-auction showings. Before a sale of antique books, scholars get to study; before a sale of rare violins, musicians may be allowed to try out the Stradivarius! For 24-hour auction and exhibition information, phone 606-7245. Admission is free, and no tickets are required, except for prestigious evening sales. To get these, you should write or call at least six weeks in advance of the sale: You may not get a seat in the main salesroom, but you will get either standing room or a seat in another salesroom with a video monitor. **Open:** Mon–Sat 10am–5pm, Sun 1–5pm.

Christie's, 502 Park Ave. (tel. 546-1000), and its lower-priced annex **Christie's East,** 219 E. 67th St. (tel. 606-0400), are New York branches of the famous British firm. Auctions are held in all fields of collecting, with items ranging from several hundred dollars to $82.5 million! Several exhibitions and auctions are held each week from September to July.

Phillips, 406 E. 79th St. (tel. 570-4830), is another prestigious London-based firm. They specialize in auctioning and appraising jewelry, paintings, prints, watches, stamps, coins, and more. **Open:** Mon–Fri 9am–5pm; some auctions held Sat.

Regularly scheduled auctions of antique American, English and continental furniture, decorations, paintings and sculpture, books and prints, as well as estate jewelry, are held at **William Doyle Galleries,** 175 E. 87th St. (tel. 427-2730). Doyle is a specialist in estates, and anything from these estates that might not be worthy of being auctioned finds its way to the **Tag Sale** store next door; this is a great source for anything from pewter tankards at $15 to a Regency style secretary/bookcase for $700. The stock changes daily, so it's always fun to stop by. **Open:** Mon–Fri 8:30am–5pm, Sat 10am–5pm (tel. 410-9285).

One of the oldest American-owned auction houses in the United States is **Tepper Galleries,** 110 E. 25th St. (tel. 677-5300), which primarily handles estate sales of antiques, fine reproductions, paintings, decorations, and accessories. Specialized auctions of artwork, jewelry, and collectibles also are held. Auctions are scheduled every two weeks through the year. Phone for schedules. **Lubin Galleries,** 30 W. 26th St. (tel. 924-3777), is always a good source for both antiques and reproductions of antique furniture, paintings, silver, Oriental rugs, jewelry, and the like; they run estate-auction sales every two weeks. Call for days and times of viewing and auctions.

For news of upcoming auctions each week, check the Antiques pages of the Friday and Sunday *New York Times*.

BED & BATH

BED BATH & BEYOND, 620 Sixth Ave., from 18th to 19th streets. Tel. 255-3550.

⭐ *Beyond* seems to be the key word in the name of this new store—as in beyond one's wildest imagination. Some 50,000 (and expanding to 80,000) square feet in an architecturally significant landmark building (originally the Siegel-Cooper Dry Goods Store, built in 1896) are stocked floor to ceiling with a dazzling array of designer home furnishings—the kinds found in better department stores—at anywhere from 20% to 40% off regular prices. Call it a never-ending white sale. Part of a chain, the store sells bed linens, bath towels, china, glassware, dinnerware, cookware, housewares, and literally thousands of gadgets. Shoppers come from all over for the selection and price.

BOOKS

BARNES & NOBLE, 600 Fifth Ave., at 48th Street. Tel. 765-0590.

This is a major midtown superstore where every book is discounted. It stocks more than 100,000 titles and has an extensive Fine Arts department. Barnes & Noble's **original store,** downtown at 105 Fifth Avenue and 18th Street, stocks nearly three million hardcovers, paperbacks, and new and used textbooks. Across the street, at 128 Fifth Ave., at 18th St., is the B & N **Sales Annex,** with huge discounts on bestsellers, as well as remainders, reviewer copies, children's books, and scholarly books. In Chelsea, on Sixth Avenue between 21st and 22nd streets, is a spectacular megastore, which includes a huge music section and a cafe. Uptown at 82nd Street and

Broadway is another megastore with a cafe, and across town at 86th Street and Lexington Avenue, still another megastore. Other Barnes & Nobles are scattered around town.

GOTHAM BOOK MART, 41 W. 47th St. Tel. 719-4448.

New York's most famous literary bookstore, in business since 1920, is dedicated to modern literature—novels, poetry, film and theater books. There are many first editions, hard-to-find and out-of-print literature, and a vast collection of literary magazines.

NEW YORK BOUND BOOKSHOP, in the lobby of 50 Rockefeller Plaza. Tel. 245-8503.

Some 4,000 new, out-of-print, and rare books about New York City can be found here. This is also a prime source for vintage photographs, old prints, maps, and ephemera relating to the city.

RIZZOLI BOOKSTORE, 31 W. 57th St., between Fifth and Sixth avenues. Tel. 759-2424.

Rizzoli boasts one of New York's most exhaustive and sophisticated collections of art and architecture books, classical and jazz recordings, and European magazines. There are two other Rizzoli outposts in town; in the Winter Garden of the World Financial Center (tel. 385-1400) and in SoHo at 454 W. Broadway (tel. 674-1616).

STRAND, 828 Broadway, corner of 12th Street. Tel. 473-1452.

Over 60 years old, Strand is the largest used-book store in the country, with some 2.5 million books on about eight miles of shelves. Collectors flock to its rare book room for signed and inscribed first editions and fine bindings, bargain-hunters to its review department for current reviewer's copies at 50% discount. Prices on its extensive collection of books on history, art, the humanities, and literature range from 50¢ to $50,000. You may send a postcard for a free catalogue. A second Strand is located at 159 John St. in the South Street Seaport (tel. 809-0875).

BRIDAL WEAR

KLEINFELD, Fifth Avenue and 82nd Street, Bay Ridge section of Brooklyn. Tel. 718/833-1100.

Planning a wedding? Prospective brides come from all over the country—and from other countries, too—just to buy their gowns at Kleinfeld, known for almost half a century for its in-depth collection, wonderfully personalized service, and fair prices (the average gown goes from $1,000 to $2,000 these days). In addition to designer bridal gowns, it also has bridesmaids' dresses, mother-of-the-bride ensembles, and other special-occasion gowns. Appointments are a must. Complimentary transportation from Le Parker Meridien in Manhattan is available by reservation.

CERAMICS

MAD MONK, 500 Ave. of the Americas, at 12th Street. Tel. 242-6678.

Those who love handmade ceramics—at very reasonable prices—should make tracks to Greenwich Village and Mad Monk. The genial Carl Monk, who presides over the store, shows the work of potters from all over the United States; their handsome teapots, casseroles, ornamental mirrors, jars, pitchers, planters, and the like range mostly from $5 to $75, although very special pieces may go much higher. Also sold at reasonable prices (discounts of 20%) is a fine collection of books on East-West philosophy.

COMPUTERS

CompUSA, 420 Fifth Ave., between 37th and 38th streets. Tel. 764-6224.

Ever since Dallas-based CompUSA opened its first superstore in Manhattan in 1994, crowds have been mobbing its endless aisles. No wonder: There are virtual acres of products—some 5,000 at last count—and they're all high value at low prices. Computer buffs' heaven.

DEPARTMENT & SPECIALTY STORES

A&S, tel. 594-8500, and A&S PLAZA, Sixth Ave. at 33rd Street. Tel. 465-0500.

A&S and A&S Plaza are the most exciting new developments in New York retailing in years. A&S is the famed emporium Abraham & Straus, which opened a Manhattan store a few years ago (on the site of the late, lamented Gimbel's). A&S Plaza, a handsome nine-floor atrium courtyard, surrounds it on three sides. It is most attractive, with its white-marble floors, pink-and-green walls, and four glass elevators that kids will love to ride. All told, there are about 60 shops here, most in a moderate price range, plus a vast, internationally minded food court.

Be sure to stop in at the **Visitor Center** on level 7, or phone them at 465-0500; they will give you specific information on seeing the city, even make restaurant reservations, car service calls, or help you get theater tickets. You may be able to catch one of the free entertainments that A&S Plaza offers several times a month.

BARNEY'S NEW YORK, 660 Madison Ave., at 61st Street. Tel. 826-8900.

The largest specialty store to open in New York in more than 60 years, the uptown branch of Barney's (the **original store** is at 106 Seventh Ave., at 17th Street; tel. 929-9000) is a $100-million emporium that features one store for men, one for women. Well-known designer names, like Armani, Comme des Garçons, Hugo Boss, Givenchy, and Azzedine Alaïa, dazzle; there are also many new designers, private labels, a golf shop, the splendid Chelsea Passage for gifts, an English shoe department for men, and much more, including three chic restaurants: Mad. 61 on the ground level, Chelsea Café on the 2nd floor, and Fred's Place on the 9th.

BERGDORF GOODMAN, 754 Fifth Ave., at 58th Street. Tel. 753-7300.

The ultimate in fine clothing and accessories, Bergdorf's in-depth collection of designer merchandise features such top names as Chanel, Giorgio Armani, Claude Montana, Ralph Lauren, and Calvin Klein, for starters. There's an outstanding gift collection on the seventh floor. Across the street at 745 Fifth Ave. is Bergdorf Goodman Men, "The Ultimate Store for Gentlemen," with everything from the most daring Italian designers to traditional clothing and formal wear. And an amazing assortment of ties.

BLOOMINGDALE'S, 1000 Third Ave., at 59th Street, main entrance on Lexington Avenue. Tel. 355-5900.

Bloomie's, as it is affectionately known to the chic sophisticates who practically make it a second home, has the latest in everything from fashions for juniors to designer clothing to the trendiest housewares and even a marvelous bakery-gourmet department. Its haute couture designer rooms on the fifth floor are outstanding, as are the frequent themed shows, when the entire store salutes the art, culture, and fashion of an exotic country.

GALERIES LAFAYETTE, 4−10 E. 57th St. Tel. 355-0022.

The only American branch of Paris's famed **Galeries Lafayette** occupies a distinguished address, adjacent to Tiffany's. The sleek contemporary structure houses a well-edited selection of exclusive European fashion and accessories, as well as gifts and housewares. Available here and nowhere else are individual styles from such designers as Emmanuelle Khanh, Corinne Cobson, and Jean-Charles de Castlebajac. Try the charming café **Demi Tasse** on the lower level for lunch, or enjoy a facial at the Clarins Institut de Beauté.

HENRI BENDEL, 712 Fifth Ave., at 56th Street. Tel. 247-1100.

Housed in three magnificently restored town houses and lighted by a spectacular set of Lalique windows, Henri Bendel has maintained its legacy of incomparable elegance and unerring style for nearly 100 years. It focuses on unique and exclusive women's clothing only, including designer collections from Karl Lagerfeld and Claude Montana. The tabletop and gifts for the home shop is outstanding, and its cosmetic department sometimes draws lines six deep on Saturdays, especially for its exclusive line of Mac cosmetics from Canada, much favored by models and celebrities.

LORD & TAYLOR, 424 Fifth Ave. at 39th Street. Tel. 391-3344.

Known as "The Signature of American Style," Lord & Taylor has promised its customers "fashion, quality, service, and value" since 1826. The Fifth Avenue flagship store has ten floors of quality clothing and accessories for women, men, and children. Enjoy three restaurants, an espresso bar, beauty salon, and Red Rose Service Personal Shopping. Its famed Christmas windows are a New York holiday tradition.

MACY'S, 151 W. 34th St., at Herald Square. Tel. 695-4400.

The world's biggest store, Macy's has it all. Selections in every department are vast and always of good quality. You can shop here for anything from children's hats to haute couture. Be sure to visit "The Cellar," a group of shops for cookware, gadgets, gifts and souvenirs, plus a pastry shop and a candy shop.

POLO/RALPH LAUREN, 867 Madison Ave., at 72nd Street. Tel. 606-2100.

Ralph Lauren's clothing and furnishings have always looked as if they were intended for the English gentry; now his showcase store looks for all the world like an English country place, complete to the family portraits on the wall, the working fireplaces, the Persian rugs and treasured antiques, and a grand baronial staircase. Polo/Ralph Lauren is a multimillion-dollar renovation of New York's 1895

Rhinelander mansion, and it's as much worth seeing as a living museum as for the merchandise it sells. The mood ranges from clublike for men's furnishings to more romantic for the areas selling women's clothing to country charm for the home-furnishings section, which contains a series of exquisitely accessorized model rooms. Service and quality are superior, and the prices match.

POLO SPORT, 805 Madison Ave., at 72nd Street. Tel. 434-8000.

Just across the street from the flagship store, Ralph Lauren's Polo Sport might well be called "Sporting Lifestyles of the Rich and Famous." This is shopping-as-theater: sections of the architecturally striking store are organized by lifestyle. Thus, the well-heeled sportsperson (or wannabe sportsperson) can shop for high-tech active wear and accessories in the nautical section, the golf area, the equestrian area, the tennis corner, the spa shop, and such: Double RL, where everything is weathered, provides a total vintage look for the ranch life. The place abounds with European accents and beautiful people, both in front of and behind the counter.

SAKS FIFTH AVENUE, 611 Fifth Ave., at 50th Street. Tel. 753-4000.

Saks Fifth Avenue—it's a name long synonymous with fashion elegance. Here you can browse and shop for the likes of Louis Vuitton luggage, Revillon furs, or the top French and American designers in their own boutiques. Some of their unique franchises include Chaumet, Charvet, N. Peal, Sahza, Peter Nygard, Nany Heller, Gordon Henderson, and Hildith and Key. In January and June, Saks runs storewide clearances, and everyone in town shows up for the bargains. The charming Café SFA, located on the 8th floor and overlooking the Rooftop Gardens of Rockefeller Center and St. Patrick's Cathedral, serves sophisticated weekday lunch and weekend brunch menus.

TAKASHIMAYA NEW YORK, 693 Fifth Ave., near 54th Street. Tel. 350-0100.

Part art gallery, part design specialty store, Takashimaya New York is a branch of Japan's largest department store conglomerate. It's very elegant, very austere, and very understated—you'd hardly know anything here is for sale. But look closely and you may find a discreet price tag or two—$18,000 for a splendid antique screen, $150 for a silk tie, or a mere $12 for a dozen tulips. Merchandise is a blend of East and West, with emphasis on superb craftsmanship. The 4,500-square-foot two-level gallery, the centerpiece of the store, presents work in various media by Asian and American artists. Tea Box Café is a serene spot for lunch or a lovely afternoon tea.

DISCOUNT CLOTHING

Here are some of the special secrets of New York shopping: how to pick up a dress for $55, a mink coat for $1,000, or a great men's suit for $200—or where to get designers' originals for one-third the price in the salons.

RETAIL

BOLTON'S, 1191 Third Ave., near 69th Street. Tel. 628-7553.

Current top-brand fashions at about one-third off department store prices—that's what you'll find at Bolton's. Fresh selections arrive daily and include a fashionable mix of famous-label dresses, suits, coats, contemporary casuals, and accessories. Dresses range from about $50 to over $100.

Bolton's also has many other locations around Manhattan, including shops at 1180 Madison Ave. (near 86th Street), 225 E. 57th St., and 4 E. 34th St. (near the Empire State Building). Check the phone book for other listings.

BURLINGTON COAT FACTORY, 45 Park Place, off West Broadway. Tel. 571-2631.

They call themselves the "Financial District's Greatest Savings Institution," and that's not a bad way to describe the New York branch of the largest retailer of coats in the country. Burlington sells first-quality brand-name and designer merchandise at prices that are considerably lower—from 20% to 60%—than those in department stores. They have woolens, cashmeres, leather coats and jackets, and fake furs. In addition to something like 15,000 coats for men and women, they also have a complete men's department (4,000 suits, even a Big Men's section); a good women's section (sportswear, suits, career clothing); a designer shoe department offering thousands of pairs at low prices; and even a children's department, which can outfit the kids from kindergarten to college. The store is two blocks from the World Trade Center. Take the 1 to Chambers Street or the 2 or 3 to Park Place.

CENTURY 21, 22 Cortland St., near the World Trade Center. Tel. 227-9092.

It's worth a trip downtown to the financial district to pay a visit to Century 21, which may be New York's most spectacular discount department store, with everything from towels to teapots, plus designer wear for women, men, and children at prices that are often 30% to 50% off the regular tabs. I've seen Jones New York pants, Christian Dior beachwear, Armani silk bomber jackets, and Vittorio Ricci shoes. The biggest bargains are in women's lingerie and shoes, but everything is well priced here, including children's clothing, electronic games, small appliances, and men's sport shoes. There are, alas, no dressing rooms, but there is a liberal return policy. **Open:** Mon–Fri 7:45am–7pm, Sat 10am–6:30pm.

DAFFY'S, 111 Fifth Ave., at 18th Street. Tel. 529-4477.

"Clothing bargains for millionaires" is the philosophy behind Daffy's, an exuberant three-level store that features stylish togs for women (and, to a lesser extent, for men and children). Daffy's buyers shop both Seventh Avenue and the European designers for terrific values and pass them on to the customers on everything from designers to name-brand clothing, plus bags and shoes. Savings range from 40% to 80% below regular retail prices. The newest Daffy's, at Herald Center, 34th Street and Broadway, occupies four full floors of that building, crammed with great bargains. At 335 Madison Avenue at 43rd Street (tel. 557-4422) is a smaller Daffy's, with less space and a slightly crowded feeling, but still those same terrific buys.

S&W FAMOUS DESIGNERS APPAREL, at Seventh Avenue and 26th Street. Tel. 924-6656.

Call S&W Famous Designers Apparel "off Seventh Avenue," if

you will. It features name brands from the Seventh Avenue houses, at discounted—but still expensive—prices. There are actually four stores in the complex. At 165–167 W. 26th St., the upper level shows designer suits, dresses, and sportswear; the lower level is the clearance section. Around the corner at 283 Seventh Ave., you'll find shoes, handbags, jewelry, and accessories; 287 Seventh Ave. has designer coats in suedes, wools, and leather, and an extensive selection of raincoats as well as petite coats and medium-priced sportswear.

SYMS, 42 Trinity Place. Tel. 797-1199.

Well worth a trip downtown, Syms is a vast store whose decor is about as dazzling as that of an airline hangar (its walls are totally black). But never mind: Its merchandise, for both men and women, is very good, and the prices are well below what you'd find in regular stores. Designer clothes sell for about one-third off regular prices, with a progressive markdown policy. Syms specializes in clothing, but they also discount handbags (wonderful buys here), shoes, luggage, linens, and more. Take the 1, N, or R to Rector Street.

CONSIGNMENT SHOPS

To find out where some of the city's smartest women pick up designer clothing at a mere fraction of their original prices, join them at New York's consignment shops. Designer or upscale merchandise, in excellent condition, is left here for resale. You'd be amazed at what can turn up at these places. And the prices are painless.

DESIGNERS RESALE, 324 E. 81st St., between Second and First avenues. Tel. 734-3639.

Beautiful dresses, outerwear, accessories, jewelry, and many selections for petite women are available here.

ENCORE RESALE DRESS SHOP, 1132 Madison Ave., at 84th Street. Tel. 879-2850.

Two floors of good finds are here, including clothing, new merchandise, handbags, and accessories.

MICHAEL'S, 2nd floor, 1041 Madison Ave., between 79th and 80th streets. Tel. 737-7273.

Some of the city's wealthiest women leave their glamorous clothing here: The top name designers are well represented.

TRANSFER, 220 E. 60th St., between Second and Third avenues. Tel. 355-4230.

This is the newest and most couture-oriented of the resale shops. Most of the extremely contemporary merchandise comes from models, celebrities, rock and movie stars, and showrooms. You might find anything from a used pair of Armani cotton pants for $25 to python pants from Prada of Milan for $3,000 (samples of $10,000 to $12,000 items). Chanel suits and dresses go anywhere from $200 to $800. Other impressive names on the tags include Jean Paul Gautier, Comme des Garçons, Gianni Versace, Azzedine Alaïa, and Emilio Pucci.

FOR MEN

With the high price of men's suits, many better-heeled men in town have left their usual haberdashers and are now shopping the outlet stores. There are many such stores advertised, but not all deliver first quality: Some simply buy last year's or unpopular styles. The ones mentioned here carry fine clothing and prices about 30% to 40% lower than elsewhere. Most levy a slight charge for alterations. The decor in some places may be pipe rack, but service is usually good—and you can't beat the prices. Already listed above, **Syms,** in the financial district at 42 Trinity Place, is very popular for menswear, carrying shoes as well as apparel and accessories.

DOLLAR BILLS, 99 E. 42nd St., next to Grand Central Terminal. Tel. 867-0212.

It looks like nothing much from the outside, but inside there are surprises! Dollar Bills buys directly from Italian designers and sells top-name, avant-garde men's suits for 40% to 50% of what they would go for in the fancy stores. Shipments vary from day to day, so it's a matter of luck as to what you'll find. Women's designer knits are also available.

GENTLEMEN'S RESALE, 303 E. 81st St., between Second and First avenues. Tel. 734-2739.

This is a resale consignment shop for top-quality designer coats, suits, jackets, slacks, ties, belts, shoes, and more.

GILCREST CLOTHES CO., 3rd floor, 900 Broadway, near 20th Street. Tel. 254-8933.

Top designer labels from Europe and the United States are represented here—Perry Ellis, Ralph Lauren, Louis Feraud, Lubian, and Emanuel Ungaro are a few. Tuxedos are stocked, too. Discounts are substantial, and alterations are free.

L. S. MEN'S CLOTHING, 19 W. 44th St., room 403. Tel. 575-0933.

This is a small family operation that's been in business for over 40 years. Their traditional woolen suits are sold at discounts of 45% to 65% off comparable prices of $385 to $950; and they have many contemporary fashions and sportswear, as well as tuxedos for sale. Suits may be custom-ordered at $495. Take the B, D, F, or Q to 42nd St.

MOE GINSBURG, 162 Fifth Ave., at the corner of 21st Street. Tel. 242-3482.

Four floors of men's clothing, furnishings, and shoes are well priced at Moe Ginsburg, and that includes European contemporary and American collections. Take the N, R to 23rd St.

NBO MENSWEAR, 1965 Broadway, near 67th Street. Tel. 595-1550.

This two-level store one block from Lincoln Center offers a top-flight selection of designer menswear at very good prices. Suits selling for $129 to $399 here go for $225 to $750 elsewhere. Service and tailoring are very good. Take the 1 or 9 to 66th St.

PARK KENNY/ROYAL FASHION, 920 Broadway, third floor, at the corner of 21st Street. Tel. 477-1948.

There are lots of good buys here: A recent sale advertised super worsted suits at $225 each, custom fabrics sports jackets at $130, and fine worsted slacks at $30 to $55. Shirts, ties, raincoats, and casual wear are always at very good prices. Take the N, R to 23rd St.

ROTHMAN'S UNION SQUARE, 200 Park Ave. South (17th Street at Union Square). Tel. 777-7400.

Rothman's buys from top manufacturers, puts its own label on the merchandise, and sells prestigious clothing for 20% to 50% off regular retail prices. This is the high end of the menswear line, the same kind of clothing you find at Barney's or Saks Fifth Avenue—but at much more comfortable prices. Sometimes you'll see labels like Hickey-Freeman, Hugo Boss, Joseph Abboud, Aquascutum, and Burberry. They also carry Canali, Jhane Barnes, Lubian, and Krïzia. A full line of menswear—from suits to socks, shirts, ties, and outerwear—is available. Take the 4, 5, 6 or N, R to 14th St./Union Square.

SAINT LAURIE, LTD., 897 Broadway, at 20th Street. Tel. 473-0100.

Saint Laurie has been manufacturing classic men's clothing since 1913, and it is sold at some of the finest stores in the country. Their exclusive Avery Lucas menswear collection is attracting much media attention. And they also offer a newly designed collection of women's classic apparel. Prices at the factory-outlet store are about one-third less than in the regular stores. Visitors are invited to take self-guided tours of the workrooms on three different floors. Take the N, R to 23rd St.

TODAY'S MAN, Sixth Avenue between 18th and 19th streets. Tel. 924-0200.

This gigantic menswear superstore features name-brand and designer merchandise from the United States, Britain, France, and Italy at way-below-department-store prices. They have more than 9,000 suits, plus shirts and ties, accessories, outerwear, and sportswear, in all sizes. Some examples: pure wool traditional suits sold elsewhere at $275, here $149; silk casual coats sold elsewhere at $135, here $69; wool gabardine blazers sold elsewhere at $135 here, $69. Cotton pinpoint shirts, sold elsewhere from $37.50 to $48.50, were $20 here. Take the F to 14th St.

LOWER EAST SIDE

You could spend a week shopping the Lower East Side, and I could write a book just telling you about the bargains here, in these narrow, tenemented streets where New York's immigrant Jewish colony once flourished. Many of the shopkeepers live uptown or in the wealthy suburbs now, and so do most of the customers. But they still keep coming down here for marvelous bargains in just about everything. I'll simply point you in the direction of a few of my favorites and let you take it from there. Bring plenty of cash, wear good walking shoes, and be prepared for sometimes inconvenient or nonexistent fitting rooms (although this situation has improved of late) and usually a strict no-return policy. Try to come during the week, since most places are closed late Friday and all day Saturday, and when they open again on Sunday, it's total insanity.

Subway: F or Q, M, or J train to Delancey and Essex streets, or D (Sixth Ave. line) to Grand St.; about 20 minutes from Midtown Manhattan.

Children's Clothing

RICE & BRESKIN, 323 Grand St. Tel. 925-5515.

This is a good place to stock up on name-brand children's clothing—brands like Healthtex, Carter's, and Renzo Rothschild.

The range goes from layettes (in which they are a specialist) to toddlers to size 14. Discount is 20% off already low prices.

Men's Clothing

G&G INTERNATIONAL, 53 Orchard St. Tel. 431-4530.

Top names—Adolfo, Geoffrey Beene, Principe Marzato, Cavelli, and Talia Hartz—are offered here at discounts of 25% to 40%. Tuxedos by Lord West and Pierre Cardin are also sold at good prices.

PAN AM MEN'S WEAR, 50 Orchard St. Tel. 925-7032.

Discounts are substantial (20% to 50%) on such top names as Polo by Ralph Lauren, Charles Jourdan, Perry Ellis, and many Italian designers.

Linens & Home Furnishings

HARRIS LEVY, 278 Grand St. Tel. 226-3102.

A direct importer of fine bed and table linens for over 100 years, Harris Levy also features a complete bath shop, closet and kitchen accessories, and a custom boutique.

Women's Clothing

FISHKIN KNITWEAR CO., 314 and 316 Grand St. Tel. 226-6538.

This old-time favorite has wonderful discounts of 20% to 40% off list on such designers as Adrienne Vittadini, Bettina Riedel, Liz Claiborne, Evan Picone, and Regina Porter—plus some of the best deals anywhere on top-level cashmere sweaters and Starrington silk shirts. Italian designer shoes and ladies' slippers are also discounted.

FORMAN'S APPAREL, 82, 94, and 78 Orchard St. Tel. 228-2500.

Prestigious designer labels, good discounts, and a store to suit your size—what more could the bargain shopper ask for? Regular-sized women should try Forman's Designer Apparel at 82 Orchard; petite women, 5′4″ and under, will find a whole store of fashion for them at Forman's Petites, 94 Orchard; and larger women, who often have problems finding stylish clothes, have a source for designer-label sportswear, dresses, and suits at Forman's Plus, 78 Orchard. *Note:* Forman's has another location in the downtown area at 59 John St. (tel. 791-4100), offering all the same features.

SHULIE'S, 175 Orchard St. Tel. 473-2480.

You've heard of the designer Tahari? Well, come meet his sister, Shulie. Her prices on her famous brother's clothing are very relaxing, and the discounts are deep—you'll pay about half of what you would uptown. She also carries well-known designer shoes at greatly discounted prices. Special orders are taken, and service is above the norm for this area.

Women's Lingerie

GOLDMAN & COHEN, 55 Orchard St. Tel. 966-0737.

This place discounts at least 20% on fine-quality women's lingerie and loungewear; you'll want to stock up when you see the prices!

MENDEL WEISS, 91 Orchard St. Tel. 925-6815.

Name-brand underwear is sold here at about 25% off regular prices: T-shirts, 30%. *Woman's Day* has called this place "one of the best mail-order houses in America."

Gloves

BERNARD KRIEGER, 216 Grand St. Tel. 226-4927.

Leather gloves, mostly imported from Italy, are a real bargain here, and so are ski gloves, wools, and suedes, for both men and women. They also carry some attractive women's hats, designer scarves, handkerchiefs, and a good line of Lycra tops and bottoms.

Handbags

FINE & KLEIN, 119 Orchard St. Tel. 674-6720.

Top name and designer bags are sold on three floors; discounts are around 35%.

Shoes

LACE UP SHOE SHOP, 110 Orchard St. Tel. 475-8040.

Current styles and colors of top designer footwear—Charles Jourdan, Arche, Yves St. Laurent, André Assous, Birkenstock, Evan Picone, and more—at very good prices. You'll pay 25% less here than in the department stores. They also carry the largest selection of both men's and women's Mephisto walking, biking, hiking, and casual footwear in the Northeast.

ORCHARD BOOTERY, 75 Orchard St. Tel. 966-0688.

Look for the top designer names here—Bruno Meli, André Assous, Delman, Ferara, Drosana, Peter Kaiser, and Martinez Valero—and more, discounted at least 30%.

GOURMET FOOD STORES

Allow me to introduce you to the word "appetizing," which is not an adjective but a New York noun (or state of mind) that means salty smoked fish and pickled herring and lusty breads and fragrant coffee beans and heady pâtés and delicate cheeses—and much more. New York has at least four appetizing emporiums to which the faithful make pilgrimages from near and very far. Each is gigantic, mind-boggling in its variety of offerings, and purveys food (including gourmet take-out) of superb quality. Make tracks to the following: In SoHo, **Dean & Deluca,** 560 Broadway, at the corner of Prince Street (tel. 431-1691); in Greenwich Village, **Balducci's,** 424 Ave. of the Americas, at 9th Street (tel. 673-2600); on the Upper East Side, **Grace's Marketplace,** 1237 Third Ave., at 71st Street (tel. 737-0600); and on the Upper West Side, **Zabar's,** 2245 Broadway, at 80th Street (tel. 787-2000), which also has a mezzanine full of housewares and gourmet kitchen gadgets at the best prices in town.

HERBAL COSMETICS & SOAPS

CAMBRIDGE CHEMISTS, 21 E. 65th St. Tel. 734-5678.

This is the kind of place that makes visiting Europeans feel right at home. Here you can buy pure and natural products by Cyclax of London (the only U.S. agent for these beauty products used by Queen Elizabeth), Floris, Penhaligons, G. F. Trumper, Taylor of Old Bond Street, Phyto Products from France (which has a unique sun-protectant cream for the hair), and a variety of other European toiletries, cosmetics, and treatment preparations. Although a listing of their clients might read like a page out of the Social Register, everyone is treated with old-fashioned courtesy. Try their John Bull Perfumery Potpourri toilet water and bath oils.

CASWELL-MASSEY, 518 Lexington Ave., at 48th Street. Tel. 755-2254.

⭐ The oldest chemists and perfumers in the United States, Caswell-Massey, in business for more than 200 years, still carries the same colognes that were favorites with George and Martha Washington and the marquis de Lafayette! Pick and choose from the largest collection of imported soaps in the world, imported shaving equipment, pomanders, potpourri, and cough drops and lozenges from England and France. A wondrous nostalgic place full of things you can't get elsewhere. For a copy of their fanciful catalog phone toll free 800/326-0500.

Other stores are located at the South Street Seaport (tel. 608-5401) and the World Financial Center (tel. 945-2630).

ORIGINS, 402 W. Broadway. Tel. 219-9764.

⭐ If the idea of Plant Spirits/Splashing Waters or Sensory Therapy Inhalations or Honey Elixirs appeals to you, visit this sparkling, environmentally sensitive store in the heart of SoHo. An alternative-cosmetic company concerned with both inner and outer beauty and well-being, Origins happily marries nature and science in its products. It uses recycled materials whenever possible and is committed to no animal testing and using no animal-derived materials: its brushes, for example, are handmade of Japanese palm-plant bristles, with birch handles. It also features such easy-on-the-environment items as handmade floral stationery, leather-looking handbags made of natural rubber, and T-shirts made of 100% natural unbleached cotton.

IRISH IMPORTS

THE IRISH SECRET, 155 Spring St., in SoHo. Tel. 334-6711.

⭐ People expect Irish import stores to be filled with traditional items such as Aran wool fishermen's sweaters, tweed jackets and walking hats, cashmere and mohair capes and coats, and the like. Well, this store has them in plentiful supply, but it also has a "secret"—some highly fashionable clothing, including ladies' linen dresses and skirts, men's silk and linen jackets, brightly colored Irish linen men's shirts, and much more—by fashionable Dublin designers.

JEWELRY

New York is the diamond center of the country, and if you're convinced that diamonds (or even pearls) are a girl's best friend, you should have a look at some of the town's outstanding jewelry shops. A stroll along 47th Street, between Fifth and Sixth avenues, where diamonds are being traded on street corners, polished in workrooms, and sold in a number of small jewelry stores, puts you right in the heart of the jewelry world. To catch the Village jewelry scene, walk on West 4th Street between Sixth and Seventh avenues; here and elsewhere in the Village you'll find any number of small shops selling avant-garde rings, pins, and brooches.

CARTIER, 2 E. 52nd St., at Fifth Avenue. Tel. 753-0111.

You'll find today's classic jewelry—plus Paris-designed watches, pens, small leather goods, china, and crystal—as well as old Cartier designs of the 1920s and '30s in the Cartier Boutique. There is also a branch of Cartier in Trump Tower, 725 Fifth Ave. at 56th Street (tel. 308-0843).

TIFFANY & CO., 727 Fifth Ave., at 57th Street. Tel. 755-8000.

Beside the splendors of its emerald brooches and diamond necklaces and the like, Tiffany also has inexpensive gift items and an affordably priced collection of sterling silver jewelry. It's *the* place for wedding gifts. Tiffany also offers a wonderful collection of time-pieces.

KILIMS

BEYOND THE BOSPHORUS, 79 Sullivan St., between Spring and Broome streets. Tel. 219-8257.

One-of-a-kind kilims, handmade flatwoven Turkish rugs and pillows that are between 50 to 100 years old can be found at this cozy little shop on the western fringes of SoHo. Proprietor Ismail Basbagi travels home to Turkey frequently to purchase the rugs, and since there is no middleman involved and since he has them cleaned and repaired in Turkey, he is able to offer them at remarkably good prices, starting at $30 for pillows. Kilims look great as wallhangings, runners, or room-size rugs, and wear practically forever. Special sales are held in January and July, when everything comes down about 30%. Mr. Basbagi will ship rugs and pillows anywhere in the country. **Open:** Tues–Sun noon–6pm (also open "by chance or by appointment"). **Closed:** Sun in summer.

MUSIC

HMV (His Master's Voice), Lexington Avenue at 86th Street. Tel. 348-0800.

This East Side store, said to be the largest U.S. recordings store (40,000 square feet), has a permanent stage where performers showcase their recordings. Both this store and the only-slightly-smaller West Side address, aim to make shopping very pleasant, with audio and visual disc jockeys and listening booths. Their West Side store is at Broadway at 72nd Street (tel. 721-5900).

TOWER RECORDS & VIDEO, 692 Broadway, at East 4th Street. Tel. 505-1500.

A "happening" since it first opened—a place where people go to be seen as much as to buy recordings—Tower still continues strong. As many as 6,000 people are said to pack the aisles on Saturday and Sunday. Tower stocks half a million recordings (in all configurations) in every conceivable category, sells many of them at discount prices, and also shows videos on 17 screens.

The Tower Clearance Center, which carries over 200,000 items in closeout, overstock, and out-of-print merchandise, is located nearby at 20 E. 4th St. (tel. 228-7317). Also nearby, at 383 Lafayette St. (tel. 505-1166) is Tower Video and Bookstore. In the Lincoln Center area, at 1961 Broadway, at 66th Street (tel. 799-2500), there's another huge and exciting Tower Records, and at 1977 Broadway you'll find another Tower Video (tel. 496-2500). Crosstown at 1535 Third Ave., between 86th and 87th streets is another Tower Records (tel. 369-2500), and around the corner, at 215 East 86th St., another clearance outlet (tel. 427-3377).

TOYS

FAO SCHWARZ, 767 Fifth Ave. at 58th Street. Tel. 644-9400.

If you have children with you, your first stop should be America's most famous toy store, a kid's wonderland, with everything from a talking tree to a 28-foot-high clock tower that sings birthday greetings. In addition to a vast array of toys, including life-sized plush lions and giraffes and a gas-powered children's car, they also have a Barbie boutique, a Bookmonster book department, a children's clothing boutique, and a hair salon.

PENNYWHISTLE TOYS, 448 Columbus Ave., between 80th and 81st streets. Tel. 873-9090.

This eclectic toy store is filled with wonderful things, all preselected by the store's savvy buyers. It carries a vast array of wooden toys, puzzles, games, educational toys that challenge a child's imagination, and arts and crafts—many items imported from Italy, England, and Sweden. It also has dress-up costumes, outdoor games, and the best in infant-care products. Because the store's in the midst of the artsy Columbus Avenue shopping area, it tends to carry things not found in ordinary stores. And the service is out-of-the-ordinary, too—very helpful and friendly; their large, neighborhood clientele is on a first-name basis.

WHIMSY

DOG LOVERS BOOKSHOP (tel. 594-3601) and EVERY-THING ANGELS (tel. 564-6944) second floor, 9 West 31 St.

A second-story shop near the Empire State Building is intriguing both dog lovers and angel aficionados. Dog Lovers Bookshop is a one-of-a-kind place selling everything for the dog lover, from books (new and out-of-print in several languages), video and audio, to periodicals, calendars, gifts, cards, and even special doggie playthings for children. Everything Angels is filled with angel treasures: angel art on watches, jewelry, tote bags, T-shirts, books, prints, plates, crystal, cards, pins, and Victoriana. Both shops have extensive catalogues and are open Monday through Saturday afternoons only.

RADIO HULA, 169 Mercer St., near Houston Street. Tel. 226-4467.

The store size is small, but there's plenty of Hawaiian merchandise, spirit, and aloha at Radio Hula. Owner Jano Cassidy and manager Robert Avilla both hail from Honolulu, and they've created a bit of the islands right here in SoHo. Everything is tasteful, in the best traditions of Hawaii's artisans and craftspeople. The store stocks superb fiber-sculpture baskets, koa-wood bowls, and petroglyph block prints. It has aloha shirts (rayon, $60; cotton, $49) that are reproductions of 1940s and '50s ones, Kona Coffee by the pound, a good collection of Hawaiian music and books, fabrics by the yard and patterns, Hawaiian jewelry, and even silk leis and fresh leis made to order. Hula workshops are given every few months by visiting Hawaiian performers (or by Jano and Robert), and they also have classes in lei-making and other traditional Hawaiian crafts. On weekends, lots of Islanders who now live in New York drop in to "talk story" and remember home.

STAR MAGIC, 275 Amsterdam Ave., corner of 73rd Street. Tel. 769-2020.

✪ This is a magical place for anyone tuned in to either inner or outer space. These "space-age gifts of science and spirit" feature everything from telescopes, globes, robots, holograms, and space shuttle models to healing crystals, pyramids, crystal jewelry, and "celestial music." There's also a Star Magic downtown at 734 Broadway (tel. 228-7770), and at 1256 Lexington Ave. (tel. 988-0300).

THINK BIG!, 390 W. Broadway. Tel. 925-7300.

✪ New York's wittiest sculpture gallery, Think Big!, in SoHo, has affordable collectibles for everyone: how about a five-foot-tall toothbrush (use it as a towel rack), a six-foot-long pencil, or a 17 × 15 foot toast replica that makes a nifty bulletin board. Prices begin around $10 and go way up. Call for a catalog; they will ship anywhere.

WARNER BROTHERS STUDIO STORE, 1 East 57th St., at Fifth Avenue. Tel. 754-0300.

The Warner Brothers Studio Stores are popular all over the country—and this one, number 39 in the chain and its flagship store—is no exception. It's always busy, both with New Yorkers and visitors alike, with kids who adore the Bugs Bunny characters wandering about, Superman holding up the glass elevator cage, and the cartoons on the big video screens; and with adults, who love the film clips of the old Warner Brothers movies. A highlight is the Batman Plane on the second-floor ceiling, which fires "lasers" every half-hour in conjunction with the video show on the big screen. Merchandise runs the gamut, everything from Bugs Bunny aprons and Looney Toons Collector's Mugs to T-shirts, sports helmets, baseball jackets, ankle socks with Bugs Bunny and "What's Up?" printed on them for a few dollars, all the way up to kinetic sculptures in the Gallery that could run as high as $12,000.

CHAPTER 10

NEW YORK NIGHTS

New York City is the entertainment capital of the nation; it's here that you will catch not only Broadway theater and New York opera but also outstanding musical, dance, and theater groups from all over the world—everything from the Moscow Circus to the Comédie Française.

New York's many beautiful parks are also sites for an extraordinary array of musical performances, plays, festivals, poetry readings, and much more. Of course, almost all of these outdoor events are in the summer. Call 360-1333 to get the **Department of Parks and Recreation's** recorded message giving free events in the parks and in the rest of the city.

TICKET-BUYING MADE SIMPLE Want to know what's playing in New York in theater, dance, and music? Talk to a computer. **NYC/On Stage,** a service of the Theater Development Fund, sponsored by the American Express Card, enables callers to find out what's playing, when, and how to buy tickets. Press a series of buttons refining your query into ever-narrowing categories. Eventually, you'll be able to make your selection and charge your tickets "by American Express or any other means." The toll free out-of-state number is 800-STAGE NY. The New York State number is 212/768-1818. Both numbers are in service 24 hours every day.

Be sure to pay a visit to the **Music & Dance Booth,** in Bryant Park, on 42nd Street just east of Sixth Avenue (behind the New York Public Library). Half-price day-of-performance tickets for music and dance concerts (including those at Lincoln Center, Carnegie Hall, 92nd Street YM-YWHA, and City Center) are available there. Advance full-price tickets are also on sale for many events. The box office is open Tuesday to Sunday from noon to 2pm and 3 to 7pm. Call 382-2323 for information about ticket availability.

See below, under "Theater," for information on how to obtain theater tickets.

1. THE PERFORMING ARTS

OPERA

METROPOLITAN OPERA COMPANY, Lincoln Center, 64th Street and Broadway. Tel. 362-6000.

One of the most prestigious opera companies in the world, the 112-year-old Metropolitan continues to enthrall opera buffs. The season usually runs from late September to mid-April. Even though most of its seats are taken by subscribers, there's a good chance you can get tickets for a single performance. The best way to do so is to phone the box office directly and ask to be put on the mailing list for a brochure. This will include a "single sales" calendar and inform you of the earliest dates when mail and phone orders will be accepted. You should, of course, mail or phone in your order as early as possible.

Failing all else, go to the Metropolitan box office or a ticket broker as soon as you arrive in town. Unless it's a *very* popular production with very popular singers, you should be able to get a seat. The only way to really save money is to stand: Standees' places go on sale on Saturday at 10am for all performances Saturday through Friday. Be sure to bring opera glasses—the house is very large. **Prices:** Orchestra tickets $60–$110 Mon–Thurs; $65–$130 Fri–Sat. Family Circle tickets $22 Mon–Thurs; $23 Fri–Sat. Standees' places $10 in Family Circle; $14 in the orchestra.

NEW YORK CITY OPERA, in the New York State Theater, Lincoln Center. Tel. 870-5570.

Now in its 50th year, the New York City Opera also has a superb company and is better than ever these days. The fall season, which opens around Labor Day, runs for 11 weeks. The spring season takes place during the months of March and April. Write to the company at 20 Lincoln Center, New York, NY 10023, for a brochure. Mail-order three or four weeks in advance will usually do the trick. Otherwise, try the box office or a ticket broker. You can also buy tickets through Ticketmaster, which will tell you if there are tickets in your price range (tel. 307-4100). Prices: $15–$73.

AMATO OPERA THEATER, 319 Bowery, at the corner of 2nd Street. Tel. 228-8200.

A New York standby for over 46 years now, the Amato Opera Theater gives full productions of the classic repertory—Verdi, Puccini, Mozart, Rossini, and Donizetti—as well as rarely performed operas. Many of its "graduates" have gone on to sing at the Metropolitan and the New York City Opera. Tickets can be reserved by calling the box office up until a day before curtain time. Performances are usually given weekends from September to May. **Prices:** Tickets $18.

CLASSICAL MUSIC

NEW YORK PHILHARMONIC, Avery Fisher Hall at Lincoln Center, 65th Street and Broadway. Tel. 875-5030.

One of the treasures of New York and of the world of music, the New York Philharmonic is the oldest symphonic orchestra in the United States and one of the oldest in the world, now in its 153rd season and under the leadership of Kurt Masur, music director. It is considered an orchestra of virtuoso players. During the subscription season, September to June, you should have no trouble buying a ticket at the box office. Or, you may write to the following address for a New York Philharmonic concert calendar: New York Philharmonic, Avery Fisher Hall, 10 Lincoln Center, New York, NY 10023-6973. **Prices:** Tickets $10–$60.

You may be able to get to hear the Philharmonic in a series of free concerts held in the city's parks in July and August: See local papers for exact listings. These concerts are *popular!* They often attract half a million or more people! Come early and bring a blanket and a picnic supper.

MUSIC IN THE MUSEUMS

On any Friday or Saturday evening from 5 to 8pm, you can join scores of New Yorkers who clamor for the tables at the balcony bar of the **Metropolitan Museum of Art,** Fifth Avenue at 82nd Street, to hear live classical music concerts of the Great Hall Balcony Bar Classical Quintet. With its subdued lighting and romantic air, this is a great dating spot (information: 535-7710). Also very popular with a young crowd are the free jazz concerts every Friday from 5:30 to 8pm at the Garden Café of the **Museum of Modern Art,** 11 West 53rd St. Performing groups change monthly. There is no charge for concerts, but you must pay the museum's admission price (see the museum listings in Chapter 7).

From September through May, free Sunday afternoon recitals by major concert artists are held in the splendid setting of the **Frick Collection,** 1 East 70th St. Call 288-0700 for details on getting tickets, preferably three weeks in advance. You can also listen to live concerts or recorded music on certain Sundays in the medieval splendors of the **Cloisters** (part of the Metropolitan Museum of Art, but located uptown in Fort Tryon Park; call 923-3700 for ticket information).

These are only a few of the many fine musical offerings in New York's major museums. Check the papers for news of frequent concerts at other museums.

MUSIC IN PARKS & OTHER PUBLIC PLACES

During summer, there is free music in the parks and other public places almost every night, from the **Summerstage** performing arts series in the Central Park Bandshell to concerts at **Damrosch Park** in Lincoln Center, the **Riverside Park Rotunda,** and **Washington Square Park;** also look for the **New York Philharmonic and Metropolitan Opera in the Park.** The **South Street Seaport** is the home of frequent free concerts, and **Summergarden,** in the Museum of Modern Art Sculpture Garden, is a particular delight. Downtown, frequent concerts are held on the Plaza of the **World Financial Center.** For timely listings, see the *New York Times, New York* magazine, *The New Yorker,* and the *Village Voice.* All are available at newsstands throughout the city.

DANCE COMPANIES

New York's dance offerings are among the greatest in the world. Its leading ballet companies perform at Lincoln Center: The **New York City Ballet** at the New York State Theater and the **Feld Ballet** at the Metropolitan Opera House. City Center is home to the exciting **Joffrey Ballet;** the **Alvin Ailey American Dance Theater;** and the **Merce Cunningham, Martha Graham,** and **Paul Taylor** companies. The Lincoln Center halls, City Center, and the Joyce Theater (a major venue for modern and experimental dance located in Chelsea) frequently play host to visiting U.S. companies (such as American Ballet Theatre), as well as to those from overseas for short seasons, as does the Brooklyn Academy of Music.

MAJOR CONCERT HALLS & ALL-PURPOSE AUDITORIUMS

LINCOLN CENTER FOR THE PERFORMING ARTS, 670 Lincoln Center Plaza. Tel. 875-5400.

New York's most important center for music, dance, and opera is Lincoln Center. Avery Fisher Hall is home to the New York Philharmonic as well as Lincoln Center Productions, which produces the Mostly Mozart Festival and Great Performers Series; Alice Tully Hall hosts the Chamber Music Society as well as Jazz at Lincoln Center and the witty-edge Serious Fun! Festival; the Metropolitan Opera House is home to the Metropolitan Opera; the New York State Theater is home to the New York City Opera and the New York City Ballet. Lincoln Center Theater is in residence at the Vivian Beaumont Theater and the Mitzi E. Newhouse Theater. The Film Society of Lincoln Center is housed at the Walter Reade Theater. Each summer, Lincoln Center Productions also presents Midsummer Night Swing, featuring dancing on the Plaza under the stars, and Lincoln Center Out-of-Doors, a free, summer-long festival of music and dance by groups from around the world—everything from Latin music to jazz to a Marathon Rockabilly Jamboree and a Mardi Gras Carnival and parade. Lincoln Center Plaza, Damrosch Park, and Guggenheim Bandshell are also the scenes of delightful free summer presentations. And the fountain plaza is surely one of New York's most glamorous meeting places (remember it from the movie *Moonstruck?*).

Also check out what's being offered by the Juilliard School (tel. 769-7406).

To find out what's happening at Lincoln Center, check local papers when you arrive. To get a two-month calendar of information in advance, send a stamped (52¢) self-addressed envelope to Lincoln Center Calendar, 70 Lincoln Center Plaza, New York, NY 10023.

For information on guided tours of Lincoln Center, see Chapter 7.

CARNEGIE HALL, 57th Street at Seventh Avenue. Tel. 247-7800.

On May 5, 1891, Peter Ilyich Tchaikovsky rose to the podium to conduct the first concert at the hall that would become known as a symbol of musical excellence all over the world. Caruso and Paderewski, Heifetz and Horowitz, Casals and Bernstein, Benny Goodman and the Beatles—they are all part of the legend. Miraculously saved from the wrecker's ball in 1960 and extensively restored in 1986 in time for its gala centennial celebration, Carnegie Hall continues to present world-renowned orchestras, chamber groups, and recitals. The gilded red-plush auditorium, with its splendid acoustics, is perhaps the best in the city. Intimate concerts are presented in its jewel-box-like Weill Recital Hall.

Tours of this National Historical Landmark are given September through July, on Monday, Tuesday, Thursday, and Friday at 11:30am, 2 and 3pm. Tickets are $6 adults, $5 seniors and students, and $3 children. For information, call 247-7800.

The **Rose Museum,** 154 W. 57th St., second floor, is open daily from 11am to 4:30pm and half an hour before a concert and during intermission. Exhibits focus on the history of Carnegie Hall: events in the theaters, the lives of its studio tenants. It is closed every Wednesday, the month of August, and on major holidays. Admission is free. For information, call 903-9629.

Single concert admissions are usually available at the box office, or in advance by phoning 247-7800. Prices vary with events.

TOWN HALL, 123 W. 43rd St. Tel. 840-2824.

Built by advocates of woman suffrage more than 70 years ago as a public forum that would enlighten women on the social and political issues of the day, Town Hall has been a platform for the great speakers of the times—from Winston Churchill to William Butler Yeats. Because of its superb acoustics and intimate sight lines, the hall also became a stage for legendary concert performances from Heifetz to Billie Holiday. With the revitalization of the Times Square area and the building's major renovation in 1984, Town Hall is once again one of the city's preeminent cultural facilities. It offers a full season of films, music, concerts, and dramatic readings and is now in the third year of a provocative 10-year New York cultural festival, "Century of Change." Tickets for many events are quite modest, from $10 up.

CITY CENTER THEATER, 131 W. 55th St. Tel. 581-1212.

Originally a Masonic temple dating from 1923–24, the landmark City Center was taken over in 1943 by Mayor Fiorello LaGuardia as a "people's theater" and a "cultural center for all New Yorkers." It is one of New York's largest, most inviting, and beloved theaters, noted for its offerings in dance, including Alvin Ailey American Dance Theater, the Joffrey Ballet, and the companies of Martha Graham, Paul Taylor, and Merce Cunningham. Ticket prices vary.

THE PARAMOUNT, Madison Square Garden Center, Seventh Ave., between 31st and 33rd streets. Tel. 465-6741.

The 5,600-seat replacement of the old Felt Forum is a stunner. *The* place for top popular artists—Cher, Barry Manilow, Barbra Streisand, and Patti La Belle have all appeared here—and other major attractions.

RADIO CITY MUSIC HALL, 1260 Ave. of the Americas, at 50th Street. Tel. 247-4777.

The world's biggest theater and perhaps its most famous, Radio City Music Hall is still alive and well, restored to its 1930s art deco splendor. Movies are not usually shown here, but the Rockettes are sometimes around, and there's a huge variety of entertainment—you might catch Bette Midler, Tina Turner, or the Gypsy Kings. At Christmas and Easter there are spectaculars for family audiences.

For tickets, the price of which varies with the event, apply to the box office or call Ticketmaster (tel. 212/307-7171) and charge with a major credit card. The number listed above provides a computerized information source of current and future events.

TISCH CENTER FOR THE ARTS, at the 92nd Street YM-YWHA, 92nd Street and Lexington Avenue. Tel. 996-1100.

The Upper East Side is home to one of New York's leading performing arts centers. Classical music concerts featuring such artists as the New York Chamber Symphony (directed by Gerard

Schwarz), Vladimir Feltsman, Isaac Stern, Nadja Salerno-Sonnenberg, Shlomo Mintz, and Andras Schiff are presented annually in a welcoming hall with great acoustics. The famous Lyrics and Lyricists series and a summer jazz festival round out the musical activities from September through July. **Prices:** Tickets $12.50–$30.

Note: Tisch Center is also home to the Y's Unterberg Poetry Center, where writers like Arthur Miller, Susan Sontag, and Philip Roth read from their own works on most Monday nights September through May.

APOLLO THEATRE, 253 W. 125th St. Tel. 749-5838.

This world-famous venue in the heart of Harlem's business district launched careers for countless influential artists, like Sarah Vaughn, Billy Eckstein, James Brown, Billie Holiday, Smokey Robinson and the Miracles, and Richard Pryor, to name just a few. The Apollo has come a long way since its early days as a burlesque theater that didn't allow African Americans in the audience. Now the Apollo hosts some of the most exhilarating concerts anywhere, with top gospel, R&B, jazz, pop, rap, rock, and soul performers commanding the stage. **Prices:** Every Wednesday is amateur night with cover ranging from $5–$20. Cover for concerts is anywhere from $20–$30. Tours of this hallowed three-floor, 1,500-seat theater are by appointment, with $4–$5 admission.

BEACON THEATER, 2124 Broadway, at 74th Street. Tel. 496-7070.

One of the city's most splendid movie palaces when it was built in 1928, the Beacon became a city landmark in 1978. It is noted for its splendid art deco lobby and an eclectic mix of other architectural styles. Now it is a favorite site for contemporary popular music performances, theater, revival films, and opening-night premieres of new movies. Ticket prices vary with events.

BROOKLYN ACADEMY OF MUSIC, 30 Lafayette Ave., Brooklyn. Tel. 718/636-4100.

This is the oldest performing arts center in the United States. Its opulent Opera House and Playhouse, and the smaller experimental theater, the Lepercq Space, are home to the famed Next Wave Festival. The complex is also an active center for dance, opera, children's programs, and theater. Music is well represented through the concerts of the resident Brooklyn Philharmonic Orchestra. A fourth theater—the BAM Majestic Theater—is a refurbished 1905 vaudeville house that has been retained in a state of suspended ruin and is home to theater, opera, and dance. It is located one and a half blocks from BAM's main building, at 651 Fulton St., about a 20-minute subway ride from midtown Manhattan. Most events are held between September and June. **Prices:** Tickets from $10.

THEATER

Many people come to New York for only one reason—to take in as much theater as possible. Indeed, the very name "Broadway" has become synonymous with the American theater, and whether you're a "tired businessperson" or an ardent avant-gardist, you will want to attend a few plays while you're in New York. But you will have two problems: first, getting seats; second, getting seats that you can afford. There are nine general tips for dealing with this sticky wicket.

TIPS FOR PLAYING THE BROADWAY THEATER TICKET GAME

1. Write ahead for tickets. As soon as you know you are coming to New York — even if it's months ahead of the date — write or phone the theater box offices for the tickets you want. This is especially important for hit musicals, often sold out months in advance. (To find out what will be playing, consult the Sunday "Arts & Leisure" section of the *New York Times.*) That way, you will be assured of a seat at box-office prices. If you wait until you get into town, you will probably have to resort to a ticket broker's services (they have branches in almost every hotel in the city), and then you must pay a commission on every seat. And you will have a hard time getting seats for the hits.

2. Pick the previews. As out-of-town tryouts for new Broadway shows have gotten too expensive and complicated, in the last few years the trend has been to substitute these with New York "previews." You can often realize considerable savings on a preview ticket, even for musicals. There will be some changes in the productions before opening night, of course, when the shows are "set," and you are taking a chance since you have no reviews to guide you. But if it's a play that's been imported after a long and well-reviewed run in England, or has top stars, or is the work of an important playwright, you're not risking too much. So be your own critic. Preview dates are listed along with the regular ads in the *New York Times, New York* magazine, and *The New Yorker.*

3. Join the long line over at TKTS. At its Times Square Theater Center outlet at Broadway and 47th Street (tel. 768-1818), theater tickets at 25% to 50% off regular prices are made available for the day of performance only from 3 to 8pm on Monday to Saturday for evening shows, from 10am to 2pm on Wednesday and Saturday for matinees, and from noon to closing for Sunday matinee and evening shows. Downtown at its Lower Manhattan Theater Center on the mezzanine of Two World Trade Center, tickets are available the day of performance for evening shows on Monday to Friday from 11am to 5:30pm and Saturday from 11am to 3pm, while tickets for Wednesday, Saturday, and Sunday matinees are sold the day before the performance. Naturally, these tickets are for shows that haven't sold out, so don't expect to get the "hottest" tickets this way. There is a $2.50 service charge (cash and traveler's checks are accepted).

4. Take the "twofers." When a show is not completely sold every night—perhaps it's at the end of its run or in previews — it often goes on "twofers." This means that, by presenting a slip at the box office, you can buy two seats for the price of one on certain nights of the week. You're running little risk here, since any show lasting long enough to go on "twofers" has some merit; you will probably not, however, see the original cast. "Twofers" are available at most hotel desks, restaurant cashier's booths, and the offices of the Visitors and Convention Bureau, 2 Columbus Circle.

5. Take advantage of standing room. If nothing you want to see is available at TKTS and you've just got to see the biggest hit in town, your best strategy is to present yourself at the box office (or phone in advance) to see if standing room is available. Some 18 theaters on Broadway sell standing-room spaces (around $15) when their house is completely sold out; sometimes they will sell these

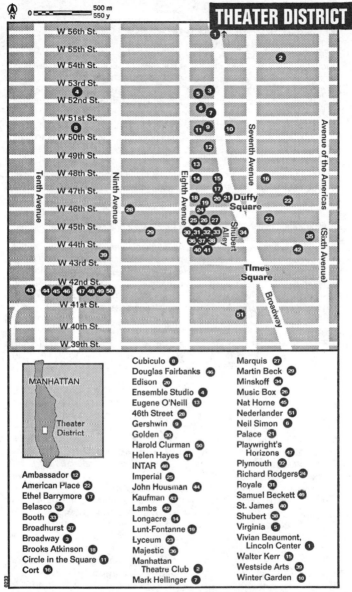

0 |===| 500 m
        550 y

W 56th St.
W 55th St.
W 54th St.
W 53rd St.
W 52nd St.
W 51st St.
W 50th St.
W 49th St.
W 48th St.
W 47th St.
W 46th St.
W 45th St.
W 44th St.
W 43rd St.
W 42nd St.
W 41st St.
W 40th St.
W 39th St.

Tenth Avenue
Ninth Avenue
Eighth Avenue
Seventh Avenue
Avenue of the Americas (Sixth Avenue)
Broadway

Duffy Square
Shubert Alley
Times Square

MANHATTAN

Theater District

Ambassador ⑫
American Place ㉒
Ethel Barrymore ⑰
Belasco ㉟
Booth ㉝
Broadhurst ㊲
Broadway ③
Brooks Atkinson ⑱
Circle in the Square ⑪
Cort ⑯

Cubiculo ⑧
Douglas Fairbanks ㊻
Edison ⑳
Ensemble Studio ④
Eugene O'Neill ⑬
46th Street ㉘
Gershwin ⑨
Golden ㉚
Harold Clurman ㊿
Helen Hayes ㊶
INTAR ㊽
Imperial ㉕
John Housman ㊹
Kaufman ㊸
Lambs ㊷
Longacre ⑭
Lunt-Fontanne ⑲
Lyceum ㉓
Majestic ㊱
Manhattan
   Theatre Club ②
Mark Hellinger ⑦

Marquis ㉗
Martin Beck ㉙
Minskoff ㉞
Music Box ㉖
Nat Horne ㊺
Nederlander ㊶
Neil Simon ⑥
Palace ㉑
Playwright's
   Horizons ㊼
Plymouth ㉜
Richard Rodgers ㉔
Royale ㉛
Samuel Beckett ㊾
St. James ㊵
Shubert ㊳
Virginia ⑤
Vivian Beaumont,
   Lincoln Center ①
Walter Kerr ⑮
Westside Arts ㊴
Winter Garden ⑩

tickets in advance. The view may be slightly obstructed in some areas, but usually it is excellent, and you can't beat the price.

6. Go to a ticket broker. If you are willing to pay full price and a little bit more, you'll find the best seats in the house are usually commandeered by them, and they will certainly get you into something. By law, they are allowed to charge 10% or $5 more than the face value of a ticket, whichever is higher. (Many abuses are reported). You can often get a ticket for a nonmusical by just going to the box office a day or two before the performance.

7. Call to purchase tickets by credit card. Tickets for many productions can be ordered via phone 24 hours a day, 7 days a week, through Tele-charge, 239-6200: they have a surcharge of $4.75 per ticket. Ticketmaster (tel. 307-4100) also has ticket-service locations at Bryant Park (42nd Street and Avenue of the Americas) and Bloomingdale's (59th Street and Lexington Avenue). They have a surcharge of $5 per ticket plus a $2.50 handling charge for the complete order.

8. Wheelchair tickets. Most theaters offer refreshingly low prices for those in wheelchairs and their companions, some as low as $7.50 and $15, up to half price. Inquire at individual theaters for information.

9. Consult the concierge. Hotel concierges often have "connections"—they may get you last-minute, "hot" tickets—for a price.

OFF-BROADWAY & OFF-OFF-BROADWAY

New York theatergoers have been going "off Broadway" for well over 50 years now, ever since the **Provincetown Playhouse** set up shop on Macdougal Street to show the works of a young playwright named Eugene O'Neill. Off-Broadway went into high gear, however, in the 1950s and 1960s, the golden years of **Circle in the Square,** the **Theater de Lys,** and the **Cherry Lane Theater.** It was at places like these that the late Geraldine Page rose to stardom, that Edward Albee tried out his first works, and that names like Eugene Ionesco and Samuel Beckett and Bertolt Brecht and Kurt Weill (his *Threepenny Opera* ran here for seven years) became household words in America. The longest-running show, on Broadway or off, Tom Jones and Harvey Schmidt's *The Fantasticks,* has run for over 35 years!

The brightest news in the Off-Broadway scene in many a year has been the creation of 42nd Street Theater Row: The transformation of the once-seedy block between Ninth and Tenth avenues into a sparkling new theater neighborhood, complete with nine theaters— including the **Harold Clurman Theater, Playwright's Horizon, Judith Anderson Theater, Samuel Beckett Theater, INTAR Mainstage Theater,** and **Douglas Fairbanks, Jr. Theater**—at least three cabarets, and half a dozen restaurants. A lot of creative work goes on in these houses, and there is often a real attempt made to keep prices down. For information, phone Ticket Central at 279-4200 after 1pm. Elsewhere around town, the **Manhattan Theater Club** mounts productions by new playwrights, usually at theaters at City Center, and **La Mama E.T.C.** on the Lower East Side is a longtime home of the avant-garde.

Off-Broadway can still afford to be more daring than Broadway theater, mainly because there is much less financial risk involved in mounting a production. The houses are much smaller than the Broadway houses (they are often converted factories, or church basements, or cellars); and the actors and technicians receive much less than a Broadway wage scale. This freedom sometimes leads to great artistic successes, to brilliant revivals of the classics, and sometimes to the merely inept and mediocre (there is, however, no shortage of the latter on Broadway, either). Occasionally, plays that open here to great success go on to Broadway.

It is usually much easier to get a ticket to an Off-Broadway production than to a Broadway one. Check the listings in the *New*

York Times, New York magazine, or *The New Yorker,* phone the theater, and pick up your reservation about an hour before curtain time. Many Off-Broadway playhouses will honor student ID cards.

Also check with theater schools, such as Actors Studio and the Juilliard School.

NEW YORK TRADITIONS

THE NEW YORK SHAKESPEARE FESTIVAL, performing in the Delacorte Theater, in Central Park. Tel. (Public Theater) 598-7100.

The Shakespeare Festival can be counted on all summer long for high-quality productions of the Bard and other entertainments in a delightful outdoor setting in Central Park. Performances are held every night except Monday from late June to early September. Two tickets per person are available at the Delacorte Theater beginning at 1pm on the day of the performance; they are also available from 1 to 3pm at the Public Theater at 425 Lafayette St. (see below). Doors open at 7:30pm for the 8 o'clock show; the theater seats 1900; all seats are reserved. The Delacorte can be approached from either 81st Street and Central Park West or 79th Street and Fifth Avenue. **Prices:** Free.

THE NEW YORK SHAKESPEARE FESTIVAL AT THE JO-SEPH PAPP PUBLIC THEATER, 425 Lafayette St., at Astor Place. Tel. 598-7150.

During much of the year, the Shakespeare Festival runs the Joseph Papp Public Theater in Greenwich Village and lets new playwrights have their fling. At this writing, there were some five theaters and a cinema under the Public's roof; the complex presents one of the most vital and compelling theatrical experiments in New York today. It was at the Public that *Hair, A Chorus Line,* and *For Colored Girls* got their start. Tickets are $15 to $37.50; Quicktix are sold on the day of the performance at 6pm for evening performances, at 1pm for matinees. Film tickets are $7. The box office is open Tuesday to Sunday from 1 to 8pm, Monday until 6pm.

2. THE CLUB & MUSIC SCENE

In general, barring Miami Beach or Atlantic City or Las Vegas, New York is the "latest" town in the country. Bars and lounges can stay open and serve liquor until 4am every morning. Informality is the mode of dress—come-as-you-will—allowed everywhere, except in the top rooms, where coats and ties are de rigueur for the men. (A few places do bar jeans and sneakers.) Nowadays, women solo or in tandem can count on being welcomed almost everywhere. Drinks average around $6 in the fancier places, somewhat less elsewhere. Even in the neighborhood pubs, the days of the $1 glass of beer are no more: Plan to spend $4 and up.

How much will it all cost? Here, the latitude is enormous, and the choice is yours. You could easily spend $100 or more (for a couple, plus tips) as you dine, dance, and watch the big names in entertainment. Or you can go pub crawling with the natives and spend lots less. *Tips:* Many places have lower prices or no covers or minimums during the week; weekend prices soar everywhere. Also, a drink or two at the bar, plus a cover charge, can often be your price of admission to some of the best entertainment in town. Note that I've given charges only where they seem to be fixed; in the changeable nightclub scene, however, most covers and admissions will vary with the performer, the time of year, and the state of business. Except in the neighborhood pubs and the bars, reservations are imperative; for the major clubs, it might be wise to phone a day in advance.

New York clubs come and go with alarming frequency. Sometimes they change their entertainment format or decide to open only on certain days of the week. It's always wise to check local papers when you come and call in advance.

Note: The legal minimum drinking age in New York is 21. Some clubs admit 18-year-olds but will not serve them alcohol; others will not admit them at all. Some clubs require double proof of age, other clubs look the other way.

NIGHTCLUBS & CABARET

Other American cities may have discos, rock clubs, and pubs, but none have cabarets to match New York's. Most of today's variety stars got their first break in New York cabarets in the 1960s. Today, talented young performers as well as major stars still strut their dreams in these beloved vestiges of vaudeville.

THE BALLROOM, 253 W. 28th St. Tel. 244-3005.

Legends and luminaries like Peggy Lee, Eartha Kitt, Blossom Dearie, Karen Akers, and Charles Pierce have all called The Ballroom home. Leading international pop and cabaret artists, including many Brazilian performers, draw the crowds. The restaurant here is quite special, featuring the oldest tapas bar on these shores, with some 50 traditional appetizers for the tasting. Come for lunch from noon to 3pm on Tuesday to Friday (except summer) and you can feast on an open tapas buffet for $18.50. In the evening, there's continental cuisine and a classical guitarist, too, on Tuesday to Sunday. **Admission:** $20-$25 cover and two-drink minimum.

DON'T TELL MAMA, 343 W. 46th St. Tel. 757-0788.

If you're lucky, you may wander into the piano room at Don't Tell Mama and catch Liza Minnelli, Michael Feinstein, or your favorite Broadway musical star casually crooning show tunes. In the back room, Don't Tell Mama presents incredibly diverse cabaret acts, from jazz combos to gospel groups to female impersonators, seven nights a week. There are also singing waiters and an open mike singalong nightly at the piano bar. **Admission:** Cabaret room, $6-$15 plus two-drink minimum. Piano bar, two-drink minimum at table.

DUPLEX, 61 Christopher St. Tel. 255-5438.

Be a star at this tree-level "entertainment complex," where the entire staff performs. Downstairs in the Piano Bar, patrons and staff sing along nightly from 9pm to 4am (no cover). Upstairs features the Game Room with pool table, jukebox, and New York's oldest continuing cabaret, with shows nightly. There's standup comedy every Wednesday at 8pm, with the "Stars of Tomorrow" contest Friday at 11:30pm. **Admission:** Cabaret, $5-$12 cover plus two-drink minimum.

EIGHTY-EIGHTS, 228 W. 10th St. Tel. 924-0088.

Cabaret fixture Erv Raible, who opened the original Duplex,

along with partners Karen Miller and Rochelle Seldin, has created one of the city's most attractive cabaret rooms in shades of lilac with chrome accents. Downstairs, friendly regulars surround the sunken piano and sing show tunes; upstairs, a diminutive stage hosts a parade of performers, from *Cats'* Betty Buckley to rising star Billy Stritch. Eighty-Eights' Sunday brunch has become a popular hangout for Village theater gypsies (dancers). **Admission:** Cover upstairs varies from $10–$12.50; two-drink minimum on both levels.

JUDY'S, 49 W. 44th St. Tel. 764-8930.

With a lively front-room piano bar and a romantic cabaret area in back, Judy's has a wonderfully intimate supper club feeling. Chanteuse Barbara Lea, singer-songwriter Arthur Siegel, and voice-and-piano partners Judy Kreston and David Lahm all frequent Judy's small stage. Judy's also serves good Italian and continental fare for lunch on weekdays from noon to 5pm. Dinner is served on Monday to Saturday from 6 to 11pm. The shows take place Sunday to Friday at 9 and 11pm, Saturday at 8 and 10pm. **Admission:** Cabaret shows, $8–$15 cover; $10 minimum.

RAINBOW & STARS, on the 65th floor of the GE Building, 30 Rockefeller Plaza. Tel. 632-5000.

⭐ This jewel box of a club is perhaps the most elegant and intimate cabaret/supper club in New York, a cousin to the famed Rainbow Room for dining and dancing. Not only can you gaze at such stars as Tony Bennett or Hildegarde, Helen Schneider or Maureen McGovern, Rosemary Clooney, but you can also gaze at the stars outside: The view overlooks Central Park, with sightings up the Hudson and as far as lower Connecticut. Curved walls display fiberoptic stars and form private nooks for two. Elegant dinners and late suppers recall the supper club days of the 1930s with caviar and lobster and lemon chartreuse; what could be more romantic? The evening of dining and show begins with a 6:30 seating for an 8:30 performance and at 9:30 for supper and a show at 11pm. Jackets and ties—and reservations—are required. **Admission:** $35 per person.

S.O.B., 204 Varick St. Tel. 243-4940.

⭐ A club with an international reputation, S.O.B. (Sounds of Brazil and Beyond) lures huge crowds to its cavernous space for the best in authentic Brazilian food and music. The throbbing sambas of Brazil alternate with African, Latin, Caribbean, and "World Music." The crowd ranges from the blue jeans set to the black tie set—there's something for everybody here.

Come to S.O.B.'s Mango Tree Café for lunch (Monday to Friday from noon to 3pm) or dinner (dinner main courses run $9.50 to $17) and sample some of the regional cuisines of Brazil and the Caribbean, partake of some of the national Brazilian drinks like caipirinhas or batidas, and enjoy one of the most unique evenings north of Rio. It's always best to call for dinner reservations and for information. Happy Hours are Monday to Friday from 5 to 8pm. **Admission:** $5–$15 cover, depending on performer; special group rates are available, and all major credit cards are accepted.

STEVE MCGRAW'S, 158 W. 72nd St. Tel. 595-7400.

⭐ Steve McGraw's is not only the best cabaret/supper club on the Upper West Side; it's one of the best in town. Count on owner Steve McGraw to pick a long-running hit: the last incumbent, *Forever Plaid,* ran four years; *Forbidden Broadway,* the one before that, even longer. Check local listings or call the club when you arrive in New York to see what's on. **Admission:** Depending on the show, around $25 to $35.

POP & ROCK

THE BITTER END, 147 Bleecker St. Tel. 673-7030.

⭐ This legendary club still continues its quarter-of-a-century tradition of showcasing up-and-coming talent. Some of the greatest names in the music business have started here: Bob Dylan, Joni Mitchell, Stevie Wonder, Linda Ronstadt, and Billy Joel. (Comics like Lily Tomlin, Woody Allen, Billy Crystal, and George Carlin are Bitter End alumni too.) Currently, the club showcases up-and-coming singer-songwriters; Tracy Chapman performed here before she became well known. **Admission:** $5.

BOTTOM LINE, 15 W. 4th St. Tel. 228-6300.

Although it's considered the preeminent rock club in the city— some say in the country—the huge, always-packed Bottom Line does not limit its acts strictly to rock. You might catch folk singers, jazz artists (of the stature of Chick Corea), even classical performers. The crowd is young, the food ordinary. No one under 21 admitted; double proof of age is required. **Admission:** $15–$25, no minimum.

CHINA CLUB, 2130 Broadway, at 75th Street. Tel. 877-1166.

You never know who'll show up—onstage or off—at this legendary record-biz hangout. David Bowie shocked the house by jumping on stage a while ago; Donald Trump makes regular appearances, as do the likes of Michael Jordan and Lawrence Taylor and friends. Lesser mortals (mostly up-and-coming bands) perform nightly. **Admission:** $10 Tues–Sat, $20 Mon.

CONTINENTAL, 25 Third Ave., at St. Mark's Place. Tel. 529-6924.

A huge fiberglass pterodactyl hovers over the roof, and inside the decor is East Village black. The expanded stage means there's room for bigger acts, from local favorites the Lunachicks to the legendary Fleshtones to punk pioneers the Dictators; the crowd and the decibel level vary depending on the bill, which features anything from punk to country to jazz to blues. **Admission:** $4–$7 cover Fri–Sat; no minimum.

DAN LYNCH BAR, 221 Second Ave., at 14th Street. Tel. 677-0911.

Dan Lynch's has just celebrated its 13th anniversary. It's popular with a young and friendly crowd. The music, usually blues, but occasionally rock/R&B, is loud, and the drinks—you must buy two—are cheap. On weekends, you might hear a hot local favorite such as Frankie Paris and friends, who rock the house monthly. Music nightly and an open jam Saturday and Sunday at 4pm. **Admission:** $5 Fri–Sat.

KENNY'S CASTAWAYS, 157 Bleecker St. Tel. 473-9870.

Kenny's Castaways is one of the hottest spots on the street, with a long bar, two levels, a back room devoted exclusively to music and a comfortable, music-art atmosphere. It's a showcase for musicians, featuring the full range of American rock and roll. More than a few of its groups—like the Smithereens—have secured record deals. A great place to catch new acts before you have to pay concert prices to see them. **Open:** Daily noon–4am. **Admission:** Varies with act.

KNITTING FACTORY, 47 E. Houston St., between Mott and Mulberry streets. Tel. 219-3055.

For something completely different, unpack your favorite all-black outfit and head down to the Knitting Factory, a dark, unpretentious performance space. Downtown New York institutions like Lydia Lunch, John Zorn, and Arto Lindsay all make regular appearances, in an atmosphere so laid-back you may think you're in your own living room. **Admission:** $5–$15 (includes one drink).

SPEAKEASY, 107 MacDougal St. Tel. 674-7346.

In the still-folksy heart of the Village, Speakeasy offers "a little bit of folk and jazz, a little blues and rock 'n roll" seven nights a week. Special events might include three women's bands playing in "New Music Seminars," a guest appearance with Speakeasy veteran David Massengill, or the annual "Bob Dylan Imitator's Contest." Open mike night is Monday.

TOMMY MAKEM'S IRISH PAVILION, 130 E. 57th St. Tel. 759-9040.

⭐ Not only is the music good at Irish Pavilion, but the Irish coffee is so delicious it must have been made by the little people themselves. Music is featured Tuesday to Saturday. It's usually Irish, but sometimes American folk. **Admission:** $8–$10 cover for special acts.

TRAMPS, 51 W. 21st St. Tel. 727-7788.

Tramps, a spacious loft, showcases eclectic, fearless (as in they'll do anything) rock, zydeco, and blues lineups seven nights a week. When the Cajun-influenced zydeco bands do their thing, there's no keeping the audience off the dance floor. Reggae bands often alternate with zydeco, keeping the Caribbean beat throbbing. Tramps serves Cajun Creole cuisine (main courses $13–$16). Tramps is open for dinner Monday to Friday from 6–11pm. **Admission:** $5–$30.

WETLANDS, 161 Hudson St. Tel. 966-4225.

Alive and open seven nights a week with a cutting-edge lineup of national and local bands, Wetlands has developed a reputation as an intimate, earthy, user-friendly nightclub. Wetlands is unique in its commitment to running a full-time eco-activist program within the club, which also offers concert-goers a variety of ways to get involved. Music ranges from rock, funk, and blues to alternative hardcore, ska, and reggae. **Admission:** Free Mondays and Tuesdays ("Grateful Dead" night), $5–$12 Wed through Sun.

COMEDY CLUBS

CAROLINE'S, 1626 Broadway, at 50th Street. Tel. 757-4100.

Forget the old image of smoky, claustrophobic comedy clubs. New York's Queen of Comedy, Caroline Hirsch, has created a soaring, sophisticated venue that feels more like a luxurious lounge than a performance room. Headliners include the hottest names in comedy, from Rita Rudner to Gilbert Gottfried to Jeff Altman. For a comedy club, Caroline's also offers a very serious Italian menu, with delicious antipasto, Caesar salad, and lasagne bolognese. **Admission:** Cover $12.50–$20, depending on headliner; two-drink minimum.

THE COMEDY CELLAR AT THE OLIVE TREE, 117 MacDougal St. Tel. 254-3630.

Known in the industry as the comic's choice of New York comedy clubs because of its intimate atmosphere and dedication to top caliber shows, the Comedy Cellar has been twice hailed by the *New York Post* as the "Best comedy room in New York." Top comedians are featured, and surprise guests have included Robin Williams, Steven Wright, and Jerry Seinfeld. Open seven nights a week. **Admission:** Sun–Thurs $5 cover, plus two drinks; Fri–Sat, $10 cover, plus two drinks.

DANGERFIELD'S, 1118 First Ave., near 61st Street. Tel. 593-1650.

You can see some of the best of the standup comics perform at comic Rodney Dangerfield's popular East Side club. Many are veterans of Letterman and Rodney's own HBO specials. Five-act shows are presented every night. **Admission:** Sun–Thurs $12.50 cover; Fri–Sat $15 cover. Special $5 Kinney parking for club patrons.

NEW YORK COMEDY CLUB, 241 E. 24th St. Tel. 888-1696.

The owners of this club swear that they aren't joking about their "Wal-Mart approach" to comedy, meaning "low overhead and top quality." The modest wood-paneled room certainly attests to their thrift, and the acts really do include the city's top names. Guests have included Damon Wayans from "In Living Color" and "Tonight Show" veterans Randy Credico and Bob Shaw. Closed Sundays, open mike Mondays. **Admission:** $5 weeknights; $10 weekends—two-drink minimum.

THE N.Y. COMIC STRIP, INC., 1568 Second Ave., near 81st Street. Tel. 861-9386.

Some of the best and brightest minds in comedy do their thing here. Comic Strip is home to Eddie Murphy; Jerry Seinfeld; Paul Reiser; and cast members of "Saturday Night Live"—Adam Sandler, Ellen Kleghorn, and Chris Rock. **Admission:** Cover varies; two-drink minimum (drinks start at $4).

THE ORIGINAL IMPROVISATION, 358 W. 44th St. Tel. 279-3446.

"Now," in the words of proprietor Silver Friedman, "celebrating 30 years of love, truth, and laughter." The Original Improv could easily be dubbed the cradle of comedy from Pryor to Piscopo. Danny Aiello, Richard Lewis, and Jay Leno all started here; so did Lily Tomlin, Bette Midler, Robert Klein, and Rodney Dangerfield. The Improv now showcases the hottest new talent of the '90s. **Admission:** Wed–Sat $10 cover, $9 minimum. Closed Sun–Tues.

STAND UP NEW YORK, 236 W. 78th St., at Broadway. Tel. 595-0850.

This is the West Side's premier standup comedy club, with the hottest comics, many of whom have appeared on "The Tonight Show," Letterman, MTV, and HBO. Drop-in guests include Robin Williams, Jerry Seinfeld, and Roseanne Arnold. A light menu is available. **Admission:** Sun–Thurs $7 cover, Fri–Sat $12 (two-drink minimum). Children's shows every Sunday at 2pm, $7 cover.

COUNTRY MUSIC

ALBUQUERQUE RODEO BAR, 375 3rd Ave., at 27th Street. Tel. 683-6500.

Albuquerque Rodeo Bar is probably the only bar in New York that's actually a converted cattle trailer. With log-cabin style walls, a 20-foot Texas State flag draping one side of the bar and loads of authentic country memorabilia, you're likely to feel like an honorary ranch hand. Along with live American roots music every night including country, blues, and rockabilly from artists like Tom Russell and the Belmont Playboys, you can enjoy a Tex-Mex menu of favorites like sizzling fajitas and quesadillas. **Admission:** No cover, no minimum.

DENIM & DIAMONDS, 511 Lexington Ave., at 48th Street. Tel. 371-1600.

A well-heeled crowd two-steps in neatly pressed jeans and spanking new cowboy hats at this upscale country/western dance club. There are dance lessons every night at 7 and 8pm, plus every cowpoke's dream disco ball—a flashy revolving saddle. Country stars Garth Brooks and Reba McIntyre have kicked up their heels here, as have comedians Bill Murray and Judy Tenuta. Denim & Diamonds is also a full-service restaurant with a Texas barbecue menu, including an outrageously delicious prime rib ($13.95). Most other main courses are about $8. Dinner is served nightly from 6pm to 1am. **Admission:** Mon–Thurs $5 cover, Fri–Sat $8.

JAZZ & BLUES

Jazz went through some lean years in New York, but now it's back, bigger and better than ever. So big has the jazz revival become, in fact, that a **Jazzline** (tel. 212/479-7888 to find out who's playing where) has been established and is flourishing mightily. On the club scene, much of the action is downtown.

Most jazz clubs charge $10 to $15 covers and/or a one- or two-drink minimum, but it all depends on the performer. And with the jazz renaissance in full swing, new clubs are opening all the time. Check the listings in the magazines (*The New Yorker* has the best), also in the *Village Voice*. It's best to make reservations, and check the credit-card policy of the club.

B. SMITH'S ROOFTOP CAFE, 771 Eighth Ave. Tel. 247-2222.

To her ultrapopular midtown restaurant, Barbara Smith has added a glass-enclosed plant-filled upstairs room where musicians like Eddie Palmieri and Will Downing entertain a well-dressed, mostly local crowd. Entertainment is on Friday and Saturday; showtimes vary. **Admission:** $10 or $20, depending on artist; $10 minimum.

BIRDLAND, 2745 Broadway, at 105th Street. Tel. 749-2228.

Birdland houses eclectic jazz and great dining. Its high ceilings, enormous windows, and inviting atmosphere make it an exceptionally warm place to enjoy cool tunes seven nights a week. Sets are nightly at 9, 10:30pm, and midnight. **Admission:** Sun–Thurs, no cover, but $7 minimum at the tables, $5 minimum at the bar; Fri–Sat, cover $10–$20, depending on who is performing, $10–$20 minimum.

BLUE NOTE, 131 W. 3rd St., near Sixth Avenue. Tel. 475-8592.

⭐ A throwback to the elegant New York nightspots of the past, Blue Note is a posh jazz bistro featuring top-name performers on a nightly basis, like Ray Charles, Nancy Wilson, Tony Bennett, Wynton Marsalis, and George Benson. Show times are at 9 and 11:30pm during the week, with sometimes a third show at 1:30am on Friday and Saturday. There is a late-night jam session every Tuesday through Saturday, after the last set, until 4am, and a $14.50 Jazz Brunch every Saturday and Sunday from noon to 6pm; show times are at 1 and 3:30pm. Reasonably priced gourmet continental dinners are served from 7pm to 1am on Monday to Thursday, until 2am on Friday and Saturday, with main courses running from $7.95 to $23.95. **Admission:** Varies, depending on performer; $5-drink minimum. Reservations recommended.

BRADLEY'S, 70 University Place, at E. 11th Street. Tel. 228-6440.

Twenty-five years old, and with a great ambience, Bradley's has been dubbed "the epitome of a New York bar" by *The New Yorker*. Its music format is famous: jazz piano trios, featuring horns, guitar, vibes, drums, and so on, as well as piano-bass duos and occasional quartets; its last set is the latest of any jazz club, and it's on seven nights a week. There's a very good kitchen, too, with reasonably priced American fare: the late-night menu runs until 2:30am (there's also an Early Bird dinner from 5:30 to 7:30). The bar is open nightly until 4am. Admission: $12–$15 cover charge (minimum $8).

CAFE CARLYLE, in the Carlyle Hotel, 781 Madison Ave., at 76th Street. Tel. 744-1600.

The eternally elegant Café Carlyle has featured top-notch entertainers covering jazz as well as the Broadway musical scene since 1965. Regular performers include Bobby Short, who has been performing here for 26 years, Eartha Kitt, and Dixie Carter from "Designing Women." Dinner (à la carte main courses $15 to $29) is served starting at 7pm for the first show, which begins at 8:45; the second show is at 10:45, and dinner is served during the show. **Admission:** $40 cover.

THE CAFE AT SIGN OF THE DOVE, 1110 Third Ave., at 65th Street. Tel. 861-8080.

A smart, stylish uptown crowd makes the scene here to listen to top-flight groups and soloists: Kenny Brawner, Sandi Blair, and Reggie Woods are regulars. While the Sign of the Dove's spectacular main restaurant is pricey, the Café is definitely not: You can have extraordinary hors d'oeuvres, sandwiches, pastas, and main courses—a great meal for under $18. Music starts most nights at 9pm (Saturdays at 10pm) and continues until closing, usually 1am or later. **Admission:** $5 music charge Sat.

CAJUN, 129 Eighth Ave., at 16th Street. Tel. 691-6174.

★ In the mood for terrific Dixieland bands and Bourbon Street blues? Head over to Cajun any Monday to Thursday (8:30 to 11pm), Friday and Saturday (9pm to midnight), or for the Sunday champagne jazz brunch, which is served from noon to 4pm (for $11.95; it's one of the best treats in town). Dine on inexpensive Cajun/Creole food or have drinks at the bar. **Admission:** Free, no minimum.

FAT TUESDAY'S, downstairs at Tuesday's Restaurant, 190 Third Ave., at 17th Street. Tel. 533-7902.

This one was a winner from the day it opened. The plush mirrored rooms with intimate seating feature the best of avant-garde and mainstream artists (Michel LeGrand, Michel Camilo, and Dizzy Gillespie, among others); food is available from upstairs. Sunday features a jazz brunch at $11.95, including champagne. **Admission:** $20 cover, $10 minimum at tables; no minimum downstairs.

THE FIVE SPOT, 4 W. 31st St. Tel. 631-0100.

A turn-of-the-century ballroom that was host to Fiorello LaGuardia's two inaugural balls is the scene of a hot new jazz club. Jazz stars of the caliber of Shirley Horn, David Sanborn, Joe Sample, and Ramsey Lewis do their sets under the golden angels and majestic icons of the restored ballroom, with marble Corinthian columns and an elaborately sculptured ceiling. A modern kitchen with a chef classically trained under André Soltner of Lutèce provides a traditional American menu with French and Italian influences; vegetarian specialties are available. There's an early show (8:30pm weekdays, 9pm weekends) and a late show (10:30pm weekdays, 11pm weekends). **Admission:** $27.50 cover charge; $10 minimum at tables.

IRIDIUM ROOM JAZZ CLUB, 44 W. 63rd St. Tel. 582-2121.

Iridium Room Jazz Club offers the same outstanding menu and crazed decor as restaurant Iridium upstairs (see p. 159). Iridium Room's all-star jam sessions are destined for greatness; everyone is welcome to bring instruments and improvise informally along with the pros every Monday at 9:30 pm. You can unwind with the cool crowd under the low lights with live piano and jazz every night after 10 and hear top names like the Pete Yellin Trio and Howard Prince and the Music Coalition. **Admission:** $5 cover during the week, $10 cover weekends, and a $15 minimum per table.

KNICKERBOCKER BAR AND GRILL, 33 University Place, at 9th Street. Tel. 228-8490.

The Knickerbocker is a cozy spot to catch some of the greats. It's known for its commendable, medium-priced kitchen, famous for its T-bone steaks for 2 for $44. **Admission:** Wed–Sat from 9:45pm; $2–$3.50 cover charge.

MANNY'S CAR WASH, 1558 Third Ave., between 87th and 88th streets. Tel. 369-BLUES.

What can be said of a Chicago-style blues bar that serves a drink called a Woo Woo (cranberry juice, triple sec, and vodka) and "World Famous White Castle Hamburgers"? There's something going on every night of the week, from 9:15pm on (from 8:45 on Sunday), on Tuesday it's Louisiana night with New Orleans blues or zydeco; on Wednesday and Thursday, nationally known and Grammy-winning musicians play. On Sunday, it's Manny's World

Famous Blues Jam. **Admission:** Mon free for women, $3 cover for men; Tues–Wed $3–$5 cover; Thurs $5–$10 cover; Fri–Sat $6 cover; Sun no cover. Two-drink minimum at tables every night.

MICHAEL'S PUB, 211 E. 55th St. Tel. 758-2272.

This English-pub style place that everybody seems to like has an eclectic entertainment policy—everybody from Vic Damone to Woody Allen's New Orleans Funeral & Ragtime Band occasionally checking in on a Monday night when the director is in town. **Admission:** Cover and minimum depend on act.

SWEET BASIL JAZZ RESTAURANT, 88 Seventh Ave. South, at Bleecker Street. Tel. 242-1785.

Highly rated among Greenwich Village jazz clubs, Sweet Basil is strong on talent. It consistently features top names in traditional and contemporary jazz, as well as very good American cuisine with some Thai touches; shows are from 9pm nightly. A special treat is the weekend jazz brunch, with the music of the Bruno Destrez Trio, on Saturday from 2 to 6pm, and the legendary trumpeter Doc Cheatham's Quartet on Sunday from 2 to 6pm. **Admission:** No music charge at brunch; $15 music charge at evening performances; $10 minimum evenings, $6 minimum at brunch.

CHESTNUT ROOM AT TAVERN ON THE GREEN, Central Park West at 67th Street. Tel. 873-3200.

★ The most dazzlingly beautiful jazz room in town, with a state-of-the-art sound system, a Hamburg Steinway grand worthy of top concert artists, and an impressive roster of jazz and other great performers, is the new Chestnut Room in venerable Tavern on the Green. Tavern's great contemporary American menu is available à la carte; an after-theater dinner is also offered after 10pm. Recent artists have included former Big Band singer Chris Connor; cabaret artists Susannah McCorkle and the Freddy Cole Trio. Showtimes are Sun and Tuesday to Thursday at 8:30 and 10:30pm, with an additional show Saturday at 12:30am. **Admission:** $17.50 cover Sun and Tues–Thurs; $23.50 cover Sat–Sun; no minimum.

THE VILLAGE VANGUARD, 178 Seventh Ave. South, just below 11th Street. Tel. 255-4037.

★ Called the "most famous jazz club in the world," the Village Vanguard has been around since the 1930s with some of the best jazz there is. Big names (like Wynton and Branford Marsalis and Illinois Jacquet) and newcomers alike appear every night starting at 9:30pm; The Vanguard Seventeen Piece Jazz Orchestra plays every Monday night. There's no food but a friendly crowd. **Admission:** Sun–Thurs $12 cover, $8 minimum; Fri–Sat $15 cover, $8 minimum.

WEST END GATE, 2911 Broadway at 113th Street. Tel. 662-8830.

You can mix with the Columbia kids and other enthusiastic music buffs at this reincarnation of the old West End Café. Renovated, and with a glittering interior, this is still an informal place that features various musical combos, jazz, rock, theater, and comedy, from 9pm nightly. Lunch and dinner are served daily, with an affordable, eclectic international menu. **Admission:** Cover depends on event.

ZINNO, 126 W. 13th St. Tel. 924-5182.

Along with wonderful Italian cuisine, Zinno dishes up top-drawer local jazz acts seven nights a week in an intimate, charming room. **Admission:** No cover; $5 music charge and $15 minimum in music room; bar minimum $10.

DANCE CLUBS & DISCOS

You should know a few things before you start out: First, nobody who is anybody arrives until very late (from 10pm on); secondly, clubs do not admit all comers (it all depends on the whim of the management); and third, note that the door fee can be very high, up to $25 per person. While clubs come and go with alarming rapidity, and many are too specialized, faddy, or ephemeral to bear listing here (see papers like *Paper* and the *New York Press* for information on these), the following, in all likelihood, will still be doing business when you come.

AU BAR, 41 E. 58th St. Tel. 308-9455.

The decidedly more "uptown" Au Bar looks like a whimsically decorated country mansion's library. Indeed, proprietor (and ex-Xenon owner) Howard Stein hired two young Britons to furnish his club with heirlooms and antiques. A supper club, Au Bar offers simple, sophisticated dinner and breakfast fare (main courses range from $12.50 to $28). A DJ entertains the Beautiful People on a small dance floor, and reservations are a must. **Admission:** $10 Sun–Wed; $15 Thurs–Sat.

BAJA, 246A Columbus Ave., between 71st and 72nd streets. Tel. 724-8890.

A smart crowd of young Upper West Siders do a lot of socializing and networking here. There is occasionally live entertainment, and there is a DJ and disco dancing every night. **Admission:** $10 Fri–Sat; prices vary Wed–Thurs by event.

THE COPACABANA, 617 W. 57th St., at Eleventh Avenue. Tel. 582-2672.

Remember the Copa, New York's legendary glamour nightclub of the 1940s? It's bigger and better than ever. With two live orchestras, disco on one level and Latin salsa on the other, it brings in the crowds on Tuesday, Friday, and Saturday. There's a free buffet between 6 and 8pm on Tuesday. **Admission:** Tues–Wed free 6–8pm; $5 women and $10 men after 8pm; Fri $10 women, $15 men; Sat $15 women, $20 men.

COUNTRY CLUB, 209 E. 85th St. Tel. 879-8400.

With a black-and-white-checkerboard dance floor and a "singin' 'n' swingin'" orchestra, this romantic retro room "reintroduces nostalgia to New York," recalling grand old clubs like the El Morocco. Sweeping trompe-l'oeil murals depict fairways, palm trees, and a swimming pool; for a moneyed old Palm Beach ambience, navy-and-white-striped canvas billows from the ceiling. Chef David Page's menu even draws 1940s favorites through a time warp, with goat-cheese fondue, macaroni with house-smoked salmon in horse-radish cream, and beef tenderloin with mashed red potatoes among my favorites. In a neighborhood not known for imaginative night-spots, Country Club makes an unusual and welcome addition. Dancing is from 10pm nightly. **Admission:** $10 cover for non-diners weeknights, $15 weekends.

DECO, 27 W. 20th St. Tel. 366-4181.

This stylish art deco club invites patrons to dress up to dance and drink, aided by a spectacular light and sound system. Deco is open from 8pm to 5am, and seafood and pasta are served until 4am. An average dinner tab, including salad and main course, is $12. On Monday, Deco often features live acts; performers have been as diverse as Debbie Gibson, RuPaul, and Tito Puente. **Admission:** $10 Fridays.

GAUGUIN, in the Plaza Hotel, Central Park South at 59th Street. Tel. 319-0404.

Paul Gauguin's Tahiti comes to vibrant, shimmering life in this stunning new supperclub with palm trees, an arched wooden bridge to walk over, Gauguin murals everywhere (it's taken over the space of the old Trader Vic's). An innovative Asian Tropical menu is served until about 11pm; then the disco dancing gets under way; nobody goes home until about 4am. Jackets required for gentlemen. **Admission:** $15 Sun–Thurs, $20 Fri–Sat.

LAURA BELLE, 120 W. 43rd St., between Sixth Avenue and Broadway. Tel. 819-1000.

Put on your party clothes (a jacket is required for men, which is meant to set the tone) and get set to enter one of the 1930s-style supper clubs that are springing up around the city. The crowd ranges in age from the 20s set to people in their 60s. You can arrive from 7 on and have a sumptuous continental dinner from 7pm to midnight (expensive: main courses $21–$31). Or arrive stylishly late anytime from 10pm on and dance, drink, and perhaps have a snack à la carte from the dinner menu. Tables and banquettes ring the dance floors, and diners may also sit in the balcony and enjoy an overview of the grand, amphitheater-shaped room with its 40-foot ceiling, faceted columns, limestone-frescoed walls, antique sconces, chandeliers, theatrical lights, and, of course, all the people who decorate the place with panache. Open Wednesday to Saturday. **Admission:** $10 after 10pm, $15 Sat. No minimum.

LIMELIGHT, 660 Sixth Ave., at 20th Street. Tel. 807-7850.

An ever-popular place to dance to the most current New York music (with up to 12 DJs) is this nightclub created out of a mid-19th-century city landmark church (it was deconsecrated some years back). Dancing takes place in the main sanctuary, and you can look down upon the goings-on from the choir loft above. There are eight bars, a library, and many cozy nooks for sitting and talking. Check out the "Smart Bar" in the first-floor lobby, which offers up nonalcoholic high-energy drinks that are said to boost one's brain power and stamina—this may be the wave of the future. Crowds line up to gain access to this cavernous place (it can hold 2,500), but the lines move quickly. Limelight also hosts occasional live acts; call Neville Wells for schedule. **Admission:** $12 Tues and Sun; $20 Fri and Sat; $15 Wed and Thurs.

NELL'S, 246 W. 14th St. Tel. 675-1567.

When it opened in 1987, Nell's broke the mold with live jazz and Victorian furnishings; although others have imitated it, the club still feels refreshing and quite distinctive. Sundays and Fridays continue to draw hordes, so expect to wait; you'll have an easier time getting in Tuesdays and Saturdays, but you'll also miss the "A" crowd. There's light supper upstairs from 10pm, entertainment from 11:30, and dancing downstairs all night. **Admission:** $7 Mon–Wed; $15 Thurs, Fri, Sat.

POLLY ESTHER'S, 1487 First Ave., between 77th and 78th streets. Tel. 628-4477.

Should you find yourself waxing nostalgic over mood rings, the Brady Bunch, Charlie's Angels, and disco, then put on your platform shoes and run, don't walk, to Polly Esther's, New York's only '70s bar and theme park. You'll love the murals of '70s celebs and the miles of memorabilia from the decade that spawned Pet Rocks and the Partridge Family. Polly Esther's is open for lunch and dinner seven days a week, with karaoke on Wednesday nights, dancing at midnight, and a weekly series of zany events, including trivia quizzes and celebrity lookalike contests. **Admission:** $3 cover Friday and Saturday.

It has less of a clublike feeling, but there's another Polly Esther's in the East Village at 21 East 8th St. (tel. 979-1971), which also has dancing. No cover charge.

ROSELAND, 239 W. 52nd St. Tel. 247-0200.

For those hankering after a nice old-fashioned ballroom fling, there's half-century-old Roseland, with a dance floor approximately the size of the Gobi Desert and a huge Chinese restaurant as well. Roseland also showcases rock singers and bands on occasional weekends (the Pet Shop Boys and the Sugarcubes were recent notable acts). Open Thursday and Sunday 2:30 to 11pm; closed Tuesday, Wednesday, Friday, and Saturday, except for special events. **Admission:** Thurs $6; Sun $10. At special events cover varies depending on performer, call for information.

ROXY, 515 W. 18th St., at Tenth Avenue. Tel. 645-5156.

This roller-rink boasts "New York's largest dance floor" in an 18,000-square-foot main room. Once you get your bearings, dance to some of the city's hottest DJs, or take a break in the glass-enclosed balcony bar overlooking all the action. Occasional live performances; call for schedules. Roller-skating to disco music is Tuesday and Wednesday. Dance Club is Friday and Saturday. **Admission:** $12–$17.

SOUND FACTORY, 530 W. 27th St. Tel. 643-0728.

On Friday and Saturday, everyone who's anyone downtown eventually lands at Sound Factory—usually *after* 3am, when the nonstop action seems almost surreal. A big black room with a massive sound system, Sound Factory has also become one of Madonna's hangouts, and rumor has it the club plays her new records long before the public ever hears them. Watch in awe as the mainly gay crowd "Vogues" or "Bus Stops" to powerhouse DJs like Junior Vasquez and Frankie Knuckles. No alcohol is served, but fruit juice and water are available; dress ranges from T-shirts and jeans to very elaborate drag. **Admission:** $20.

SOUND FACTORY BAR, 12 W. 21st St. Tel. 206-7770.

More a club than a bar, this fresh Chelsea hotspot sometimes shares DJs, like Frankie Knuckles, with its namesake nightclub (see above). Small and dark, Sound Factory Bar changes hours, covers, and crowds depending on the night of the week; call first to check the evening's program, which could run the gamut from techno to industrial noise. **Admission:** $8 Mon–Fri; $10 Sat–Sun.

TATOU, 151 E. 50th St., near Third Avenue. Tel. 753-1144.

An opera house in the 1930s, then the club Versailles (where Edith Piaf, Judy Garland, and others sang the night away), Tatou has resurrected the bygone glamour, even to the grand chandelier and imposing bronze Amazons beside the rococo stage. To be assured a place amid all this glitter (painstakingly tarnished for effect), dine at Tatou (reserve days in advance), and segue onto the floor when the dancing gets under way—around 11pm, when dinner service is over. The food ranges from fantastic to incredible. Then, doors are selectively opened to those who arrive for disco dancing, until 4am.

Dinner, with live jazz, is from 6 to 11pm (average check about $45, sans wine). Late supper is 11pm to 2am. There are shows nightly. On Monday, it's Monday Night Live!—rhythm and blues and popular music. Tuesday through Friday, it's David Raleigh and his "little big band" with guest singers. On Saturdays it's the jazz sounds of the Nat Jones Trio. Lunch is served weekdays noon to 3pm. Jacket required. **Admission:** $10 Mon–Thurs; $15 Fri–Sat.

USA, 218 W. 47th St. Tel. 869-6103.

Perhaps the ultimate playhouse for the MTV generation, USA caters to a trendy high-profile crowd and has been visited by the likes of Madonna, Brooke Shields, and Prince. Carrying on in the tradition of the legendary New York megaclub, it has five levels and even an enclosed 50-foot tubular slide as a special attraction. The main floor is a satirical paean to Times Square with huge neon light fixtures and illuminated billboards, some in Japanese and Chinese. House music is the usual order of the day, but clubgoers can also sweat to retro, progressive, and alternative music, loll about on furniture designed by Jean Paul Gaultier, and mellow out in Thierry Mugler's "Big Bottom Lounge." **Open:** Thurs–Sun. **Admission:** $20.

WEBSTER HALL, 125 East 11th St. Tel. 353-1600.

When it opened 100 years ago, Webster Hall was the first dance club in Manhattan; in the '50s, it was an RCA recording studio where Sinatra, Elvis, and other greats cut records. Now Webster Hall is 40,000 square feet of adventure, with five levels and four dance floors. You can move to classic disco on Saturday nights in the Balcony Lounge and enjoy Psychedelic Night on Thursdays. Most nights it's quite the downtown scene, filled with "club kids" galore. Doors open at 10pm; you can dance until 5am. Celebrity parties here have included Prince, Mick Jagger, Madonna, and Depeche Mode. **Admission:** $12 cover Wednesday and Thursday, $15 Friday and Saturday.

---

3. THE BAR SCENE

'Tis pleasant in the cool of evening to drop into a warm and atmospheric public house and slake the thirst with a brew, a drop of the grape, or a belt of the grain. Below is a sampling of some favorite watering holes around town. (A number have been reviewed as restaurants in Chapter 6.) At most places, mixed drinks cost at least $6; for wines by the glass, expect to pay $4 to $6, or more.

DOWNTOWN MANHATTAN

NORTH STAR PUB, 93 South St., at the South Street Seaport. Tel. 509-6757.

★ More than just traditional English brews, food, and atmosphere prevail at the jolly North Star Pub. There's usually a zany celebration of some sort taking place: A recent one, for example, was a "British Forgive George Washington" bash! Their major celebrations are St. George's Day (April 23) and Boxing Day (December 26); others occur "as the spirit (or spirits) move us." For anyone who's counting, they boast a 60-plus collection of single malt scotches.

LOWER BROADWAY

ACME BAR AND GRILL, 9 Great Jones St. Tel. 420-1934.

Any noise on quiet Great Jones Street is likely to come from Acme Bar and Grill, where solid Southern food is served in what looks like a converted garage, albeit a stylish one. After your hush puppies and collard greens, head downstairs for jams—of the musical variety. Under Acme, Acme's funky underground bar, hosts live music acts nightly.

AMSTERDAM'S GRAND BAR & ROTISSERIE CORP., 454 Broadway at Grand Street. Tel. 925-6166.

Amsterdam's, in the heart of SoHo's gallery district, draws a quiet, party crowd. There's usually a long wait for restaurant seating, but it's easy to get to the 30-foot bar, active every night.

BAYAMO, 704 Broadway. Tel. 475-5151.

Pulsatingly popular Bayamo, named for a Cuban town where many Chinese and Cubans intermarried, offers an upscale version of Chino-Latino fare, plus a bar scene that hops all week. Tuesday is mambo night with Cruz Control; dancing from 8pm to midnight.

GONZALES Y GONZALES, 625 Broadway, between Houston and Bleecker streets. Tel. 473-8787.

Come fiesta time, the crowds also gather here for Mexican food—and music from both sides of the border—in an atmosphere of frenetic fun. The mostly Latin and World Beat acts like Samba Novo and La Nor Este perform nightly for a friendly crowd. The decor (wild colors, oversized sombreros, and peppers) adds to the ambience. There is dancing, yes, and cover, no.

TIME CAFE, 380 Lafayette St. Tel. 533-7000.

Expert people-watchers gather to see and be seen in this strikingly simple space, with whitewashed walls and a single blown-up black-and-white mural photograph. There's a lot going on under one roof here. Upstairs is an environment-conscious restaurant, with a moderately priced menu that serves some organic dishes, and a very popular lounge called Fez; downstairs is Fez Under Time Café, a performance space where one might catch music, poetry, theater, or film presentations (tel. 533-2680 for weekly updates).

SOHO

I TRE MERLI, 463 West Broadway. Tel. 254-8699.

The most glamorous of the wine bars? That's I Tre Merli, a SoHo outpost of Italian chic. *I tre merli* means "the three blackbirds," and it's the brand name of the wine imported from northern Italy by the owners. It's served here, along with about 27 other wines by the glass; the cuisine is of Genoa in the region of Liguria. A very popular spot for a fashionable crowd in the late evening.

SOHO KITCHEN AND BAR, 103 Greene St. Tel. 925-1866.

The biggest of SoHo's wine bars, SKB offers an astonishing number of wines by the glass—some 110 types—as well as "Flight Tastings," a serving of three to eight glasses (each 1.5 ounces) of wine categorized into certain groups, which allows wannabe oenophiles the chance to explore many different types of wine in a professional tasting process. On top of all that, a DJ spins "the hippest music out" on Thursday to Saturday evenings from 9pm to closing.

GREENWICH VILLAGE

THE LION'S HEAD, 59 Christopher St., just off Sheridan Square. Tel. 929-0670.

The Lion's Head attracts young writers, newspaper people, and TV news personalities like Linda Ellerbee and Chauncey Howell. Doors stay open until 4am.

WHITE HORSE TAVERN, 567 Hudson St. at the corner of 11th Street. Tel. 243-9260.

Bookish types touring the Village will want to knock back an "arf 'n arf" at the White Horse Tavern, where Dylan Thomas dwelt and allegedly drank himself to death, and where such American literary lights as Norman Mailer and Louis Auchincloss used to be regulars in the back room. A large and comfortable outdoor cafe offering light foods is open during the warm weather, usually from May 1 through early fall.

GRAMERCY PARK AREA & EAST VILLAGE

PETE'S TAVERN, 129 E. 18th St. at Irving Place. Tel. 473-7676.

Pete's Tavern, the oldest original bar in New York City, a 130-year-old shrine, was a favorite haunt of O. Henry (who lived across the street). It was commemorated by the author in one of his stories.

SUGAR REEF, 93 Second Ave., between Fifth and Sixth streets. Tel. 477-8427.

Caribbean food and drink are "hot" in New York right now, so to see what that scene is all about, calypso over to the East Village, to Sugar Reef. Dine on sizzling hot Caribbean food, cooled by the sounds of calypso, merengue, and reggae. At the bar, sip a long, cool, rum something while you munch on conch fritters or shrimp-and-coconut fritters or the like. The bar, by the way, is a "beach-style" affair, its base made of multicolored steel drums; other decor includes native art, plus plastic plants, bananas, and birds.

MIDTOWN & THE THEATER DISTRICT

B. SMITH'S, 771 Eighth Ave., at 47th Street. Tel. 247-2222.

Cover girl–turned–restaurateur Barbara Smith attracts a stunning, stylish, multiethnic crowd to the bar of B. Smith's Restaurant. Lots of show-business folk gather here.

BLUE BAR, in the Algonquin Hotel, 59 W. 44th St. Tel. 840-6800.

Although recently ensconced in slightly larger quarters, this may be the most petite, chummy lounge in Manhattan—you'll surely be privy to every conversation. Here, too, you'll find celebrities, often itinerant actors or authors from Britain.

CAFE NICOLE, in the Novotel Hotel, 226 W. 52nd St. Tel. 315-0100.

If you'd like to combine a spectacular view with a view of celebrities, then try Café Nicole, which is blessed with a commanding view east and downtown on Broadway from its glass-enclosed lounge; for city watching, it's hard to beat the outdoor terrace, open in warm weather. A pianist performs six nights a week, and the cuisine (American with a European slant) at breakfast, lunch, brunch, and dinner is excellent here, too.

CLARKE'S BAR, 915 Third Ave., at 55th Street. Tel. 759-1650.

Only the noncognoscenti persist in calling Clarke's—incorrectly—P. J. Clarke's. This is truly a landmark and one that began its life as a workingman's saloon—and still looks the part. Now *tout le monde* turns up there. (Jackie Onassis went there for the burgers.) The time to go is late (well after midnight), in time to catch the celebrity flow. Incidentally, sequences for that classic film *The Lost Weekend,* starring Ray Milland, were filmed here.

GOLD ROOM, in the New York Palace Hotel, 455 Madison Ave., at 50th Street. Tel. 888-7000.

The Gold Room is perhaps the most splendid cocktail lounge in New York. Designed by Stanford White, the two-story room with vaulted ceiling has decorative panels based on the 15th-century Luca della Robbia panels in the cathedral of Florence, and demi-lunette paintings and stained-glass windows by artist John La Farge. And the drinks served from 5pm to midnight nightly aren't bad, either. You can have tea, too, in the Gold Room from 2 to 5pm every day.

HARRY'S NEW YORK BAR, in the New York Helmsley Hotel, 212 E. 42nd Street. Tel. 490-8900.

Harry's, a convivial spot for a drink, is madly popular during the 5 to 8pm Happy Hour, when they offer a free selection of hors d'oeuvres—shrimp, hot appetizers, and the like—with drinks.

O'FLAHERTY'S ALE HOUSE, 334 W. 46th St. Tel. 246-8928.

This authentic Irish tavern in the heart of the theater district is a favorite spot for musicians, actors, dancers, and others from the various shows playing in the area. The food is good and plentiful, and the setting is impressive, with two working fireplaces. Games are a high priority here. Choice single-malt Scotches, premium ales, and a full range of beers (from light-amber Irish lager through the rich-golden Scottish brown ales and English reds to the dark full-bodied stouts and ports from Ireland, served by the Imperial pint) are the usual order of the day at O'Flaherty's. Don't worry about getting here late: The merriment continues until 4am.

PEACOCK ALLEY, in the Waldorf-Astoria, Park Avenue at 50th Street. Tel. 872-4895.

★ Nostalgia reigns in Peacock Alley, a posh watering spot in the Waldorf-Astoria. Cole Porter's splendid Louis XVI–style Steinway piano is played nightly and at the fabulous Sunday brunch, by leading pop/jazz pianists. Gourmet-inspired French Provincial fare adds to the enjoyment.

SAMPLINGS BAR, in the Holiday Inn–Crowne Plaza Broadway at 49th Street. Tel. 315-6000.

Samplings offers a stunning view of the Broadway scene; the multitiered room also offers drinks, a large selection of wines by the glass, and a moderately priced grazing-style menu of light fare.

SARDI'S, 234 W. 44th St. Tel. 221-8440.

Almost all visitors to the Big Apple find themselves at a Broadway theater on at least one evening. The most obvious suggestion for a nightcap is Sardi's, a landmark institution in the area. A contingent of authentic Broadway personalities sometimes still arrives after the last curtain, around 11:30pm, and the supreme vantage point for checking all comings and goings is the bar, just inside the entrance. Continental cuisine is also available daily from noon until 1am.

UPPER EAST SIDE

BEMELMAN'S BAR, at the Carlyle Hotel, 781 Madison Ave., at 76th Street. Tel. 744-1600.

A New York perennial, Bemelman's Bar takes its name from Ludwig Bemelman, the artist behind the popular children's book character Madeline, who comes to life in the wall murals. A smart crowd gathers here for piano music and pop/jazz singing, often by artists Barbara Carroll and Ronny Whyte. Entertainment is on from 6:30 to 8pm and later from 9:30pm to 12:45am. **Admission:** $10 cover at tables starting at 9:30pm.

ELAINE'S, 1703 Second Ave., between 88th and 89th streets. Tel. 534-8103.

Elaine's is an old-timer, famous for its celebrity clientele—the people at the next table could easily be Joan Rivers, Woody Allen, or one of that crowd.

KING COLE ROOM, in the St. Regis Hotel, Fifth Avenue at 55th Street. Tel. 753-4500.

Newly restored to its former elegance and with the famous Maxfield Parrish mural looking better than ever, the King Cole Room is one of the city's smartest watering holes. Food and drinks are both pricey, but this place is full of history: It was here that Fernand Petit invented the Bloody Mary, over 60 years ago.

NEAR LINCOLN CENTER

O'NEALS', 49 W. 64th St. Tel. 787-4663.

A charming watering hole with period-piece fixtures, this is an old-time favorite, owned by Michael and Patrick O'Neal.

THE SALOON, 1920 Broadway, at 64th Street. Tel. 874-1500.

This huge restaurant with a bar and, in summer, a sidewalk cafe has enjoyable food, good drinks, and roller-skating waiters to serve them all.

UPPER WEST SIDE

THE FIREHOUSE, 522 Columbus Ave. at 85th Street. Tel. 362-3004 or 787-FIRE.

Firehouse paraphernalia adorns the walls and also refers to the spiciness of the inexpensive food, particularly the Buffalo Chicken Wings and the European Pan Pizzas with exotic toppings, which the mixed crowd (mainly 25 to 35) often doesn't wait for a table to enjoy. The cheap beers attract rowdy softball teams who come to celebrate after a game, and on Thursday, Friday, and Saturday nights the management turns the CD jukebox way up.

HI-LIFE BAR AND GRILL, 477 Amsterdam Ave. Tel. 787-7199.

Miami Beach—circa 1962—meets Manhattan at this clever, kitschy restaurant and watering hole that's always packed, especially in summer, when tables and crowds occupy the sidewalk. **Admission:** No cover, no minimum.

COCKTAILS WITH A VIEW

RAINBOW PROMENADE, on the 65th floor of 30 Rocke-feller Plaza. Tel. 632-5000.

In a class by itself is the Rainbow Promenade, just outside the fabulous, recently restored Rainbow Room, and around the bend from Rainbow and Stars, the complex's intimate night-club. A sophisticated crowd will be drinking champagne by the glass, or 1930s-style cocktails, or grazing on precious "little meals." Open until 1am on Monday to Saturday, 11pm on Sunday, and for Sunday brunch from noon until 2:30pm. It's also great for a theatrical after-theater stop. No reservations required.

TOP OF THE TOWER, at the top of the Beekman Tower, 3 Mitchell Place, First Ave. near 49th Street. Tel. 355-7300.

Top of the Tower has breathtaking views along with songs and music at the piano. The entertainment is from 9pm to 1am on Tuesday to Saturday. **Prices:** No cover.

THE VIEW, on the 48th and 49th floors of the Marriott Marquis Hotel, 1535 Broadway at 45th Street. Tel. 398-1900.

If the room is spinning before you've even had your first drink, it's likely you're at The View, New York's only revolving restaurant and lounge. Relax and watch as the city lights seem to spin around you; it takes about 60 minutes for the room to make one complete rotation. In The View Lounge, open nightly, there's live entertainment and dancing Friday and Saturday from 10pm to 2am. No T-shirts, jeans, or sneakers allowed. (For information on The View Restaurant, see Chapter 6.) **Price:** $5 cover during entertainment, plus one-drink minimum.

4. MORE ENTERTAINMENT

TELEVISION

So you want to see "Donahue," "The Late Show with David Letterman," "Geraldo," or some of the other popular shows taped in New York. Although standby tickets are sometimes available, it's better to do a little advance planning. Here's how:

For the "Donahue" show, you should request tickets 1½ months in advance. Write: "Donahue" Tickets, NBC, 30 Rockefeller Plaza, New York, NY 10112. Limited standby seats may be available at the Information Desk at 30 Rockefeller Plaza the day of the show; tapings are Monday through Thursday at 4pm and also Thursday at 1pm.

Securing tickets for NBC's "Saturday Night Live" is an art: Send a postcard in August of the year before your trip! Lottery winners get tickets, either to the regular show or to a dress rehearsal. Standby tickets may be available on Saturday at 9:15am at NBC on the mezzanine level of the 49th Street side of Rockefeller Plaza; they are limited to one per person and do not guarantee admission.

Tapings of "Late Show with David Letterman" are held Monday to Friday at 5:30pm. Send a postcard as far in advance as possible to "Late Show Tickets," Ed Sullivan Theatre, 1697 Broadway, New York, NY 10019. Standby tickets may be available at noon at the theater box office; they are limited to one per person and do not guarantee admission.

Tapings of "Geraldo" are held Tuesday through Thursday at 1 and 3pm. Send a letter with a self-addressed stamped envelope requesting tickets 1 month in advance to "Geraldo" Tickets, CBS Television, 524 W. 57th St., New York, NY 10019 (tel. 265-8520). Standby tickets may be available at 530 W. 57th St., 45 minutes before the show.

Write at least eight months in advance to request tickets for "Live with Regis and Kathie Lee"; the address is "Live" Tickets, Ansonia Station, P.O. Box 777, New York, NY 10023-3054 (tel. 456-1000). Standby tickets may be available at 8am Monday through Friday.

Standby tickets may be available for "Sally Jessy Raphael" on Monday through Thursday morning at 9:45am at 515 W. 57th St. Or request tickets 2 to 3 months in advance by writing to "Sally Jessy Raphael" Tickets, P.O. Box 1400, Radio City Station, New York, NY 10101 (tel. 582-1722).

Note that most shows will give tickets only to those 16 years or older (17 or older for "Sally Jessy Raphael"). Tickets are sometimes given away in the morning at the New York Convention & Visitors Bureau, 2 Columbus Circle, New York, NY 10019; you can write to them in advance for a brochure listing all the shows taped in New York and for information on how to obtain tickets.

You will be well entertained and educated by taking the 55-minute **NBC Studio Tour** of its television and radio facilities. In summer, tours leave from 30 Rockefeller Plaza every 15 minutes from 9:30am to 4pm (early arrival is advised) every day; admission is $8.25. Children under six are not admitted. Phone 664-4000 for information.

ACCOMMODATIONS

RESTAURANTS

Key to abbreviations E = Expensive; I = Inexpensive; M = Moderately priced; VE = Very expensive.

Please Send Me the Books Checked Below:

FROMMER'S COMPREHENSIVE GUIDES
(Guides listing facilities from budget to deluxe,
with emphasis on the medium-priced)

	Retail Price	Code		Retail Price	Code
☐ Acapulco/Ixtapa/Taxco 1993–94	$15.00	C120	☐ Morocco 1992–93	$18.00	C021
☐ Alaska 1994–95	$17.00	C131	☐ Nepal 1994–95	$18.00	C126
☐ Arizona 1993–94	$18.00	C101	☐ New England 1994 (Avail. 1/94)	$16.00	C137
☐ Australia 1992–93	$18.00	C002	☐ New Mexico 1993–94	$15.00	C117
☐ Austria 1993–94	$19.00	C119	☐ New York State 1994–95	$19.00	C133
☐ Bahamas 1994–95	$17.00	C121	☐ Northwest 1994–95 (Avail. 2/94)	$17.00	C140
☐ Belgium/Holland/ Luxembourg 1993–94	$18.00	C106	☐ Portugal 1994–95 (Avail. 2/94)	$17.00	C141
☐ Bermuda 1994–95	$15.00	C122	☐ Puerto Rico 1993–94	$15.00	C103
☐ Brazil 1993–94	$20.00	C111	☐ Puerto Vallarta/ Manzanillo/Guadalajara 1994–95 (Avail. 1/94)	$14.00	C028
☐ California 1994	$15.00	C134	☐ Scandinavia 1993–94	$19.00	C135
☐ Canada 1994–95 (Avail. 4/94)	$19.00	C145	☐ Scotland 1994–95 (Avail. 4/94)	$17.00	C146
☐ Caribbean 1994	$18.00	C123	☐ South Pacific 1994–95 (Avail. 1/94)	$20.00	C138
☐ Carolinas/Georgia 1994–95	$17.00	C128	☐ Spain 1993–94	$19.00	C115
☐ Colorado 1994–95 (Avail. 3/94)	$16.00	C143	☐ Switzerland/ Liechtenstein 1994–95 (Avail. 1/94)	$19.00	C139
☐ Cruises 1993–94	$19.00	C107	☐ Thailand 1992–93	$20.00	C033
☐ Delaware/Maryland 1994–95 (Avail. 1/94)	$15.00	C136	☐ U.S.A. 1993–94	$19.00	C116
☐ England 1994	$18.00	C129	☐ Virgin Islands 1994–95	$13.00	C127
☐ Florida 1994	$18.00	C124	☐ Virginia 1994–95 (Avail. 2/94)	$14.00	C142
☐ France 1994–95	$20.00	C132	☐ Yucatán 1993–94	$18.00	C110
☐ Germany 1994	$19.00	C125			
☐ Italy 1994	$19.00	C130			
☐ Jamaica/Barbados 1993–94	$15.00	C105			
☐ Japan 1994–95 (Avail. 3/94)	$19.00	C144			

FROMMER'S $-A-DAY GUIDES
(Guides to low-cost tourist accommodations and facilities)

	Retail Price	Code		Retail Price	Code
☐ Australia on $45 1993–94	$18.00	D102	☐ Israel on $45 1993–94	$18.00	D101
☐ Costa Rica/Guatemala/ Belize on $35 1993–94	$17.00	D108	☐ Mexico on $45 1994	$19.00	D116
☐ Eastern Europe on $30 1993–94	$18.00	D110	☐ New York on $70 1994–95	$16.00	D120
☐ England on $60 1994	$18.00	D112	☐ New Zealand on $45 1993–94	$18.00	D103
☐ Europe on $50 1994	$19.00	D115	☐ Scotland/Wales on $50 1992–93	$18.00	D019
☐ Greece on $45 1993–94	$19.00	D100	☐ South America on $40 1993–94	$19.00	D109
☐ Hawaii on $75 1994	$19.00	D113	☐ Turkey on $40 1992–93	$22.00	D023
☐ India on $40 1992–93	$20.00	D010	☐ Washington, D.C. on $40 1994–95 (Avail. 2/94)	$17.00	D119
☐ Ireland on $45 1994–95 (Avail. 1/94)	$17.00	D117			

FROMMER'S CITY $-A-DAY GUIDES
(Pocket-size guides to low-cost tourist accommodations and facilities)

	Retail Price	Code		Retail Price	Code
☐ Berlin on $40 1994–95	$12.00	D111	☐ Madrid on $50 1994–95 (Avail. 1/94)	$13.00	D118
☐ Copenhagen on $50 1992–93	$12.00	D003	☐ Paris on $50 1994–95	$12.00	D117
☐ London on $45 1994–95	$12.00	D114	☐ Stockholm on $50 1992–93	$13.00	D022

FROMMER'S WALKING TOURS
(With routes and detailed maps, these companion guides point out
the places and pleasures that make a city unique)

	Retail Price	Code		Retail Price	Code
☐ Berlin	$12.00	W100	☐ Paris	$12.00	W103
☐ London	$12.00	W101	☐ San Francisco	$12.00	W104
☐ New York	$12.00	W102	☐ Washington, D.C.	$12.00	W105

FROMMER'S TOURING GUIDES
(Color-illustrated guides that include walking tours, cultural and historic
sights, and practical information)

	Retail Price	Code		Retail Price	Code
☐ Amsterdam	$11.00	T001	☐ New York	$11.00	T008
☐ Barcelona	$14.00	T015	☐ Rome	$11.00	T010
☐ Brazil	$11.00	T003	☐ Scotland	$10.00	T011
☐ Florence	$ 9.00	T005	☐ Sicily	$15.00	T017
☐ Hong Kong/Singapore/			☐ Tokyo	$15.00	T016
Macau	$11.00	T006	☐ Turkey	$11.00	T013
☐ Kenya	$14.00	T018	☐ Venice	$ 9.00	T014
☐ London	$13.00	T007			

FROMMER'S FAMILY GUIDES

	Retail Price	Code		Retail Price	Code
☐ California with Kids	$18.00	F100	☐ San Francisco with Kids		
☐ Los Angeles with Kids			(Avail. 4/94)	$17.00	F104
(Avail. 4/94)	$17.00	F103	☐ Washington, D.C. with		
☐ New York City with Kids			Kids (Avail. 2/94)	$17.00	F102
(Avail. 2/94)	$18.00	F101			

FROMMER'S CITY GUIDES
(Pocket-size guides to sightseeing and tourist accommodations and
facilities in all price ranges)

	Retail Price	Code		Retail Price	Code
☐ Amsterdam 1993–94	$13.00	S110	☐ Montréal/Québec		
☐ Athens 1993–94	$13.00	S114	City 1993–94	$13.00	S125
☐ Atlanta 1993–94	$13.00	S112	☐ Nashville/Memphis		
☐ Atlantic City/Cape			1994–95 (Avail. 4/94)	$13.00	S141
May 1993–94	$13.00	S130	☐ New Orleans 1993–		
☐ Bangkok 1992–93	$13.00	S005	94	$13.00	S103
☐ Barcelona/Majorca/			☐ New York 1994 (Avail.		
Minorca/Ibiza 1993–			1/94)	$13.00	S138
94	$13.00	S115	☐ Orlando 1994	$13.00	S135
☐ Berlin 1993–94	$13.00	S116	☐ Paris 1993–94	$13.00	S109
☐ Boston 1993–94	$13.00	S117	☐ Philadelphia 1993–94	$13.00	S113
☐ Budapest 1994–95			☐ San Diego 1993–94	$13.00	S107
(Avail. 2/94)	$13.00	S139	☐ San Francisco 1994	$13.00	S133
☐ Chicago 1993–94	$13.00	S122	☐ Santa Fe/Taos/		
☐ Denver/Boulder/			Albuquerque 1993–94	$13.00	S108
Colorado Springs			☐ Seattle/Portland 1994–		
1993–94	$13.00	S131	95	$13.00	S137
☐ Dublin 1993–94	$13.00	S128	☐ St. Louis/Kansas		
☐ Hong Kong 1994–95			City 1993–94	$13.00	S127
(Avail. 4/94)	$13.00	S140	☐ Sydney 1993–94	$13.00	S129
☐ Honolulu/Oahu 1994	$13.00	S134	☐ Tampa/St.		
☐ Las Vegas 1993–94	$13.00	S121	Petersburg 1993–94	$13.00	S105
☐ London 1994	$13.00	S132	☐ Tokyo 1992–93	$13.00	S039
☐ Los Angeles 1993–94	$13.00	S123	☐ Toronto 1993–94	$13.00	S126
☐ Madrid/Costa del			☐ Vancouver/Victoria		
Sol 1993–94	$13.00	S124	1994–95 (Avail. 1/94)	$13.00	S142
☐ Miami 1993–94	$13.00	S118	☐ Washington,		
☐ Minneapolis/St.			D.C. 1994 (Avail.		
Paul 1993–94	$13.00	S119	1/94)	$13.00	S13

SPECIAL EDITIONS

	Retail Price	Code		Retail Price	Code
☐ Bed & Breakfast Southwest	$16.00	P100	☐ Caribbean Hideaways	$16.00	P103
☐ Bed & Breakfast Great American Cities (Avail. 1/94	$16.00	P104	☐ National Park Guide 1994 (Avail. 3/94)	$16.00	P105
			☐ Where to Stay U.S.A.	$15.00	P102

Please note.
we may have
tion. Call cust

DS,
CO
2
SHOP
E.Y.
2
P
S
een 20ᵗʰ + 21ˢᵗ Sts.
ME CH THRIFT SHOP
ᵗʰ Sts.